CW00801614

Imperial Conversations

Imperial Conversations

Indo-Britons and the Architecture of South India

Shanti Jayewardene-Pillai

YODA PRESS

YODA PRESS
G 93, Connaught Circus
New Delhi 110 001

Published in India
by YODA PRESS

© Shanti Jayewardene-Pillai 2007

The moral rights of the author have been asserted
Database right YODA PRESS (maker)

First published 2007

All rights reserved. No part of this publication may be reproduced, stored in a retrieval system, or transmitted, in any form or by any means, without the prior permission in writing of YODA PRESS, or as expressly permitted by law, or under terms agreed with the appropriate reprographics rights organisation. Enquiries concerning reproduction outside the scope of the above should be sent to YODA PRESS at the address above.

You must not circulate this book in any other binding or cover and you must impose
this same condition on any acquirer.

All efforts have been made to obtain permission to reproduce the images used in this volume, without success in a few cases. On seeing this edition if the copyright holder/s would like to come forword, YODA PRESS would be happy to come to an agreement with them.

ISBN: 81-903634-2 5

Typeset in Lepdiary333 BT 12/15.6
By Excellent Laser Typesetters, Delhi 110 034
Printed at Roopak Printers, Delhi 110 032
Published by Parul Nayyar and Arpita Das, YODA PRESS
G 93, Connaught Circus, New Delhi 110 001
Distributed by Foundation Books Pvt. Ltd.
Cambridge House, 4381/4, Ansari Road
Daryaganj, New Delhi 110 002

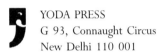

FOUNDATION
BOOKS

Contents

List of Illustrations

CHAPTER 3

Chapter 6

List of Abbreviations

BL	British Library
CUP	Cambridge University Press
FSG	Fort St. George
INTACH	Indian National Trust for Art and Cultural Heritage
IESHR	Indian Economic and Social History Review
MAS	Modern Asian Studies
MPED	Madras Proceedings Education Department
MPMC	Madras Proceedings Military Consultations
MPPC	Madras Proceedings Public Consultations
MPPWD	Madras Proceedings Public Works Department
OIOC	Oriental and India Office Collection
PP	Parliamentary Papers
PPIE	Professional Papers on Indian Engineering
RIBA	Royal Institute of British Architects
SKM	South Kensington Museum
SRPI	Selections from the Records of the Madras Government—Reports on Public Instruction, TNA
TNA	Tamil Nadu State Archives
TNCHI	The New Cambridge History of India
TRIBA	Transactions of the Royal Institute of British Architects
VV	Vintage Vignettes

Preface

Chepauk Palace, home to the royal house of Carnatic, was a powerful physical and political symbol in colonial Madras. Its present dilapidation and neglect masks an intriguing and important colonial history. When British architect and planning consultant Donald Insall, ardent conservationist and a member of the Historic Buildings Council of England, visited Madras in the 1980s, he was charmed by the Arcot Palace which he called Chepauk, but was positively bowled over by Senate House, a stone's throw away. In Insall's view Senate House was a work of 'sheer genius', designed to harmonise and integrate with the palace.[1] The palace, begun in the late eighteenth century was, arguably, designed by Indians for an Indian king, but Senate House, flagship building of the new crown state and the University of Madras, was commissioned in the late 1860s. Sources credit its Islamic/Byzantine designs to Robert Chisholm, a British engineer attached to the Public Works Department.

My Masters research into the work of Geoffrey Bawa—Sri Lanka's foremost modern architect—convinced me that my capacity to understand the modern architecture of the region was hampered by a lack of knowledge of the architectural history of the nineteenth century, undertaken from a perspective different from that of the erstwhile rulers of the subcontinent. My own introduction to the above buildings came with the decision to focus on a regional archive as the main source for my doctoral work. My research theme was the interface between native and British architects in nineteenth-century South Asia. I was curious to discover how this strange cultural maze—the incongruous juxtaposition of the so-called palace, Senate House and several other buildings in hybrid styles (to be introduced in due course)—came to be? Why

[1] S. Muthiah, *Madras Discovered* (Madras, 1992), p. 135.

were these landmark official British buildings, built in an Islamic style, set adjacent to an Indian palace, in the heart of 'Hindu' South India? Why were they commissioned? How were they designed and who built them?

The existing literature could not provide satisfactory answers to such questions. In supplying my own, I was reluctantly but inexorably drawn into the controversial minefield of imperial history. This book is a result of that journey. It chronicles the turbulent nineteenth-century architectural world in Madras where Indians and Britons met to design and construct buildings. I was little concerned then that these individuals, whom I call Indo-Britons, had a long history of cultural sharing. Now, however, the fact that they began enjoying and developing a mutual exchange of architectural design and construction knowledge as early as the seventeenth century defines the outer limits of my narrative.

The eighteenth century was a time of profound upheaval when economic and political control of southern India passed from native kings to the East India Company. 'The Company', as it was commonly known, was the instrument by which the British state forged its empire in India. By the end of the eighteenth century, those regions that came to be known as British India were governed by a military state. Further conquests and the consolidation of power depended on the vastly expanding British colonial army. The army became a major patron of building, cramming the colonial building world with soldier-engineers, fostering a deepening exchange of knowledge about engineering, aesthetics and building construction between European soldier-intellectuals and Indian engineers and architects. That world of overlapping cultures, in which Indo-Britons exchanged ideas about architecture continued into the nineteenth century, but has, for some reason, failed to engage the serious interest of historians.

This oversight is remarkable when contrasted with the rapid strides made in recent anthropological studies in exploring cultural exchange; especially those concerning the 'ethnoscience' of Enlightenment scientific travellers who were known to solicit information from the people they encountered, and use the rhetoric of science to evaluate and verify the knowledge claims of other societies. For instance, Michael Bravo, in a study of late eighteenth-century European contact with Inuit cartographic knowledge, shows how Europeans assumed that maps were universal and that everybody in the world thought in terms of 'mental maps'. He points to the paradox of this ethnoscientific exchange as that which 'on the one hand, suggests the existence of an indigenous tradition, while on the other hand, it is intrinsically cross-cultural, invoking the procedures and ideals of the sciences as a yardstick of comparison'.[2]

[2] Michael T. Bravo, *The Accuracy of Ethnoscience: A Study of Inuit Cartography and Cross Cultural Commensurability* (Manchester, 1996). Also Steven J. Harris, 'Jesuit Scientific Activity in the Overseas Missions, 1540–1773' in *Isis*, 96 (2005), pp. 71–79 or

The Indo-European exchange of architectural knowledge in eighteenth- and nineteenth-century India has yet to benefit from like scholarship.

The writing of the history of eighteenth- and nineteenth-century architecture in India began in earnest in Europe in the late 1960s. Sten Nilsson's excellent *European Architecture in India 1750–1850* (1968),[3] was the first of this genre. Nilsson did not discuss Indian patronage of European architecture. In his foreword to the book, Sir John Summerson remarked that the architectural enterprises of the French and British in eighteenth- and nineteenth-century India must surely have worn a veil of almost mythical remoteness to a Swedish scholar; the first to have 'so sharply and delightfully profiled the subject for us' in the twentieth century. In his wonderfully open manner Summerson asked whether an English scholar could have written the book. The answer was 'yes'. The reasons as to why no English scholar had done so needed to be sought for within the 'embarrassing load of apprehensions, prejudices and inhibitions about India and about imperialism which most educated Englishmen still carry around with them'.

Until the late 1980s most writers were content to remain safe in an art-historical cul-de-sac, producing descriptive accounts of style and building types with a casual mention of politics. They had found that on stylistic grounds it was easier to study British and Indian buildings separately, and to portray imperial architecture as something that happened without Indians. Typical of this genre is Philip Davies' rather splendid survey of the *Splendours of the Raj* published in 1985. The insularity of this method, however, has proved a disincentive to engaging with exciting developments taking place in other disciplines, especially imperial history. The break with art-historical methods occurred when Anthony King linked buildings more emphatically with imperial history in his books *Colonial Urban Development* (1976) and *The Bungalow* (1984). King approached the subject tangentially, from an urban development perspective. In her book *A Fatal Friendship: The Nawabs, the British and the City of Lucknow* (1985), Rosie Llewellyn Jones provided the first systematic descriptive account of Indian architectural patronage and design of the period, but in doing so she also managed to exclude empire altogether.

In a ground-breaking study published in 1989 Thomas Metcalf used orientalist discourse methods to examine imperial architectural visions. Unfortunately, in his account Indians featured only as an audience for British architectural activity: 'rarely did Indians themselves

---

Sujit Sivasundaram, 'Trading Knowledge: The East India Company's Elephants in India and Britain' in *The Historical Journal*, 48, 1 (2005), pp. 27–63.

[3] Sten Nilsson, *European Architecture in India 1750–1850* (London, 1968).

participate in the erection of a monumental architecture.'[4] Nevertheless Indian patrons were never completely excluded. The ones who most commonly appeared were the princes who built fabulous European or hybrid-style palaces often designed by Europeans. Metcalf upheld the view that the British began a self-conscious 'revival' of 'Indian' architecture; a view he qualified with the note that this was a 'revival' only from the very distinctive perspective of the late Victorian ruler.

Also in the same year, Giles Tillotson offered an appreciative and spirited defence of the 'Tradition' of 'Indian' architecture. On the one hand, from his art-historical perspective it appeared rather 'late in the day to harangue British imperialism',[5] on the other hand, unlike Metcalf, he was able to admire the work of a few named Indian designers[6] who had 'learned' Indian architecture from Samuel Swinton Jacob, executive engineer to the Maharaja of Jaipur in 1867. Tillotson identified Swinton Jacob, who hailed from a line of Indian army officers and was a graduate of the East India Company military academy at Addiscombe, as the instigator of a genuine 'revival' of Jaipur arts. It is a historiography that begs the question: what happened to Indian architecture that it had to be revived by British engineers?

The idea of the need for a 'revival' of Indian architecture must rest on the assumption of its 'decline'. But where did such overwhelmingly self-assured and sweeping ideas about decline come from? They originated in more general theories addressing the decline of Indian society as a whole. Theories of decline were integral to British political discourse and deeply embedded in the material reality of the political and military power that was being established in India. Their roots were put down early, in the historical traditions of Scottish enlightenment, developed by men such as the utilitarian intellectual and senior Company official, James Mill, in his massive and influential six volumes on *The History of British India* (1817).[7] It has to be said nonetheless that notions about European cultural superiority were in circulation from around the 1500s, long before Mill, and it was of no matter that he had never visited the places he wrote of. His writing exemplified a growing imperial trend, convinced of European superiority in all things.

The notion that colonial conquest was in part justified by the divine right to rule and the necessity to subdue created realms is too well-rehearsed to repeat here. It is equally well-known that the masquerade of the 'mission to civilise' was also justified by a belief in European

[4] Thomas Metcalf, *An Imperial Vision: Indian Architecture and Britain's Raj* (London, 1989), p. xii.

[5] Giles Tillotson, *The Tradition of Indian Architecture: Continuity, Controversy and Change since 1850* (New Haven, 1989), p. viii.

[6] Ibid., p. 78.

[7] James Mill, *The History of British India* (6 vols., London, 1817).

supremacy, which held in turn that Asian societies were degraded by the rule of unenlightened despots, and in such societies art could not flourish. From Mill also sprang the belief that excellence in architecture rested on the ability to build arches.[8] He asserted that Hindus had to learn this technique from their Moslem [*sic*] conquerors. This peculiar example of ethnoscience could be attributed to the fact that Europeans had begun to report that 'Hindus' were incapable of building arches. Lumped in with Hindus were Egyptians, Mexicans and Peruvians, also ignorant of architecture, lacking as they did the secret of building vaults. As I will show later, 'Hindu' inability to build vaults had significant ideological and practical ramifications in Company engineering circles and in subsequent colonial discourses on archaeology and architecture of the eighteenth and nineteenth centuries.

It was during this time that the older European view that had guardedly celebrated the wonder and beauty of Indian architecture came to be displaced by the new imperial notions. The latter became the leading theory, but by no means the only one, steering intellectuals of empire in their interactions with the colonial bureaucracy. It guided the practice of East India Company officials and administrators confronted with the realities of practical building. On the whole, imperial theory denied excellence in Indian art and architecture; instead, it found a way to offer grudging praise to craftwork. Indians were allowed to excel at 'applied' art, which only required a manual skill, but not at 'fine' art which exercised the intellect and emotions. Through this distinction colonial intellectuals fostered a blindness to the existence of Indian architects and engineers, and assiduously promoted the Indian 'craftsman'.

By confining Indian employment to that of craftsmen (the state never employed Indians as architects because architects were thought to practise a 'fine' art), the nomenclature of state policy succeeded in making an ideological distinction real. The intellectual and institutional erasure of the Indian architect stemmed any threat to the rising star of building professionals imported from Britain. The notion that there were no engineers and architects in India was so well-entrenched in mainstream thinking that even a liberal, orientalist art teacher and prolific writer like E.B. Havell endorsed it in the following century, albeit for other reasons as well.[9] Thus although the 'mission to civilise' is a well-worn cliché in other disciplines, it still retains a stealthy seductive hold on architectural history. There is no mystery surrounding the theory of decline present in the modern literature on Indian architecture, and even though Metcalf did feel able to point to the ideological ramifications of the British-led idea of a 'revival' of

[8] Ibid., vol.1, p. 340.

[9] E.B. Havell, *Indian Architecture,* 2nd edn. (London, 1917). Havell was echoing the Romantics' bias towards craft methods.

Indian architecture, he did not need to explore the question of 'decline'—he began with the assumption that Indians did not contribute to the making of imperial architecture.

Except for nawabi Lucknow, studies of Indian architectural patronage and design of the period are rare. Madhu Trivedi provided a brief exposé of European impact on the architecture of Awadh in 'Encounter and Transition: European Impact in Awadh (1765–1856)' in Ahsan Jan Qaisar and Som Prakash Verma (eds), *Art and Culture: Endeavours in Interpretation* (1996). She was of the opinion that in the final phase of this architectural encounter, Indian architects produced 'a synthesis of the best of the two traditions'. Neeta Das offered a short pamphlet on the subject *Indian Architecture: Problems in the Interpretation of 18th and 19th Century Architecture, A Study of Dilkusha Palace Lucknow* (1998). The most recent book in this vein is Banmali Tandan's painstakingly detailed catalogue of nawabi building types and styles, *The Architecture of Lucknow and its Dependencies 1722–1856* (2001). Nineteenth-century architecture has also interested cultural historians who have discovered that certain buildings, as imperial artefacts, are fertile ground for discussing that niggling topic of 'hybridity' which they say, defies the production of stable meanings.[10] Naturally such studies open up the art-historical debate in new ways and are a window into architecture as material culture.

This very brief overview of historiographical themes introduces a range of approaches adopted by scholars from a number of specialities, who have studied nineteenth-century Indian architecture from a variety of theoretical positions, using different methodologies. It is almost self-evident that these approaches are not, however, as numerous or as nuanced as those adopted for the study of Western architecture.[11] Overall it may be fair to say that the art-historical survey continues to be the most popular approach to the subject and our understanding of it is largely regulated by the analytical and interpretative limits of that school; its more obvious legacy is a neglect of the study of architecture as material culture.

This is not to advocate a preferred method of architectural history or one exclusively correct way of interpreting architecture; rather it is to suggest that a combination of interpretations may yield a more balanced understanding, granting that no single study can present all possible interpretations or cover all aspects of historical events. Perhaps, it is this fundamental imbalance in the modern literature that has allowed several powerful assumptions to remain unquestioned. Was Indian architecture really in decline? What happened to those highly trained Indian architects, and the wonders of Indian architecture, in the nineteenth century?

[10] See for instance Ian Baucom, *Out of Place: Englishness, Empire and the Location of Identity* (Princeton, 1999).

[11] This discussion is set out in Iain Borden and David Dunster (eds.), *Architecture and the Sites of History: Interpretations of Buildings and Cities* (London, 1995).

Answers to these questions cannot possibly be supplied in one book or in looking at a single region. This book hopes to make a preliminary contribution in providing some answers. Its focus is the design/build interface itself where the raw struggle of patronage, knowledge and power entangled patron, designer and builder in a changing building world. This was the place where people with very different world-views met to make buildings, in the context of the imperial matrix that was taking shape and shaping southern India.

On the building site, irrespective of patron or style of building, the builders were always Indian men, women and children; a point of cultural overlap rarely discussed in architectural history. Thus it is fiction, in the form of a short story by Rudyard Kipling that yields an explicit, fey tale of Indo-British interdependence on a building site. The story of *The Bridge Builders*,[12] set in the last quarter of the nineteenth century, recreates sights, sounds and scenes from a great construction site, employing 5,000 (Indian) men to build a bridge across the Ganges. The Kashi bridge was a double-storey, lattice-girder structure, trussed with the Findlayson truss, designed by chief engineer Findlayson of the Public Works Department. Findlayson was also in charge of construction, ably assisted by young Hitchcock.

'The bridge was two men's work unless one counted Peroo, as Peroo certainly counted himself.' Peroo was a *Lascar* sailor, a Kharva from Bulsar, familiar with every port between Rockhampton and London having served on British India boats. Men of his calibre were sure of inland employment for their knowledge of tackle and handling of heavy weights. The indispensable and widely travelled Peroo spoke wonderful English and a still more wonderful lingua-franca, half-Portuguese and half-Malay and participated 'without fear' in the field-councils of Findalyson and Hitchcock. Just prior to completion and the ceremonial opening by His Excellency the Viceroy, 'Mother Gunga' threatened to destroy Findlayson's bridge and with it his reputation, with a flood. In his moment of despair Kipling turned Findlayson over to his companion and (adequately subordinate) right-hand Peroo for refuge and succour. As the river raged, the friends traversed a dreamscape to attend a gathering of Indian deities, deliberating the fate of the bridge. The soothing opium-induced journey began with a few brown pellets supplied by Peroo from a tin-box. Peroo's faith ultimately saves Findlayson's life, the bridge and colonial engineering hubris, but the reader is left in considerable doubt as to whether the Indian gods themselves would survive the onslaught of the new gods.

Like any work of history the sources emphasised are subjective and the interpretations offered are my own; I am heavily indebted to other writers for ground already covered. This

[12] Rudyard Kipling, *The Bridge Builders*, A Penn State Electronic Classic Series, first published in 1898 (The Pennsylvania State University, 2002).

story has in a sense been structured and limited by the nature of its sources, which were fragmentary and difficult to access. Private sources on colonial building design and construction are rare, whilst scattered descriptive accounts of architecture abound. By contrast, the official British public works and military archive is extensive. It is probable that this archive has recorded in English, many a multi-lingual conversation; almost all senior Company servants, intending to be in India for long periods, were expected to learn Indian languages. After 1806, those who attended the Company academies were given some, probably rudimentary, language training. To be posted in the south, Company officials were expected to have learnt one or another of the major regional languages: Tamil, Telugu, Marathi, Kannada or Malayalam. High-ranking Indian civil servants knew one or more European languages, as did some of the lower cadre who actually compiled the records. It is a fair guess that the professional Indo-European staff engaged at the building interface was, for the most part, bi-lingual.

Where possible I have tried to balance the deficiency in textual sources with material evidence from the buildings themselves. The scarcity of South Indian sources for building in this period, in any language, reduced the choice of buildings I could write about. Therefore, of the buildings studied only one was, partly, commissioned by Indians. For the same reasons it was not possible to write about Indian architects and private building projects. I have set out the sources in the context of British military and political vulnerability which led to a shuffling array of alliances and compromises with Indian élites. Manifold fugitive alliances dispel the idea that there ever was a single Indian or British response to one another, or to anyone else.

Chapters 1 and 4 lay out the general historical scene in which architectural events were situated. Four building studies, chapters 2, 3, 5 and 6, presented chronologically, make up the core of the book. In these chapters I use the sources to try to unravel how and why the buildings were commissioned, designed and built. The buildings are in Chennai; St. Andrew's Church maintains a semblance of its original glory, and after years of neglect Senate House was refurbished and re-opened in 2006. The others, although neglected, are still in use by the authorities who commissioned their design.

Acknowledgements

I incurred many debts in the writing of this book. It gives me great pleasure to acknowledge them. First, my gratitude goes to my teachers Adrian Forty and Mark Swenarton who, in addition to so much else and not quite meaning to, sent me in search of empire. Second, I thank those scholars, Thomas Metcalf and Giles Tillotson in particular, whose seminal work has guided and inspired me in untold ways.

In India I wish to thank V.R. Muraleetharan, D. Veeraraghavan, M. Varagunan, M. Gunasegarran, M.D. Srinivas and the staff at the Tamil Nadu State Archives, the Roja Muthiah Research Library, INTACH and the University of Madras for their assistance. I thank the Prince of Arcot and his staff at Amir Mahal, Prince Rajah Bhonsle Chattrapathy of Thanjavur, the Pachaiyappa Trust and Pachaiyappa School, St. Andrew's Church, Senate House, University of Madras and the Central PWD Offices at Chepauk and the many scholars who befriended me while I was conducting research in Chennai, and Neeta Das and Ayesha Rao. I owe very special thanks to Srivatsan and Raju Poundurai for enjoyable discussions and site visits; K.M.C. Cherian and Celine; Rajan, Selvi and the staff of the Madras Medical Mission for making me welcome and comfortable in Chennai and my travels in India. I am grateful to P. Manohar and Koppalu Raju for assistance in Tiruchirapalli, Hyderabad and Karnataka.

In London I have to mention the staff at the British Library; especially the Western Manuscripts and Oriental and India Office Collections and the British Architectural Library. In Oxford I thank Anna-Maria Misra, Nandini Gooptu; the staff at the Faculty of History; the Bodleian Library; the Beit Foundation for financial support to travel in India, and the wonderful team at the Indian Institute Library where I spent many pleasant hours.

The following kindly gave me permission to reproduce their images; I mention them with thanks: the British Library, the Bodleian Library, Cambridge University Press, Christopher Bayly, Sten Nilsson, Douglas Annan, Graham Reed, George Michell and Ranjith Alahakoon.

Finally I express my gratitude to David Washbrook; without whom this book would not have happened, and thank friends and colleagues: Julian Turton, Carina Montgomery, John McKean, Murray Fraser, David Christie, Penny, Sandra, Hugh, Shanthi, Chandi, Nitthi, Faiz and Shoba for diverse help and encouragement. Special mention has to be made of my editor Arpita Das for her unwavering enthusiasm and sound counsel, and Parul and Supriya at Yoda Press; together they made this a truly collaborative endeavour. I am delighted to thank Hassan Kattach for his technical wizardry and those long, happy, uncomplaining spells with computers, my sisters Ru, Jeeva and Usha for Chennai visits, pictures and ferrying books across continents; Ran and Suhi for food and beds, and Rajesh, Shahila and Laura for constructive boredom, critical reading and more. Last but not least I thank Ravi, for incalculably generous financial and moral support during all the time it has taken to bring this book to completion.

Introduction
Mutual Fascination and Conflict

Imperialists—All respectable, polite, peaceable, genteel people.

Gustave Flaubert[1]

It was late in 1870 that Lord Francis Napier, Governor of Madras, delivered a lecture on architecture, in India. It was then that he made the startling announcement that the Government, with the help of Mr. Chisholm, an accomplished architect, had 'set the first example of a *revival* [italics added] in native art'.[2] The revival constituted improvements made to a building of the Chepauk Palace in Madras—until 1855, home to the nawabs of Carnatic. The Government ordered improvements to the original 'Saracenic' style of the building, as well as changes to its internal spaces now to be used as offices for the Revenue Board. In his long and detailed talk, inter alia, Napier remarked that 'the moment a native of this country becomes educated and rich he abandons the arts of his forefathers and imitates the art of strangers whom, in this respect, he might be competent to teach.'

Napier arrived in India in 1868. Within a brief span of two years he was making authoritative and wide-ranging pronouncements on the subject of Indian art. Almost in the same breath he outlined several paternalistic and proprietorial ideas that were to prove influential in casting imperial art policy in India. Aside from personal observations, which reveal him to

[1] Gustave Flaubert, *Dictionary of Received Ideas*, first published 1913 (London, 1994).

[2] 'Modern Architecture in India', *The Builder*, 10 September 1870, pp. 722–23.

be far from open-minded, his sources had to be the long European tradition of writing on Indian art, and the views of senior colonial statesmen and Madras civil servants. Broadly speaking his arguments may be summarised as follows: 'Indian' architecture was being abandoned by educated Indians who should confine themselves to 'Indian' architecture rather than experiment with 'modern' European architecture. Britons would henceforth assume guardianship of 'progress' and 'modernity' and thus also protect what in their own definition was to be regarded as 'Indian' architecture. Hidden in this prescription was a view that Indo-European architecture built by Indians was somehow not 'Indian'; it defied British ideas about what 'Indian' architecture was and should be. At face value and compared to the more philistine of his predecessors Governor General Lord Bentinck—who wanted to demolish the Taj and sell the marble—Napier's thinking on architecture can be regarded as enlightened. And yet, the legacy of his manifestly partial views was not straightforward, and indeed, its rhetoric remains unchallenged.

The problem lay not so much with Lord Napier's imagined need for a British-led revival in Indian art and architecture per se, but the enormity of what it implied—the underlying unspoken assumption that Indian architecture was somehow dying or, indeed dead. In a broad sense Napier was simply repeating a crude well-established European cliché that depicted oriental societies as stagnant. But, by branding experimental and innovative tendencies in modern Indian architecture as 'decline', he brought this knowledge to bear on the state practice of architecture. Such ideas framed imperial state policies that strove to control modern architectural aesthetics and knowledge. There was thus no irony in the new colonial government's patronage of the very same Indo-European stylistic mode that was purportedly killing Indian architecture. The relationship between empire and modern Indian architecture is complex. I suggest that it remains in shadow precisely because the colonial rhetoric that invented the decay of Indian architecture still silently frames our understanding of it.

Therefore, any account of a nineteenth-century story of architecture requires taking rather a longer view in order to tease out the overlap between empire and decline. This story really begins somewhere in those earlier times from 1600–1800—when the serious European appreciation of Indian architecture began—in the wake of the Portuguese occupation of western coastal regions of the subcontinent. The threat of force that underlay the European presence in India meant that, from its inception the relationship between the two communities was to some extent unbalanced. This was no golden age of partnership and early cross-cultural encounters were hardly symmetrical. As Sanjay Subrahmanyam points out, while describing a slightly different encounter in the same period, 'the problem we are dealing with here is not one where knowledge is shaped by actual power. . . : rather it is one of a will to power.'[3] It was this will to power that introduced an element of conflict into what might otherwise have been relatively 'innocent' moments of cultural sharing.

Jesuit hostility to Indian religions did not deter their offering hesitant tributes to the magnificent architecture they encountered. Beginning with Garci do Orta, a Portuguese botanist in 1534, a long line of humanists and men of letters wrote about the wonder and beauty of the cave temples at Gharapuri (known to the Portuguese as Elephanta), on the western coast. Other Europeans, travelling in southern India during the early sixteenth century, also found their imagination struck by Indian architecture. Domingo Paes, travelling in the regions of the great Vijayanagara Empire, was full of admiration for the magnificent city of the same name, 'as large as Rome and very beautiful to the sight'. The intricate layout of the huge city-temples at Tirupati, the lavish use of precious stones for the massive Jagannath temple at Puri and the temples of Benares impressed the French jeweller, Tavernier. The Dutchman, Jan Nieuhof, wrote appreciatively of the lofty ancient pagodas at Pulicat.[4] The northern temples of Baroda, Benares and Chittor too were described in appreciative tones by late sixteenth-century English travellers.

At the same time, European architecture could not have compared well with the magnificence and grandeur so easily admired in the architecture of India. European response to architectural aesthetics in India was therefore often guarded and even ambivalent; especially troubling to the Christian ethos were unfamiliar 'Hindu' buildings: encrusted with lascivious ornament, blurring the boundaries of architecture and sculpture. It was a problem that refused to go away. Three hundred years later, Lord Napier was still ambivalent. He thought Brahmanical architecture had qualities of vastness, mystery and the lapse of incalculable time; it was imposing and even poetical but manifestly defective from the scientific and aesthetic point of view. Napier's views show that the science rhetoric had gained a high point in architectural discourse by this time and was easily matched by cavalier aesthetic judgements. Art historian Partha Mitter argued that European admiration for various facets of Indian culture never included an aesthetic appreciation of the visual arts.[5]

[3] Sanjay Subrahmanyam, *Explorations in Connected History: Mughals and Franks* (New Delhi, 2005), p. 171. He dismisses the time-honoured cliché that this was an 'Age of Partnership'.

[4] A useful account of this interaction is found in Partha Mitter, *Much Maligned Monsters: History of European Reactions to Indian Art* (Oxford, 1977), chapter 1.

[5] Ibid., p. 1.

It was during the seventeenth century that Indo-European cultural sharing began to be established. An early instance of literary sharing survives in the form of a book written jointly by Abraham Rogerius, a missionary living in the Dutch enclave on the Coromandel coast at Pulicat, and Padmanava, a fugitive Brahmin from Goa. *The Open Door* (*De Open Deure tot het verbogen heydondem)* was published in 1651: it announced the opening of the door to the secrets of paganism. French fascination with Indian art began as early as 1568. French Indomania of the seventeenth century led to 287 volumes of text, collected by Indian scholars for their Jesuit counterparts, reaching Paris by 1730. French and German philosophers found in Indian knowledge a source of ideas and a liberating intellectual tool. Their seventeenth- and eighteenth-century analyses of Indian and Chinese knowledge partly spawned both the Enlightenment and the French Revolution.

Anquetil Duperron, a founder of European Indology, and a key figure in *la renaissance orientale* which excited and inspired European intellectuals, travelled extensively in India in search of material and teachers to instruct him in Asian languages. With their help in learning Pahlavi and Sanskrit, he made sensational translations of the *Zend-Avesta* and the *Upanishads*. In 1782, Duperron wrote that Indo-European economic exchange should be founded on mutual respect;[6] perhaps sensing the horror of an impending imperial ideology that would soon close India to all travellers and restrict European scholarly access to the thrills of Indian knowledge. This was the age when westernised Indian gentlemen of Persianised upbringing began writing of their European travels, partly encouraged by their British patrons whom they accompanied to England.

The precise methods by which Europeans gained information on Indian architecture in the seventeenth and eighteenth centuries are not known. But the tasks of surveying, drawing, interpreting texts, space and building iconography required Indian help. Similarly, learned texts gained authenticity with a deeper access to Indian knowledge. Indo-European cultural collaboration grew from a mutual intellectual curiosity; Indians too were learning European languages and pursuing European culture through books, European teachers and local institutions. Indian sailors, merchants, diplomatic and business agents travelled extensively and had physical access to European metropolitan buildings. In the eighteenth century, many sites and shades of Indo-European cultural sharing co-existed.

The late eighteenth century was a period of profound upheaval in the rich production zones of the southern region. Their promise of wealth provoked savage conflict amongst several

[6] Jean-Marie Lafont, *Indika—Essays in Indo-French Relations* (New Delhi, 2000).

warring factions: the Carnatic rulers (nawabs), appointed by the Mughal Emperor, Aurangazeb, in 1692; military officers from Awadh and the Deccan;[7] the major regional powers—the Maratha generals and the Hyderabad Nizams—along with the French and the British were all seeking southern supremacy. Muhammad Ali, in a so-called 'subsidiary alliance' with the British, emerged as Nawab of the Carnatic in 1751,[8] Britain's first political ally in India. His base was at Arcot, near Madras. By the 1760s the East India Company was also nominally in control of Bengal in the north and the Northern *Sircar*s; a string of eastern coastal districts ceded by the Nizam of Hyderabad. But the house of Hyder Ali and Tipu Sultan of Mysore remained intact. A formidable foe, it stood between the British and those tempting southern revenues they coveted. After four Mysore Wars, begun in 1767, Tipu was finally defeated in 1799 and Mysore dismantled. Britons had finally transformed from petty chieftains into a major regional power. If a British empire in India was unthinkable in 1750, it was not so now.

There was no longer any need for a dual government in the South; the partnership with the nawabs of the Carnatic was ended. Following fierce suppression of a further rebellion in the southern Carnatic in 1801, Britons assumed complete military control of the South. With the Indian kings and population totally disarmed, London and the Company were free to interfere in the making of kings and drawing the boundaries of the new princely states of Travancore, Mysore, Hyderabad, and the newly constituted Madras Presidency of British India. This region of India was now ruled by a martial pro-consular aristocratic élite, flying the flag for the new 'British' nation-state. At their command was an expanding war-machine inexorably sweeping the north and the west, greedy for further conquests. This militant élite championed the ideology of Western cultural superiority in their aggressive state-building activities. Indian architecture too was not to be spared their assault.

Late eighteenth-century English orientalists inherited the conflicting traditions of European reactions to Indian art. A deepening English appreciation of Indian architecture is attested to by articles which began to appear in various learned publications. In 1780, the

[7] Deccan is an Anglicised version of the Prakrit *dakkin*, meaning south. The Deccan is a vast plateau, south of the Indo-Gangetic plain. It has an average elevation of 500 metres and is bound by the Vindhya and Satpura ranges in the north, the Nilgiris in the south, the Western Ghats on the west and the Eastern Ghats on the east. The northern plateau is drained by the Godavari river, the central by the Krishna river and the southern by the Kavery; all rising in the Western Ghats and draining east into the Bay of Bengal.

[8] Carnatic (elevated land) was the name Muslim conquerors gave to a region of southern India between the Western and Eastern Ghats, in the modern states of Tamil Nadu and southern Andhra. Europeans used it to designate an area between the Eastern Ghats and the Coromandel Coast, bound by Guntur in the north and Cape Comorin in the south and divided into north, central and southern regions. Thanjavur and Trichinopoly were in the south, Madras and Arcot in the centre and Ongole was the chief town of the north.

seventh volume of *Archaeologia*, the journal of the Society of Antiquaries, gave an account of Elephanta. The first serious essay on the great southern city-temple of Madurai appeared in 1792. The author, Adam Blackader, spent three years making the drawings. He also included a description of the complex iconography of the columns of the *choultry,* community hostel, based on temple records translated for his use. The text, drawings and paintings of the enormously popular volumes of *Oriental Scenery* (1795), by the Daniell brothers were praised by none other than Turner himself who said that 'the artists had succeeded in increasing our enjoyment by bringing scenes to our fireside, too distant to visit, and too singular to imagine'.[9]

The inauguration of the Asiatic Society of Bengal, in 1784, and its journal, *Asiatick Researches*, provided a forum dedicated to the English study of Asia. The first contribution published in this journal on Indian art was by William Chambers and it dealt with the arresting Mamallapuram pagodas on the coast near Madras. The establishing of British power encouraged the first professional approach to archaeology in India because it gave army personnel greater access to monuments, with less resistance from local notables.

By the end of the century, empire defined ever more conflictual contours of cultural sharing. The dawn of the new century found English polemicists formulating approaches to Indian architecture that closely interwove ideologies of race, church and empire. The Company's hitherto adequate minimalist fare of military and commercial building, that had satisfied the aristocratic republican ethos of older leaders, did not stand comparison with the opulent landscape of new and old buildings unfolding to a budding imperial gaze. An example of this new breed of rulers was Lord Wellesley, Governor-General in 1798. Driven by grandiose pretensions to set the imperial domain on a proper symbolic footing, Wellesley aimed to build for the British Empire an architecture that surpassed what Britons found in their new territories. But in contrast to the vast lands and rich, ancient and unknown societies these Britons desired to conquer and rule, they were a small people from a small place. How were they going to reconcile the self-engineered contradiction of a subject 'inferior' people possessing a clearly 'superior' architecture? It was a dilemma that seduced nineteenth-century imperial statesmen into a contest of pleasure and power with Indian élites and their designers, and continued, unabated, until the end of empire.

Meanwhile, metropolitan artists and intellectuals were busy foraging the globe to concoct an imperial 'British' architecture. The Gothic and the Classical styles they eventually opted for were European. But even the most prestigious products of European architecture did not

[9] Quoted in Partha Mitter, *Much Maligned Monsters*, p. 130.

compare well with their 'Islamic' counterparts; found in the Mediterranean, familiar to Europeans long before those of India. The paradise gardens of Islam were seen in Spain as early as the tenth century; in the sumptuous 277-acre palace complex of the Umayyad caliphs, at Madinat al-Zahra, five kilometres from Cordoba.[10] The complex comprised a series of regularly arranged arcaded courtyards with ornamental pools. Fountains, aviaries and shaded arbours embellished the stylised cruciform garden plan. The caliphs at Cordoba were carrying on design themes from the ninth-century Umayyad palaces in Samarra, on the south bank of the Tigris, renowned for their gardens and the ethereal delicacy of their polychrome brick buildings. Compared with the Spanish palace and the extensive seventeenth-century city-palace complex of Moulay Ismail, in the imperial Moroccan city at Meknes, the contemporary palace of the French king Louis XIV, at Versailles, was a 'compact structure'. And the equivalent 'English palace of William III, at Hampton Court, appeared small and toy-like in comparison.'[11] It must be said, however, that although prior to 1750, Islamic societies had appeared bigger, richer, and stronger to most Europeans, by the 1800s they were beginning to appear less so.

It was around this time that influential social critics A.W. Pugin and John Ruskin argued that architecture had the power to help construct our identities. Mourning the loss of an idyllic golden age, they suggested that the nation could be spared the evils of capitalism and recover the spirit of its lost medieval past by producing and inhabiting the vaulted spaces of Gothic architecture. Ruskin expanded his argument to include England's imperial mission; speaking at the Kensington Museum in 1858, he expressed outrage that Indians had dared to defend themselves against 'gentle and unoffending' Britons during the rebellion of 1857. Ruskin saw Indians as 'bestial, degraded and abominable',[12] he contended that Gothic architecture (a Christian architecture with a debt to Islamic architecture) would reform, discipline and render into Englishness the identity of the English labouring classes, variously seen as Gypsies, Arabs and Irish navvies and England's colonial subjects. Architecture then was inextricably woven into questions of national identity and modernity. The most complete triumph of Victorian-Gothic architecture was to be realised not in England but in Bombay. It is important, to note that mainstream historiography generally accepts Ruskin's thinking as the major socialist tradition in architecture, prior to the modern era.

The British intellectual milieu induced a variety of imperial responses to the spectacle of modern Indian architecture. Lucknow affords a glimpse of one strategy that became a model

[10] Henri Stierlin, *Islam from Baghdad to Cordoba: Early Architecture from the 7th to the 13th Century* (Koln, 2002), p. 102.

[11] Linda Colley, *Captives: Britain, Empire and the World 1600–1850* (London, 2003), p. 110.

[12] Cited in Ian Baucom, *Out of Place: Englishness, Empire and the Location of Identity* (Princeton, 1999), p. 76.

for British urban development. Lucknow, capital of the independent state of Awadh, was the largest and most prosperous eighteenth-century city in India, and Awadh the most coveted province of Mughal India. In 1764 the Nawabs of Awadh entered into a fatal embrace with the British: for 80 odd years there co-existed, uneasily, two centres of power in Lucknow: the nawabs in their magnificent palaces and the British in their dull, austere residency, tucked in between two nawabi palaces.

The modern constructions of Lucknow rulers and their architects were also highly eclectic affairs; having emerged from informal sharing between the people of the subcontinent and the wider European, Arabo-Persian and East Asian regions. Lucknow was an Indian city with a European cultural presence. It was cosmopolitan and Indo-European—an 'Indian interpretation of the mysterious West.'[13] One observer commented that: 'There are perhaps no buildings in Britain equally brilliant in external appearance as the palaces of Lucknow.' The gargantuan building programmes of Lucknow aroused almost incessant interest and sent Howard Russell, the correspondent of *The Times*, in 1858, 'into a transport of rapture'.[14] It is worth spending some time on Russell because his view of the city, from the rooftops of the Dilkusha Palace, is a memory all but lost today. He pronounced Lucknow

> a vision of palaces, minars, azure domes and golden cupolas, colonnades, long façades of fair perspective in pillar and column, terraced roofs—all arising up amid a calm still ocean of the brightest verdure. Look for miles and miles away and still the ocean spreads and the towers of the fairy city gleam in its midst. Spires of gold glitter in the sun. Turrets and gilded spheres shine like constellations... is this a city in Oudh? Is this the capital of a semi-barbarous race, erected by a corrupt, effete and degraded dynasty?[15] ... a city more vast than Paris and more brilliant.... Not Rome, not Athens, not Constantinople... appears to me so striking and beautiful as this.[16]

But Russell was in a minority. The ignominious dismissal of nawabi architecture was more symptomatic of the colonial era, with one qualification—only the European-style buildings of Lucknow came in for vituperation. Critics were silent about the mass of private housing in the city and usually flattering about nawabi structures free of European influence.[17] James Fergusson, the doyen of Indian architecture wrote,

[13] Rosie Llewellyn Jones, 'A Fatal Friendship: The Nawabs, the British and the City of Lucknow' *The Lucknow Omnibus* (New Delhi, 2001), p. 237.

[14] Banmali Tandan, *The Architecture of Lucknow and its Dependancies 1722–1856* (New Delhi, 2001), p. 188.

[15] Quoted in Veena Talwar Oldenberg, 'The Making of Colonial Lucknow 1856–1877', *The Lucknow Omnibus* (New Delhi, 2001), p. 11.

[16] Banmali Tandan, *The Architecture*, p. 188.

[17] Rosie Llewellyn Jones, 'A Fatal Friendship', p. 236.

of course no native of India can well understand either the origin or motive of the various parts of our Orders—and in the vain attempt to imitate his superiors he has abandoned his own beautiful art to produce the strange jumble of vulgarity and bad taste we find at Lucknow and elsewhere. [18]

These views were published in the 1890s, but he had expressed similar views in 1862 when he berated colonising races for having no sympathy with 'Art', and the conquered for being unable to rise to the level of their masters.[19] Other visitors used equally harsh invectives: 'degenerate', 'grotesque', 'execrable taste' are just a few of them.[20]

Rosie Llewellyn Jones, a modern defender of nawabi architecture, argued that the buildings Russell described were expressions of the vision and innovative design skills of Indian architects—and, it may also be said, the vitality of modern Indian architecture. The high emotions these buildings aroused in Europeans leave little doubt that they recognised the competition such buildings represented. Giles Tillotson, however, sees nawabi architecture as an example of the 'decline' of Indian architecture and is dismissive of 'Lucknow apologists' who have little understanding of what is 'bad'; the 'proper occupation for the art historian' is, in his view, distinguishing good from bad architecture.[21] It would appear that the issue remains as controversial today as it was in the nineteenth century.

How could the spare military classicism of Company building match the hybrid, exuberant aesthetics and monumental scale of the buildings of nawabi Lucknow? The Company's long-planned annexation of Awadh took place in 1856. The nawab was exiled in Calcutta, a 'shameless and unjustified act' that swept Awadh into a furious rebellion in 1857. British victory and the 140-day siege in the Residency gave the Britons an opportunity to display their vision of urban development for India. Steered by Colonel Robert Cornelius Napier of the Bengal Engineers, who arrived in Lucknow in 1858, two-fifths of the city was wilfully destroyed with dynamite laid by Company sappers. Napier later became the illustrious military hero, Lord Napier of Magdala. The blueprint for the destruction was spelt out in a little-known 'Memorandum on the Military Occupation of the City of Lucknow', dated 26 March 1858; it claimed to make the city invincible.[22] Awadh was the last state to be conquered before the roar of the British lion was heard throughout the length and breadth of the subcontinent; its visionary buildings paid the price. Britons had now achieved the military and political power to destroy, control and intervene in the future course of modern Indian society and architecture.

[18] Cited in Rosie Llewellyn Jones, 'A Fatal Friendship', p. 235.

[19] James Fergusson, *History of the Modern Styles of Architecture* (London, 1862), Book VIII, pp. 409 and 417.

[20] Rosie Llewellyn Jones, 'A Fatal Friendship', pp. 234–35.

[21] Giles Tillotson, *The Indian Tradition*, p. 17.

[22] Veena Talwar Oldenberg, 'The Making of Colonial Lucknow', p. 30.

'The hybrid style of the architecture of Lucknow has always been regarded as an assault on classicism,' says Banmali Tandan, because, in 'seeking to borrow the language of classicism nawabi architects appeared to have displayed an appalling contempt for its grammar'. They randomly grafted European stylistic elements, as details and motifs, on to a skeleton deriving from the Indian-Islamic school. They never followed the aesthetic dictatorship of the orders and played the same architectural game that many Europeans did. As with any artistic exercise, it is reasonable to say that depending on one's point of view, some buildings were abidingly fascinating in their quite novel aesthetic mix and others far less so. According to Tandan, this hybrid style was the chrysalis for the formation of the 'vernacular British empire style upon which so much of the architecture of the Indian subcontinent was based in the 19th and 20th centuries'.[23] But this claim seems to contradict his own observations and Veena Oldenberg's evidence, demonstrating colonial statesmen's excessive disrespect of European-style nawabi architecture. Their objective was to destroy, not reproduce it. This is a dilemma I will come to later. For the moment, I wish to turn to another aspect of the cross-cultural encounter—pleasure.

Pleasure was rarely linked with those early colonial journeys when intrepid travellers and men of science set out to make money, observe, and record other worlds and people. Nevertheless, pleasure, often undiscussed, maintained a steady quiet presence.[24] Charles Darwin, when confronted with the tropical jungles of South America in 1832, was ecstatic. He wrote: 'Here I first saw a Tropical forest in all its sublime grandeur. Nothing but the reality can give any idea, how wonderful, how magnificent the scene is.... I never experienced such intense delight.'[25] Darwin wanted his friend Fox to think of him enviously, as he collected oranges and pineapples in the lush tropics, staining his fingers with ripe oranges; meanwhile, Fox, wretchedly cold in tame Nottinghamshire, picked insects off a hawthorn hedge, staining his fingers with dirty blackberries. Darwin was only extolling God's work. But we find Darwin's counterparts, exploring the building world in India, expressing similar feelings of delight, with equal abandon, in regard to 'traditional' things.

William Emerson, who went on to become President of the Royal Institute of British Architects, wrote excitedly for his peers in England in 1866 about why Agra and the Taj Mahal stood pre-eminent in the impression they made upon his mind. Venice with its Grand Canal and St. Marks, Constantinople with its St. Sophia and Suleiman mosques, Cairo with its Tooloun,

[23] Banmali Tandan, *The Architecture,* p. 215.

[24] Edward Said, *Culture and Imperialism* (London, 1994), p. 159.

[25] Peter Raby, *Bright Paradise: Victorian Scientific Travellers* (London, 1996), p. 19.

and Bijapur with its big dome and the elaborate Ibrahim Rauza, all fell into the shade when contrasted with Agra and the Taj. He purred that:

> Its romantic situation, dazzling brilliancy, excessive elaboration, and the particularly refined, though lavish display of wealth in its ornamentation, make it beyond all other places in which a cold-blooded Caucasian can perhaps realise somewhat of the poetical and luxurious feeling of the voluptuous Easterns... through this gateway, at the end of a long avenue of cypress trees, the centre of the avenue being occupied by marble fountains, basins and flower beds, the Taj Mahal dazzling the eye with its whiteness is seen. On walking up the avenue and through the gardens, I could not help feeling it to be a more beautiful place than I ever dreamed of. There is almost every description and variety of flower, and on a hot day the cool sound of water trickling along the little aqueducts which carry it to all parts of the grounds, the shady walks, and parts of the path arched over by creepers, covered with flowers of the most gorgeous colours; and the mango, guava, orange, lime and loquat trees, combine to make it a most pleasant resort.... And if heaven consists in the gratification of the senses, I should say these people realised it; for, on a sultry afternoon—the heat hushing even the birds, and the cool, refreshing splash of the glittering fountains, seen from, and resounding through the beautiful attar-scented marble halls—these children of luxury, in languid repose, sipping their sherbet, in the calm and full enjoyment of their hulwar and their hookahs, might have been excused if they did almost fancy themselves in heaven.[26]

Emerson's extravagant prose can almost transport us to the hushed heat of an exotic orientalist heaven. His quest to acquire knowledge of Indian architecture yielded immediate sensual and vicarious pleasure. We find him revelling in the completely new visual and spatial beauty of the gardens and buildings and enjoying voluptuous Eastern lifestyles through fanciful intellectual reconstructions. Heavenly pleasure was enhanced by a suspicion that the Taj was designed by Italians. Moreover, he knew for a fact that it was 'traditional', and the contemporary 'Hindoo [was] incapable of following the rush of modern science introduced by the English, and [would] only work in his own way'. Fortunately, British ethnoclassifications had decided that the Taj was built by Muslims. What Emerson was really doing in India was earning a living. He was expanding his reputation by learning how to build Indian domes, copying Indian designs to produce what he considered a 'hybrid' style suitable for India, and pretending that Indians knew little about so-called science.

An important site of the Indo-European architectural encounter was the acquisition of 'useful knowledge'—an activity avidly pursued by some Europeans. It could satisfy an altruisitic desire to understand and learn from others and serve as an instrument of the colonial project. Gaining knowledge, in acquiring an imperial state-sponsored dimension in the late eighteenth century, came to encapsulate the contradiction of humane activity based on a threat of force.

[26] W. Emerson, 'On the Taj Mahal at Agra', *TRIBA, 1st Series*, vol. 20 (1869–70), pp. 195–203.

Architectural pleasure reveals how the pursuit of knowledge camouflaged and eased access to an absolutely new type of pleasure—impossible to imagine—the world over.

The enormous British output in the field of studying subject peoples is testimony to a wide-ranging pleasure that accompanied the often onerous tasks of patient surveillance, painstaking classification and meticulous attention to detail that so marked the project of gathering knowledge. The opportunity to probe, pry and exhaustively survey and document the lives of others, with impunity and without permission, came to Britons as a by-product of colonial subjugation. Douglas Peers writes in a recent article that little research has been done on the relationship between colonial knowledge-gathering and the military. He maintains that intellectual pursuits were taken up by military men not only for utilitarian reasons, but also on account of boredom, curiosity, professional aspirations, and because the army provided opportunity for travel and technical training.[27] There is perhaps a clearer way to say this—it was, quite simply, pleasurable. Gathering knowledge offered a covert avenue for a particular form of inter-community fraternising and companionship. Naturally, gaining Indian knowledge required Indians.

It is tempting to regard British passion for Indian architecture as an innocent dalliance born of humane intellectual curiosity. There is surely a kernel of truth in this popular view that somehow ignores the intimacy between the British passion and the structures and pulses of imperial state power. Architecture was inseparable from the expansive spaciousness of the Indian landscape. Travel in India was increasingly difficult for outsiders. Thus it came to be that dominion over land gave a few privileged Britons untrammelled freedom to roam in it; territorial conquest was the pathfinder for a certain sort of pleasure in architecture peculiar to imperialism. Indians could not traipse over Britain with such compelling authority (assuming they might have wanted to) in search of pleasure in its equally rich heritage.

It was in 1898 that a Rajput chieftain said to a curious Briton: 'You admire what is ours because it is strange; for similar reasons we like the work of Europeans.'[28] There is sufficient material evidence to show that some Indian élites were curious and excited by European architecture, but written accounts are rare. Indian occidentalists often belonged to a cosmopolitan cultural avant garde, and were very like Britons enamoured with European classicism: they enjoyed experimenting with it in their buildings; but theirs was a private enterprise, without any backing from a powerful imperial state. Imperial Britons thus approached

[27] Douglas M. Peers, 'Colonial Knowledge and the Military in India 1780–1860', *The Journal of Imperial and Commonwealth History*, 33, 2 (May 2005), pp. 157–80.

[28] T. H. Hendley, 'Decorative Arts in Rajputana', *Journal of Indian Art and Industry*, 3 (1898), p. 45.

Indian architecture differently; they admired, destroyed, censured, conserved, drew, studied, classified, theorised, wrote about, photographed, regulated, imitated and experimented with it. It was an intimate engagement that offered a peculiar and contradictory delight. In the architecture of subject peoples, Britons discovered intellectual and sensual gratification. Not only did they enjoy the sensuality of Indian buildings, they satisfied their intellectual curiosity by gaining access to details of hidden design and construction knowledge and Indian architectural canons. All this was underlined by a freedom to experiment at will. The liberation of designing with mysterious, unknown and ancient aesthetic and construction systems was theirs.

Access to such aesthetic delights, however, was not the privilege of Britons alone: French imperial architects practising in Africa and Asia were equally fortunate. Gwendolyn Wright described French architect Joseph Marrast's sheer delight in designing the Casablanca court house, in Morocco, using the elemental volumes and intricate detailing of Moroccan architecture.[29] There was no real time gap between this early twentieth-century (1920s) exercise in imperial pleasure and Le Corbusier's innovative slant on African architecture emerging at the same time as Picasso's fascination with African art, or Henri Rousseau's with tropical jungles. Le Corbusier's International Style housing at Pessac in 1926 had been derisively dubbed 'the Moroccan district'. Norma Evenson mentioned that when the International Style was first introduced in the West, to the eyes of many Westerners, 'plain white walls and flat roofs had north African associations'. The Werkbund exhibition in 1927 in Stuttgart, inspired a photomontage of the houses juxtaposed with camels and caftan-clad Bedouins. Whilst a 'German critic once denounced the new architecture as inappropriate to the German climate and customs.... It [was] immediately recognizable as the child of other skies and blood.'[30] The sources of the elementary shapes and pristine simplicity of modern European architecture that continue to give pleasure are seldom linked to empire. And it is unlikely that the historiographical gap that underscores this disassociation can be bridged until imperial history is integrated with the mainstream history of modern architecture.

There is no single reason to explain adequately what set imperial pleasure apart, but it is tempting to ask the question: what gave it its subtle, indefinable *frisson*? Does the answer ease into view a less benign domain of pleasure, absent in the pre-colonial encounter? Was it, on the whole, an institutional pleasure, complacent in a noble state purpose that appeared to set it on a plane separate from mere private interests? Since the imperial pleasure domain was unshared, the teasing issue of its moral underpinnings remains wide open.

[29] Gwendolyn Wright, *Politics of French Colonial Urbanism* (Chicago, 1991).

[30] Norma Evenson, *The Indian Metropolis: A View Toward the West* (New Haven, 1989), p. 168.

One of the most enduring, if baffling, products of the Indo-British architectural encounter was the emergence in Madras, in the 1860s, of an imperial style that fused Eastern and Western aesthetics. This is the style that Tandan claimed was based on the architecture of Lucknow. British art intellectuals gave the Indo-British style the somewhat misleading name, Indo-Saracenic—a name that also happened to efface its Britishness.[31] In fact, the British had first coined the term 'Indo-Saracenic' to denote 'Islamic' architecture in India. The term 'Saracen' made oblique concession to the view that Muslims in India were interlopers; it harked back to an older genealogy deeply embedded in Anglo-Protestant culture. Since the late sixteenth century, Reformation theologians in Scotland and England, as part of the propaganda of 'demonising' Islam, began to use the term 'Arab' and 'Saracen' to separate the cultural aspects of the medieval Arab civilisation from militant Islam. In the new historical scheme, 'Saracen's' became the militarished disseminators of Islam. Nabil Matar has shown how the emergent ideology, not only confirmed 'Anglo-Protestants in their own godly superiority, it also allowed them to be pro-Israelite but anti-Jewish, pro-Arab but anti-Islam and pro-Roman but anti-Catholic.'[32]

By 1900 modern architecture in British India was led by the British. The princes in their own states and British grandees in British India continued their architectural contest by experimenting with an eclectic bundle of styles. Ultimately, it was the mixed cultural idiom of the Indo-Saracenic that defined Edwin Lutyens's enigmatic designs for the new imperial capital at Delhi in 1913: one of the major architectural statements of the twentieth century and the largest and most prestigious building programme the British would undertake anywhere. Although the buildings of imperial Delhi are not usually mentioned in the same breath as the Indo-Saracenic, I use the term to include them because they were hybrid Indo-British buildings; Indian volumes and motifs were randomly mixed with largely classical themes. The classical frame was adorned with the Indian dripstone, domed pavilions, balconies, pierced screens and that unforgettable dome of Viceroy House, leaning unequivocally towards Buddhist architecture at Sanchi.

A high Edwardian imperialist such as Lutyens could afford to believe that there was no such thing as real Indian architecture. The dome and ornaments were his reluctant concessions to his imperial patrons' demand for Indian architecture; it was their intention to imprison, in

[31] I use the name inclusively to refer to all British Indo-European architecture.

[32] Nabil Matar, *Islam in Britain 1558–1685* (Cambridge, 1998), p. 161. That the British went on to call their own hybrid architecture in India 'Indo-Saracenic', despite obvious inaccuracy and incongruity, admits to the suspicion that they were rather less than assured as to exactly what they were doing.

the stone and bronze of their new monument, the spirit of British sovereignty. The classic explanation given for the British use of Indian architectural forms in imperial buildings is that it announced British mastery over Indians and their history; it expressed as it helped shape, 'the self-confident Age of Imperialism'.[33] But this explanation begs the question as to why, if until this time the Classical style had sufficed to express imperial purpose, did senior Madras officials take the daring decision in 1869 to shift to an Indo-European style to express that very same, if not heightened, imperial purpose? There is no evidence to suggest that Indians were fooled into reading this architecture as expressing British mastery over themselves or their history. Even if this were the case, we are still left with having to explain why this style of self-confident imperial power did not originate in the capital Calcutta, or in cosmopolitan Bombay, or, at the very least, why was it not replicated there? And, patently, this did not happen.

My story follows beguiling glimpses of other imperial visions that may shed light on the early appearance of this hybrid architecture in Madras. I would like briefly to return to Tandan's claim that the architecture of Lucknow was the chrysalis for the formation of the Indo-Saracenic style. This is true to the extent that the nawabs of the Carnatic and Lucknow patronised a regional Indian-Islamic architecture. The efflorescence of Lucknow architecture might be attributed to the wealth of Awadh and its nawabs' ability to resist British dominance till 1856. As the following story will show, the south was not so lucky.

[33] Thomas Metcalf, *An Imperial Vision,* p. 250. His is the only serious monograph on Indo-Saracenic architecture. Metcalf's analysis of Lutyens' designs for New Delhi has been challenged by Jane Ridley, 'Edwin Lutyens, New Delhi and the Architecture of Imperialism', in Peter Burroughs and A.J. Stockwell (eds.), *Managing the Business of Empire: Essays in Honour of David Fieldhouse* (London, 1998).

Figure 1: Muhammad Ali Khan, Nawab of Arcot, George Willison, oil on canvas, 1795

1

A Pluralist Society
Patrons and Designers

Kingdoms to Presidency: Madras—A City and a Region of Nation and Empire

When in 1640 the powerful regional Velugoti lords of Kalahasti and Chandragiri, in south-eastern India, ratified a trade arrangement made between a small group of Telugu lords and a band of armed merchant adventurers from overseas, it secured for the British the right to set up a home in close proximity to several urban formations sited on the Coromandel coast; these were the old settlements of Mylapore, Triplicane (*Tiru valli kadi*, lake of the sacred lamp) and Tiruvoyur. They were walled compounds, centred on ancient temples, surrounded by a market place, production units, tanks (reservoirs), gardens and residential zones. The foreigners were permitted to rent land comprising four villages and a stretch of beach, build an enclosure and pursue trade. The British outpost called Madras expanded gradually, with further acquisition of land through rent, purchase and conquest.

During the course of the following two centuries the tiny enclosure was transformed into a powerful city-state. Its power and prosperity was founded on the contributions of plural communities organised in a stratified and segmented socio-political system. No one community quite managed to dominate or exploit the rest. The result was a polity with a multi-ethnic culture and a complex arrangement of power-sharing amongst several élite groups. At the commencement of the nineteenth century, the British, with the help of their local allies, emerged as the supreme military power. A legacy of intertwining loyalties between élite families and East India Company servants, and the traditional corporate consensus that had governed the

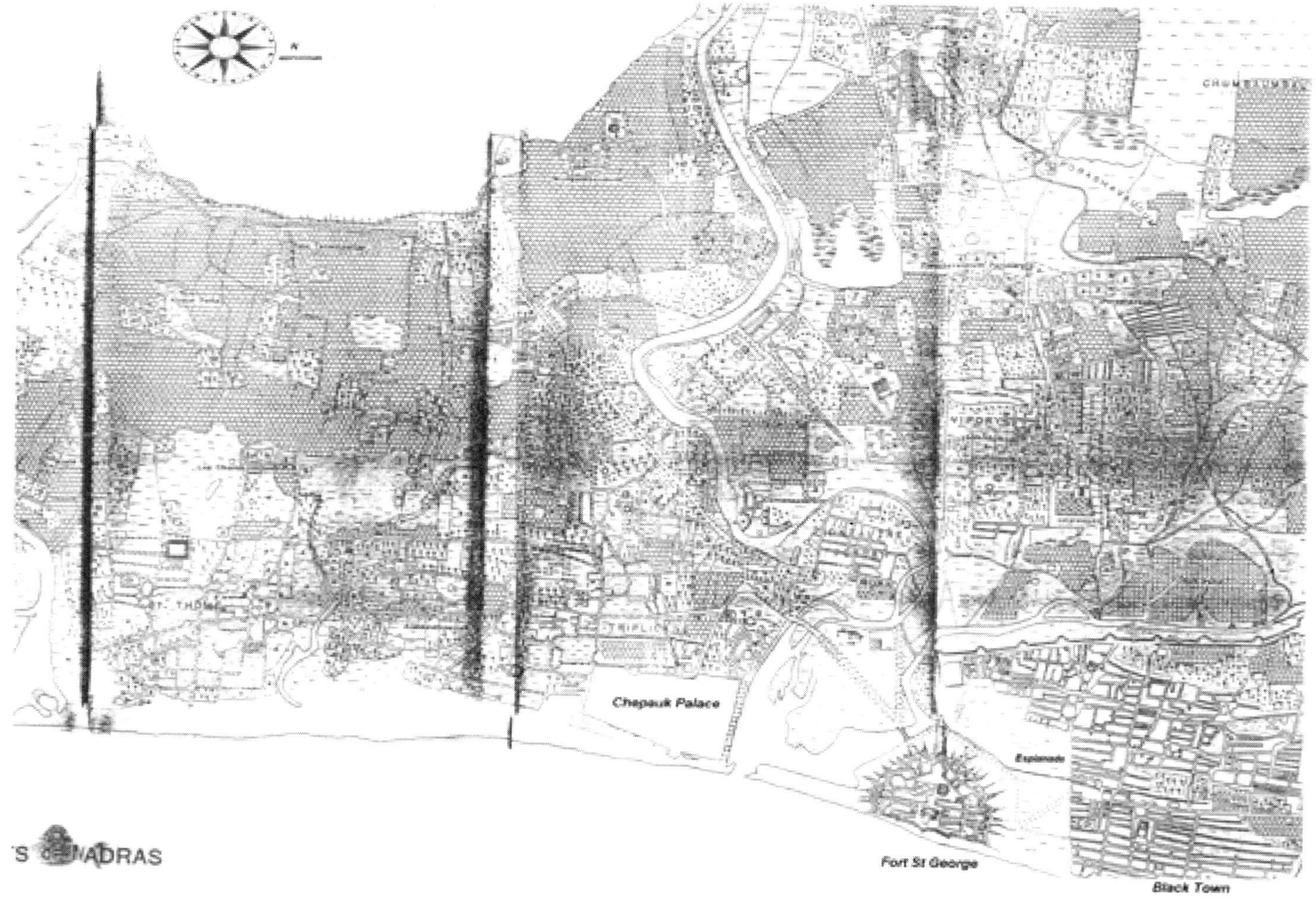

Figure 2: Map of Madras, 1798

growth of the city, impeded any automatic British dominance in the politico-cultural sphere. A continual renegotiation of the terms of power-sharing between communities defined the political and cultural configuration of Madras since its inception. It remained hybrid and plural even in its imperial heyday. In 1700 the population of the city was estimated to be around 300,000, whilst Arcot, the short-lived capital city of the Carnatic, at its peak in the mid-seventeenth century, had a population of 500,000 or so.[1]

At the opening of the nineteenth century Madras was a port city without a harbour. Passengers arriving by ship were rowed ashore by *mosullah* boatmen. It was a very pleasant place to live in, graced with a long gentle shoreline with the Indian Ocean, salubrious neighbourhoods adjoining the two rivers running through it, and shady leafy streets and buildings interspersed with many fruit gardens. Its built form was made up of one very large walled settlement—Black Town, with a population of around 120,000 persons—and several smaller walled units. Immediately south of Black Town was the open expanse of the esplanade and heavily armed and garrisoned Fort St. George (FSG). South of FSG was the larger, 117-acre walled compound of the Chepauk Palace—home to the House of Carnatic—the premier royal house of South India, whose kings were now forbidden to maintain an army. These large walled units were set amongst a series of smaller walled temple complexes, villages and hamlets (see Fig. 2).

Village-like settlements were of two distinct types: *kaniyatchi* villages, home to the rural élites who held dominion over land, and the *paracheris* in which resided the lowliest of people. The old *paracheris* attached to *kaniyatchi* villages survived the breakdown of the communal agricultural formations in the eighteenth century and drew new residents. By the 1830s there were at least forty of these untouchable settlements in the city whose residents comprised one-fifth of its total population of around 250,000–300,000. Several suburbs were founded by Indians on contract from the British—Chintadripet was a densely populated locality, founded for weavers as early as 1734. Its planning attended to the location of houses, trees and temples.[2] Washermanpet was similarly founded for cloth dyers and Royapuram for the *mosullah* boatmen, just north of Black Town. Black Town was the commercial centre and home to the bulk of the Indian population, the East Indians (mixed race persons) and poor whites. Schools, churches, temples, mosques, *choultries*, traditional community hostels, inns, hospitals and commercial buildings of all private

[1] Susan Neild, 'Colonial Urbanism: The Development of Madras City in the Eighteenth and Nineteenth Centuries', *MAS*, 13, 2 (1979), pp. 217–46, is still the most empirically useful study of Madras. She estimated that the total population of Madras in 1875 was 400,000, with 3,600 Europeans, i.e., less than 1 per cent. The figures are disputed. In 1700 Thanjavur had a population of 100,000 and Seringapatam 150,000; see Tsukasa Mizushima, *Nattar and the Socio-economic Change in South India in the 18th–19th Centuries* (Tokyo, 1986), p. 281.

[2] J. Talboys Wheeler, *Madras in the Olden Time*, vol. 3 (3 vols., Madras, 1862), p. 145.

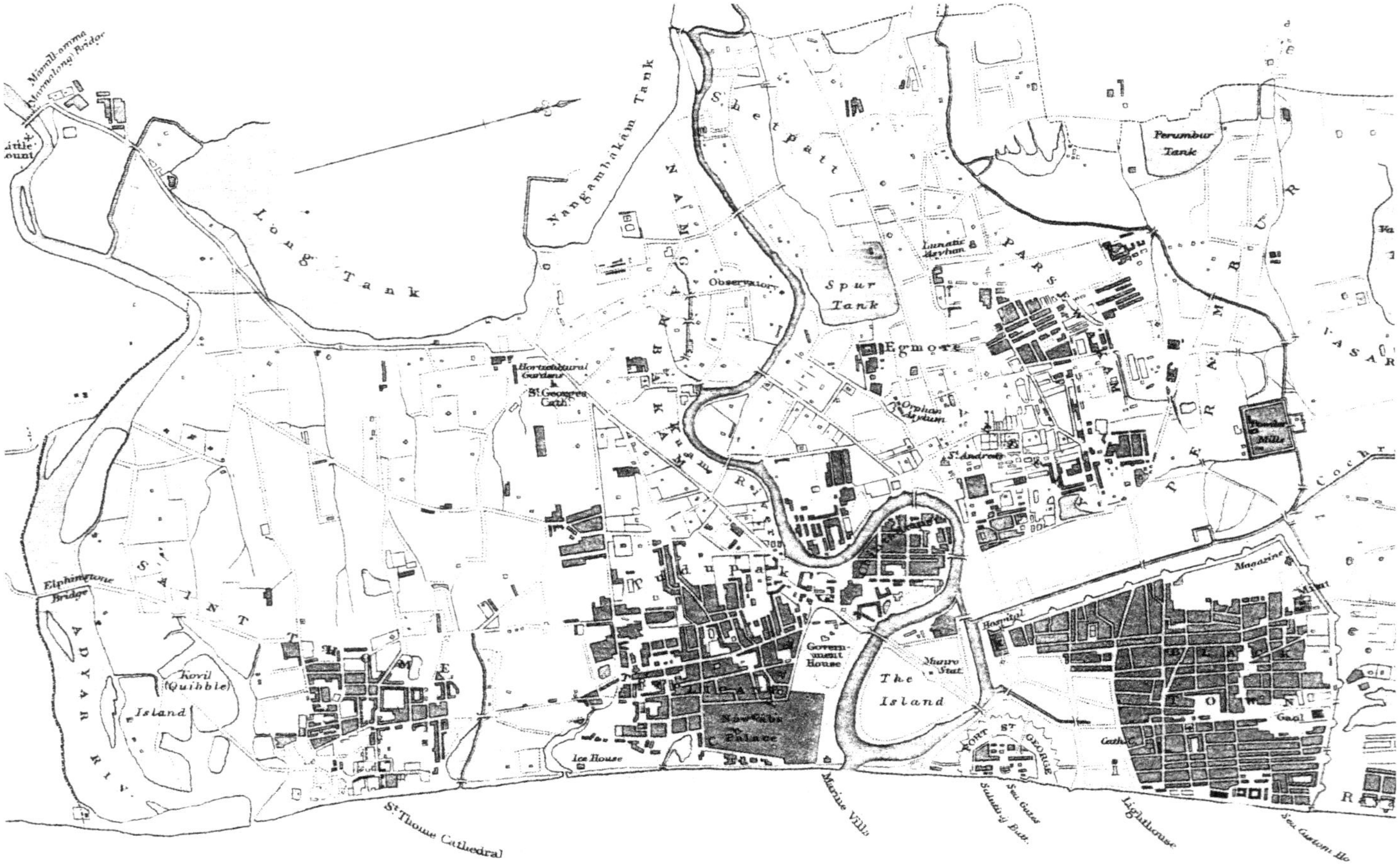

Figure 3: Map of Madras, 1859

merchants were located here. The town was administered by Indo-Britons. A few activities like justice and defence were, on occasion, shared with FSG.

FSG contained the British garrison, the church, administrative buildings, the godowns and some British and Indian dwellings. The Chepauk Palace compound housed the residential, administrative and military buildings of the Carnatic Nawabs. Nawab Muhammad Ali moved his residence to Chepauk, near Triplicane, around 1768. It is estimated that this move added a community of about 20,000 northern Muslims to the indigenous Tamil-speaking Muslim, Marakayyar population.[3] In addition to being an ancient urban/temple centre, Triplicane developed into the largest Muslim town south of Hyderabad. The nawab's militia patrolled the streets and he maintained his own duty-free bazaars.[4] Until the turn of the century local disputes were settled by Muslim law. The Company was forced to maintain a battalion at Chintadripet, in order to overawe the considerable Mahommedan population of Triplicane.[5]

Triplicane was bounded by the Choultry Plain on the west and by Adyar on the south. These salubrious regions by the river were inhabited by rich Europeans and some Indians, who lived in garden houses, protected by several redoubts or small suburban forts in San Thome, Egmore, Puraswalkam and Nungambakkam.[6] Due to land shortage in the city, the native battalions comprising the garrison of FSG were cantoned, in unmilitary fashion, in several parts of the city. The Madras cantonment, initiated in Munro's Minute of 1822, was located three miles outside the Fort, at Palaveram, beyond St. Thomas' Mount; it provided the city with an efficient garrison. Only the élite artillery corps was garrisoned at St Thomas' Mount. The governor was protected by a regiment of European bodyguards, resident inside the fort.[7]

The spatial configuration of the city in the early nineteenth century yielded a sense of its conspicuous cultural mix. When approached by sea, from the south, the long undulating skyline began with the fort walls of the Portuguese stronghold of San Thome, rising to the spires of its famous church. The high boundary walls and the lofty *gopuram* gateways, of the Kapaleeswaram and Parthasarathi temples in Mylapore, and the minarets of the Nawab's big mosque, at Triplicane, continued the fretted theme of the skyline. Further north, the domed and flat roofs of the palace buildings flashed through the dense tree-line that rose above the forbiddingly high wall surrounding the compound (see Fig. 3).

[3] Christopher Bayly, *Indian Society and the Making of the British Empire* (Cambridge, 1988), p. 69.

[4] H.D. Love, *Vestiges of Old Madras* (3 vols., London, 1913), p. 189.

[5] Alexander Arbuthnot, *Major General Sir Thomas Munro Governor of Madras,* new edn., vol. 3 (3 vols., Madras, 1886), p. 369.

[6] Susan Lewandowski, 'Changing Form and Function in the Ceremonial and the Colonial Port City in India: An Historical Analysis of Madurai and Madras', *MAS*, 11, 2 (1977), pp. 183–212.

[7] Alexander Arbuthnot, *Major General Sir Thomas Munro*, p. 369.

Immediately north of the palace, the glacis, ramparts, bastions and battlements of the British FSG came into view. Its harsh outlines were softened by the pastel shades and long low lines of colonnades, flat roofs and cupolas of public buildings. The lighthouse, situated high up on the roof of the exchange building, led the eye upwards and on to church spires and lofty flagpoles. Moving further north, the domes, minarets, spires, and *gopurams* of Black Town emerged from behind the snowy white, regular, three storey neo-classical façades of the customs buildings fronting the beach. Here, *mosullah* boats waited to transport passengers from the large sailing ships anchored in the sea-roads. The buildings lining the Madras shore-front when seen from ships impressed many a visitor. In 1780 the romantic traveller Eliza Fay wrote of public buildings and houses as being very extensive. The rich and beautiful buildings had long colonnades, porticoes and flat roofs and were covered in shell-lime, which was polished like marble and produced a wonderful effect. It is reputed that the first views of eighteenth-century Madras had the effect of transporting visitors to ancient Greece and Rome. Fay found the rising spires communicated 'such harmony, softness and elegance to the scene as to be altogether delightful'. More like a fairy tale from the Arabian Nights than anything in real life.[8] Maria Graham, of the imperial naval Dundas family, who arrived in the Madras roads shortly after Fay, wrote that 'the town and fort [were] like visions of enchantment.'[9] A cloudless blue sky, a green sea and white beach, seen against shimmering white buildings set in green foliage, perhaps made for a startling change of scene for people more accustomed to intemperate weather and bleak urban scenes in Britain.[10] The 'evening silhouette of *gopurams*, minarets, domes and spires' etching the skyline reminded the historian Robert Frykenberg that the city-state was founded upon a covenant of mutual respect and communal restraint. Below this picturesque sight were the mud and thatch shelters of the city's labouring population (see Fig. 4).[11]

Conflict

The idea that the built landscape alluded to above was the product of a pluralistic society in which political power was not centralised was most forcefully presented in 1984 by the

[8] Eliza Fay, *The Original Letters from India,* 2nd edn. (Calcutta, 1908), p. 120 and Sten Nilsson, *European Architecture in India1750–1850* (London, 1968).

[9] Maria Graham, *Journal of Residence in India* (Edinburgh, 1812), p. 123.

[10] For an interesting account of this contrast as projections of Greece and Rome see Sten Nilsson, *European Architecture*, chapter 1.

[11] Robert E. Frykenberg, 'Socio-Political Morphology of Madras', in Kenneth Ballhatchett (ed.), *Changing South Asia* (London, 1984), pp. 20–41.

Figure 4: Beach of Madras, William Simpson, 1867

American historian Robert Frykenberg. He said that the 'British were never, either in Madras or in India as a whole, all of one piece. Before the nineteenth century it was hard to find many British at all, and impossible in Madras to find them united.' The Hindu elements too were not monolithic: there were just 'too many cross-communal or Anglo-Indian alignments in opposition to each other, and to other indigenous alignments within local society, for us to take such monoliths too seriously'.[12] Even in 1875 there were only 3,600 Europeans in Madras, making up less than 1 per cent of its population.

It is indeed remarkable that Frykenberg chose to overlook the violence and conflict of a half-century of Anglo-French and Indian wars that paralysed the region from around the 1750s: wars which saw almost all the local forts deliberately destroyed and FSG enlarged to assume its unmistakably belligerent built form. He also failed to regard as significant, the fact that indigenous kings and the southern population were disarmed after 1801. Thereafter, the army was controlled by the British, albeit tenuously. The building of the army cantonment and

[12] Ibid.

reorganisation of the army in the 1820s, attest to fundamental shifts in political and military power. The Company's army was frequently deployed to crush any rebellious tendency in the newly configured Madras Presidency; this too was unworthy of mention in Frykenberg's assertion of a commonwealth of interests.

The Madras Army was racked by dissent, prone to mutiny and anxiously watched by London. But British control of all Indian forts and the virtual stranglehold it had on the Carnatic House, bestowed on FSG the unchallenged status of the first military/political base of the ruler. Moreover, the impressive military artery, Mount Road, connected other military centres at The Mount and Palaveram to FSG. Together they represented a formidable military presence, defining FSG as the focus of British power. Mount Road's importance to the city was such that in 1839, it was embellished by the equestrian statue of the popular governor Sir Thomas Munro.

In one sense, relative to the other Presidency capitals of Calcutta and Bombay, Madras was unique. Madras was the only Presidency capital to have in residence a native king who had historically regarded the Company, not as his equal but as his servant—a factor influential in the shaping of its peculiar architectural culture. The 1763 Anglo-French Treaty of Paris marked the end of the Anglo-French wars of the Carnatic. It left Muhammad Ali Walajah as Nawab of the Carnatic, with all his territories intact. However, in practice, the victorious Company in Madras refused to respect its content. Notwithstanding this, the Nawab's importance to London was unequivocally expressed in the Company's headquarters in Leadenhall Street—the East India House—the most imposing building in the City of London in 1817. The Room for the Committee of Correspondence in East India House was adorned with the 'portraits of Clive, Hastings, Cornwallis and the resplendent nabob of Arcot':[13] three Governor-Generals and the Nawab. (The names Arcot and Carnatic were interchangeable. It must, of course, be remembered that Arcot, the largest fort and capital city of the Carnatic region, was completely destroyed in the Carnatic wars).

Relations between the British and the House of Carnatic were volatile and ambiguous. These took material shape in Madras where the nawabs lived in their forbidden palace, tucked in between the British power houses, Government House and FSG. Until it was taken over in 1855 the palace remained an unwanted and uncomfortable reminder of ancient kingship and dual authority, forever undermining British legitimacy and challenging their claims to unassailable, supreme sovereignty. The nineteenth-century history of the palace compellingly illustrates the shifting alliances and interdependence between the two regimes and the unstable

[13] Ray Desmond, *The India Museum 1809–1879* (London, 1982), p. 1.

balance of political power; this is discussed at some length in Chapter 5. The nineteenth-century city retained many of the important cultural unities and continuities of the social and physical morphology of the eighteenth century. Nevertheless, its physical structure was substantially altered to accommodate the shift in regional power alignments. The changes reflected the city's enhanced status as the capital of the recently created British administrative zone—the Madras Presidency.

In contrast to the almost harmonious evolution of the city of Madras, the birth of the Madras Presidency was violent. The foundations of the modern state in the south were laid during the eighteenth century. The Presidency was forged through the dispossession of several major and minor South Indian dynasties of which the royal lineages of Hyderabad, Mysore, Thanjavur and the Carnatic were the major players. British military supremacy came after the third Mysore War in 1799, and the brutal annihilation of rebellious chieftains of the southern Carnatic in 1801. The Madras army had a striking history of unrest during the early nineteenth century. Some historians have gone so far as to claim that the latter wars and the 1807 Vellore uprising of the sepoy army against the British and not the alleged northern 'mutiny', were the first wars of colonial independence. The victorious British expropriated the wealth of the royal Houses of Carnatic and Thanjavur. The dynasties were reduced to begging for recognition of their royal status and money, even as their ancestral lands became the base and the assets of the conqueror. The remaining dynasties at Mysore, Travancore (Kerala) and Hyderabad negotiated various concessions through treaties to establish some independence but Britons held overt military and covert political control in the newly constituted 'princely states'. Native kings and powerful British political residents competed to rule these vast regions, just as subjugated native courts and British courts jostled for power and patronage in the struggle to forge the contours of the new colonial state in the recently founded geo-political unit called the Madras Presidency.

Several modes of kingship co-existed in southern India in the eighteenth century. Beside the powerful royal dynasties, smaller sovereigns ruled states like Ramnad, Sivaganga, and Pudukottai, and shared power with the *poligar* chieftains in control of the extreme south. Although modern state-building programmes were adopted by all the would-be rulers, they were hardly intended to displace politico-cultural continuity. Agrarian settlements were of two types: the riverine high-agriculture zones of the lowland Kaveri basin and the extensive upland areas of low yield and dry-cropping. The former, requiring high labour intensity, were concentrated in the irrigated valleys. The latter, needing only a modest labour input, were widely dispersed in the uplands, giving rise to different social formations. The economic stability of the region was founded on a part fluid and part enduring communal system of land-holding

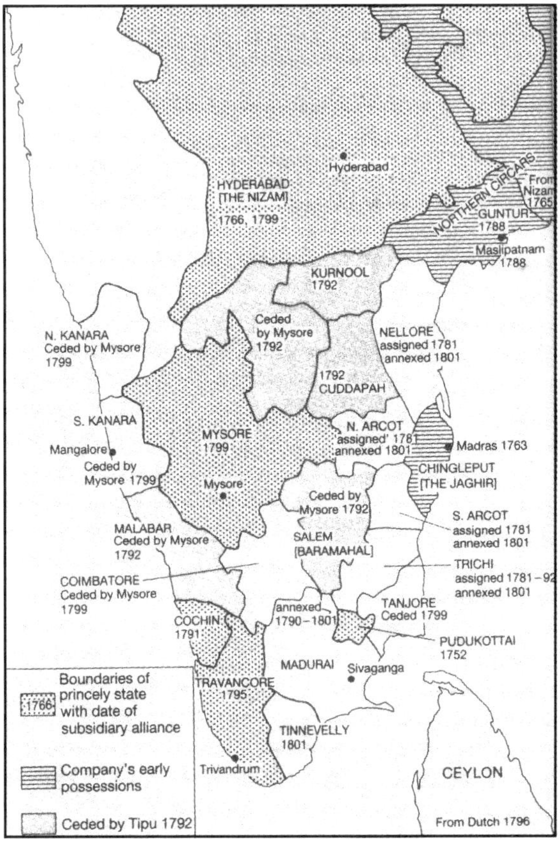

Figure 5: Map of British Expansion in South India

that had come into existence around a 1,000 years earlier, and which no foreign power had succeeded in displacing.

The governance of agrarian settlements was carried out by a powerful, largely autonomous and self-contained élite who ruled over a steeply descending order of lower castes and untouchables. The élite was made up of farmer-warrior lords and scribal castes who controlled the enormous sacro/commercial centres (the temple-towns), merchant-bankers and traders. These notables, mediating between the labouring groups and kings, constituted a sub-ruling class of land managers known as *nattars* in Tamil country. The extreme complexity of the communal social structures of wealth meant that, so long as the tax was collected, the British, emulating the policy of native sovereigns, largely left the existing administrative structures in place.

By 1801 British territory comprising what would soon become the Madras Presidency had trebled in size (see Fig. 5). The first region, acquired in 1759, was the rich and highly productive Northern *Circars* belonging to the Nizams of Hyderabad. Thereafter, a complicated process of gifting and military acquisition ensued. The nawab's land, the Jagir, was acquired in 1763, the Baramahal, Kurnool, and Salem were ceded by Mysore in 1792. Finally, following Tipu's defeat in 1799, huge tracts of Mysore lands were confiscated. The deep southern regions of Tinnevelly and Madurai were subdued and the remaining lands annexed by 1801. Leading colonial administrators in the south were of the view that the newly acquired regions should continue to maintain the existing indigenous administrative structures, with the superimposition of a thin veneer of European management.

It is noteworthy that this approach was very different from the more interventionist strategies then being adopted to govern and transform north India (see Fig. 6), particularly

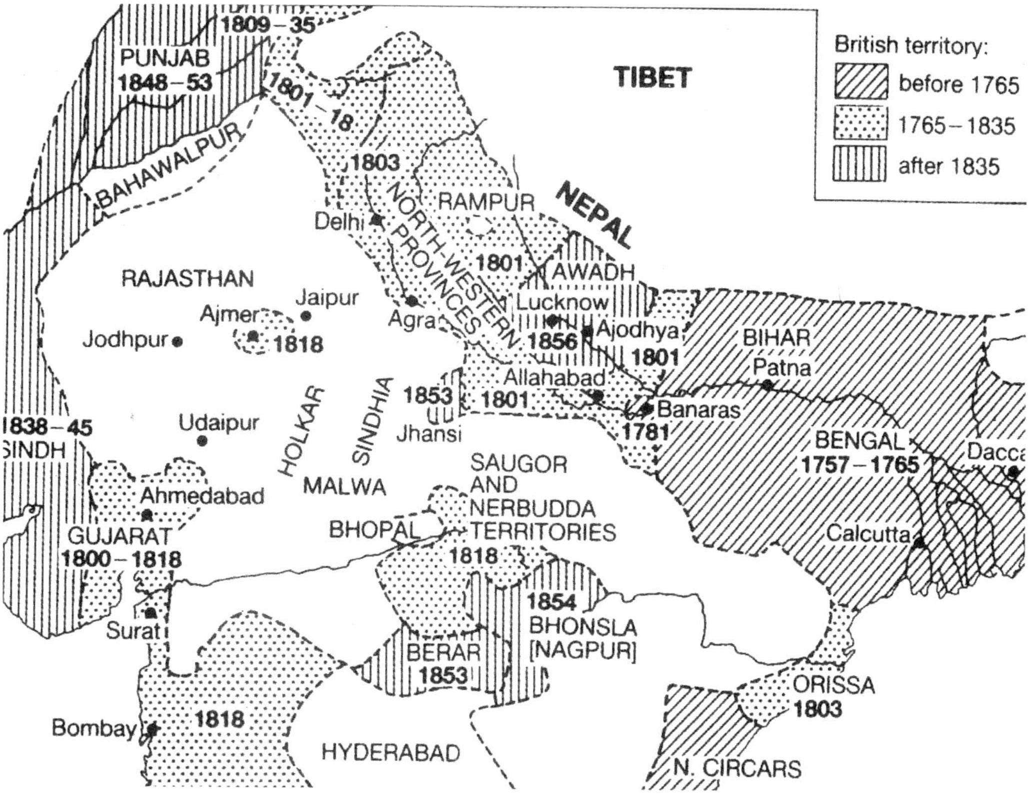

Figure 6: Map of British Expansion in north India

Bengal. In the closing years of the eighteenth century, competing ideas led to the development of an alternative model for the British colonial state in India. Imperial ideals, inclined to continuity with existing Indian institutions, grew from a convergence of the shared politico-cultural experiences of southern Indo-Britons. Sensitivity to pre-colonial governance did not, however, preclude major socio-cultural shifts. These in turn led to the emergence of new patrons of architecture.

Interdependence—An Indo-British Élite

At the opening of the new century there were five powerful élite communities in Madras whose social life overlapped in ways significant to architectural commissioning and design. These were the older royal houses of the Carnatic and Thanjavur and the warrior aristocracy, new *zamindar*s or landlords, *nattar*s or native leaders and their client groups, private European merchants and the Company. The south Indian *dubash*, speaker of two languages, familiar in English writing of the period, is an interesting enigma in the shared cultural life of the Indo-Britons.[14] *Dubash* appointments in European service ranged from those of household servant, to diplomat and investment banker. High-ranking *dubash* performed sophisticated functions at the highest level in native courts and European circles. For instance, Pachaiyappa Mudaliar, the archetypal *dubash*, served the Nawab, the Company and the Thanjavur court. There were several other instances where similar associations have been known to have developed. The relationship between Lord Clive, who later became the Governor-General of India, and his companion-in-arms, Mohammed Yusuf Khan, the Tamil warrior-general, during the Carnatic wars; or that of Colonel Mackenzie, intellectual and collector and his circle of scholar/Brahmins; or of Thomas Munro, who became a general, was knighted and appointed governor of Madras, and his exclusive cadre of advisors and civil administrators, are some such instances. They attest to deep levels of friendship and mutual service between Indians and Europeans;[15] and indeed, the intertwining and interdependence between the two communities, over such a long period, hints at a degree of mutual respect and sharing.

The Court of Directors, in London, greatly feared its servants' friendships with *dubash,* local merchant princes, landowners and financiers. The intimacy between some Englishmen and Indians, jointly engaged in southern state-building, aroused fear and envy. Simple financial digression is inadequate to explain the vituperative reactions against such Indo-British association, both in England and Madras. There was a very real danger that fraternisation between wealthy and influential Indo-Britons could jeopardise the consolidation of Company rule. Some Englishmen, drawn into the Indian world of politics and business investment, had indeed forged intimate local alliances that had financial power to sway parliament in London.

It is alleged that the Nawab of Carnatic and his allies were sufficiently powerful to have an influential 'parliamentary squad' in London. The Nawab's London agent was the powerful Sir John Mac Pherson. It was his task to seek the king's protection for Nawabi interests, against those of the Company. Mac Pherson's contact with the Prime Minister led to the king sending his emissary, Sir John Lindsay, to Madras, in 1770. Sir Lindsay arrived in the dual capacity of Naval Commander-in-Chief and Minister Plenipotentiary at the Carnatic court, and not the Company headquarters at FSG. He had the authority to treat with Indian rulers and to enquire

[14] Susan Neild-Basu, 'The Dubashes of Madras', *MAS*, 18, 1 (1984), pp. 1–31. Short biographical notes are supplied by C. Vadivelu, *The Aristocracy of Southern India* (2 vols., Delhi, 1984).

[15] For Yusuf Khan, hero of the French siege of Madras of 1758, see P.R. Krishnaswami, *Tom Munro Saheb: Governor of Madras* (Madras, 1947) and D.M. Reid, *The Story of Fort St. George*, 2nd edn. (New Delhi, 1999).

into the past conduct of political affairs, much to the annoyance of the Madras Council whose status was as a result degraded in the eyes of the Nawab.

Lindsay's successor, Sir Robert Harland, also supported the Carnatic court against the Company. Sir Edward Hughes, who followed Harland, was dubbed 'Edward Durbar' by the Calcutta papers because he spent his time at Chepauk Palace, instead of on his ship.[16] The fortunes of London parliamentarians were so covertly enmeshed with those of the Carnatic that the Nawab became the dispensable pawn in the confrontation between Parliament and the Company.[17] Parliament had a clear national agenda. It wanted total control of the Company itself. With the passing of the Regulating Act of 1773 and the Pitt's India Act of 1784 the Company became an organ of the British state. It came under a minister known as the President of the Board of Control, with Bombay and Madras in unwilling subordination to Calcutta. The new Acts made independent alliance between London and the Carnatic Nawabs superfluous. It was only a matter of time before the British state sacrificed the interests of its one time royal ally for the more rewarding prize of building a global empire through the Company.

To create loyalty and unity of vision in their servants, the Company, now a 'national' state enterprise, was compelled to undertake the training of the men they would send out to create and rule the future imperial India; accordingly, in 1806, it opened the East India College, at Haileybury. The imperial military élite was trained at the Company's military academy at Addiscombe, opened in 1809. These men were bred to maintain a moral order superior to that of the earlier breed of ill-educated, self-serving adventurers. They were highly paid and groomed to serve king and state. Learning about Indian culture and acquiring local languages was an essential part of their training.

The class of men occupying the highest ranks of the colonial service around 1800 were Welsh, Scottish and Anglo-Irish patricians, trained largely at Eton, Harrow and Oxbridge, fast moulding themselves into Britons in a 'new and intensely profitable fashion'. English patricians reserved the top jobs in the civilian establishment at home for themselves and shared their quota of patronage and employment in the army and imperial service with provincial counterparts.[18] By the early nineteenth century, the cultural reconstruction of the élite witnessed the growth of a genuinely British ruling group. Little is known of how patrician education

[16] For an account of the times see B.S. Baliga, 'British Relations With the Nawabs and Princes of Arcot' in B.S. Baliga (ed.), *Studies in Madras Administration* (Madras, 1960), pp. 310–29 and H.D. Love, *Vestiges of Old Madras*, vol. 3, p. 47 and p. 220.

[17] P.J. Marshall (ed.), *The Writing and Speeches of Edmund Burke, vol. 5, India: Madras and Bengal 1774–1785* (5 vols., Oxford, 1981), p. 6.

[18] Linda Colley, *Britons: Forging the Nation 1707-1837* (London, 1992), chapter 4.

shaped attitudes to the British nation, but some historians suggest that a patriotic duty, informed by classical literature, Christian values and heroism was stressed. It was only natural that this class would seek a common ground for friendship with like-minded Indians, not merely for pleasure but also to develop secure political alliances which required knowledge of local society.

The local counterparts of the new British élite were the *nattar*s whose economic interests included agriculture, trade and production. *Nattar*s were influential city patrons who partook of life in multiple worlds—urban and rural, Indian and European. It is their social life in village houses and gardens that is adroitly captured in the *Sarva Deva Vilasa*, a eulogy to the city life of merchant princes, written around 1800.[19] *Nattar*s were cultured high-caste *Vellalar*s or brahmins with reputations gained from local social status and service to indigenous regimes. They played an important role as representatives of multi-skilled *jati*s, collective bargaining/kinship bodies, at the higher councils or the *nadu*s.

Nattars were of orthodox religion, supported temples and patronised Sanskrit learning and the arts. Although they maintained homes in Madras and in FSG (a privilege only accorded to influential Indians), their village links were never severed. Individuals like Manali Mudaliya were owners of extensive tracts of land in the city, but most seemed to prefer smaller suburban gardens in the older temple centres or villages outside the city wall. In the city, Pachaiyappa Mudaliar and his friends lived in the leafy exclusive residential suburb of Komaleswaran Kovil on the banks of the Cooum River. *Nattar*s travelled regularly to their country homes to fulfil their traditional duties, *kaniyatchi* associated with dominion over land.[20]

The Tamil identity, high social status and intimate knowledge of diplomacy and local social and political networks made the *nattar*s indispensable to the Company as its administrative role expanded. Some Telugu and Maratha Brahmins, with *kaniyatchi* status, served as agents in the revenue administration of the Carnatic and offered their skills to the British. Members of such establishment families served on the Madras Council that governed the city. They were the Company's chief merchants and military *dubash* which made them influential in commercial and political life. It was their lifestyle that the British aspired to and began to imitate when they built the Company Garden in the late seventeenth century and acquired private gardens outside the fort and town in Muthialpet and Peddanaikpet in the 1730s.

[19] V. Raghavan (ed.), 'The Sarva Deva Vilasa: a Critical Historical Study', *The Adayar Library Bulletin* 21.3-4 and 22.1-2 (1958).

[20] *Kaniyatchikarars* were resource controllers of land, but less than proprietors. K. Rajayyan, *Administration and Society in the Carnatic 1701–1801* (Tirupati, 1969) and *South Indian Rebellion: The First War of Independence 1800–1801* (Mysore, 1971). Indespensible background reading for the period are Burton Stein, *TNCHI, 1:2, Vijayanagara* (Cambridge, 1989) and Sivakumar Chitra and S. Sivakumar, *Peasants and Nababs: Agrarian Radicalism in late 18th Century Tamil Country* (Delhi, 1993).

Figure 7: Tottik-k-kalai Vedacal Mudaliar

Tottik-k-kalai Vedacal Mudaliar (see Fig. 7), Sriranga and Kalingaraja were the great citizens of the day who were even described as incarnations of the divine trinity. As lavish patrons of the arts they enjoyed a sumptuous lifestyle, served by large establishments of staff including secretaries, pandits, musicians and courtesans.[21] *Nattar*s used their country estates for hunting and riding, for *sada*s or literary dancing and musical events, held in tents, and for bathing and dinner parties. Almost all the city magnates, scholars and artists attended these functions. The gardens were intended for relaxation and had rest houses, plantations, deer and other animals and tanks or pools for boating and bathing and were open to the public.

It is significant that the *Sarva Deva Vilasa's* mention of social interaction between this class and Europeans is perfunctory. But the authors certainly imply that the élite was flexible, having developed a taste for things western, especially music and European women as riding companions. Vedacal took his morning rides 'on horse-back with numerous hounds, and accompanied by English ladies who had decked themselves with wild flowers'.[22] From the interest in Arabo-Persian literature shown by their counterparts later in the century, we can infer that these men shared in the 'Islamicate' world of high culture patronised by the courts of Chepauk and Thanjavur.[23, 24] The royal family amused itself in its many gardens and pavilions with singers, dancers and poets. The nawabs had boating parties on lakes and made zenanas for the women to watch the full moon on the sea-shore. For this cosmopolitan, consummately sophisticated privileged class, the pursuit of European friendships, science and culture may have been as intellectually stimulating as it was politically expedient. It is unfortunate that we will perhaps never know for certain the nature and extent of friendship between members of the Indo-British élite because of fragmentary nature of extant sources and also because a mature imperial society did not encourage such interactions.

[21] V. Raghavan, 'The Sarva Deva Vilasaya'.

[22] Ibid., p. 114.

[23] Life at the Chepauk court is described in Muhammed Karim, *Swanihat-I-Mumtaz*, vol. 2 (2 vols., Madras, 1940–44).

[24] The term Islamicate was first applied to the Deccan by Richard Eaton, in 2000 in an attempt to unite a trans-regional cosmopolitan cultural zone in a purely non-religious sense and inclusive of a material culture inspired by Islam, practised by non-Muslims. Richard Eaton (ed.), 'The Articulation of Islamic Space in the Medieval Deccan', *Essays on Islam and Indian History* (New Delhi, 2000), pp.159–75.

The presence of large numbers of illegitimate children in Madras of the 1780s suggests that a very definite social intercourse was taking place between communities. The Eurasians were a problem with wide and potentially embarrassing social ramifications. In 1786 the Court had forbidden the transport of mulattos to Great Britain. It intended instead to render them serviceable in the colonies.[25] Institutions like the Upper Military Orphan School protected the officer class from the social implications of children born of native women. Lower-class needs were catered to by Company-regulated prostitution.[26] The presence of Indian servants at all levels of European life sets finite limits to a definitive assertion of separateness between the two communities, but it leaves the question of friendship necessarily obscure.

Letters between the Governors Bourchier and Stratton and their families and those of their Indian *dubash*, Venkatanarayan Pillai and their families, span a hundred years. They reveal feelings of intimacy and sympathetic understanding and hint at common material connections. The first such contact was between Venkatadri Pillai and Governor Elihu Yale, in 1687. Again in 1788 George Stratton thanked Venkatanarayana for the bottle of peacock oil sent to help his little boy's arm. Intimate social and service relationships are indicated when Charles Bourchier was appointed power-of-attorney to attend Privy Council appeals from the Mayor's Court of Madras, on behalf of the Pillai family. James Bourchier promised to buy wall-paper in London for Umdat-ul-Umara, one of the Nawab's sons. These accounts suggest that personal friendships across communities prevailed in the upper social ranks. Studying the letters in the 1930s Govindaswami queried the possibility of a real meeting on equal terms in the 1760s.[27]

Indo-Britons in the army had integrated lives at one level or another. Some idea of this intimacy 'between races' is present in the accounts of the immensely anglophile Swami Nayak, hailing from a medical military family with a tradition of serving the British from the 1760s and under whom they rose to high rank and affluence. Swami Nayak was a favourite of Lord Clive who appointed him chief medical practitioner, in the vaccination division, under Dr. Horseman, and gifted him with gold bangles and a rich house in 1802. In 1812 he received a silver palanquin, a proper conveyance for great men and a 20 pagoda allowance for bearers. His indigenous knowledge was especially helpful with the small-pox vaccine and he devised

[25] Indrani Chatterjee, 'Colouring Subalternity: Slaves, Concubines and Social Orphans in Early Colonial India', *Subaltern Studies* X (1999), pp. 49–97.

[26] For an introduction to this subject see M. Sundararaj, *Prostitution in Madras: A Study in Historical Perspective* (New Delhi, 1993). Indispensible background reading for the period are Burton Stein, *TNCHI, 1:2*, *Vijayanagara* (Cambridge, 1989) and Sivakumar Chitra and S. Sivakumar, *Peasants and Nababs: Agrarian Radicalism in late 18th Century Tamil Country* (Delhi, 1993).

[27] S.K. Govindaswami, 'Some Unpublished Letters of Charles Bourchier and George Stratton', Madras Tercentenary Committee (ed.), *Madras Tercentenary Commemoration Volume*, reprint (New Delhi, 1999), pp. 27–33.

antidotes for sea-snakes, hydrophobia and cholera which saved many lives during the outbreak at Tirupati.[28]

James Wathen, a gentleman touring India in 1811, on a visit to the upper rooms of Government House, peered into the neighbouring palace and gardens of the Nawab of Arcot (see Fig. 1). He observed the 'lower room to be surrounded by a gallery, from which are suspended a great number of lamps and lustres in a very elegant taste'.[29] This noble salon sat 200 persons at dinner. Wathen implied that the pavilion had European furniture. We can imagine a warm moonlit evening where the nawab entertained guests in the palace gardens lit with a myriad lamps. The soft sounds of musicians and singers mingled with the tinkle of the fountains and the boom of the ocean. Dancing girls were a popular item of entertainment, as was the wide variety of food served by servants to guests who lounged on carpets and cushions on the floor, or on divans in courtyards and sumptuously decorated marquees and garden pavilions.

Some of the guests wore flowing Indian robes of fine cottons or embroidered silks, and their bodies were adorned with gold, pearls and other precious stones. Often their heads were covered with jewelled headdresses and prominent religious marks on the forehead denoted sectarian affiliation. Others preferred the long brocade tunic and trouser, with the muslin skirt, made fashionable by the *nayaka* rulers. Cloth or leather shoes and slippers were worn on the feet. British men wore tailored dark suits. Sashes with stars of rank or the braids, buttons, and medallions of military regalia provided bursts of glitter and colour. Swords or pistols were carried on formal occasions. British women were gowned and jewelled but it is unclear whether upper class Indian women attended public functions. The entertainment was multi-cultural; guests conversed in many languages and the fashions and customs of diverse ethnic groups overlapped.

Similar lavish entertainment was common amongst all the élite groups. Governor Lord Clive's daughter, Charlotte, visiting her father in the late eighteenth century, was impressed by the wealth, dress and deportment of the Indians she encountered at the round of parties, balls and assemblies the family attended and held.[30] In 1807 the *Madras Courier* reported a magnificent fête held at Brodie Castle, by Lady Theodosia Craddock, to bid farewell to the commander-in-chief. The extravagant display began at the entrance to the compound. Peons with flambés were stationed along the mile-long road leading to the house and troopers

[28] 'Historicus', *Sawmy Naick and his Family* (Madras, 1951).

[29] James Wathen, *Journal of a Voyage in 1811 and 1812 to Madras and China* (London, 1814), p. 46.

[30] See C.F. Clive, *Journal of a Voyage to the East Indies and During a Residence There A Tour Through Mysore and Tanjore Countries Etc. and the Return Voyage to England* (1798), Prints and Drawings Catalogue, WD 4235, OIOC.

paraded it at intervals. Lamps at three feet from each other added an air of gaiety and splendour difficult to imagine. The decoration of the house itself made it look like a palace of eastern enchantment. The guests could almost feel like they were entering a fairyland. A truly elegant *pandal* was erected as a supper room. It was a square structure with a central dome and the whole structure was lined with a red and gold ornamented fabric. The floor was carpeted with a rich scarlet cloth.[31]

Despite having stripped the royal house of its wealth and power, Government House was still unsuccessfully competing with Chepauk Palace for recognition as the most exclusive social venue in Madras. Viscount Valentia, the only English aristocrat to privately tour India in the nineteenth century (having received Company permission), had to contrive an invitation to the Palace.[32] The Company had by now abandoned its earlier image of merchant frugality. It was acquiring the social accoutrements of an imperial Indian state power and could not afford to be outshone by the private display of wealth and style of the competing élites. In keeping with this, during the annual ball, held in the monsoon, the entrance to Government House was protected by a temporary arcade stretching from the long drive to the main door. It was decorated with boughs and illuminated with festoons of lamps. The windows of the ballroom were also ornamented with festoons of interwoven lamps and flowers.[33]

Wathen described a party thrown by an eminent Persian diamond merchant, prior to his departure for Canton. The garden house had a flat roof where eating and nautch dancing took place under an awning. European gentlemen, army officers and Indian merchants were among the thirty guests.[34] The élite Madras society that Wathen entered exhibited free and uninhibited intercourse between the various communities. Inhibitions did, however, exist due to orthodox religious practices that generally prevented Hindus from eating with outsiders. It may have been this that led to the practice of all respectable natives retiring when Europeans proceeded to take supper at the Governor's Ball in the 1830s.[35]

Bishop Heber, on his tour of Baroda, in 1824, wrote of the 'remarkable familiarity between natives of rank and Europeans'.[36] He attributed this to Mr. Williams, who spoke Hindustani

[31] *Madras Courier*, 18 February 1807.

[32] Viscount George Valentia, *Voyages and Travels to India, Ceylon, the Red Sea, Abyssinia and Egypt in 1802–1807*, vol. 1 (3 vols., London, 1809), p. 381.

[33] *Madras Courier*, 19 August 1807.

[34] James Wathen, *A Journal*, p. 82.

[35] Julia Charlotte Maitland, *Letters from Madras during the Years 1836–39* (London, 1843), p. 241.

[36] Reginald Heber, *Narrative of a Journey Through the Upper Provinces of India from Calcutta to Bombay 1824–1825*, vol. 1 (2 vols., London, 1928), p. 126.

well, the Maratha temperament or the fact that the Geakwar (king) and the British were allies. His remarks offer a rare glimpse into an unfamiliar social world. Maria Graham, on her travels in India at the turn of the century, found difficulty in getting acquainted with any native families in Calcutta and Madras, as she had been able to in Bombay. She wanted a society where British and Indian social interaction was more common.[37] However, on her trip to Mamallapuram she mentioned receiving the offer of the services of a Brahmin named Sreenivasie, one of Colonel Mackenzie's 'servants'. It was her opinion that during her visit, every Briton prided himself on being 'outrageously a John Bull', and it is likely that this led her to depict as master-servant, relations that were not necessarily so.

Also in Madras in the 1840s, Reverend Acland noticed some Englishmen going out for a walk, carrying a whip with which to lash troublesome natives.[38] Yet other men like the Advocate General of Madras, George Norton, 'established a sort of conversations once a week at his own house for the better class of natives to meet and discuss subjects of general interest and information in the hopes of leading them to think of something a little beyond their monthly salaries and diamond earrings.'[39] The condescending overtones of the text derived from the pompous pen of Julia Maitland, wife to the magistrate at Rajahmundry. In 1836, she described the natives, also known as 'Blackies,' who visited her husband, as a cringing set who behave 'to us English as if they were dirt under our feet'. Their servility, while disagreeable, was partly explained by the 'rudeness and contempt' with which the English treated the natives, 'quite painful to witness'.[40] Maitland's writing exhibited a full blown air of racial supremacy, tempered with a noble measure of shame, and she described a perfect patron-client employment market. She had a large staff at her service and employed an eminent native *munshi*, a standard part of the English domestic establishment, to teach her Tamil.

Maitland was also privileged to have rich natives like Armogum and Sooboo invite her for a feast. Their home was furnished like a French lodging house with comfortable sofas and ottomans and the walls were covered with looking glasses. They had powdered musicians, dancers, and cooks from the nawab, so she might see Mussulman and Hindu entertainment. A large orchestra played Hindu music. Armogum had consulted his English friend to discover how best to treat a lady. Despite Maitland's curiosity she was debarred from meeting the ladies

[37] Maria Graham, *Journal of Residence*, p. 136.

[38] Charles Acland, *A Popular Account of the Manners and Customs of India* (London, 1847), p. 5.

[39] G.S. White (ed.), 'The Norton Family and Pachaiyappa's', *Pachaiyappa's Charities 125th Year Foundation Celebrations Commemoration Volume* (Madras, 1968), pp. 89–95.

[40] Julia Charlotte Maitland, *Letters*, p. 40.

of the house. We can read between the lines that her Indian hosts treated her with respect and entertained with refined courtesy. Servility did not feature on this plane of social intercourse. The cultural fusion of Muslim and Hindu communities displayed here is revealing. Julia Maitland's hosts arranged a plural cultural entertainment and she writes that 'the upper classes are exceedingly well bred and many are descendants of native princes.' Maitland joined Governor-General John Shore in condemning military and civilian incivility towards natives, of which the military were, in her view, the worst offenders.

Alexander Arbuthnot schooled at Rugby, and trained for the Indian Civil Service at Haileybury, where he became proficient in Sanskrit and Telugu. He arrived in Madras in 1842 and served for thirty years; rising to the apex of the service, holding the appointments of acting governor, member of the governing council and director of public instruction. He spoke fondly of his valued friend V. Ramiengar 'on whose integrity and sound principles [he] had always relied'.[41] The great Komati merchant family member Gajalu Lakshmanarasu Chetty owned the Crescent newspaper. In 1844 he placed it under the editorship of his trusted aide Edward Harley. Under Harley, an ex-naval officer and teacher in a Vepery school, 'the paper emerged as the outspoken advocate of Hindu interests in South India.'[42] The Tinnevelly anti-Christian riots of 1845 saw many rioters charged by the police. When these convictions were squashed at the Madras High Court, the government stepped in to question the judges' decisions. Such actions led to conflict between the judiciary and the executive, resulting in the suspension and later dismissal of one of the judges, Malcolm Lewin. The urgency to maintain the independence of the judiciary was keenly supported by élite Indians who backed Lewin. Moreover, in his support, they sent a memorial to the Court, alleging collusion between Governor Tweedale's administration and the missionaryism of some European officials.

In the mid-1850s there was considerable Indo-British distaste for what were seen as Governor-General Lord Dalhousie's excesses inflicted on the royal houses of the Carnatic and Thanjavur, erstwhile allies of the British. Dalhousie simultaneously deployed the army and the law to deprive them of their hereditary wealth, status, homes and titles.[43] John Bruce Norton sent his letter, '*On the Condition and Requirements of the Presidency of Madras*' straight to London, to Sir Robert Lowe, Joint Secretary to the Board of Control. It supported the Madras Native Association's Petition protesting against the very high rate of taxation in the Presidency relative to Bengal and the North West Provinces. The letter made a case for crown

[41] Alexander Arbuthnot, *Memories of Rugby and India* (London, 1910), p. 181.

[42] R. Suntheralingam, *Politics and Nationalist Awakening in South India 1852–1891* (Arizona, 1974), p. 38.

[43] Evans Bell, *The Empire in India: Letters from Madras and Other Places* (London, M.DCCC.LXIV).

rule.[44] In 1859 Governor Charles Trevelyan threw open the doors of Government House to natives in an atmosphere of cordiality, politeness and freedom. (It seems that the closing of the doors had come about due to the extreme prejudices of a few of his predecessors). Trevelyan held monthly durbars attended by officials and non-officials alike and by Europeans, Anglo-Indians, Hindus and Muslims. Born into a cultured family of clergymen, Trevelyan schooled at Charterhouse and Haileybury and entered Company service in 1826. He married Lord Macaulay's sister and possessed impeccable connections to powerful patrons. He was dedicated to native education and paradoxically associated with Macaulay's infamous Anglicist minute on Indian education. Trevelyan's career captured the contradictions and duality of one type of imperial official—evangelical and paternalistic.[45]

A Tradition of Sharing

The cause of the demise of the traditional élite is not well studied, but it is certain that their share of revenue was heavily cut in favour of the Company. Reorganisation of Company administration, in the closing years of the eighteenth century, gave rise to a socially exclusive realm of 'heaven born', highly paid civil servants, with a racially stratified service where Indians were subordinate. Political and economic power for the English now lay not in trade but in the army and civil service. Contest for social and political status took place sometimes alongside and often beyond fault-lines of ethnic difference. Indo-British alliances disagreed with and challenged the Board of Revenue, the Council, the Supreme Government and the Home Government, institutions which were themselves ridden by fundamental clashes of opinion. Rich Indians and their English friends never hesitated to sue the government or appeal directly to parliament in London; a common practice since the early days when Indians had a place on the governing council of the city. The presence of supra-ethnic factions and counter-factions, united in temporary alliances, was a feature of the polity.

Sir Thomas Munro was the son of a Glasgow merchant, with a family firm that was neither large nor as well established as the great companies in the American trade able to withstand the revolt of the colonists. But he received the excellent education demanded by substantial citizens of the town for their children. He attended the Grammar School of Glasgow

[44] John Bruce Norton, *A Letter to Sir Robert Lowe Esq. from John Bruce Norton Esq. On the Condition and Requirements of the Presidency of Madras* (Madras, 1854).

[45] B.S. Baliga, 'Sir Charles Trevelyan, Governor of Madras 1859-1860', in B.S. Baliga (ed.), *Studies in Madras Administration* (Madras, 1960), pp. 338–86.

and the University. He could speak Spanish, Italian, Latin and some Greek; mathematics and chemistry were his favoured subjects. Grinding poverty compelled his father, as with other poor, ambitious Scots, to place three of his sons in the Company's armies in the 1780s. It is known that in the 1790s his brother Alexander sent a dark girl-child named Mary back to Scotland as his illegitimate daughter. Of the sons, only Daniel was married. Burton Stein writes it is probable that Thomas had a 'black lady' in India. He had an illegitimate daughter called Jessie Thompson, whose education, care and marriage he made his responsibility and whom he later settled in England and provided for in his will.[46] Munro climbed up the Company ranks in India to eventually become governor of Madras in the 1820s. In 1825 a grateful nation awarded him a hereditary baronetcy. Munro began his civil administrative career after his contribution to the downfall of Tipu Sultan's regime. Munro and his peers formulated the alternative to the Bengal model of the British colonial state in India. They welded European ideas with their knowledge of local society, gained from Indians during their tenure as senior administrators of lands conquered from Tipu and the nawabs. Their theories matured in the 1790s and were founded on the premise of continuity and innovation within existing Indian structures.

Burton Stein claims that it was 'self-interest' which prompted poor men like Munro to advocate a model of imperial governance, where 'the play of Indian traditional forms had to be directed by men like himself, knowledgeable and sympathetic, with great and concentrated authority'.[47] If 'knowing India was the basis of the careers of such men' it is difficult to see how Indian thought did not seep into their mental universe. Munro advocated a bureaucratic structure of governance based on Indian institutions; not one of divided functions but a segmentary one in which governors, collectors and village headmen held the same kind of executive authority. It contrasted with the Governor-General, Lord Bentinck's (1828–35) more conventional hierarchical structure which came to prevail in India by mid-century. There was, nevertheless, considerable common ground between the two. It is said that Bentinck acquired first-hand knowledge of southern intellectual currents during his tenureship as Governor of Madras from 1803–7; especially those ideas which he espoused regarding the moral and pragmatic necessity for 'native agency', first outlined by Munro. But were there other reasons, besides self-interest, that appealed in the alternate model proposed by the Munro school? It is possible that the power-sharing model may have proved attractive in its own right to many senior officials and

[46] Burton Stein, *Sir Thomas Munro: The Colonial State in India and His Vision of Empire* (New Delhi, 1989), p. 12.
[47] Ibid., p. 353.

intellectuals, who worked closely with the Indian intelligentsia. They preferred to maintain politico-cultural continuity. For such Britons survival and advancement depended partly on Indian help and cooperation. Concern for the welfare of the people they subjugated was an uplifting theme present in the views of all but the most extreme of imperial administrators, however violent their rule would prove for its intended and alleged beneficiaries. It was this contradiction that allowed the Indian view of Munro as a simultaneous local hero and colonial exploiter.

During the eighteenth century a rich tradition of Indo-European education and shared culture had evolved in the South. It pre-dated colonial rule. Indians acquired knowledge about and familiarity with European culture on their own terms, through mission schools and private education. This was especially true of the royal houses and certain Saivite scribal families who had access to Jesuit learning during the seventeenth century. Europeans acquired Indian knowledge by seeking Indian teachers. Indian occidentalists were certainly not a new phenomenon. They joined forces with British orientalists in the early part of the nineteenth century to develop a shared intellectual tradition around the themes of history, linguistics and culture. Their work has been identified as a Madras School of Orientalism, seeking to assert its authority over the study of the Indian south, as a counter-argument to the views of the orientalist establishment in Calcutta and the Asiatic society.[48]

The site of these activities was the Madras College of FSG, opened in 1812, ostensibly to train British civil servants in Indian culture and language. The Madras College aspired to continue the Indian intellectual traditions associated with the defunct but illustrious Madurai Academy, known to European intellectuals via Jesuit channels. Eighteenth-century Madurai luminaries had bestowed the academy's highest degree on the renowned Italian Jesuit, Father Beschi, in honour of his work in Tamil. Moreover, Madurai Brahmins were the sources behind Colonel Colin Mackenzie's collections, now treasured by the British Library. The Madras College attracted Indian intellectuals from decentralised scholastic institutions which previously orbited native courts for patronage. The Company, city magnates and the College replaced such institutions as new sources of patronage for cosmopolitan and dynamic modes of cultural exchange with international reach.

Architecture featured early in this cultural dialogue in the form of a book published by the Royal Asiatic Society of Great Britain and Ireland, in 1834. Ram Raz's *Essay on the Architecture of the Hindus* was one of the first examples of modern scholarship produced for

[48] T.R. Trautmann., 'Hullabaloo About Telugu', *South Asia Research*, 19, 1 (1999), pp. 53–70.

westerners anxious to unravel the secrets of Indian architecture. It also 'set out to prove the antiquity and the early advanced development of Indian civilisation'. The author was a local judge from Bangalore. While the British were relying on a 'Hindu' to decode the 'aesthetic canons of Hindu architecture, Ram Raz himself had to depend heavily on traditional Brahmins and the local practising clan of builders, of the Cammata tribe, in deciphering the difficult text and its technical vocabulary.'[49] The essay introduced the Sanskrit text, the *Manasara*, and attempted to convey its aesthetic content to a western audience.

The art wing of the Madras orientalist circle more self-consciously expressed itself by promoting the 'rediscovery' of the Amaravati marbles. Amaravati featured as a crucial site for the maturing of colonial archaeology.[50] In 1855, Edward Balfour, in charge of the Government Central Museum, asked Rev. William Taylor, on behalf of the governor, to draw up a 'Memoir on the Amrawutty Sculptures'. Taylor's memoir was given the grand title *On the Elliot Marbles, Being a Report by Reverend William Taylor, Madras* (1857).[51] The Madras art orientalists made a bold bid to pitch these sculptures in range of the highly acclaimed Elgin marbles; dubiously acquired from Athens, and brought to London for exhibition by Lord Elgin in 1807. In doing so, they were seeking a global niche for their scholarship as well as the Elliot marbles: which for delicacy of workmanship 'have perhaps never been surpassed', on the world stage. International recognition was not long in coming. The sculptures were shipped to London where they became 'the object of a momentous discovery by the self-acclaimed historian of world architecture, James Fergusson'. They formed the core of a display of photographs of Indian architecture which Fergusson organised at the Paris International Exhibition of 1867. Fergusson himself belonged to a fascinating new breed of Indo-Britons: merchant-turned-aspiring imperial scholar. Having made his fortune in India, Fergusson strove to secure a reputation for himself as an architectural historian in Europe, in the 1840s, by writing on what was then virgin territory—the history of Indian architecture. As mentioned in the Preface, as an imperial visionary, Fergusson had few qualms about writing the first history of the architecture of the world, in English. He did so in the 1850s.

[49] Tapati Guha-Thakurta, *The Making of a New Indian Art: Artists, Aesthetics and Nationalism in Bengal 1850–1920* (Cambridge, 1992), p. 118.

[50] Tapati Guha-Thakurta, 'The Museumised Relic: Archaeology and the First Museum of Colonial India', *IESHR*, 34, 1 (1997), pp. 21–51.

[51] Apparently, Colonel MacKenzie first 'discovered' the sculptures in the Guntur district in 1801. See Appendix B, of Edward Balfour, *Report on the Government Central Museum and the Local Museums of the Provinces for the Years 1855–66* (Madras, 1857), p. 191.

Training for a Multi-culture

In 1841, just prior to crown rule, the Company state opened its own prestigious school to train a new layer of exclusive Indian administrators, destined to hold high office both in British and princely territories. The opening of the Madras University in 1858 assured the new civil servants of state-sponsored access to European higher education. The new mandarins, although trained by the British, were, like their predecessors, equally well steeped in indigenous culture and comfortably spanned two worlds. The foremost among Indian statesmen trained, fêted and employed by the British were Sir Madava Rao, *Dewan* of Travancore and Baroda (see Fig. 8) and Sir Seshaya Sastri, *Dewan* of Travancore and Regent of Puddukottai; both of whom later became influential patrons of the arts.[52]

Figure 8: Sir Madava Rao and Lord Napier

Madava Rao, born in Kumbakonam to an eminent Brahmin family, was one of Presidency College's most distinguished alumni. Seshaya Sastri, born to a poor family, cultivated the patronage of Henry Montgomery, Member of the Board of Revenue, and was rewarded with a clerkship in the Board. Runganada Sastri, a High School alumnus of the 1840s also received a classical Indian education. He knew French, Latin and Arabic, and Hafiz and Sadi were his favourite poets. Sanskrit literature, Cicero and Virgil graced his library of 3,000 books. He surrounded himself with an array of scholars fluent in different languages whom he rewarded munificently. In addition, Sastri fed and educated several students in his home and is known to have been the first among Madras Indians to wear boots and trousers, for which he was 'ridiculed by his countrymen'.[53]

The Maharajah of Travancore, although not educated by the British, was accorded a rare honour as an educated native when, in 1861, Governor Denison, impressed by his erudition, appointed him a fellow of the university. This recognition was repeated by several western scientific societies like the Royal Geographical Society, the Statistical Society of London and

[52] For Sir Madava Rao's rather limited views on social reform, see S.C. Srinivasa Charier, *Opinions on Social Matters of Raja Sir T. Madava Row K C S I Fellow of the Madras and Bombay Universities* (Madras, 1890).

[53] Parameswaran Pillai, *Representative Indians* (London, 1902), p. 153.

the Royal Asiatic Society. The Maharajah cultivated the arts, literature and the sciences of the east and west; he was also a Sanskrit scholar and a devout Hindu who performed religious ceremonies with zeal. The Maharajah of Thanjavur, Rajah Serfoji, privately educated under British auspices, was also known as a man cultivated in European science and culture, looking and talking more like a French general officer than any other object of comparison.[54] He remained a great patron of indigenous art, promoting a neo-traditional revival in painting, music and dance, under the watchful eye of British Residents who stood masked in the shadows. Such Indian aristocrats were leading occidentalists as well as innovative patrons of a syncretic modern Indian culture.

A parallel tradition of Islamic scholarship flourished in the mosques and *madrasas*. At Chepauk, the Nawabs pursued a Muslim court culture patronising scholars and poets from all over India, including the prestigious Sufi lineages of the scholar-mystics of the Vellore Hazarat Makan and scholars from Lucknow's famous Farangi Mahal. Scholarship and poetry in Arabic, Persian and Dakhni were encouraged by Nawab Muhammad Ali Walajah who had been associated with important Sufis from Hyderabad, Arcot, Chicacole and Medak, before his move to Madras. The nawabs were also conversant with English. The later Carnatic dynasty was ostracised by the British and held as virtual prisoners in the palace until it was appropriated in 1855. Their overall contribution to the culture of the time is obscure.

In 1874 the Honourable Mr. Cunningham founded the Cosmopolitan Club in the city, as a means of 'bringing the two races in India into friendly relations'.[55] Pundi Runganananda Mudaliar, educated at Presidency College was appointed a fellow of the University of Madras in 1872 and was known for actively participating in the deliberations of the University Senate. He associated with the British during the proceedings of the Madras municipality and 'was the life and soul of the Cosmopolitan Club'.[56] It would appear that unbroken traditions of multilingual and multicultural male Indo-British interaction were continued officially and socially in the confines of such old and new institutions.

This brief foray into less well-known aspects of Indo-British relations in the south has revealed that such interactions defy easy classification. Throughout the eighteenth and early nineteenth centuries ruling Indians and Britons met as friends and enemies, united and divided on small and large issues, across and within boundaries of *jati* and kinship. For the British, the

[54] Mildred Archer, 'Serfogee: An Enlightened Thanjavur Ruler and his Patronage of the Arts', *The India Magazine* (1985), pp. 9–19.

[55] *Asylum Press Almanac* (Madras, 1874), p. xxvii.

[56] Parameswaran Pillai, *Representative Indians*, p. 187. He introduces many South Indian men of similar ilk.

act of conducting friendship across communities grew increasingly difficult as the two worlds separated to become racially exclusive. Nonetheless, there were those whose intellectual curiosity and desire to continue with friendships were accommodated through cross-cultural institutions. The late appearance of the Cosmopolitan Club shows that affinities amongst the old guard of the two communities remained. For élite Indians too, such friendships were no longer without serious political consequence; even as the southern élites cooperated in the establishment of the colonial state, they were in danger of abrogating many of their historic rights to rule. The unwillingness of these élites to abandon their traditional obligations and the ways in which they negotiated satisfactory compromises with the British shaped the ideologies and the contours of the so-called modern colonial state in South India. It softened the impact of colonial rule.[57]

The mixed culture of the Madras pro-consular élite produced a peculiar and unexpected hybrid imperial architectural style. The material evidence urges consideration that cross-cultural conversations continued in the nineteenth century despite the overbearing climate of racial segregation. If this aspect is overlooked then we are left with the explanation that this architecture appeared in Madras almost solely due to Lord Napier's ambition and vision where the Indian contribution was confined to a technical one. This is a possibility that cannot be ruled out entirely.

Three Hundred Years of Indo-European Architecture

When Europeans began building in India they confronted ancient and well-organised aesthetic, educational and architectural practices. The sources on this subject are few and dispersed and here I only attempt to provide a bare overview of a vast and complex building scenario. This overview is intended to function as a broad historical canvas for the rest of the book. Indigenous architecture received theoretical guidance and a remarkable degree of consensus and uniformity from a trans-regional group of texts, technical treatises, originally in Sanskrit, called the *Silpa Sastra*s or *Vastu Sastra*s.

The literature on the *sastra*s is both voluminous and scattered and is matched by a vernacular literature even more scattered and less well known. Bruno Dagens' *Mayamata: An Indian Treatise on Housing Architecture and Iconography* illustrates some of their architectural concerns.[58] The *Mayamata* is considered to be a revealed text, expressed by Maya, the divine architect. Its theory of architecture has been extrapolated from existing monuments belonging to an easily identifiable

[57] Pamela Price, *Kingship and Political Practice in Colonial India* (Cambridge, 1996), p. 4.

[58] Bruno Dagens, *Mayamata: An Indian Treatise on Housing Architecture and Iconography* (New Delhi, 1985).

school. Originating in South India and written in the Chola period, it is part of the Saivite agamic literature, lacking any sectarian connection. It comprises 36 chapters, written in 3,300 verses, on palm leaf manuscripts in Tamil, Telugu and Malayalam script. The text makes many references to a classical India and is said to belong to a slightly different South Indian school of architecture than the other equally renowned treatise, the *Manasara*. The monuments covered by the text are broken up into elements, with a norm established for governing the circumstances of their use. There is dispute as to whether the *sastras* can be accurately regarded as treatises on architecture. Some believe that the social hierarchy of objects set out in the *Manasara* also designate a material hierarchy. In other words, they have a wider social purpose which is to designate man-made things and the position of the people who have access to them in society.[59]

Until the nineteenth century, European building needs in India were chiefly utilitarian and it was natural that the sophisticated and scholarly world of texts and aesthetics bypassed the range of most early European builders. They engaged the indigenous construction industry for practical purposes and built domestic, religious, military and commercial structures in a mixed Indo-European mode. European monumental secular building began when the French built an extravagant government house in their fort at Pondicherry (south of Madras), in 1752. This is usually regarded as the first building to make a significant civil statement about European aesthetics, monumental civil architecture in the European style was accessible in and around all the various European enclaves. The British began their monumental building in Madras and Calcutta almost simultaneously (see Fig. 9). To celebrate Tipu Sultan's defeat, in 1800 the governing élite built a vast pile of a Banqueting Hall in Madras. It was in reality a temple for the worship of war heroes, modelled on the Banqueting Hall at Whitehall. In Calcutta they began work on a splendid government house—a new residence for the Governor-General. This was the first instance where Britons deployed classical architecture with a view to announcing political power. Prior to this time Company men were hardly on competing terms with Indian élites for conferring architectural patronage. Only with the passing of the wealth and power of the Indian élites to the British did the latter begin to emerge as competing patrons of architecture.

Indians too experimented freely with European aesthetic conventions. By the early nineteenth century they had acquired a fair repertory of Indo-European built forms, popular with a range of patrons, from royalty and land owners to minor urban dwellers in colonial port-cities. Colonial wars and histories have bequeathed a dim understanding of Indian patronage of European architecture. Here I refer to the architecture of Lucknow and Thanjavur—sites

[59] For a new reading of the scope of the *sastras* to include all material objects, see Jennifer Howes, 'Kings, Things and the Courtly Ideal in Pre-Colonial South India 1500–1800' (University of London, Ph.D., 1999), p. 25.

Figure 9: A view of part of St. Thome Street, Fort St. George, 1803

where royal Indian patrons commissioned lavish monumental Indo-European architecture on the eve of the transfer of power. For Indian patrons, unlike for Europeans, Indo-European architecture was not always a practical necessity. It was instead an exciting opportunity to indulge an intellectual curiosity and an invitation to experiment with fascinating new forms, spaces and details.

The notion of an Indo-European discourse in architecture, spanning the period between 1500 and 1800, has not yet appeared in architectural writing. It is very likely that such a discourse began and matured in avenues of informal association between Europeans and Indians since the early days of Portuguese arrival. Indo-European architecture represented one strand in the changing scene of contemporary Indian architecture. As mentioned in the Introduction, modern Indian architecture reached the apogée of its efflorescence in the nawabi city of Lucknow. The range of robust European responses it evoked attests to its political and not simply aesthetic impact. There is good reason to believe that the architecture of Lucknow was well known in some high-level metropolitan architectural circles in England.

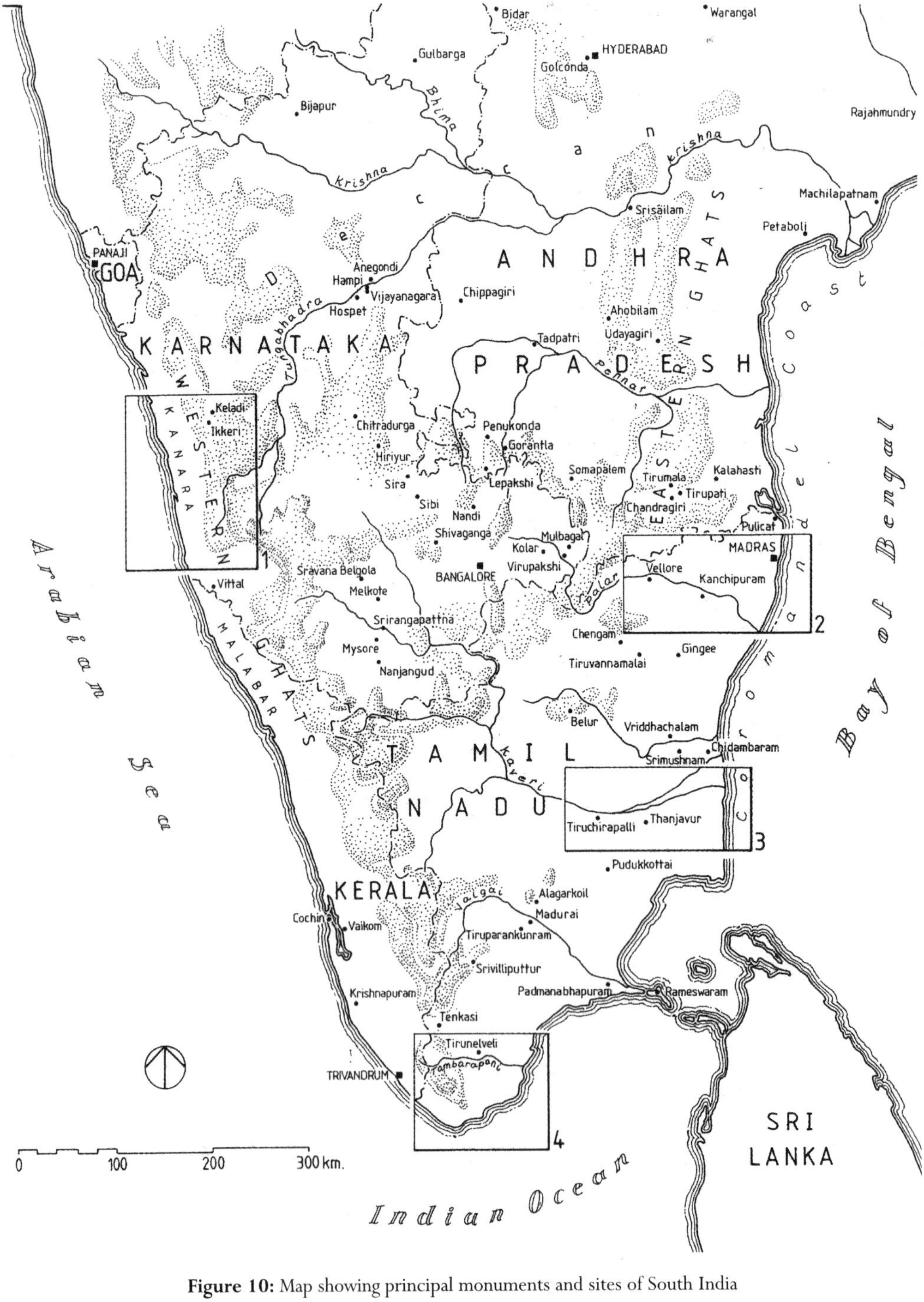

Figure 10: Map showing principal monuments and sites of South India

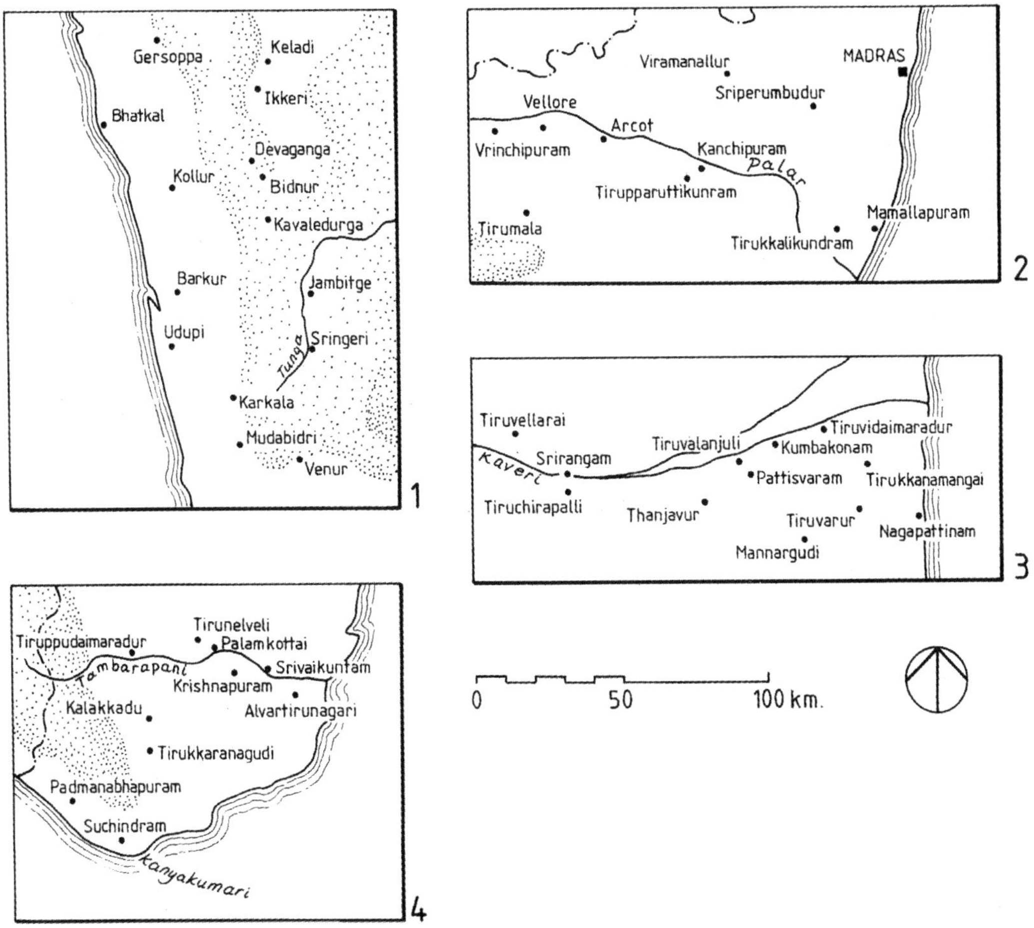

Figure 11: Insets for Map 10

In fact, it was the British reaction to the architecture of Lucknow that prompted Rosie Llewellyn Jones to write a book to answer the question, 'How could mere buildings excite such vituperation from writers, politicians and architects?'[60] She described the Qaisarbagh Palace, commissioned by the nawabs between 1849 and 1850, as one of the most remarkable palace complexes ever erected; 'designed with a virtuosity, panache and fantastic vision to create buildings that have a truly surreal quality'. The palace design endeavoured to simulate the tradition of great tent cities by using terraces and walls to divide up gardens, and encircle these and the buildings from the plains outside. It was one of the many Nawabi palaces that had served as

[60] Rosie Llewellyn Jones, *A Fatal Friendship*, preface. Her book offers a descriptive introduction to the subject.

Figure 12: Trichinopoly Palace, top-lit wagon vault, eighteenth century

military strongholds for those who fought the British. The British regarded the palaces as symbols of rebellion and occupied them for military purposes after their victory of 1857. Lord Canning, the Viceroy, declared in 1858 that 'from this day it [Avadh] will be held with a force which nothing can withstand, and the authority of the government will be carried to every corner of the province'.[61] All the palaces fell victim to Robert Napier's brutally destructive plans to make the city safe for the red-coated army of its new rulers.

Descriptions of the Thanjavur and Madurai palace complexes and the extant remains there and in Hyderabad suggest that similar architectural experiments were conducted in the south. And it is fair to assume that in varying degrees, the same was true of the lost palaces, temples and gardens of the massive forts of Chingleput, Ginjee, Arcot, Rajagiri, Chandragiri and Trichinopoly in the vicinity of Madras (see Figs. 10–14). But they were victims of bitter rivalry in the Carnatic wars and blown up by the British, long before the courtly buildings of Lucknow were destroyed. The point to be made here is that Europeans were familiar with the impressive fortifications, architectural splendour and cultural significance of these sites.[62] There are indications early on itself in the century that Indian architecture in the metropolis was regarded with some esteem. It was hardly coincidental that in 1835, the Council of the fledgling Royal

[61] Veena Talwar Oldenberg, 'The Making of Colonial Lucknow', p. 27.

[62] Jean-Marie Lafont, *Chitra: Cities and Monuments of Eighteenth-Century India from the French Archives* (Oxford, 2001).

Figure 13: Madurai Palace, top-lit dome

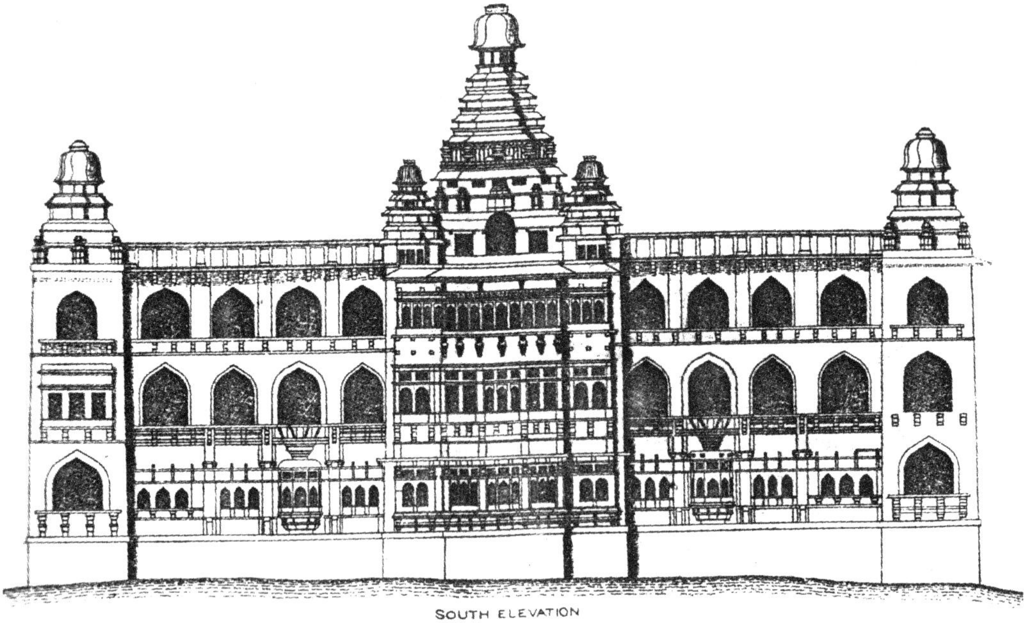

Figure 14: Chandragiri Palace, Tirupati, Chisholm, 1883

Institute of British Architects invited His Highness, Rajah Sivaji of Tanjore (Thanjavur), and His Majesty the King of Oude, and two architectural writers trained at Cambridge, to be its first honorary members.[63] At the request of the Council, Rajah Sivaji gifted the Institute a set of 18 architectural drawings of buildings in Thanjavur.[64]

But this still leaves us wondering why the Indo-European architecture in the smaller states that succeeded the Mughal Empire in the north and the Vijayanagara Empire in the south, proved so appealing and threatening to the British? To European eyes this oriental architecture was strange. In their struggle to capture its essence within familiar visual patterns, Lucknow, for instance, was variously described as redolent of handsome European cities such as Paris, Dresden, St. Petersburg, Moscow, Oxford and Constantinople, albeit with an oriental flair. It was without precedent. The historian Hermann Goetz, writing in 1938, was willing to censure the luxury of eighteenth-century Indian courts, but unwilling to deny their high cultural achievement. For Goetz, the mingling of Western Baroque, Rococo and Classicist

[63] RIBA Council Minutes, No. 42 and 152, 1834–1844, RIBA British Architectural Library. Lucknow was the capital of Awadh known to the British as Oude.

[64] Rajah Seevajee, RIBA Archives, Letters to Council, Box 2, Folder 1,LC/2/1/6,30,1, (1838). The drawings are held at the British Architectural Library, Folder F3, London.

styles created architecture of 'solid refined elegance' and 'delicate sweet splendour'. It was magical and possessed a complete synthesis of buildings, gardens, and landscape, dreamy, musical and unreal. He attributed the mystic quality of refined aesthetic culture to political and economic decay, but conceded that the architecture of northern states like Udaipur, Jaipur, Deeg, Jodhpur and Lucknow was one of transformation, not evolution.[65]

Perhaps the appeal of this architecture lay in its mystery and inaccessibility—it combined allure and threat. One tradition of Indian palace design possesses a quality of 'elusion' (a term used by Giles Tillotson) where a deliberate indefinability creates a sense of mystery. He noted that such buildings defy simple, direct apprehension, although the devices by which such an effect was achieved could be learned, analysed and understood.[66] The architecture fused spatial ambiguity with aesthetics to create something faintly familiar to Europeans and yet whimsical and unknowable. Its threat lay in that it was something the British coveted but could not possess. Even as they assumed political and cultural overlordship the British élite knew they lacked the resources to match modern Indian architecture. As the soldier-engineers demolished the fabled buildings of Lucknow, less philistine Britons were beginning to seek control of Indo-European architecture. They were realising that to hold India something more than force was required.

At no stage however was there an observable coherence or singularity in the British response to Indian architecture. The army and the church, heavily reliant on native knowledge and labour, had unhesitatingly built using Indian technical and aesthetic systems. A more formal conduct ensued when the Ecclesiological Society entered the scene in 1845, in response to requests for suitable church designs for colonies, as far flung as Australia and Hong Kong. But for the *Ecclesiologist*, the architectural periodical of the High Church movement, 'style was a matter of religious identification and national prestige'; it remained hostile and intransigent in its refusal to support church building in local styles.[67] However, real dissent arose in the ranks of colonial patrons only after military success, when public buildings became prestigious symbols of conquest and state power.

Even then, British response was diverse and contradictory. In Calcutta, the leading repository of colonial power, the conservative grandees' favoured architectural style was to

[65] Hermann Goetz, *The Crisis of Indian Civilisation in the Eighteenth and Early Nineteenth Century and the Genesis of Indo-Muslim Civilisation* (Calcutta, 1938), p. 21.

[66] Giles Tillotson, *The Rajput Palaces: The Development of an Architectural Style, 1450–1750* (New Haven, 1987), p. 38.

[67] In April 1845 James Millard put forward this idea to the Oxford Society for promoting the study of Gothic Architecture. It is discussed in Mark Crinson, *Empire Building: Orientalism and Victorian Architecture* (London, 1996), p. 117.

remain strictly European and classical; but as early as the 1860s one strand within the imperial élite expressed a preference for the aesthetic language favoured by Indian royalty. This move paralleled the mounting technical tyranny of the newly empowered bureaucrats in the Public Works Department. Soldier- engineers taught an austere, bare classicism in their new engineering schools. Wherever Britons sought to control Indian architecture they transformed it. The buildings they produced were of a different order from the pre-colonial Indo-European architecture created by Indians. British architects, designing for the colonial state, rarely achieved in their Indo-European architecture the mystical, surreal quality of modern Indian architecture. The latter derived its élan from a degree of independent contact between Europe and pre-colonial South Asia and it was built for royal patrons by Indians trained in indigenous modes.

On the other hand, it has to be remembered that several wealthy Europeans in Lucknow had their own Indo-European palaces designed and built by Indo-Europeans. Claude Martin's adventurous buildings come to mind, especially Constantia, that four-floor concoction of Gothic towers and Grecian pilasters. 'A strange and fantastical building of every species of architecture, and adorned with minute stucco fret-work, enormous red lions with lamps instead of eyes, Chinese mandarins and ladies with shaking heads and all the gods and goddesses of the heathen mythology.'[68] The most amazing feature of the building was its summit, crowned by stucco statues, and two bisecting arched ribs springing from the four octagonal towers ascending from the core of the building. The ribs float in mid-air, giving the structure a fairy tale touch. Apparently Constantia, designed by Martin himself, was a prototype for many Indian buildings. Honoria Lawrence who visited in 1842 commented on the inappropriate use of innumerable stucco statues of every imaginable design from gigantic soldiers, to Jupiter, Venus and Hercules that adorned this 'Musulman' city, which must be a 'sore abomination to true believers'. She claimed they were introduced by 'a certain General Martin about half a century ago'. The mixing across cultures and people was diverse and vibrant if not always 'good' by purist standards.

The Designers—Indian (*sthapathi*)

From the literature presently available for study it is difficult to extract much more than a fragmented and incoherent idea of who designed buildings and how this information was transmitted to the builder in pre- and proto-colonial times. It is in some ways easy therefore to assume that those who designed and built were the same people. The *Mayamata, Manasara*

[68] Lord Valentia, cited in Rosie Llewellyn Jones, *A Fatal Friendship*, p. 140.

and other treatises, however, suggest that the division of labour was, at least in theory, of greater complexity.[69] The *Samarangana* depicted the qualifications of the *sthapati* architect, as knowledge of the *sastras*, practical experience, intuitive insight and righteous conduct. The *Mayamata* described a four-fold division of technical personnel. The *sthapati* was 'from a renowned land and of mixed caste; a man of quality who must know how to establish buildings and must be well-versed in all the sciences, learned in mathematics, able to draw, and must have crossed the ocean of the science of architecture'.[70] Another was the *sutragrahin*, the disciple, or the son of the architect who followed his directions. He was skilful in all the arts. Then there was the *taksaka*, who cut the stone, wood, bricks and lastly, the *vardhaki* who assembled and erected them. These texts imply a fair degree of learning on the part of the *sthapati* and the *sutragrahin* and outline a deeply hierarchical social organisation with an expert architect at the apex.

The monuments, which pertained to the architectural school which the *Mayamata* represented, covered a period of fifteen centuries and an area which encompassed a large part of the Indian peninsula, as well as of South East Asia. It appears that the plans of Mughal palaces of the late medieval period also followed the dictates of the *sastras*, although they assumed forms which appeared to be 'Arabic' or 'Persian' (this distinction refers to the fact that they did not look like 'Hindu' temples).[71] Naturally, some historians have proved more willing than others to treat the *sastras* seriously, as possible secular design guides. In the domain of temple studies, however, it is reasonably well accepted that the *sastras* were consulted as design manuals, although the intricacies of how they were used have not been unravelled.[72] The scope of the *sastras* allowed them to function as canons on urban design and architecture: they specified the layout of different types of cities, villages, dwelling places, palaces, as well as details of columns, doors, windows, materials and techniques.

The information was always written and not drawn, and the list of dimensions given for a moulding, for example, was not intelligible unless the description was read and drawn simultaneously. Similarly, plans and elevations could not be read easily unless they were transposed to drawings, which the use of regular patterns made simple. This ambiguity afforded the specialist a chance to interpret the text in a personal way or in a way guided by the fashions of the time

[69] For some early work on treatises, see P.K. Acharya (ed.), *Manasara on Architecture and Sculpture* (4 vols., Allahabad, 1927) and D.N. Shukla (ed.), 'Hindu Science of Architecture', *Vastu Sastra* (5 vols., Lucknow, 1960).

[70] Bruno Dagens, *Mayamata*, p. 10.

[71] Jon Lang, Madhavi Desai, and Miki Desai, *Architecture and Independence: The Search for Identity, India 1880–1980* (New Delhi, 1997), p. 29.

[72] For an interesting discussion see Adam Hardy, 'Form, Transformation and Meaning in Indian Temple Architecture', in Giles Tillotson (ed.), *Paradigms of Indian Architecture* (London, 1998), pp. 107–35.

and place. Since this puzzle is not peculiar to medieval India, I would like to refer to an interpretation of grid-based plans in an Ottoman context of the fifteenth and sixteenth centuries in an article that also discussed the painting of the figure holding a grid-plan in the Mughal emperor Babur's chronicle the *Baburnama*, c.1580. Necipoglu-Kafadar wrote that 'The key points in the elevation of a standardized building could be computed by traditional formulae deriving from proportions inherent in the geometric ground plans with modular grids.'[73]

Little is known of the training of architects or craftsmen although it seems that a thorough knowledge of drawing was essential to the superior craftsman, even if it was not used to make technical drawings, for accurate estimating and costing purposes. Art pupils were first taught to prepare colours, sharpen chisels, burnish paper, make hair brushes and become wholly familiar with the tools of their trade.[74] Later, they were taught to draw repeating patterns with a geometrical construction, and all the different types of conventional floral ornaments made use of in design. The aim was not to enable the pupil to copy a design before him but to enable him to reproduce from memory, certain well-known designs and figure subjects and to make use of the traditional elements of design. For years, the disciple was not allowed to try his hand at drawing a full sketch. At no time was the pupil taught to draw from nature. Those who did not know the traditional forms and those who drew after their own vain imagining were often scorned.[75] In this instance, although the academic learning of the ordinary artist was limited, his training was most rigorous.

Craft trades were usually hereditary and learned in the actual workshop and in the home by precept, example and practise. From the outset the disciple absorbed the technique, tradition and metaphysics. The third-eye (considered the eye-of-wisdom) opening ceremony was performed at the age of seven. The artist was expected to cultivate a certain degree of asceticism. In 2001, I interviewed *sthapathi* K.P. Umapathi, of the *Visvakarma* (the divine architect) community, in Kumbakonam, near Thanjavur. He revealed that, from a young age, his father taught him the principles of proportion and design using a secret three-dimensional system of linking dots in space. He was reluctant to offer any further clarification of what this might be. Design was also taught by precedent through visits to temples and building sites, in the company

[73] Necipoglu-Kafadar, Gulru, 'Plans and Models in 15th and 16th Century Ottoman Architectural Practice', *Journal of the Society of Architectural Historians*, XLV, September (1986), pp. 224–43. Alexandrina Buchanan discusses how this process occurred in medieval church architecture, Alexandrina Buchanan, 'The Power and the Glory: the Meanings of Medieval Architecture', in Iain Borden and David Dunster (eds.), *Architecture and the Sites of History* (Oxford, 1995), pp. 78–92.

[74] B.N. Goswamy, 'The Pahari Artists: A Study', *Roopa Lekha*, xxxii, 2 (1961), pp. 31–50.

[75] Ananda Coomaraswamy, *Medieval Sinhalese Art*, 2nd edn. (New York, 1956).

of senior family members. The families had their own *sastra*s which contained code words and ciphers. Umapathi claimed that his community possessed an exclusive higher knowledge of Sanskrit, rituals related to design and building and drawing. A significant feature of design knowledge systems was secrecy and cryptography to which access was regulated by birth.[76]

Alice Boner's article on *Economic and Organisational Aspects of the Building Operations of the Sun Temple at Konarka* is a translation and edited version of a manuscript called the *Baya Cakada*—a book recording the day-to-day expenses incurred in the construction of the gigantic temple of Konarka, around the middle of the thirteenth century.[77] She claims that comparable records have not been found in Europe for any of the great cathedrals of the Middle Ages. The manuscript offers, amongst other things, an account of a most exclusive and sophisticated design consultation practice. It recorded the presence of a group of Atreya Brahmanas who were experts in the *silpa sastra*s and acted as design consultants: they gave advice and guidance to workmen as and when required. They were settled in a special camp near Konarka, called Vedapura. Whether these sculptors and workmen were members of professional corporations, bound by strict rules of conduct and enjoying certain privileges as they did in medieval Europe, is not known. Boner believes that they did have some professional organisation on patriarchal lines in the form of caste associations. The executive architect, Gadadhara Mahapatra, was the head of a very large regional association of stone masons. He had additional titles bestowed as rewards for distinctions merited by individual work; his payments were recorded in land, cash and in kind.

The works of the great masters were not executed single-handedly. On site each master had a team of specialists and in each contract the number of men they could have was stipulated. It seems that the design of the sculpture was the work of one person and its execution that of many. At the time of building a wise disposition of information-sharing in the team kept it conversant with the master's intentions at all times. On very large projects a change of plan or any major addition, after receiving client approval, was notified across many camp sites by a drum beat. There were meetings with the *sutradhara* disciple or junior, to discuss new work and masters and, *silpin*s or artisans often made individual suggestions which were accepted, rejected or sent to the patron for arbitration.

[76] He volunteered the information that Velayuta Acharya, of the Madras School of Art, had assisted E.B. Havell with the drawings and information contained in the latter's prodigious output on Indian art.

[77] Alice Boner, 'Economic and Organizational Aspects of the Building Operations of the Sun Temple at Konarka', *Journal of Economic and Social History of the Orient*, 13 (1970), pp. 257–72.

The existence of powerful guilds that functioned with jurisdiction over several *nadus* or villages has been attested to.[78] The assembly, officiated by a chief or elder, fixed the rules of work, the quality of the product and its price, and therefore safeguarded both artisan and customer. Its decisions were binding on the whole community and it acted as an intermediary between members and the state. It has been suggested that the larger assemblies were in turn affiliated to certain *math*s or academies, to which their members showed special deference. It is generally held that the artisan or architect in Mughal India had low social status, while those in some areas of the medieval south appear to have enjoyed a position of eminence.[79]

Temple design was sharply differentiated into a small, exclusive group of prodigiously talented, highly trained, skilled and literate men and the bulk who were ordinary artisans trained in several crafts. Complex designs were the responsibility of an élite, fluent in the mysteries of the *sastra*s and practical skills. Specialist guilds were restricted to sculptors and architects, giving the leading masters a powerful and independent voice. They were the men who directed the gigantic temple building programmes, moving with great ease from architectural planning to monumental sculpture, to fine chisel work and even engineering designs. Since architects travelled and lived on work sites, it is possible that clients could choose their designers either through local contacts or on the basis of reputations of masters of established workshops.

The earliest Indian paintings done for Europeans are said to have originated in the Andhra region in the seventeenth century. But the origins of the genre of paintings called 'Company paintings' are assigned to the early eighteenth century. They were prepared for Company officials by unemployed native artists who were gradually losing court patronage. The paintings covered a variety of different subjects and from around 1800 large architectural drawings were made for a European market, as well as for native rulers. The Maratha court at Thanjavur, with its Telugu speaking *moochy* artists (originally leather workers), reinforced by migrant artist families from Hyderabad, developed into a flourishing school of Company painting in the late eighteenth and early nineteenth centuries. Army survey drawings created a large demand for Indian draftsmen in the eighteenth century causing the establishment of the first survey school in India, in Madras, in 1794.[80]

[78] Kellson Collyer, *The Hoysala Artists: Their Identity and Styles* (Mysore, 1990), p. 105.

[79] Ahsan Jan Qaisar, *Building Construction in Mughal India: The Evidence from Painting* (Delhi, 1988), p. 43, and K. Sundaram, 'The Artisan Community of Medieval Andhra (A.D.1000–1600)', *Journal of Indian History*, 43 (1965), pp. 905–15.

[80] S. Ambirajan, 'Science and Technology Education in South India', in Roy MacLeod and Deepak Kumar (eds.), *Technology and the Raj* (New Delhi, 1995), pp. 112–33. Mildred Archer also gives a South Indian provenance—Andhra, date 1686—for the first European paintings by Indians. Mildred Archer, *Company Paintings: Indian Paintings of the British Period* (New Jersey, 1992), p. 23.

Popular demand had also produced a pool of Indian architects specialising in European architecture. It was not unusual for Europeans to draw on their specialist skills. William Hickey, living in Calcutta in the 1790s, availed himself of the services of an Indian architect to build his European-style houses.[81] In 1802 the British Resident at Hyderabad, James Kirkpatrick, especially requested the services of a 'Madras Native Architect' (*ruaz*—an expert mason conversant with the European orders of architecture) to help with the 'perfect European classical form of the Palladian Hyderabad Residency'—second only to the Government House in Calcutta.[82] The livelihood and status of this group ultimately came under threat from the imported military engineers who were soon to dominate the world of colonial building.

The Designers—Britons (soldier/engineers)

British designers practising in India were not professionals to the extent that their practice was often eclectic: it included surveying, engineering, architecture, mechanical works and whatever else their patron might demand of them. Although they were, like Indians, apprentice-trained, the colonial market place created a demand for military engineers, not architects. Military engineers have been called a 'deliberate instrument of British Imperial authority';[83] they brought a very different world-view and social relations to the local architectural interface. In the early days the army competed with Indian rulers as a patron offering regular work. The Company's engineers were granted commissions in the army after January 1759. It was a ruse to attract staff by giving them some status relative to the king's officers—royal engineers—serving in Madras. The Engineering Corps was placed entirely on a military footing in 1775. It was the shortage of officers for the so-called scientific arms in India—engineering and artillery—that compelled the Company to open its Military Training Academy at Addiscombe, in 1809. Addiscombe was modelled on the Royal Military Academy at Woolwich, opened in 1741, which together with Royal Military College, Marlow, opened in 1802, had produced efficient officers for the King's Engineers and Artillery. The burgeoning demand for specialisation resulted in the opening of a new school in Chatham, in 1812, whose purpose was to train the Corps of Royal Military Artificers or Sappers and Miners and the junior officers of the Royal Engineers.[84]

[81] Rosie Llewellyn Jones, *A Fatal Friendship*, p. 159.

[82] Quoted in William Dalrymple, *White Mughals: Love and Betrayal in Eighteenth Century India* (London, 2002), p. 351.

[83] John Weiler, 'Colonial Connections: Royal Engineers and Building Technology Transfer in the Nineteenth Century', *Construction History*, 12 (1996).

[84] E.W. Sandes, *The Military Engineer in India*, vol. 2 (2 vols., Chatham, 1933), pp. 346–50.

The pioneering and innovative scientific training supplied by the academies was not however the norm. Apprenticeship was the preferred training method for artificers or scientific personnel in England. Unlike the French, Britain did not possess state-sponsored training programmes for engineers or architects in the eighteenth century.[85] The science schools of eighteenth-century France were steeply ranked, leading to heavy social stratification. The Grand Ecoles of Artillerie and Genie headed the list. One strand of the French military enlightenment envisioned a society controlled by a corps of men of the state, armed with new forms of knowledge, transferred to practical instruments of power. Their social ideology broke with the privileges of birth and patronage and was founded on meritocratic striving. The colonial state gave the military engineer in India a similar patronage base and access to knowledge, employment and power unavailable in England. No formal training for civil architects was offered in Britain till the 1890s.

The origins of modern engineering possessed an interlocking epistemological and social base. Students were drawn largely from the sons of civil servants and the rentier classes trained in abstract mathematics and science and bound for state service at the highest level, often in the military.[86] Moreover, the training emphasised mathematics and drawing, both of which produced a common body of knowledge instilling uniformity and precision. It gave rise to a new way of seeing and behaving and was the technicians' equivalent of *esprit de corps*. Drawing was the key to production control. It defined the engineer's role in the hierarchy of knowledge and shifted production control from the artisan atelier to the drafting studio. Drawing also made possible the exercise of power by enabling the possessor to master phenomena on a scale and at a distance, inaccessible to others. Descriptive geometry (mechanical drawing), developed by Gaspard Monge, was the universal language necessary to all those who worked in the mechanical arts. Its function was to discipline the artefact. With it the path was open to incorporate the secret drawings of artisans into an objective drawing system which eliminated individual idiosyncrasies. Monge's drawing technique remained a military secret until 1794, and was unknown in England till much later.

Whatever knowledge the engineering system in Britain provided it excluded architectural design and aesthetics. The absence of aesthetic training amounted to only one facet of the two

[85] For a useful discussion of the French approach, see Antoine Picon, *French Architects and Engineers in the Age of Enlightenment* (Cambridge, 1992).

[86] Ken Alder, *Engineering the Revolution: Arms and Enlightenment in France 1763–1815* (Princeton, 1997), p. 138. English machine builders and craftsmen used technical drawings extensively but they did not formally learn mechanical drawing. They were all apprentice-trained.

very different cultural universes that met at the Indo-British architectural interface. One group of men highly trained in the aesthetics and design modes of Indian indigenous knowledge, but rapidly losing wealthy patrons, converged towards another who possessed access to European indigenous knowledge and a powerful new patron.

A New Code of Taste

A measure of self-delusion and prejudice underscored the British bid to seize intellectual leadership of Indo-European architecture. By the 1860s art intellectuals had developed a hierarchical code whose Eurocentric ideological component staked a claim for sole custodianship of legitimate 'taste' in architecture. The new code of 'taste', international in reach, placed western aesthetics at the apex. It swung into action fabricating a static 'tradition' of 'Indian' architecture, which took its assigned place lower down. Certain buildings designated as 'traditional' were duly banished to a golden, dead and distant 'past'. In the new 'past', the imperial soldier-archaeologist safely admired and interpreted their petrified beauty. The code now discovered that in comparison with a golden 'past' modern Indian architecture was in 'decline'. The ideology of 'decline' embraced the wider Christian notion that redemption was impossible without European intervention. The truth of 'decline' was verified by the pure 'Indian tradition' to which modern architecture was an unworthy successor. The European intelligentsia, heavy with the obligation to civilise those inferior to themselves graciously assumed the added burden of guarding the new 'Indian tradition'.

Military control of building and demography denied nineteenth-century British India a pool of talented western intellectuals and designers. And a state policy that excluded Indian designers from senior posts created a leadership vacuum that was filled by the scholar/soldier/engineer. Indigenous designers were accorded subordinate status in the new establishment cadre. The 'neutral' tools of the 'modern sciences' of engineering, archaeology, anthropology and history were charged with defining and regulating new models of cultural sharing. The new disciplines, conducted in European languages, afforded ambitious Europeans posturing as 'scientists' unimpeded access to Indian architecture and the intellectual leadership of its history and contemporary development. The poverty of English architecture in the colonies and its imitation by native princes was ridiculed by the self-proclaimed 'authority' on 'world' architecture—James Fergusson, whose inimitable words, written in 1862, were that:

> With the knowledge we possess of the tastes of our countrymen, it is no matter of wonder that they should have carried with them their great principle of getting the greatest possible amount of accommodation at the least

possible expense.... Had the French ever colonized the East, their artistic instincts might have led to a different result: but as the inartistic races of mankind seem the only people capable of colonization, we must be content with the facts as they stand, and can only record the progress of the flood-tide of bad Art as we find it.[87]

Fergusson was, on the whole, a great admirer of the art of the East.

State command of Indo-European architectural design became so thorough that by the twentieth century it acquired the peculiar distinction of being identified as the architecture of empire. It is ironic that the shift in leadership compelled twentieth-century nationalist ideologues to ignore the indigenous birth and vitality of this architecture. They preferred to summon western sources of inspiration for the new architecture of Indian independence. The principal designer for the new city of Bhubaneswar, 1948, in the state of Orissa, was the Berlin trained Otto Koenigsberger; Chandigarh was first designed by the American pair Albert Mayer and Matthew Nowicki. With the latter's death in 1950, the French architect Le Corbusier took over, assisted by Jane Drew and Maxwell Fry from England. A further irony was that an Indo-European trend, now termed 'revivalist', was pursued by foreign and Indian 'professional' architects in the twentieth century. The most notable examples of 'professional revivalism' were the Osmania University in Hyderabad, 1934, a joint design by Belgian and Indian architects; the neo-Dravidian style Vidhana Soudha, Bangalore, 1950, designed by R. Manickam and Hanumanthe Rao Naidu of the Mysore State, Public Works Department. It is significant that both are located in South India. The nation builders of independence failed to recognise that what they were marginalising as 'revivalist' also had a dynamic, modern Indo-European component. In a sense this brings us back to Lord Napier's insinuation in 1870 that Indian architecture was decaying or dead. The truth of the matter was very different—Indian architecture was changing. Indian patrons and architects were experimenting with modern forms in ways that the British could not control nor imitate. It was necessary for the British to curb this particular trajectory. As a safety valve, henceforth, Indians were encouraged to 'revive' tradition.

[87] James Fergusson, *History of the Modern Styles of Architecture* (London, 1862), p. 409.

2

Invisible Indians and 'Science Experts'

Thomas Fiott de Havilland and St. Andrew's Kirk 1816–21

In 1844 British readers of the *Foreign and Quarterly Review* were told that 'nowhere within the wide circle of civilised society, will we meet with individuals more mild, more unassuming, more refined, more intellectual, in one word, more completely gentleman, than the officers of the Indian Army'.[1] According to Douglas Peers, it is only recently that historians of India have come to regard as important, the role of the Indian army in determining the political and economic directions of the colonial state, as well as in shaping social interactions between Indians and the British; but they still pay insufficient attention to the army's legacy in intellectual, cultural and imaginary terms. This chapter tells the story of the building of a Presbyterian church commissioned by the East India Company. It was designed by a military engineer, Thomas Fiott de Havilland. The only modern writing on the building are two short notes by Sten Nilsson (1968) and Philip Davies (1985).[2] They discussed it simply as a British building; any special qualities it possessed were attributed to the talent of the designer. The documentary records pertaining to the building are scant and exclusively British. To recount the story of building it was necessary to read the written evidence in the context of the nineteenth-century building

[1] Cited in Douglas M. Peers, 'Colonial Knowledge and Military in India', pp. 157–80.

[2] Sten Nilsson, *European Architecture;* Philip Davies, *Splendours of the Raj* (London, 1985).

world. This revealed a hitherto silent Indo-British conversation on architecture and the great pleasure architecture opened up to high-ranking colonial officials and their military technicians.

Indo-European Christians and Indian Vaults

Tradition ascribes the origins of Christianity in South India to the Apostolic Church, established when St. Thomas preached on the Malabar and Coromandel coasts. When the Portuguese arrived on the Malabar coast in 1492, they discovered a flourishing native Christian community who called themselves Syrian Christians. In 1605 the Jesuits sent the Roman nobleman, Roberto de Nobili, to Madurai, on a conversion mission.[3] The Jesuits led the modern intellectual exchange between Europe and South India. When the servants of the East India Company began building large churches in the south, they confronted an ancient and well-established native as well as a European Christian tradition of church building.

The oldest Protestant Church in Madras is the fort church of St. Mary, built in 1678. It was designed by William Dixon, chief gunner and designer of bastions to the East India Company. In the early days, because fort guns came off ships, naval gunners were also fort designers. The placement and use of guns required specialist knowledge: only to be found in artillery schools—the first to provide science education in Europe.[4] In the isolated conditions of early colonial forts, a link was forged between the army, the navy, design and building knowledge. Important buildings like St. Mary's were doubtless built using Indian materials, labour and knowledge. It has a peculiar bomb-proof, five-foot thick barrel vaulted roof, allowing it to double up as an arsenal or shelter; in this respect it was similar to its indigenous counterpart, the walled Hindu temple.

The nearest church of similar date and construction was the Church of Zion (see Fig. 15), in Tranquebar (Tarangambadi), the official church of the Danish East India Company, built in 1701. This too had a wagon vaulted roof rising above an Indian-style parapet ornamented with turrets.[5] The architectural historian Sten Nilsson noted that,

> The roof was vaulted in the same way as the Hindu temples in the town [see Fig. 17]; its section looks like a pointed arch. This [was] undoubtedly a strange borrowing, when one thinks of the old symbolism of church building, where the vault represent[ed] the heavens, but the reason [was], of course, purely practical: the Indian craftsmen were allowed to use the vaulting technique to which they were accustomed.[6]

[3] Vincent Cronin, *A Pearl to India: The Life of Roberto de Nobili* (London, 1959), p. 35.

[4] Ken Alder, *Engineering the Revolution*, p. 57.

[5] Frank Penny, *The Church in Madras*, vol. 1 (2 vols., London, 1912), p. 251.

[6] It is interesting that Nilsson confirms the use of a pointed arch roof in Hindu temples of the Tranqebar region. Pointed arches are usually associated with Islamic architecture, not with Hindu temples. See Sten Nilsson, *European Architecture*, p. 49.

Figure 15: Zion Church, Tranquebar, c. 1717, official church of the Danish East India Company

The New Jerusalem Church in Tranquebar, built in 1717 for the Protestant missionary Ziegenbalg, had a Greek cross plan. As it combined both Dutch and native traditions, Nilsson designated this hybrid style—the Euro-Indian Baroque. Thus, at the start of the nineteenth century, we find that there were many different types of Indo-European church designs circulating in southern India. And European patrons were accustomed to using Indian vaulting: a central feature of the design and construction of St. Andrews. The earliest Anglican Church built in the classical style was the Presidency Church of St. John, in Calcutta, 1787, designed by James Agg, an engineer officer.

Aristocratic Competition
St. George's—A Church for the English

The witty pen of the former Reverend William Taylor (Munro) informs us that the Madras aristocracy was shut out from the 'church' (St. Mary's) because it was usually filled by the military. Outside the fort, the only churches were either Roman, or unsuitably Anglican, serving poor white and native congregations. Thus, even if the 'bigwigs' wanted to go to church, they had no church to go to.[7]

[7] W.T. Munro, *Madrasiana* (Madras, 1889), p. 15.

This élite civilian need was met with the building of the appropriately imposing and spacious neo-classical St. George's Church on the Choultry plain. Funded partly by the state and partly by subscription, it was constructed around 1814–15, and consecrated by the good Bishop Middleton, of Calcutta, in 1816. The Bishop wrote to the Governor of Madras that he had been quite struck by the plainness, or even the ugliness, of buildings being erected as churches. His view was a clear warning to the Company that in some circles at least, building aesthetics could no longer simply be dismissed on pecuniary grounds, even for minor buildings like out-of-station churches.[8]

Reverend Taylor was 'much impressed by the beauty and grandeur of the large Ionic pillars of the St. George's portico' (see Fig. 16), a portico with a carriage drive being a novelty in Madras, save at Government House. And St. George's naturally had much affinity with Government House. It was unequivocally built to gratify the pious wish of the upper-class laity. The church was designed by the incumbent Chief Engineer, Colonel James Caldwell, and erected under the supervision of Major Thomas Fiott de Havilland.[9] It made a splendid gathering for English colonists, owing to its size, white *chunam* (a highly polished plaster finish) façade and elegant interior ornamentation, glowing in the soft light filtered through stained-glass fanlights. It also sealed de Havilland's reputation. When de Havilland became the new presidency engineer he was to distinguish himself as an architect designing in the manner of James Gibbs:[10] none other than London's favourite Tory architect, trained under the Italian Baroque master Carlo Fontana.

Several commentators noted the weakness in the Gibbs design selected as the prototype for St. George's. The rectangular church looked like a Roman temple with a peculiar tower. It was no more classical than it was neo-classical. Here was an Anglican church with nave, aisles and an eastern chancel, looking like a pagan basilica. It had a portico on the short side and to add to the discomfort—a preposterous tower dwarfed the main body of the church; with a complicated design composed of different elements mounted on each other. The tower 'constituted a Baroque element'.[11]

In view of such criticism it is no wonder that the prototype adopted for St. Andrew's Kirk was rather more special. Gibbs remained the preferred choice for copying, but this time the

[8] Frank Penny, *The Church*, vol. 2, p. 343.

[9] MPMC, P/260/5, 86, 29 September 1818, Major de Havilland was Superintending Engineer for the Presidency Division by September 1818.

[10] Sten Nilsson, *European Architecture*, p. 129.

[11] Ibid., p. 127.

Figure 16: St. George's Church, Madras, side elevation

Figure 17: Tank on the Shiva Temple at Chidambaram, showing standard use of barrel vault over *gopuram* and wagon vault elsewhere, by Francis Swain Ward, oil on canvas, c. 1782

patrons chose his 'very wonderful' circular design for St. Martin-in-the-Fields. The latter had served as a model for several churches built in England in the late eighteenth century.[12] The notion that the Scottish church, when built, attempted to upstage the recently completed English church of St. George's had much currency and led to amusing banter in Madras. The Company's court of arms on the eastern pediment of St. Andrew's was flanked by lions with bullock-like humps, said to represent the temper of the British lion when his church—St. George's on the Choultry Plain—was eclipsed by St. Andrew's ostentatiously proclaiming itself as the Company church!

Aristocratic Competition
The Kirk: St. Andrew's, a Church for the Scots

'The Kirk', as it was referred to in common parlance, has in its time received a variety of superlative accolades. It has been described as the 'most splendid church in Madras',[13] as 'the finest 19th-century church in India'[14] and as one of the 'finest examples of Georgian Church architecture in Asia'.[15] Its origins lay with the decision taken by the House of Lords to renew the Charter of the Company, by the Act of 1813, with certain conditions attached. It was the wish of certain members of Parliament to press upon the Company the obligation to appoint Presbyterian ministers to the Presidency Towns in India. The Company, forced to oblige, increased its clerical establishment with the appointment of one minister of the Church of Scotland to each of the Presidencies. He was to be granted the same salary as that of a junior chaplain and was to be given a suitable place of worship or allow to have one erected.

The first Presbyterian Church to be erected following the official decree was in Calcutta, in 1816. It was of the basilica type with a plain Tuscan order. It was judged a handsome edifice, though some difficulty arose on the score of steeples proposed to be added to the Kirks. Doctor Middleton, the Bishop of Calcutta, had opposed it as an unusual and unconstitutional measure, inadmissible out of Scotland. Dr Bryce, head of the Scottish Church in India, persisted in support of his own establishment and carried the point. Kirk steeples rose in proud majesty among those of the English Church.[16]

[12] John Summerson, *Architecture in Britain 1530–1830*, *Pelican History of Art* (Somerset, 1977), p. 353.

[13] W.T. Munro, *Madrasiana*, p. 36.

[14] Philip Davies, *Splendours of the Raj*, p. 4.

[15] Peter Millar in the 'Introduction' to a copy of de Havilland's *An Account of Saint Andrew's Church Madras* (1982) held in St. Andrew's Church, Madras.

[16] Jeremiah Losty, *Calcutta: City of Palaces* (London, 1990), p. 87.

Nearly all the free merchants in Madras at the beginning of the nineteenth century were 'Scotchmen' [*sic*] though they were not all Presbyterians. But there was sufficient national feeling among them to desire a Kirk in Madras, even though they might prefer to attend the services at St. Mary's Church. The demand from Ireland and Scotland for jobs was pronounced in the civil service in late eighteenth-century Britain. It explains how Sir Henry Dundas, an élite Scot and President of the Board of Control, is said to have brought about 'the Scottisisation of India'. (The Board of Control was an organ of state, set up in 1775, to allow Parliament to control the Company. It included the Secretary of State and the Chancellor of the Exchequer, effectively making the Company a state department). Dundas explained to Sir Archibald Campbell, the Governor of Madras, that with a Scotchman [*sic*] at the head of the Board of Control, and a Scotchman at the Government of Madras, all India will soon be in their hands.[17] India in the eighteenth century was seen by some as a 'corn chest for Scotland' where, in the words of Sir Walter Scott, 'we poor gentry must send our younger sons'.[18] The Scottish Governor Mr Elliot and the Indian Scottish church establishment spared no expense to provide the Madras Scottish élite with a flashy flamboyant Kirk, the details of which largely bypassed the Court of Directors in London.

With the institution of parliamentary control, the more republican forms of corporate government of the older East India Company were transformed. Members of the aristocracy, armed with a more coherent imperial theory, were now assigned to build empire; they were not to be restrained by the vulgar counting-house values of merchant princes. What they set out to create was a sophisticated and splendid British empire, ruled from the finest examples of English architecture, not from the hand-me-down palaces of native kings or merchant houses. The new Governor-General and Anglo-Irish peer Lord Mornington (later Richard Wellesley), used the Lord-Lieutenancy of Ireland as his model to enhance the ostentatious viceregal pageant begun under Lord Cornwallis. He was determined to set British rule in India on a proper symbolic footing that interwove Indian rank with European chivalry. Wellesley developed his own patronage system with his own sycophants and modelled the new Calcutta Government House of 1801, on Kedleston Hall, Derbyshire (or the viceregal lodge in Dublin?).[19] For all his vainglory and

[17] David Cannadine, *Aspects of Aristocracy* (London, 1995), p. 23.

[18] Quoted in Anne Buddle 'The Scots in India', in Anne Buddle and Pauline Rohatgi (eds.), *The Tiger and the Thistle: Tipu Sultan and the Scots in India 1760–1800* (Edinburgh, 1999), pp. 55–58.

[19] It is usually accepted that Kedleston Hall, home of Lord Scarsdale, was the model, but it is also possible that the Irish building, like the concept of viceroy, used by the British to govern Ireland since the eighteenth century was known to Wellesley.

colonial posturing the English rewarded him with a mere Irish peerage—Lord Mornington became Marquess Wellesley. His brother Arthur Wellesley, on the other hand, who also began his military career in South India, went on to become a national hero, honoured in 1814 with the Dukedom of Wellington: a hereditary title and senior peerage in Britain.

St. Andrew's Kirk was an imperial building, replete with political symbolism, in the grand manner of design inaugurated by Edward Clive, Governor of Madras, in 1798. The tradition of building grand, regal European government houses began with the French at Pondicherry, in 1752. The French edifice at Pondicherry convinced Lord Clive that British claims to rule lacked credibility, unless they were able to match and surpass the French and the Indians in their capacity for sumptuous living and high culture.

An opulent imperial building programme marked the victorious end to a quarter century of war with the formidable enemy Tipu Sultan, the Tiger of Mysore. It began with Lord Clive commissioning the grand and showy Triplicane Banqueting Hall (see Fig. 18) and extensions to Government House (see Fig. 19). For this purpose he appointed the astronomer and mathematician John Goldingham, Civil Engineer, in 1800, and gave him the task of design. The Hall took the form of a pagan temple on a high podium, approached by a giant stairway guarded by sphinxes. The order was a huge two-storey Tuscan-Doric pilaster which rested on a terrace on three sides, built over a lower-level rustic arcade. Spoils of war decorated the metopes and pediments. The names Seringapatam, 1799, and Plassey were inscribed on the pediments. The portraits of famous military men, hung inside the Banqueting Hall, unequivocally celebrated war. It was a '*Heroum*, a neo-classical temple for hero worship'.[20] Less aggressive liberals like Bishop Heber deplored its great expense and 'vile taste'.[21] It is also possible that the sheer scale of the building and its ornate interior strove to echo royal metropolitan pomp, epitomised in the sumptuous interior of the Banqueting Hall at Whitehall, which it resembled. The Court of Directors was strongly critical of Clive, who possibly excused himself on the grounds of needing to surpass the 'neighbouring magnificent residence of the Nawab of Arcot'.[22]

Ordinary church building was funded by semi-private lottery, subscription and some state assistance. The purchase of land and the enormous building cost of St. Andrew's was met by the Company. The site was situated along the Poonamale High Road: one of the two main roads leading out of town. Despite the prime location, the site was declared insalubrious.

[20] For a well-researched defence of this claim, see Sten Nilsson, *European Architecture*, pp. 108–9.

[21] Bishop Heber, *Narrative of a Journey*, vol. I, p. 273.

[22] Sten Nilsson, *European Architecture*, p. 109.

Figure 18: Banqueting Hall, Madras, c. 1800

Figure 19: Government House, Madras, c. 1800

It bordered the banks of the Chintadripettah River, which held stagnant and unwholesome water for many months of the year; the soil near the banks was marshy and unsuitable for building and adjacent to it was a noisy village and temple. It did nonetheless possess certain advantages, chief among which was the bargain price of 4,000 pagodas (gold coins used in South India). Moreover, proximity to the esplanade made it convenient for any part of the garrison of Fort St. George.

Flashy Patrons and their Designers—Thomas Fiott de Havilland[23]

Thomas Fiott de Havilland was born in Guernsey in April 1775. He was the eldest son of the Bailiff, Sir Peter de Havilland, and received his early education at Queen Elizabeth College, Guernsey. He began his Indian sojourn around the age of 20, when he joined the Madras Army. It was the custom of the times to purchase high-level commissions in the Indian army. It is therefore likely that de Havilland gained his medium grade posting through patronage networks accessible to his family. The sources are unenlightening as to the nature of de Havilland's engineering training. In 1795 we find him employed as an assistant engineer, under the great collector-engineer Major Colin Mackenzie who regarded him as 'an active enterprising man' aspiring to 'éclat as a Geographer'.[24]

Between 1798 and 1800 de Havilland had prepared sketch maps of Coimbatore, Dindigul and the regions to the west of Thanjavur (Tanjore).We have to assume that this early map production enterprise involved a string of ethnoscientific encounters with local knowledge, where de Havilland used the geographical and drawing knowledge of native informants to produce the type of maps needed by the army. In the context of the day, when the British were at war, in what was to them virgin territory, maps were rare and valuable documents. Map preparation was a labour-intensive entrepreneurial exercise, undertaken by enterprising engineers or surveyors, with a view to selling them to the state. In 1801 de Havilland was sent to Egypt where he performed survey work in Cairo and the Suez. On his return trip on a Company ship, he was captured by a French Privateer but safely released.

Military Engineers were one of the most professional groups among the amateur 'science' men floating around the empire in the late eighteenth century—a function of their indispensability in war. They had developed a codified corpus of knowledge, within an *esprit de corps*. As noted already, this was serviced by a drawing system that was as an objective medium of distant communication and discipline. Colin Mackenzie is one of the few imperial engineers to have attracted the attention of modern historians. Peter Robb observes that Mackenzie's drive to collect displayed the 'single mindedness and egotism of the self-made ethos' but was

[23] Sir Thomas Munro himself had a high opinion of de Havilland's talents. For something of a short eulogy to de Havilland, see H.M. Vibart, *The Military History of the Madras Engineers and Pioneers from 1734 to the Present Times*, vol. 2 (2 vols., London, 1881–1883), pp. 1–3.

[24] R.H. Phillimore, *Historical Records of the Survey of India*, vol. 2 (2 vols., Dehra Dun, 1950), p. 394. For bio-data see Phillimore, vol. 1, p.334. De Havilland served in Ceylon and Egypt for the Madras Army, was dismissed after the mutiny in 1809, and reinstated in 1814. For further details see MSS Eur E232, *A Narrative by Captain de Havilland*.

raised above mere ambition by the 'intellectual excitement in his enquiries, a lively curiosity and the pursuance of scientific method'. With some reservation, the same could be said of de Havilland's encounter with Indian building. Robb refers to Mackenzie's work as:

> observation and exchange between Indians and Europeans; participant observers recorded what they were told by Indians, at the same time as they imposed Western measurements and classifications. Both sides of the process were equally necessary. On the other hand, it is true that Europeans made significant changes in the perceptions of India—in this instance in the understanding of *place*. The selection of elements for mapping and their measurement helped establish a new image of the land.[25]

In 1805 de Havilland was appointed as engineer to the Hyderabad Subsidiary Force of His Highness the Nizam with directions to complete the survey of the Deccan, begun by Major Mackenzie. De Havilland occasionally revealed a reliance on native knowledge and assistance in the execution of his work, such as when he referred to 'valuable information' from natives regarding his coastal survey for a new harbour[26] and he admitted to paying draughtsmen to copy Company maps for his private collection. 'While employed with the Hyderabad Forces in the hope of my appointment being extended to the whole of the Deccan, I collected a large quantity of maps, sketches and other documents and materials for the construction of a general map.'[27] The general map of the Deccan, comprising six sheets, was done at his leisure and expense and gifted to Lord Minto, the Governor-General. The map project speaks of de Havilland's great personal ambition and initiative. Map production relied on the labour and knowledge of so-called Indian assistants; he privately employed local draughtsmen to survey the southern division and draw the maps. His map collection was the only one of its kind, and the Military Board was eager to purchase it on his dismissal from service. Judging by his voluminous output we can conclude that, like Mackenzie, de Havilland's early success as a surveyor relied heavily on his own large circle of technically competent native partners, as did his later reputation as an architect.

De Havilland married Elizabeth Saumarez in 1808. Whilst appearing to have a comfortable life in Mysore, he took a leading part in the Madras army's European Officers' Mutiny at Seringapatam (Srirangam). The Srirangam island contained a fort, a palace and a *pettah* (walled suburb). It was described as the most beautiful spot possessed by any native prince in India. It

[25] Peter Robb, 'Mysore, 1799–1810', *Journal of the Royal Asiatic Society*, Series 3, 8, 2 (1998), pp. 181–206.

[26] T.F. de Havilland, *The Public Edifices of Madras* (Kingsbury, 1826), p. 32.

[27] 27 April 1810, F/4/379, 9460, Board's Collections. De Havilland complained that his allowance as surveyor and engineer was less than what had been given his predecessor Major Mackenzie. The Military Board was interested in purchasing his collection of instruments and maps on his dismissal from service, see 15 March 1811, F/4/379, 9460.

is likely that de Havilland lived in the *pettah* which had many two-storey houses and was divided into regular streets, all wide and shaded. Tipu Sultan's Lal Bagh garden was situated at the end, filled with orange, mango and pomegranate trees, laid out in straight walks, many of them luscious with blossom. Despite de Havilland's defence that he had 'all to lose and naught to gain.... Not only my life and commission might be forfeit but the provision of my family depended on my conduct. I had considerable property and works on hand at Seringapatam to a large amount', he was court-martialled and released from Company service.[28]

De Havilland was an enterprising and ambitious man caught up in the rapidly changing events in Mysore, long before his arrival in Madras. His work was eclectic; surveying appears to have been his better-known skill in the army, although he was involved in repair work of the Srirangam Fort. De Havilland first made an architectural name for himself at Mysore, in 1807, when he was sought by a powerful political patron, John Malcolm. In the image of his magnificent master Governor-General Lord Wellesley, Malcolm entertained extravagant ideas of empire and was, at the fairly tender age of 34, British Resident at the recently conquered Mysore Court.[29] Malcolm desired a great banqueting hall to be built at the Residency as a wedding gift for Lady Malcolm. (She was the daughter of a Madras officer and may have opened up avenues of patronage in Madras for de Havilland). The new hall had to be not only handsome and imposing, but unique. It was to be the largest room in South India whose roof was unsupported by columns. In order to achieve his ambition Malcolm sent for Captain de Havilland who had built a great arch in his garden with a hundred-feet span, to dispute the assertion that he could not make a stable arch of that span using country bricks. It even bore his name and was standing in 1930.[30]

It was no accident that imperial opulence, vaulted spaces and army engineers converged in this Mysorean building experiment at the turn of the century. The great block of territory acquired with the defeat of Tipu in 1799 needed to be known and governed. The fertile plateau of Mysore 2,000 feet above sea level was one of great beauty. For some British soldiers it seemed almost like paradise. Sugarcane groves, mulberry farms and silkworm factories, coconut, coffee and cotton plantations, vineyards and extensive paddy fields were mostly unknown in Scotland and England. Its natural riches and prosperity added greatly to the appeal. The scientific

[28] MSS Eur E232, *Narrative by Captain (later Colonel) Thomas Fiott de Havilland (1775–1866) Madras Army 1793–1825, of his part in the Mutiny of European Officers of the Madras Army at Seringapatam in 1809 and subsequent events up to the court martial.*

[29] Philip Woodruff, *The Men Who Ruled India: The Founders* (London, 1953), p. 206.

[30] This was in the context of building a bridge over the Kaveri river for which de Havilland had proposed a support of five brick arches. See Constance Parsons, *Mysore City* (Oxford, 1930), p. 112.

ferment in Mysore bore a direct link to the government's desire in 1804 to 'facilitate and promote all enquiries which may be calculated to enlarge the boundaries of General Science', as one of the duties imposed by its present exalted situation. Grand pioneering surveys such as William Lambton's famous Trigonometrical Survey of India which commenced in the South, Francis Buchanan's Botanical Survey of Mysore and Colin Mackenzie's much more general Mysore Survey—now the Mackenzie Collection—received official sanction around this time. The aim was to institutionalise the link between scientific knowledge and the state. The men chosen to lead such projects belonged to the often self-taught scholarly military élite. As events testify, Mysore was a political and scientific magnet. If you were an ambitious and adventurous man of science, it was quite the place to be.

The parvenu officer-class of swaggering Britons was not satisfied with the mere use of Indian palaces, acquired as spoils of war. However desirable vaulted Indian buildings were, they came with a price: they were Indian buildings. Men like Malcolm actually wanted British-built vaults. For this he needed English men with mastery over the theory and practice of Indian vaulting. Mediating between the imperial patron who desired Indian knowledge and skill, and the Indian architect, was the military-engineer—the new 'science' specialist.

It is not clear which vaulted spaces served to inspire Malcolm; although there was no shortage of domes. They were present close by in Hyder's mausoleum or farther afield, on a grander scale, in the renowned tombs of Bijapur. The majestic proportions of the hall of the Gol Gumbaz, built in 1660, vied with those of the Roman Pantheon and the St. Sophia at Istanbul. If only on account of its stupendous proportions, the Gol Gumbaz is regarded as one of the unquestionable structural triumphs of the Indian builder (see Figs. 22 and 23). It covered the largest domed space in existence. The dome itself is 135 feet across and 178 feet high.[31] The dome of the second-century Roman Pantheon spanned 142 feet internally and rises to a height of 143 feet. The dome of the fifteenth-century cathedral of Santa Maria del Fiore, in Florence, is 143 across and 270 high, but for what it is worth, it is believed to cover a smaller ground area than the vaulting system of the Gol Gumbaz. Smaller lofty vaulted halls could be encountered at the palaces of Madurai, Thanjavur (see Figs. 24–27) and Tiruchirapalli. Indirect access to southern domes was also at hand; vaulted interior spaces were handsomely depicted in the Thomas and William Daniells' drawings of the Madurai Palace, published in 1795 (see Fig. 20). William Hodges' drawings of 1786 showed the soaring Brihadisvara Temple tower of Thanjavur, whose hollow inner sanctum representing cosmic space, was forbidden to non-believers.

[31] See Percy Brown, *Indian Architecture (Islamic Period),* 4th edn. (Bombay, 1964), pp. 73–79 and Ross King, *Brunelleschi's Dome* (London, 2000), p. 9.

Figure 20: Ruins of the Palace, Madura, Thomas and William Daniell, aquatint, c. 1798, showing vaulted chamber domes and wagon vaults

Figure 21: Bara Imambara, Lucknow, eighteenth century

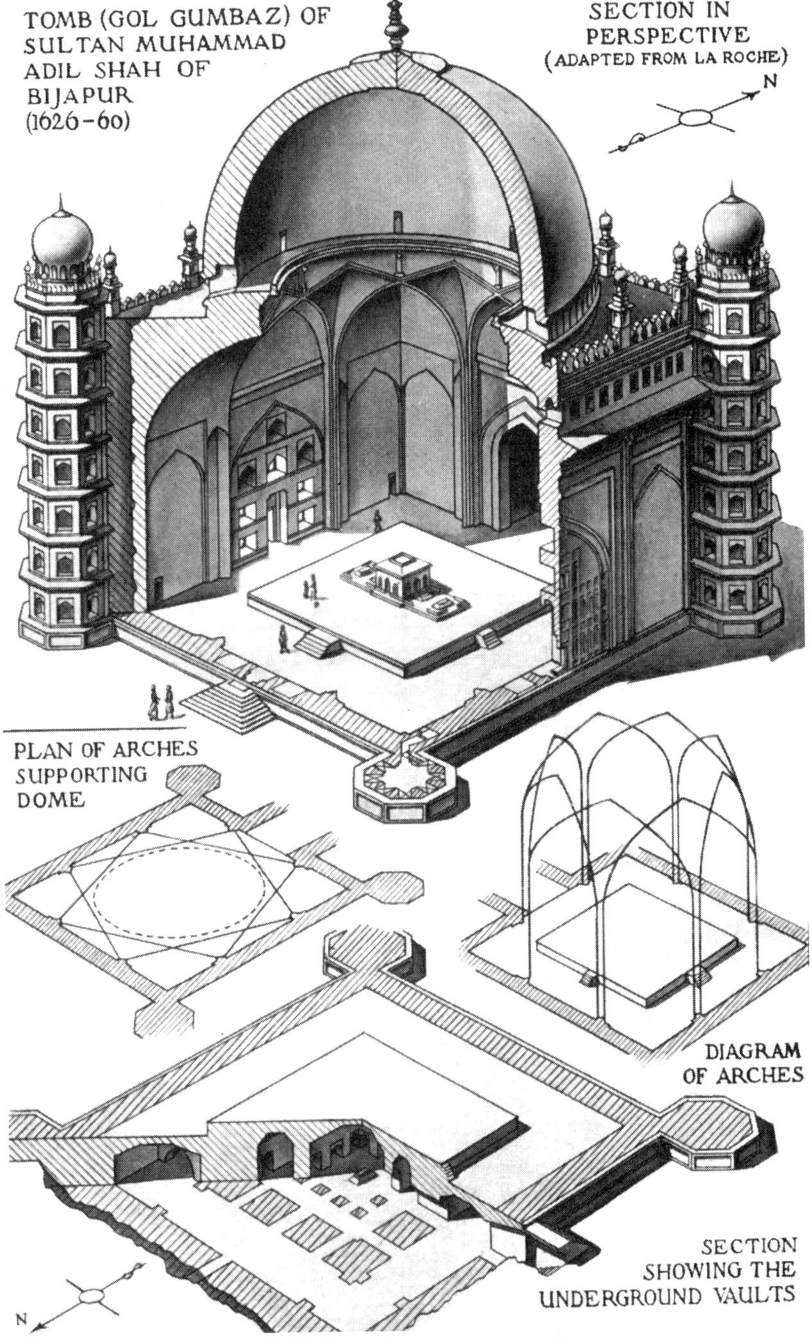

Figure 22: Gol Gumbaz, Bijapur, c. 1660, cross section

Figure 23: Gol Gumbaz, Bijapur

Figure 24: Thanjavur Palace, seventeenth century, interior view of wagon vault over throne

The magnificent eighteenth-century Bara Imambara in Lucknow (see Fig. 21), possessing an enormous vaulted brick chamber 163 by 63 feet and 49½ feet in height represented a unique building type found elsewhere only in the seventeenth-century Madurai Palace hall which measured 125 feet by 69 feet and 56 feet in height.[32] The Imambara was a major technological achievement because it had the 'largest vaulted hall that ever spanned an uninterrupted space'.[33] Banmali Tandan noted that the Imambara did not resemble anything in north India and speculated as to whether the two edifices represented a lost or as yet unrecorded building type? Tandan failed to mention earlier South Indian vaulted halls: a sixteenth-century pavilion at Vijayanagara and a seventeenth-century one at Ginjee.[34]

The fact that vaults with pointed sections were rare in the Deccan[35] and the early appearance at Vijayanagara of large rectangular wagon-vaulted buildings, repeated at Ginjee and Madurai, raise the likelihood that this form of vault construction belonged to an older mainstream subcontinental tradition. I say this because brick vaulting appeared somewhere between the second and fifth centuries in the regions south of Lucknow. It was a feature of the sumptuous Buddhist architecture that pre-dated Islam, to which I shall shortly return. For the moment it is only necessary to remember that the existence of such buildings shows that imported and local vaulting techniques may have overlapped and merged, supplying the designer with a greater creative range of outwardly different forms. It cannot be discounted that the dome builders of Bijapur and Madurai could have drawn on an older tradition of local vault construction whose precise contours are as yet unknown. Until the 1860s the British unhesitatingly tapped into this indigenous mode.

The secret skills of Indian arch and dome building could not be gained from books or drawings, but only by making things happen. Ken Alder called this tacit process a 'grappling with the thick things'. He deems the presence of tacit skill as unavoidable in the transfer of new technology because no device can be made from drawings alone.[36] The site of de Havilland's experimental brick arch offers insight into a 'tacit' process of knowledge transfer. By commissioning the construction of the experiment in his backyard, de Havilland became the proprietor of a range of tacit and direct Indian building knowledge. Indians prepared the materials and built the arch whilst he could watch, record and have hands-on contact with

[32] Banmali Tandan, *The Architecture of Lucknow*, p. 34.

[33] Catherine Asher, *TNCHI I:4 Architecture of Mughal India* (Cambridge, 1992), p. 324.

[34] See George Michell, *TNCHI 1:6 Architecture and Art of Southern India* (Cambridge, 1995), illustration no. 94, Rectangular pavilion with gabled vault, Vijayanagara sixteenth century and no. 106, Granary Ginjee, seventeenth century.

[35] Elizabeth Merklinger, *Indian Islamic Architecture: The Deccan 1347–1686* (Warminster, 1981), chapter 4.

[36] Ken Alder, *Engineering the Revolution*, p. 146.

Figure 25: Thanjavur Palace, domes over throne area

Figure 26: Thanjavur Palace, stepped vault and flat roof, with tower on the right

Figure 27: Thanjavur Palace, tower over throne, note European details

the raw matter of bricks and mortar, if so inclined. Once again he was engaging in an ethnoscientific venture.

Through payment, de Havilland tested and absorbed information direct from the building activity of the Indian builder, without requiring an informant. In northern European medieval guilds, masons were the zealous guardians of the 'mysteries' of their profession. The Bishop of Utrecht, for example, managed to extract knowledge of the secret of laying out the foundation of a church from a junior member. The Bishop was murdered for his efforts. [37] Economic gain accruing from the monopoly of knowledge was the spur for the Bishop.

As Indian intellectual property passed into the British domain, the economic benefits in this example accrued to de Havilland. Above all he gained confidence in Indian building methods, in order to direct Indians to build what he designed; as an imperial engineer he had the added bonus of sensual and intellectual pleasure. The social process which transferred Indian knowledge to Britons went unacknowledged. It is also true that Indian designers too gained first-hand experience of the volumes, proportions and ornamental details of European aesthetic canons and new structural systems that served to enhance their reputations as designers in the private sector.

It has been said that de Havilland built a test dome in his garden in Mount Road, before the Kirk dome was built, because 'he wanted the Kirk to be a domed building and to work out all the calculations himself'.[38] There is no evidence to sustain the claim that theoretical knowledge was involved in the design of the dome. Since it is unlikely that de Havilland learnt his engineering at a prestigious military academy (although a French training cannot be wholly discounted due to the proximity of Guernsey to France), we have to assume that he acquired his formidable knowledge as an apprentice, through private learning and actual building with Indians. Private learning was not unusual amongst builders in England. For example, John Soane, the famous English architect, was a bricklayer's son, deeply committed to the private study of not only beauty and aesthetics, but also materials and building science.[39]

The engineering training schemes in Britain and France had, on the other hand, provided candidates with a certain social profile with pretensions to élite status. The meritocracy, when set against the corporate order of the *ancien regime*, emerged as a deliberate social construct

[37] See Ross King, *Brunelleschi's Dome*, p. 132.

[38] Frank Penny, *The Church*, vol. 2, p. 254.

[39] See David Watkin, *Sir John Soane, Enlightenment Thought and the Royal Academy* (Cambridge, 1996). Gillian Darley made the point that Soane's equal absorption with building science and materials was carefully excluded from the 'polite' discourses of his academy lectures. Gillian Darley, *John Soane: An Accidental Romantic* (New Haven, 1999), p. 40.

where poor nobility, comfortable commoners and bold adventurers in the colonies found a particular kind of achievement rewarded. This was the beginning of the new social space of the modern professional, designed to serve not the king but the state.[40] It is in this exciting world of new knowledge and opportunity that the actions of men like de Havilland begin to make sense. We can understand the eagerness and freedom with which they grasped at innovation, individual preferment and the social status gained by rhetorical claims to 'new' knowledge, under the incipient guise of 'science' or 'art'. The Company state provided a secure income and patronage for 'scientific' experiment and industrial production. It rewarded its loyal servants with commissions and promotions and gave engineers power over Indian subordinates. De Havilland's egotism, ambition and reputation for professional arrogance as an engineer made him the butt of fun in certain Madras circles. The following extract was written after the building of St. Andrew's and related to overt competition between the English Church establishment in Calcutta, and the Scottish Church of India as to the height of steeple building:

> allowing for the Calcutta-Middleton vs Bryce controversy, inducing Scotia to resolve to have the best, and highest steepled churches, at whatever cost; allowing, I repeat, for this chivalrous feeling, the suitable inscription on the building would have been 'Erected to the honor and glory of F.de Havilland, Major of Engineers'.[41]

For the overall system to work, however, Indians capable of reading and making 'academic' drawings were required at the subordinate levels of the new state-controlled system. Since Indians with private access to this knowledge found better remuneration in the private sector, to fulfil its burgeoning requirements, the Company state was compelled to undertake the production of a low-level technical cadre. In 1794, Michael Topping, the East India Company's Astronomer, and Geographical and Marine Surveyor-in-Chief set up, in Madras, a specialised training school for surveyors. The small intake was drawn from poor European and East Indian (the name then given to mixed race persons) children from schools in the Presidency. On behalf of the British, these young men would oversee the main civil work of repairing tanks and civil buildings. They were trained in algebra, geometry and arithmetic, levelling, drafting and estimating, and taught the elementary principles of hydraulics.[42] State-sponsored and armed with the new knowledge, they were set to compete with traditional

[40] For this argument see Ken Alder, *Engineering the Revolution*, p. 82.

[41] W.T. Munro, *Madrasiana*, p. 38. For further evidence see MSS Eur E232, 'A Narrative by Captain Thomas Fiott de Havilland'. The narrative is accompanied by innumerable 'handsome testimonies I possess from almost every officer I have served under as well as from the Court of Directors and the Supreme Government'. Allowing for what he would legitimately need in his defence the rest borders on vanity.

[42] S. Ambirajan, 'Science and Technology'.

Indian engineers who had for centuries performed such tasks, reliant on their own secret training methods.

In 1821 Thomas Fiott de Havilland, Chief Engineer of the Presidency, wrote *An Account of St. Andrew's Church*. It appeared, with additions, in his book *Public Edifices of Madras* (1826).[43] Included in the latter were two other projects: *St. Andrew's Bridge* and *An Account of the Armogham Shoal and Blackwood's Harbour on the Coromandel Coast of Madras*. The *Account* is an exercise in science rhetoric and self-promotion. It draws attention to advantages that may accrue to the Company by having commissioned officers superintend the new civil building programmes incumbent upon it in its expanding functions as a territorial government. This was outright advocacy by the military engineering profession for state privilege and civil office. Another remarkable feature of the *Account* is that it is immensely informative on certain technical and aesthetic aspects of the church project and curiously silent on others.

The Round Church Design—From Westminster to Madras

De Havilland claimed that by 1816 the elders of the church had determined on a circular plan and were keen to start work; so was Lieutenant Grant, acting temporarily as Presidency Superintending Engineer, for fear of being superseded.[44] It was Grant's duty to provide designs for the new church. Grant and the church elders took the decision to copy Gibbs' proposed circular plan for St. Martin-in-the-Fields (see Figs. 28 and 29), which they found in Gibbs' *A Book of Architecture,* published in 1728.[45] In 1720 Gibbs was the architect most 'in vogue' in London. His unbuilt circular design for St. Martin-in-the-Fields was said to ultimately derive from the Pantheon and his admiration for the heroic grandeur of Imperial Rome.[46] Gibbs had asserted that his round design for St. Martin's was rejected on grounds of cost, even though he had intended the dome to be a wooden structure with a metal covering. Notwithstanding this, in Madras, the Grant proposal was hastily approved: 'The Right Honourable, Mr. Elliot, the then Governor, being favourable'. For the Kirk roof, Colonel Caldwell, Chief Engineer, officially recommended a wooden dome covered with lead or copper.

[43] The date 1821 is given in Peter W. Millar's Introduction to the copy of de Havilland's, *An Account*, see fn. 18. T.F. de Havilland, 'An Account of St. Andrew's Church' *The Public Edifices of Madras* (Kingsbury, 1826) may be found at the British Library.

[44] The Edinburgh St. Andrew's, of 1785, was probably the first oval Kirk to be built on British soil. It was refined classicism with an elegant steeple and pedimented portico. The designer was a Captain of the Engineers. See George Hay, *The Architecture of the Scottish Post-Reformation Churches 1560–1843* (Oxford, 1957), p. 97.

[45] James Gibbs, *A Book of Architecture* (London, 1728), plate 8. The book was popular.

[46] T. Friedman, *James Gibbs* (New Haven, 1984), p. 36.

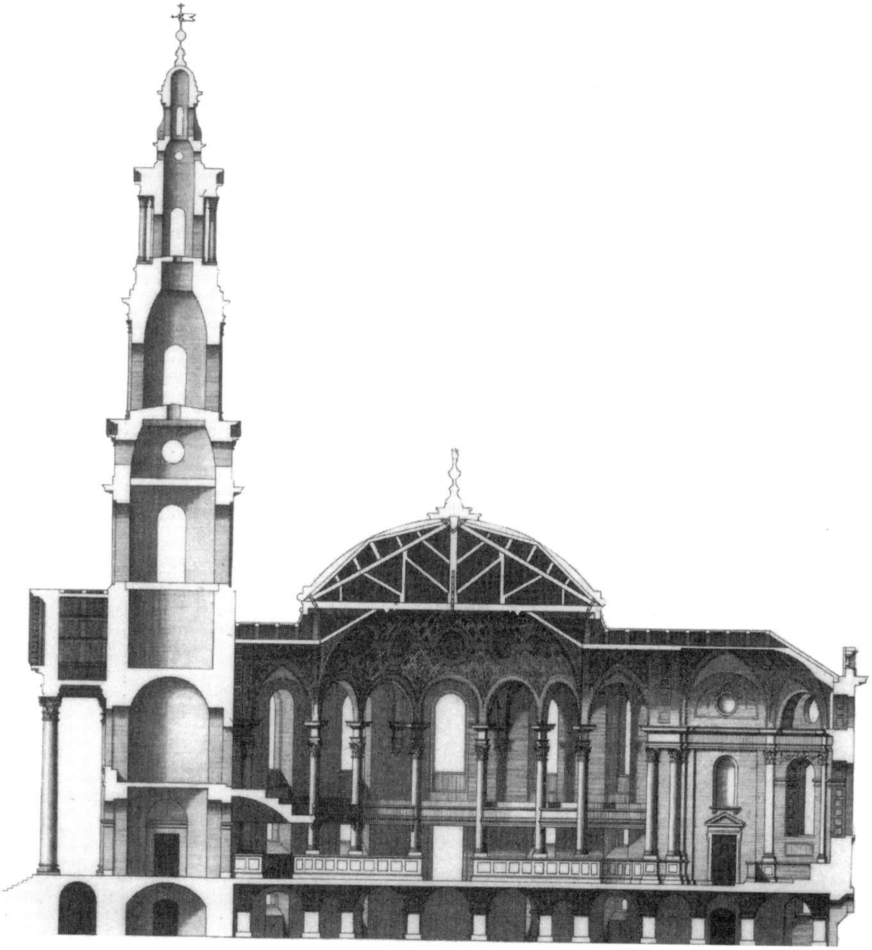

Figure 28: James Gibbs' circular design for St. Martin-in-the-Fields, London, section

Meanwhile, in 1818, the dynamic de Havilland, backed by a growing professional reputation as a surveyor and architect, and with the prestigious St. George's Church added to his expanding string of commissions, had been called to Madras to take over the coveted post of Superintending Engineer. On aesthetic and scientific grounds and familiarity with local conditions, he dismissed the Caldwell suggestion:

which would have rendered the church scarcely sufferable in the heat: besides, that it would have been very difficult, if possible to have secured the wood-work from the white ants, as has been evinced in St. George's Church . . . and want of taste was also thought to pervade the architectural proportions and combinations.[47]

[47] T.F. de Havilland, *An Account*, p. 5.

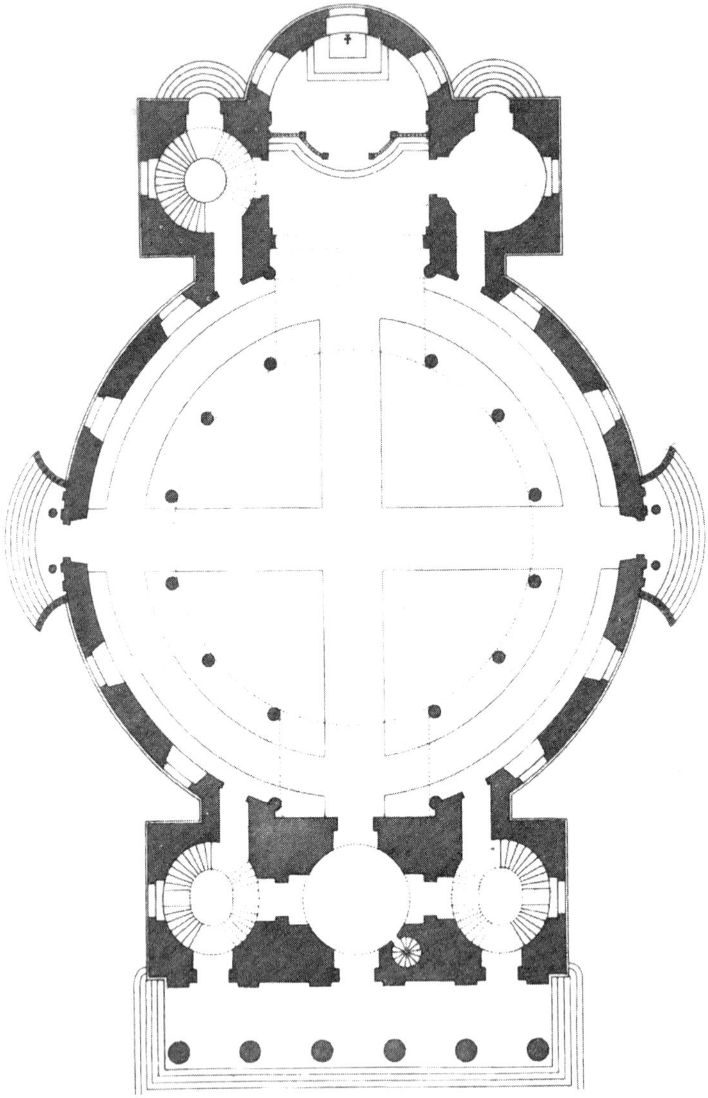

Figure 29: James Gibbs' circular design for St. Martin-in-the-Fields, London, plan

He persuaded his patrons to alter the material of the dome from wood to bricks and obtained their approbation in the 'most flattering and unqualified terms'. The Kirk was meant to be viewed from all sides. To achieve this end it was placed in the centre of the site. The circular form lent itself well to the function of high visibility and, in this sense, the building appropriated and sat in space in a manner alien to Indian design traditions. It made a grand statement of form and façade which was new.

An Indo-British Dome

In 1740, when construction work on James Gibbs' Radcliffe Camera, in Oxford, reached the top of the balustrade crowning the rotunda, the trustees decided to stop work because of 'the uncertainties of attempting an entirely masonry structure for no stone dome of such size had been built in England'.[48] Eventually, on Gibbs' advice, the fifty-foot diameter dome was finished in wood and lead. In eighteenth-century England, large domes were popular and usually built in wood.[49] The only famous masonry domes are attributed to John Soane who used terracotta hollow-cones to lighten the fireproof vaulting at the Bank of England in 1793. It is thought that the hollow-cone technique was evolved in France around the 1780s and came to England from there.[50] Soane's pendentive domes were 'modest' and structurally different from Gibbs' wooden

Figure 30: St. Andrew's, south-west elevation

[48] T. Friedman, *James Gibbs*, p. 250.

[49] John Summerson, *Architecture in Britain*, p. 458. The London Pantheon was designed by James Wyatt. It followed the plan of the Santa Sophia and the dome of the Roman Pantheon. The wooden superstructure was built in 1772. Sir John Vanbrugh's celebrated 'English' domes have been shown to have strong Indian influence from his two-year stint in Surat; see Robin Williams, 'Vanbrugh's, India and his Mausolea for England', in Christopher Ridgway and Robert Williams (eds.), *Sir John Vanbrugh and Landscape Architecture in Baroque England* (Stroud, 2000).

[50] The cones were made at a kiln on site; see Christopher Woodward. '"Wall, Ceiling Enclosure and Light"; Soane's Designs for Domes', in M. Richardson and Mary-Anne Stevens (eds.), *John Soane Architect: Master of Space and Light* (London, 1999). Gillian Darley noted that John Summerson felt that Dance, with his Indian style work in the Guildhall, may have had a hand in the dome designs for the bank; although a more recent study argued differently; see Gillian Darley, *John Soane*, p. 129.

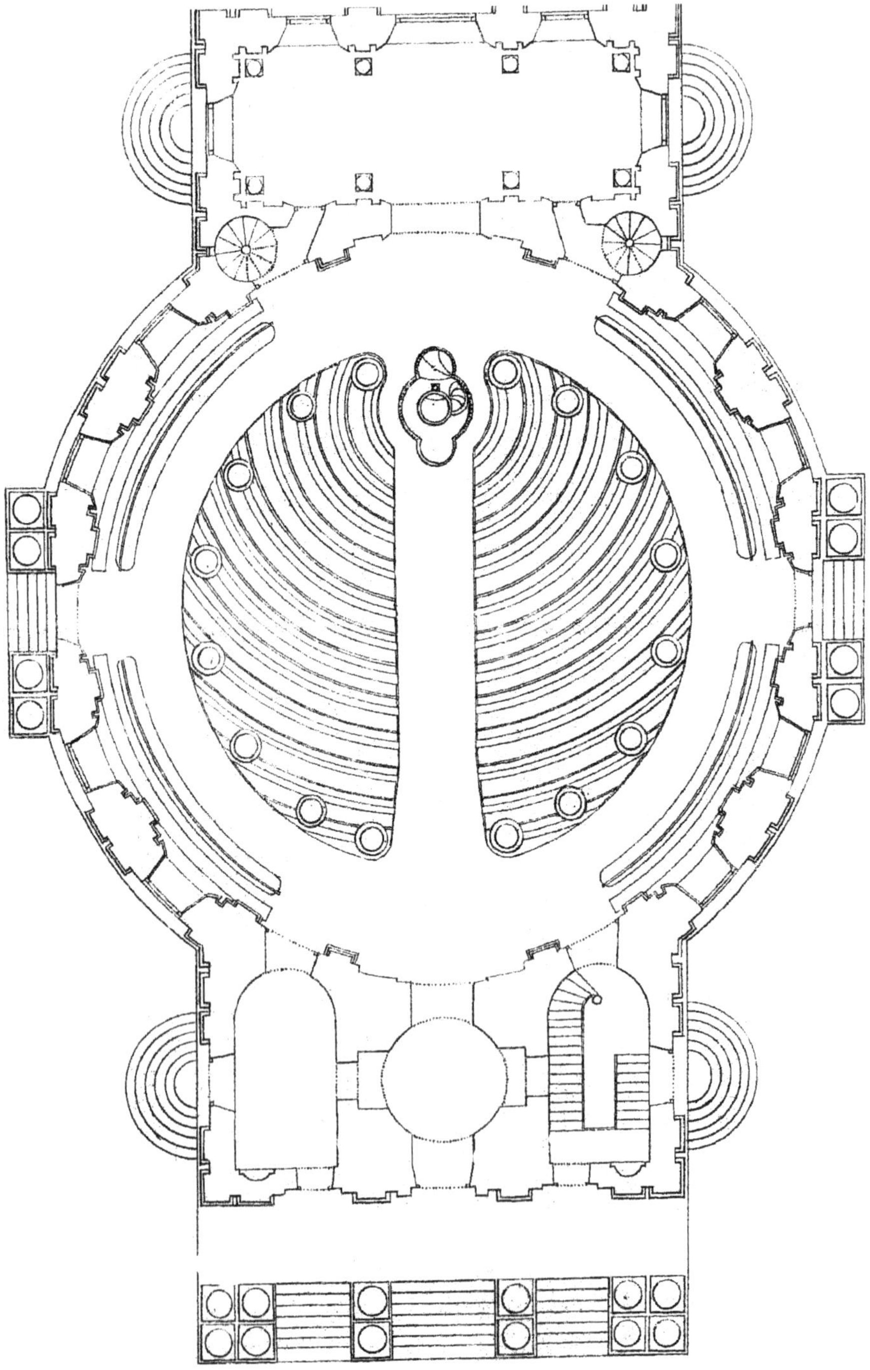

Figure 31: St. Andrew's, ground floor plan

dome for the Camera. At St. Andrew's (see Figs. 30–34), de Havilland used a shallow profile masonry dome, lower and smaller than the 95-feet diameter wooden one proposed by Gibbs. He also increased the number of columns from the original twelve to sixteen, to accommodate the extra weight of masonry.

Figure 32: St. Andrew's, section

There is no evidence that construction drawings were used; they were in any case superfluous since the builders would have followed sketch drawings and used their own 'secret' structural methods. The foundations and the dome were the design aspects most susceptible to structural failure. For these items and the flat roof and arched pediments connected with the structure of the dome, it is likely that de Havilland used tried and tested local methods. It is indeed peculiar that he freely admitted his indebtedness to Indian knowledge and skilled labour in the design and execution of the foundation and flat roof, but was silent regarding any Indian contribution to the design and building of the dome. What follows is a précis of de Havilland's views on his dome: 'Above all the abstraction of timber-work in the roof is desirable; first, because, in the vicissitudes of that climate, even the best-seasoned wood soon perishes; and secondly, that it never can be completely secured against the depredations of white ants.'[51]

On these grounds it was resolved to dome and arch the building with masonry, if it could be safely contrived without making it heavy or taking away from the elegance of the design. 'Such an undertaking was of no small difficulty without incurring very great expense and was even by many considered impracticable.'[52] He never tells us why this was so or how he surmounted the difficulty of constructing this rather large dome. The body of the church was a circle, 81½ feet diameter in the clear, with a rectangular compartment east and west of it and a portico extending beyond the latter to the westward. Over the circular parts was a dome covering as it were the nave of the church, with an annular arch round it, over what may be termed the aisles. St. Andrew's dome measures 51½ feet in diameter internally and was borne on sixteen columns, disposed at unequal distances.

Of the sixteen columns above-mentioned, the four bearing the principal inter-columniation are of granite; the remainder are of the same kind of stone as the architrave and frieze, and of what is at Madras termed *iron-stone*: an indifferent sort of material, apparently composed of clay and scoria of iron, more or less honey combed, but which by experiment has been found to be of a consistency sufficient to resist a pressure, three times as great as bricks would bear without being crushed.[53]

On each capital stood a block of granite, against which the straight arch of the entablature pressed and was supported. The voussoirs were about three feet high for the whole breadth of the entablature and one foot thick.

The dome is constructed as to relieve the entablature by means of arcades, wrought into it and resting on the columns; while at the same time it was, as it were, but a framework of brick, running upwards from the columns also towards the crown, where these ribs are terminated and united together by a circular arch of the same

[51] T.F. de Havilland, *An Account*, p. 5.

[52] Ibid., p. 4.

[53] Ibid., p. 5.

description. This framework is then filled in with masonry formed of *cones* of pottery, such as are used in *Syrian roofs*.... The interior of the dome was twenty four feet high including the entablature making the whole height under the key from the pavement about fifty-four feet. In the interior of the dome, above the entablature of the order [stood] in relief a balustrade, through which is seen, as it were, the azure sky, the canopy of heaven; represented by the stucco of the dome coloured with *lapis lazuli*. This appearance gives to the whole an awful grandeur, which could not have been expected in so small an edifice.[54]

The thickness of the dome at the crown was only nine inches, whence it gradually increased to nearly twice that dimension at the cornice. Three courses of flat tiles were laid over the Syrian cones over which stucco was applied. The flat roof surrounding the dome was an integral part of its construction and balanced its outward thrust. The structural design of the flat roof, pediments and the brick dome with its shallow stepped profile, arched base and lapis lazuli chunam finish, place it within the South Indian vaulting tradition. Besides, Captain Underwood of the Madras Engineers, in a detailed article written in 1836, tells us exactly how natives built small domes using hollow cylinders:

The centrings were principally composed of crooked old bamboos laid over and tied to jungle-wood Malabar trusses, supported on sun-burnt bricks and mud pillars—sun-burnt bricks were packed closely together on the bamboos, earth strewed on these, and a plaster of wet mud applied over all, to render the curve smooth.[55]

Figure 33: St. Andrew's roof, arches in the pediment

[54] Ibid., p. 5.

[55] George Underwood, 'Memorandum Regarding Syrian or Cylinder Roofs', *Professional Papers of the Madras Engineers* (1836), pp. 92–95.

Figure 34: St. Andrew's, stepped dome and arches

The article included drawings of domes built in the Ice House and Medical School buildings in Madras. De Havilland's description of the use of temporary brick pillars to support the centerings of the sacramental room was the only clue he supplied as to how the main body of the church may have been built. At the RIBA in 1905, Robert Chisholm (who had worked in India for forty years), discussing the building of his design for a little semi-dome at the First Church of Christ Scientist, Sloane Street, London, said that 'if the dome was turned on true Hindoo principles without a centre, the cost of doming was very little more than the cost of walling.'[56] Discussions with *sthapathis* in Madras suggest that there were several modes of dome construction in use, of which corbelling was one. For small domes, the easiest was to make a full-size bamboo frame with a mud cover, a form of shuttering on which the brick-mortar was laid. De Havilland's brick piers seem to bear out the fact that substantial but cheap temporary mud structures were used as supports for vaults during construction. Fergusson, writing on the subject of the buildings of Bijapur in 1891, after querying as to whether the Adil Shah sultans were of European descent, proceeded to assign the largeness and grandeur of the Bijapur style to the sultans' quasi-western origin.[57]

[56] Chisholm spoke at the end of the talk made at the RIBA by the Consulting Architect to the Government of India, James Ransome; see James Ransome, 'European Architecture in India' *Journal of the Royal Institute of British Architects*, Third Series, XII, 6 (January 1905), p. 200.

[57] James Fergusson, 'History of Indian and Eastern Architecture', *History of Architecture*, vol. 3 (London, 1891), p. 558.

No modern consensus prevails on the history of dome-building knowledge in medieval Europe or in India. Most authors point vaguely in the direction of West Asia as a point of origin for masonry domes built without centering (i.e., a temporary wooden framework to support the masonry structure until it is stable). Ross King queried the construction of the colossal brick dome of the Santa Maria del Fiore, built in Florence in 1420 (without centering), using a masonry technique then unknown in Italy. He speculates that the mysterious herringbone brick building techniques were learnt by Brunelleschi from Muslim slaves in Florence, or from possible visits to Persia, Byzantium or Asia Minor.[58] In his 1989 study on domes, Felix Escrig noted that the Ottomans and the Mughals were also experimenting with a cultural renaissance, parallel to the western one, which produced many innovative buildings; domes featured in many of them. The famous Ottoman architect Sinan's builders knew the construction techniques of domes from experience, even if they did not articulate or understand the theory of their design. It is generally held that for this knowledge, we had to await the 'shell theory', not developed by mathematics till 1940.[59]

This is a rather confused subject. It is worth a little attention because a great deal of controversy arose amongst Britons in the nineteenth century as to whether Indians did construct 'proper' (i.e., not corbelled) arches and vaults. As I mentioned in the Preface, by the early nineteenth century, discussion on dome and arch construction had already acquired an ideological charge with British intellectuals pushing the view that Hindus could not construct 'true' arches and naturally it followed that they were unable to construct domes.

Figure 35: Mahabodhi shrine, c. second century, conjectural reconstruction

The impact of such ideas on the built form can be gauged by the British decision to rebuild the Mahabodhi shrine (see Fig. 35), minus its mighty vaulted porch in the 1880s. To understand this controversy it is necessary to introduce,

[58] Ross King, *Brunelleschi's Dome*, p. 100.

[59] Felix Escrig argued that Muslim science went to Italy from Sicily, after the fall of Constantinople in 1435, and oriental craftsmen were used to build the Florentine shell dome. See Felix Escrig, *Towers and Domes* (Southampton, 1998), pp. 54–60.

very briefly, a popular but lost temple-type aptly named 'Buddhist skyscrapers' by Benjamin Rowland, with the caveat that towers of one form or another were built for all the major religions of the day. The towers I refer to were hollow image houses built of wood or brick, and present in many of the subcontinental sites stretching from Pakistan to Bengal and the deep South. The most renowned was the thirteen-storey wonder of the Buddhist world, 'built of every kind of wood,' by the Kushan King, Kanishka, in Peshawar. Its date of construction is not known, but in the sixth century, it rose to a height of 700 feet. The tower best known today is the internationally revered and heavily rebuilt Mahabodhi shrine at Bodh Gaya, located in the Ganges valley, near Patna, in modern Bihar; the site associated with Lord Buddha's enlightenment. The brick tower, thought to have been first built in the second century, rose 180 feet above ground.

Rowland claimed that the construction technique of the arches and brick vaults of the original tower were 'so completely un-Indian', and closely resembled the arch construction of the Sassanians (Persians). 'It is just possible that this method of vaulting was introduced through Kushan contacts with Sassanian Iran.'[60] The Sassanian empire had its capital and imposing court at Ctesiphon, in Iraq, where remains of huge third-century brick vaults are in evidence. The construction of domes on squinches appears to have been known in the region from about the second century BCE.[61] He goes on to tell us that the buildings and splendid art of the Mathura school (as art-historians like to call Kushan art from the southern capital at Mathura, near Delhi), was made by Indians trained in workshops under 'Near Eastern supervision'.

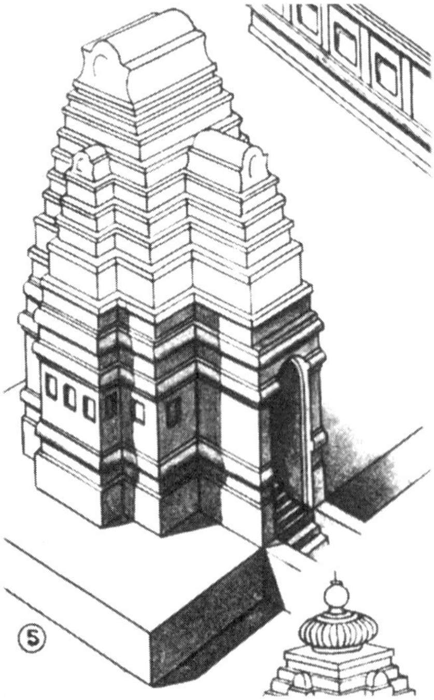

Figure 36: Bhitargaon shrine, c. fifth century, conjectural reconstruction

The best preserved Buddhist skyscraper is the unique and important fifth-century Bhitargaon tower (see Fig. 36), situated on the Ganges, near Kanpur; one of the few surviving examples of Indian

[60] Benjamin Rowland, *Art and Architecture of India: Buddhist, Hindu, Jain*, 3rd revised edn. (Middlesex, 1967), p. 163.
[61] Arthur Upham Pope, *Introducing Persian Architecture* (Tehran, 1976), p. 28.

architecture in brick. It has a barrel vaulted vestibule, domical vaults over the sanctuary and porch and a tower crowned by a 'hull-shaped roof'.[62] The architecturally impressive monasteries at Nalanda, the last stronghold of northern Buddhism, were described by Hsuan-tsang, at the height of their splendour, in the seventh century. According to him, the tallest brick tower was about 300 feet high and resembled the tower at Bodh Gaya. Excavations at Nalanda revealed nothing of this grandeur. The only recovered brick tower, known as stupa at site no. III is smaller and capped with a 'saucer-like dome'. Rowland does not date the latter, but the Pala-Sena dynasty, who patronised Buddhism, ruled from the eighth to the twelfth centuries.

To add to the confusion, a rare South Indian Buddhist skyscraper at Nagapatam (a port city south of Madras) was destroyed by Jesuits in 1867. Its date of construction is uncertain, although nearby ruins were dated to 1267 in Chinese records. The Nagapatam tower possessed an irregular, square plan and the portion remaining, at the time of demolition, was thirty metres high; built of enormous bricks with clay cement used externally and very hard cement internally. In the opinion of the eminent scholar Debala Mitra, it was evidently built by a Chinese architect because it looked like a brick Chinese pagoda.[63]

According to architectural historian Percy Brown, Indian brick domes of the seventeenth-century Deccan consisted of 'a homogenous shell or monobloc of concrete reinforced with bricks', as do those further south. Brown thought that Indians learnt their vaulting technique from the Persians.[64] And George Michell attributes the great constructional triumph of the Gol Gumbaz dome of Bijapur, to vaulting systems imported from the Middle East.[65] Perhaps the only escape from the bewilderment of these 'diffusionist' theories is to allow the idea that there existed in India, a much older indigenous legacy of dome building that evolved in parallel with that of the Sassanians. This more or less frees us to introduce the idea that a Turko-Persian-Chinese-Indic cultural overlap, possibly from the thirteenth century onwards, was responsible for the vaulting systems of medieval South India.

We are now in a position to say that the St. Andrew's dome was unequivocally the product of conversations on aesthetics, construction and materials between Indo-Britons.

[62] Benjamin Rowland, *Art and Architecture*, p. 227.

[63] Debala Mitra, *Buddhist Monuments* (Calcutta, 1971), p. 195.

[64] Percy Brown, *Indian Architecture (Islamic)*, p. 77. For 5th century brick vault construction see Percy Brown, *Indian Architecture (Buddhist and Hindu Periods)*, 3rd revised edn., (Bombay, 1983), p. 41.

[65] George Michell and Mark Zebrowski, *The New Cambridge History of India I:* vol. *7 Architecture and Art of the Deccan Sultanates* (Cambridge, 1999), p. 271.

The cost incurred, in rupees, for the building was as follows:

Building	178,037
Original cost of site	16,443
Further land purchase paid by the lottery fund	2,406
Commission to Engineer	14,746
Alteration to kill echo	4,800
Total	**216,432**

The Directors were displeased with the exorbitant sums spent on the church. They pointed out that churches more capacious than St. Andrew's had been completed in various parts of India for one-fourth the sum. The Kirk at Bombay for example cost Rs. 45, 354. Besides, the Kirk in Madras, meant to hold a congregation of 440, was frequented on average by only 40 or 50 persons. Although payment of commissions to army staff engaged in building work was inconsistent (it could be as high as 15 per cent), on the whole, building design/construction was a lucrative activity for commissioned officers.[66] In truth it is likely that the Madras Government was not contrite in regard to the cost of the Kirk. It had achieved its object:

They had provided the gallant Scotchmen [*sic*] of the Presidency, who had in many ways helped to build up the British power in the South, with a church they could be proud of; one that cost as much as the seven new military churches at Trichinopoly, Secunderabad, Cannanore, Arcot, Bangalore, Poonamallee and Bellary altogether.[67]

A commission was appointed in 1829 to consider how to reduce the cost of military and ecclesiastical buildings, but by then the glory of the Scots in Madras was already petrified.

Martial Technocrats on the Rise

In 1819 the Company's building programme in territories of the Presidency was split into three divisions, each under the charge of a civil engineer with a suitable establishment. The whole was placed under the control of an engineer at the Presidency, styled 'Inspector General of Civil Estimates'.[68] De Havilland was the first engineer to hold the office of Inspector of Estimates for the Repair of Tanks and Water Courses under the Board of Revenue

[66] T.F. de Havilland discussed army officers and their commissions for building work in his petition to the Court for payment for the bulwark at the sea-face in 1821, L/MIL/5/387 (105). John Goldingham received a commission of 15 per cent when the standard was 8 per cent. Subalterns received 5 per cent. The practice at the time was to give the entire project under one contract.

[67] Frank Penny, *The Church*, vol. 2, p. 255.

[68] C.D. McLean, *Manual of Administration of the Madras Presidency*, vol. 3 (Madras, 1885), p. 365. This I believe was the post first held by T.F. de Havilland though the records title it differently.

in 1818.[69] His appointment marked the beginning of soldier-engineer intervention in the civil arena. This period also records the appearance of the influential and extensive fusion-institution, the *Maramut* (maintenance) Department, whose control passed to the Board of Revenue in 1825. It will be discussed more fully in Chapter 4.

Latent in this organisational structure it is possible to see one vision of empire; an empire controlled by European martial technocrats, who had achieved high status through meritocratic striving and administered largely unchanged Indian institutions. Between 1836 and 1858 official building in Madras was organised in three divisions: the *Maramut* Department was in control of irrigation and navigable canals, civil buildings in the provinces and all roads and bridges not under the military or the Trunk Road Department. The Engineering Department of the Military Board supervised all fortifications, and the building work of the military and Presidency Towns. A separate Trunk Road Department had sole control of the great lines of communication known as the Trunk Roads.[70]

The most impressive irrigation scheme in India was at Thanjavur and still functioning when it came under British control in 1801. It is therefore hardly surprising that senior military engineers of the *Maramut* Department built their reputations on their contributions to hydraulic knowledge and the building of great 'British' irrigation works. The Bengal Military Board encouraged de Havilland to translate the book, *Principes Hydralique*, in 1821.[71] It ordered one hundred copies, while the Bombay Government ordered fifty.[72] Arthur Cotton achieved fame as a pioneer irrigation engineer following his extensive tank rehabilitation work in the Madras Presidency. Direct military control of civil building was officially relinquished only in 1858.

It was in this context of military building activity that the Military Board in Bengal became enamoured with masonry vaulted roofs. For pragmatic and pecuniary reasons it began encouraging a series of experiments with this unfamiliar (to the British) building technique. In 1818, the Board indicated to the supreme government, its indebtedness to Major General Garstin for the general adoption of this 'superior and durable description of roof, in particular the vaulted roof of pottery or hollow cones'.

The most visible and costly state-sponsored 'experiment' for purely practical purposes was John Garstin's Gola (see Fig. 37), of 1786. It 'stands like a colossus on the banks of the

[69] 10 February 1818, Z/P/2486, MPPC. According to 29 September 1818, P/260/5, 86, MPMC, he was Superintending Engineer, Presidency division.

[70] C.D. McLean, *Manual of Administration*, vol. 1, part 3, p. 365. It is noteworthy that the largest department retained its Indian name suggesting its Indian origins. *Maramut* is Hindi for maintenance.

[71] I have not been able to locate the original which was presumably published in France.

[72] L/MIL/5/391 (136a) pp. 226–39.

Figure 37: The Gola, Bankipur, designed by John Garstin, 1786

Ganges'.[73] It was an experimental prototype for large masonry granaries (the largest radius of the Gola was 120 feet). To build it Garstin adapted Indian designs and building techniques derived from his interest in Indian architecture. The social process designated 'experiment', concealed a tacit transfer of practical knowledge from Indians to Garstin. The potential military and utilitarian value of the Gola placed it in a different experimental class from St. Andrew's. It was never used as a granary and remained empty. However, the Board felt that its officers could not:

lay claim to the merit of the invention of the vaulted roof whether Syrian or made with an Arch of common bricks and mortar or even to their first introduction to this country. Some of the buildings of the Ishapore Powder Works have Syrian roofs which have stood many years and are still standing with little repair. Ramparts and barracks at Fort William and other buildings in the Presidency have vaulted roofs of common masonry.[74]

[73] Sten Nilsson, *European Architecture*, p. 99.

[74] 17 November 1818, P/260/8, 465, MPMC.

The Board's experience confirmed the superiority of this roof over all the others for military buildings, especially for frontier stations. It was happy to note the introduction of this building type whenever new buildings were required. It had had few failures, even though 'our Executive Officers were practically strangers to this form of building'.

Interestingly, the Board recorded the aversion and distrust of native workmen when 'anything novel or contrary to their usual practice was introduced'. It was, they said, 'comprehended with difficulty'. If, as the Board suggested, native workmen and English engineers were both unfamiliar with this technique, it remains a mystery as to who built the recent vaults described in the letter. Since the records do not say anything about the builders not being local, it is reasonable to conclude that local brick-workers were indeed familiar with vaulting techniques. In this event it is difficult to see precisely what was being resisted.

Assuming the builders were local, the contradiction inherent in the Board's position regarding Indian knowledge of vaulted roofs may have arisen because its members and informants had difficulty accepting that masonry vault construction was indigenous to the region, and already understood by the workmen. Perhaps what aroused distrust was the interlocking of social and technical engineering in British-controlled building activity which appropriated the workmen's knowledge by means of 'experiments' over which they had no control.

There existed a huge gulf between Britons who amassed knowledge and the 'Indians whom they controlled or thought they controlled'. Indian resistance to the prestigious state-sponsored surveys, undertaken by other famous military men of science at the turn of the century, is well recorded.[75] The state's attempts to appropriate Indian intellectual heritage rendered knowledge exchange unfree and unshared. It was a contested site. M. Harrison argues that the idea that what we think of as 'western science' was produced in the colonies rather than exported to them is a very recent one,[76] implying that the writing of the history of imperial science has hardly begun. Here I isolate aspects of this so-called ethnoscience, not to assign priority or to dismantle the divide, but to take a closer look at the entangled processes of informal exchange of information.

The Bengal Board was experimenting with vaulting at several sites. The officers who stood to be commended by its success were as follows: Captain Arnold, a promising officer in the Kurnaul Cantonment, Lieutenant Moulin in the Fort Allighur barracks and Captain Barron at Futtehgurh.

[75] Peter Robb, 'Mysore, 1799–1810', *Journal of the Royal Asiatic Society*, and Matthew E. Edney, *Mapping an Empire: The Geographical Construction of British India 1765–1834* (Chicago, 1997), p. 332.

[76] M. Harrison, 'Colonial Science and the British Empire' *Isis*, 96 (2005), pp. 56–63.

The last two have reduced the expense of buildings at the stations where they have been employed and we already experience the advantages of Captain Barron's practical science skill, and his knowledge. We have had occasion more than once to bring under the notice of government in the most favourable terms the merits and services of these officers, particularly Captain Barron who has been employed as an executive officer in the Building Department with occasional intervals since 1818.[77]

The warm, paternal tenor of the communication implies that promotion for Barron was imminent. What was particularly admired was his 'practical science skill'. The Board continued that not enough time had elapsed to compare this system with the roofs formerly in use from practical experiment and concluded that, at present, the cheapest roof was the pitch roof with tiles or thatch. The attention paid by the Court and Supreme Government to the progress of engineering science hints that meritocracy was taking its place alongside patronage as an avenue for personal advancement. Moreover, the process whereby colonial social relations permitted practical 'experiment' to verify and test Indian building knowledge and commandeer it, if suitable, was sanctioned at the highest levels of the state.

De Havilland's claim to fame, however, took a slightly different and ambiguous tack from the strictly utilitarian domes of Bengal. He presented himself as the supreme specialist combining a theoretical and practical knowledge of science and art. Despite the scent of mutiny, his slick packaging proved irresistible to some among his superiors. De Havilland was well aware that his Indian engineers and workforce were perfectly able to build a masonry dome and he possibly knew that the Bengal savants had made it clear that no officer was to lay claim to the merit of inventing dome techniques in India.[78] Undeterred, he proceeded to use the masonry version of Gibbs' domed church design to stake his claim in the history books, assuring us of his modesty at all times. De Havilland educates us as to why the St. Andrew's dome was exceptional:

Without arrogating to himself any particular merit in the edifice, the engineer may safely say that it is the only building extant, or at least generally known, in the world, wherein a dome of masonry of those dimensions is supported on a colonnade of that height the entablature of which is a straight arch, without beam or lintel. Many larger domes exist, doubtless, but they are supported on solid walls or strong arcades; and if any there be resting on colonnades, it is where the intercolumniations are small, and not by means of strong beams or massive stone lintels crampt together and not acting as voussoirs against each other.[79]

[77] 17 November 1818, P/260/8, 465, MPMC.

[78] As I noted previously, Davies, for instance, attributes the complex construction of the dome to de Havilland who had experimented with huge brick spans for many years. Philip Davies, *Splendours of the Raj*, p. 44.

[79] T.F. de Havilland, *An Account*, p. 8.

It is difficult to verify this particular design claim, but as noted earlier, the principle of bricks and special mortar, acting as a composite material, was a familiar mode of construction for Indian vaults. Almost all the pyramidal *gopurams*, gateways set in the high walls that surrounded sumptuous southern temples were towers constructed of corbelled brick and plaster on an internal timber framework, crowned with a partly hollow barrel-vaulted *shala* roof; the ends were marked with horse-shoe shaped arches.[80] They functioned as lookout towers with stairs on the inside. The base of the tower consisted of a solid structure with a central passage often covered by a pointed barrel-vault. The profuse external decoration consisted of painted brick and stucco. They displayed an ease and fluency in the handling of these materials. Moreover, the composite material brick-mortar, deployed as a flat arch, was the standard construction mode for the Madras Terrace—a flat roof or flooring method—where bricks in mortar were laid on wooden beams. Variations in the composition of the mortar were achieved with the use of jaggery (palm sugar), differing local additives and setting agents. Differing types of clay and the burning process of bricks made this composite material extremely versatile.

De Havilland's claim that the 51-feet diameter Kirk dome, supported on free standing columns which were 35-feet tall, and connected by a flat arch, was the only such one generally known in the world, may well be true. Without the benefit of structural engineering history it is difficult to comment on the finer points of the design and construction of the Kirk dome. The building illustrates the convergence of several layers of Indian and European aesthetic and scientific knowledge. The aesthetic design of the building was European and it is probable that the dome design and construction relied heavily on Indian science and technical skill.

In the eyes of the Europeans, the spatial symbolism and design sophistication of dome building were regarded as a European preserve, effortlessly linked to antiquity and Rome. The domes of Florence, the Vatican and St. Paul's were after all reinterpretations of the Pantheon and the Hagia Sophia. Besides Imperial Rome, they had spiritual associations with the vault of heaven and Christianity. Dome building was associated with high culture and civilisation. The European aesthetic and ecclesiastical building tradition invested domical space with a special ideological value.[81] We may guess that this ideological status played a significant part in why the Indian dome builder was rendered invisible and why de Havilland and the Military Board had

[80] George Michell, *Architecture and Art*, p. 28 and J. Harle, *Temple Gateways in South India* (London, 1963).

[81] Indians invested their domes with similar properties. Muhammad Ali, when appointed ruler of Trichinopoly around 1750, built a dome to sanctify the resting-place of the saint Nathar Wali. 'The illuminating dome which is so high as to surpass the sky brings under the shade of its protection the fort which is within an arrow shot.' See Burhan Ibn Hasan, *Tuzak-i-Walajahi*, vol. 1 (Madras, 1934), p. 132. This was a multi-functional dome affording sanctity and protection.

difficulty conceding that in some regions, dome building was a reasonably common Indian practice. It is then easy to understand why de Havilland was eager to arrogate a part of the dome mystique to himself.

De Havilland continued to enhance his practical science skill by 'experimenting' with Indian building construction methods, constantly reporting his results to the Board and seeking ways to introduce new methods in the projects he handled. He tested the native method of using jaggery in mortar, 'so prevalent throughout India' to discover its advantages. For the purpose, he built small pillars, some of which had mortar with sugar water; others that had mortar with limewater. After testing the strength of these columns he concluded that not much benefit was derived from the use of saccharine matter, except that the mortar appears more plastic and masons find it works better. He thus discontinued the use of jaggery in mortar in the St. Andrew's bridge project and recommended its disuse for large works. It is interesting that experiments with a new material, natural hydraulic cement made from magnesia limestone, were carried out by Dr. MacLeod, in Madras in 1825, and followed up by Captain John Smith of the Madras Engineers who wrote the second work in English on the subject of cement in 1837.[82]

Indians used thin bricks and special mortar as a composite material. It allowed the construction of buildings with very different technical and aesthetic properties from English structures. De Havilland's orders for altering the composition of mortar indicates an unwillingness to allow for such differences. It must be said though that his interest in the Indian construction system was manifold and marked by persistent curiosity and enthusiasm. Aside from seeking personal pleasure, he used this interest primarily to market himself as a scientist and an architect/contractor with practical and aesthetic skills.

Bricks—Engineering Social Conflict

Extracting jealously guarded scientific information on building from European or Indian designers and builders was not a simple contest of bringing secret craft knowledge out in the open and organising it into a new universal codified scientific knowledge. It was an interlocking technical and social process where coercion was often employed in the early years. In India it is possible to trace how Company intervention threatened substantial changes in the technical and social life of Indian architects, craftsmen and builders.

[82] John Weiler, 'Colonial Connections: Royal Engineers and Building Technology Transfer in the Nineteenth Century', *Construction History*, vol. 12 (1996), pp. 3–18.

In late eighteenth-century Calcutta the state interfered to alter indigenous production of building materials. The engineer in charge of constructing Fort William had introduced regulations to stop the malpractices of the *banyans* (banias in other sources), Indian agents of merchants, who supplied the large quantities of bricks and scantlings needed. The *banyans* deserted the works and bricklayers and coolies followed. The state was forced to take control and appointed a 'Superintendent of Brickmaking', allowing him a premium of several annas on every 1,000 bricks which he produced from his kiln. He was authorised to collect all the brickmakers in Calcutta and to prohibit any other person from making bricks, on pain of confiscation. This action broke the ring of contractors, but the post of Superintendent of Brickmaking proved to be so lucrative that it was very much in demand. The fortunate holder enjoyed an income equal to the Chief Engineer himself! Naturally, such affluence perturbed the Directors who abolished the post in 1762 and ordered the Committee of Works to arrange to carry on the work.[83]

In 1817 de Havilland was engaged in the construction of St. Andrew's Bridge. It was on this site that he claimed to have initiated the mixing of mortar in a mill, in Madras. Because he found the mill system efficient, 'it [was] pursued in most works of magnitude in lieu of beating it in troughs with small hand pillons or stampers by women and children in the Indian manner.'[84] When de Havilland made an even stronger effort to intervene in the production of building materials at the same site we can see how the coercive arm of the state joined the soldier-technocrat to effect technical and social change in craft work and the labour force. He persuaded the Military Board to seek permission from the government for the Superintending Engineer to prepare 200,000 bricks for the public service, because the production of bricks in Madras had deteriorated. The cause for the deterioration was identified as the failure of the police to enforce regulations.

De Havilland informed the Board that rules for brick production in England deemed that the clay used was dug early, and left to be rid of its salt, but in India soil was not given this opportunity. In India the pricing of bricks was such that engineers made a deal with the manufacturers to try and stop the abuse of producing too many brickbats, as it provided an opportunity to the producer and the carter, who transported the bricks, to cheat. In 1818 de Havilland urged amendment of the regulations as follows: soil intended for brickmaking was to be dug before the monsoon, three large or four small bats, none less than a half brick were accounted as one brick, a dimension was to be fixed for bricks and no deviation allowed, at

[83] Sandes, *Military Engineer*, vol. 1, p. 124.

[84] T.F. de Havilland, *The Public Edifices*, p. 25; this was adopted in the building of the St. Andrew's Bridge in 1817.

least for those used in public works. A mould, stamped by the police, should be used for making bricks, after the Superintending Engineer had certified its dimensions. He compared the strength of European bricks, able to withstand loads of 1,000 lbs/sq.inch to Indian bricks which only withstood a load of 350 lbs/sq.inch.

De Havilland assumed that the practice of laying bricks end on arose from a scarcity of whole bricks, which prevented the laying of a header and a stretcher alternately as in Europe. He further observed that interior plastering was needed because of the badness of bricks, whose uneven surface prevented proper joints, and exposure to air caused disintegration. His final suggestion was the trial preparation of 1,500,000–2,000,000 bricks, using a pug mill and block mould, as in England. His English experience made him confident in undertaking the work; he begged to offer his services in the superintendence of the manufacture of bricks on the principles he had suggested.[85] The steady appeal to intercontinental precedent gave his work a metropolitan cachet, evidently not available to Indian competitors.

Five months later, the Superintendent of Police submitted an amended version of the 1804 *Regulations for Controlling the Manufacture of Bricks, Tiles and Pots and the Burners of Chunam* for the consideration of the government.[86] It suggests that the original had lapsed and the superintending engineer was prodding the police to revive it. When first framed, responsibility for the supply of bricks and chunam for the use of the honourable Company's work rested with the executive engineer at Madras. The amended regulations were as follows: no person was permitted to burn bricks, tiles or pots for sale or otherwise without a license; no person could erect a chunam kiln or burn chunam without a license, any person defying the order was liable to be fined Rs. 50 by the police, and the material so burned confiscated for the use of the Company. Application for license should be first made to the executive engineer who would give a certificate that the soil was fit for manufacture. Next, the Collector of Madras would examine the situation of the ground to ascertain if the kiln may be erected in the spot without becoming a nuisance.[87] The Collector should accurately describe the plot and countersign the application, before forwarding it to the police.

The police was to issue the license at a fee. The license fee, Rs. 4 for brick and chunam, and Rs. 2 for tiles and pots, was renewed annually. A condition of the license issue was that 'the Company shall be entitled for the construction of public works, to have the choice bricks

[85] 29 September 1818, P/260/5, 86, MPMC. He was by now Superintending Engineer of the Presidency Division.

[86] 8 January 1819, P/444/77, 61,62, MPPC.

[87] In 1787 the residents of Luz had complained of potters and brick and tile makers making a nuisance, see H.D. Love, *Vestiges*, vol. 3, p. 370.

of every kiln, on paying the market rate which shall be determined from time to time and published by the Committee of Police.' Such choice of bricks was to be furnished on the production of a requisition signed by the Superintendent of Public Works and the Secretary of the Military Board. A further condition of the license was that the holder would give, for the use of public roads, the bottom of all kilns, after the removal of all bricks and tiles fit for building. The Committee of Police would determine the length, breadth and thickness of all bricks manufactured and insert in the license, the obligations to conform. The Committee was also to regulate and determine the measure by which chunam would be sold.

The Commissary General roundly declared that without police authority, it was not possible to control the manufacturers altering the dimensions of the bricks and the *parrah*, a vessel of measurement. He wanted the latter changed in order to reduce cheating, if the 'prejudices' of the burner could be overcome. Although we are not told exactly what this prejudice was, its mere existence indicates that there was resistance to the regulations. However, the government of FSG in January 1819 was 'averse to the reenactment of the Police Regulation'.[88] The official reason given was that the governor wanted the manufacturers left free to reap their profits and felt it would be 'inexpedient and improper' to press the proposed reenactment. The 'prejudice of the burners' may refer to their resistance to draconian state efforts to change their way of life. There plainly were contending views as to the degree of state control acceptable in the production of building material. In this instance administrators overruled technocrats angling for more control.

Well-foundations

The Kirk rests on 150 well-foundations of two types: four-feet diameter brick wells and three-feet diameter pottery ones (see Fig. 38). De Havilland was unstinting in his praise for well-foundations. He went as far as to advocate that the 'time immemorial Madras method of well sinking' be substituted for the European pile foundation and recommended its use for the tunnel 'now constructing under the Thames'. The process of sinking the wells required bricks shaped in the form of the well which were utilised to construct a cylindrical wall the size of the intended well, built on a base ring of wicker-work. The cylindrical wall was raised to a convenient height and the cylinder thus formed was firmly bound outwardly, with straw ropes wound round it, from bottom to top.

[88] 29 September 1818, P/260/5, 80, MPMC.

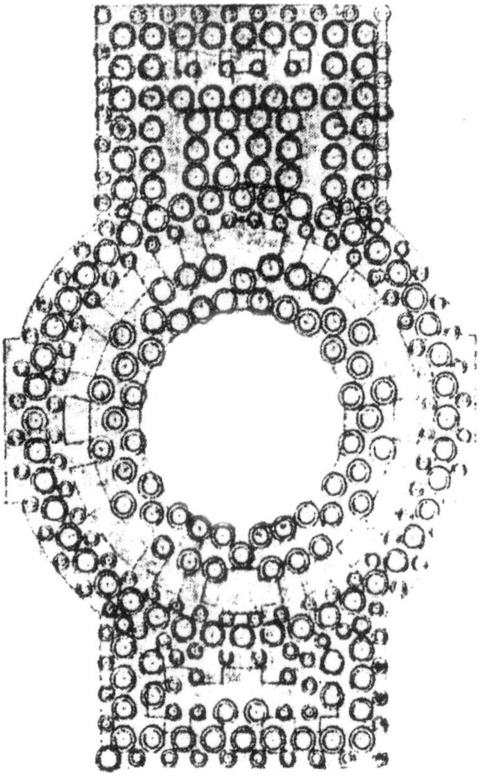

Figure 38: St. Andrew's, foundation plan showing 150 brick and pottery wells

> This done, the well sinker gets into the cylinder with a basket, and with his hands chiefly when the mud is soft, sometimes with a *mammotty*, large, short-handled hoe, and other fit tools, he excavates the soil from the bottom, and fills the basket, which is then hauled up by other workmen on a scaffolding above, and handed out of the way. In this operation great care must be taken to excavate *evenly* all round under the wicker ring, that the cylinder may preserve its perpendicularity.[89]

The process was continued until it disappeared beneath the soil, until the bottom was found. If the cylinder was too short, it was raised and bound round as before and the well sinker continued in this manner until the correct bearing was attained. The well was then filled with brickbats, sand, shingle, small stones or any other substance which would not dissolve, nor alter its volume in water and would admit of being rammed solid.

The wells having been placed as near to each other as was practicable, the interstices were also filled and rammed and the whole space levelled to a uniform surface, perfectly firm and impenetrable on which the masonry foundation was laid. Pottery wells were fitted up and sunk like the others, but the cylinders were formed of baked rings and only used for wells of not more than three-feet depth. Brick wells were often sunk to a very great depth. Sophisticated knowledge defined the varying diameters and depths of the water wells which were constructed on the same principle. The clay mortar used in this case was laid very thin and the well could be as much as fifty-feet deep. The plans show the larger wells disposed under the more essential parts of the building. The foundations were connected by vaults which rose to receive the pavement at the top of the basement, the spandrils being filled with broken brickbats and lime mortar called 'jully' in India. The total foundation depth below the pavement was twenty-six and a quarter feet.

[89] T.F. de Havilland, *An Account*, p. 16.

Discovering Well-sinkers

From the days of the Carnatic wars, military engineers in southern India were associated with the recruitment and management of labour. Artillery officers were in charge of supervising labour gangs who were apt to, 'down tools and fly', on the first appearance of the enemy. In September 1780 Lieutenant Moorhouse of the Madras Artillery proposed the raising of a Company of Pioneers to replace his 'Momaty Men', a reference to the *mammoty*, a local digging tool. The Pioneers were to have a uniform, be armed, and employed to clear and mend roads during field campaigns. They were relied upon in the building of saps and batteries for siege warfare and paid heavily for leading the way in assault. Engineers of FSG were also called upon to strengthen the defences of the fort and in emergencies; they 'swept the surrounding country clear of coolies, labourers and tank-diggers, and so managed to keep 4,000 men at work daily'.[90]

The same problem was faced in the building of Fort William, Calcutta, where bricklaying presented an acute problem. Since labour was much better paid in private work, it forced the Company to legislate that, 'nobody should be allowed to employ any artificers without special permission' and that any artificer found at work without a certificate should be severely punished and obliged to work on the fortifications for five days on half pay. Such stringent rules were never fully enforced, possibly because the private employers were also state officials and could and did reach private arrangements with Indian labour contractors. In principle though, the Company was not averse to resorting to legislation and physical violence to coerce labour.

De Havilland's *Account* furnishes valuable information on the specialist skills and social organisation of certain types of labour associated with Indian irrigation and building construction. The well-sinkers he documented were:

> a distinct set of people, of the agricultural or labouring class in Lower India. They intermarry amongst themselves only, not even, is said, with the tank-diggers, whose avocations and labours are of so similar a nature. They travel about the country in small companies or families with tents or sheds, in search of employment, but in the vicinity of Madras where their labours are constantly in request, they have had for the last forty years a settled place of habitation and reside there in small huts and houses. They are very hard working people but not provident though well paid while employed. They are given to drinking, perhaps more than other classes of labourers from their practice of taking spirits while sinking the wells, in order to sustain them in their great exertions, and to preserve them against the effects of cold and wet.[91]

[90] E.W. Sandes, *Military Engineer*, vol. 1, p. 76.

[91] T.F. de Havilland, *An Account*, p. 17.

During well-sinking the men were almost always immersed in water, having no more clothing than required by decency. Although the water rose above them they continued to dive, remaining below a considerable time at each immersion. The practice of allowing the water to rise over the men was to save the expense of bailing, which would be considerable. It further avoided the greater evil which would accrue if bailing were attempted; 'for the water, forcing itself through the interstices of the bricks, would wash away the mortar and derange the cylinder which would fall in'. In pottery wells, however, it was often done. The narrow diameter of pottery wells made it difficult for the sinker to surface for breath if the water was very deep. As the exertion of working under water was great the workers relieved each other frequently; the one employed in drawing up the basket taking the place of his fellow below. The women and children did not assist in this work but they received and removed the soil from the man who raised it out of the well.

This detailed account exhibits a sustained interest and deep respect for the hard work performed by well-sinkers as well as their corporate social life. It is confirmed by de Havilland's approval of a petition for pension made by the wives of two men killed during the sinking of the well-foundations for the new furnace at the powder mill. He commended the petition to the Board, in his capacity as Superintending Engineer of the Presidency, attesting that the men were killed by the 'falling in of earth on them' and wished their case to be well considered on the grounds of humanity and policy. He regarded the well-sinkers as a peculiar class of men, 'exceedingly useful', whose work needed encouragement on account of its danger and hardship. To strengthen his case he mentioned a precedent of 1808 when men were drowned in the sea while constructing the bulwark of the sea-face; the Governor was pleased to sanction the petition and requested the Military Board to fix the amount.[92] The incident affords insight into another side of de Havilland who comes across as a man who believed that humanity demanded an official policy of protection for this labour force, at least with regard to pension facilities if death was caused by work.

However, against the individualism of colonial state officials, another view of the *Wudders, Odde* (Telugu), *Odda* (Tamil) suggests that they possessed strongly defined modes of community action which offered protection to their own and enforced an advanced notion of justice. The name *Odda* appears to encompass persons associated with skilled and non-skilled activity which ranged from quarrying stone, well-sinking, tree felling and the making of roads, tank bunds and all earthwork associated thereto, who worked in gangs where everyone, except the very

[92] 29 September 1818, P/260/5, 80, MPMC.

young, shared the work. Edgar Thurston, in his book on *Castes and Tribes of Southern India* (1909) registered the case of the tank diggers in Kurnool. The diggers had been paid for their work, when a bitter dispute arose in the apportioning of the share because one of the women had not received what she deemed her fair amount. On enquiry it turned out that she was 'in an interesting condition' and therefore could claim for herself and a share for the expected child. This anecdote hints that although the women in the earlier mentioned petition were seeking a state pension, it is unlikely that the community would have left them totally destitute. By the same token justice was sought from elders within the community.[93]

What is striking in these accounts by de Havilland and Thurston, written almost a century apart, is not merely the minute attention to detail, but the immense intellectual curiosity of the authors and the variety of avenues which afforded pleasure to colonial officials. A staggering amount of patient surveillance, enquiry and writing was done by the 'detached observer' such as de Havilland, unilaterally accumulating 'factual' information in the course of his work. It was the exalted social status of the engineer in imperial society that opened up the opportunity for a man from Guernsey to peer into the lives of a South Indian work-force, uninvited. Although there must have been one, de Havilland does not record Indian participation in this knowledge-gathering exercise.

Not content with the above, de Havilland was also instrumental in pioneering the use of colonial convict labour in construction. The government, investigating Major de Havilland's new plan for repairing roads at the Presidency using convict labour, had instructed the law officers to explore the possibility of bringing within the precincts of the Supreme Court judicature, persons convicted by the *zillah* provincial courts. It was keen to use convicts on more important projects and was of the opinion that de Havilland had 'not maturely considered the extreme difficulty of providing shelter for such a number of convicts' and how to transport them daily to scattered work sites.[94] Despite such reservations the Military Board instructed the Road Committee, of which de Havilland was a member, to try an experiment using convict labour in road repair.

In obedience to this order the Committee chose the road leading from the new bridge (St. Andrew's bridge which de Havilland had just completed) through Chintradripettah for the purpose. The Governor, Lord Denison, however, instructed the Committee to choose another road less liable to frequency by foot passengers since he was apprehensive that this mode of

[93] Edgar Thurston, *Castes and Tribes of Southern India*, vol. 5 (Madras, 1909), pp. 422–25.

[94] 10 February 1818, P/244/69, p. 531, MPPC.

repair would be 'inconvenient for a footpath for natives'.[95] It is difficult to understand the Governor's apprehension unless we imagine gangs of chained convict labour, patrolled by police *peons*, armed men in the service of Indian chiefs (British in this case), unknown in the pre-colonial building world.[96] Evidently chained labour was not a familiar sight in Madras and the Governor believed it had the potential to cause offence to the natives who frequented the road. It transpires that the Madras Government wished to conduct a discreet experiment with a potentially socially offensive mode of road building.

By mid-century the use of convict labour for building work was a well-recognised colonial state practice. It is interesting that de Havilland, representative of an evolving breed of technocrats, wanted the labour of convicts to render an 'advantage' to the government. The Company was covertly willing to sanction a source of cheap bonded labour and its ideologue, on this occasion, was the military engineer. Convict labour was particularly offensive because it physically removed the labour force from access to wider structures of territorial corporate organisation, which traditionally protected each labour group and its rights associated with terms of work and payment. It appears to be a British colonial practice. Prasanna Parthasarathi's fascinating study of weavers in a transitional colonial economy shows how the pre-colonial South Indian moral order set stringent limits on the use of force and the coercion of labour by rulers.[97]

A Single Building World

Many types of contract were in use in the official building world in Madras. When the Company needed buildings for special public purposes, it called for tenders from contractors who would prepare a brief and usually find, alter and rent a building for the purpose.[98] Lack of specialisation in the industry dictated that design and building were part of the same job.

[95] 7 April, 1818, P/244/69, p. 1055, MPPC.

[96] Denison was a Captain of the Engineers and Governor of Van Diemen's Land in 1847, where he observed that the labour used for road building was 'convict men in irons guarded by soldiers'. See W. Denison, *Varieties of Vice Regal Life*, vol. 1 (2 vols., London, 1870), p. 24.

[97] Prasanna Parthasarathi, *A Transition to a Colonial Economy: Weavers, Merchants and Kings in South India 1720–1800* (Cambridge, 2000). For a discussion of corporate organisations and labour resistance see David Washbrook, 'Land and Labour in Late Eighteenth-Century South India: The Golden Age of the Paraiah?', in Peter Robb (ed.), *Dalit Movements and the Meanings of Labour in India* (Delhi, 1993), pp. 68–86. Ian Kerr in his detailed study of construction labour in the railway industry did not discuss convict labour in later railway building, indicating perhaps that it was a privileged practice of the colonial state, not available to private road contractors; Ian J. Kerr, *Building the Railways of the Raj* (London, 1995).

[98] See the contract for the Supreme Court, 16 December 1816, P/244/58, p. 4842, MPPC.

De Havilland's agreement to design and build St. Andrew's Church was executed by him 'on oath' as to his disbursement. What de Havilland was referring to was the ancient *mamool* local custom—the final arbiter and highest court of appeal—that governed the social and commercial life of the highly pluralistic pre-colonial segmented city-state.

He defended this as a practice that has 'successfully prevailed, almost uninterruptedly at Madras for the last thirty years, and has been found to answer in every respect better than the contract system':[99] a defence mounted in reference to the thrice-failed attempt to introduce the British contract system in Madras, though it was generally established in the Bengal Presidency. De Havilland believed that success of the oath system lay with having commissioned officers to superintend public works. Such men had all the inducements, like other men, to serve their employer honourably and, in addition, stood to forfeit their military commission if guilty of fraud. It also offered the government an opportunity to usefully employ its military staff in times of peace; 'in which employment scientific men cannot fail of improving themselves, both in theory and practice, and of thus combining the several branches of the profession, a knowledge of which can alone form the perfect engineer'.[100]

The school-trained engineer was non-existent. The design-and-build contracts offered potential European engineers an opportunity to learn both theory and practice on the job. Until 1800 the Company had on the whole remained aloof from undertaking new building work except for the military. When buildings were needed they were designed, and contracts run, by general 'science' men. The largest civil building programmes were the irrigation works, maintained by Indians in the *Maramut* Department. Most military and civil building was largely done by Indian designers and contractors, some of whom may have teamed up with European partners.[101]

A case in point is the founding and settling of the entire new weavers' town of Chintradripettah. In 1734 Governor Pitt issued a *cowle,* an agreement in writing, for the erection of the town, with an advance of five hundred pagodas, as part of a total of two thousand, to be paid on completion to Chintomby Moodeliar and Vennala Narrain Chetty. The following account of their work is an extract from a petition for payment submitted by them to the Company.[102] The contract stipulated that they were to advance the money to settle the place

[99] T.F. de Havilland, *An Account*, p. 27.

[100] Ibid., p. 28.

[101] 16 December 1816, P/244/58, p. 4842, MPPC. There were some private European contractors at the time. The Military Board was to examine the tender of Mr Sherson to provide a Court House for the Supreme Court. De Havilland tendered for the same, as did Mr. Maconochie and Messrs D'Fries and Company, see letter dated 6 February 1816, P/244/ 5.

[102] J. Talboys Wheeler, *Madras in Olden Times*, vol. 3, p. 133. The accounts are provided on p. 147.

and prepare to produce large quantities of calicos (white or printed cotton cloth) to benefit the Company. The contractors first sent persons to the weavers' *pettah*s, walled suburbs or towns, with presents and money, to persuade the weavers to relocate and help with their travelling expenses to Madras, and to lodge them till their new houses were built. They then explored the site and took care to transplant the trees of the garden which stood there. Thereafter, the ground was levelled and all materials needed for building purchased.

The costs incurred were as follows: digging foundations where *chank*s were buried with a ceremony of feeding poor Brahmins, transplanting the trees from where the streets were to be, levelling ground and making streets, costs for house poles, country reapers and palmera reapers, clay for mud walls, palm coir, coolie for making mud walls, carpentry coolie, sawers, brick layers, coolie for making upper part of the house, tiles, brick kilns, coolie for digging sand for clay work, planks for doors from Jafnapatam, coolie for bringing country wood from sea-side, bricks and tiles from the kiln, coolie for transplanting trees, coolie for watering trees, and coolie and *peons* employed at Chintradripettah for 10 months. The most expensive item in the list was the labour cost.

We have here a picture of an Indian business that possessed skills ranging from labour persuasion and relocation for textile production, to human resettlement, land management and the building of new towns. Besides which, the entrepreneurs appeared to have possessed the capital to withstand the risk of late payment. The entire project of capital and labour investment was undertaken on oath. The purpose of the petition was to remind the Company to meet the terms of the oath. It bound both parties. The contract de Havilland entered into with the Company 83 years later was similar. It was a self-confessed Indian method, tying the Company into what was essentially a regional indigenous construction industry. This was the customary method by which transactions were conducted in Madras.[103] It is doubtful whether European contractors on their own could have matched indigenous skills in competing for contracts. The state was unable to effect radical changes in the contract system in the 1820s. The Indian and British contract systems and patronage arrangements possibly began to diverge only after the Company initiated its major public works programmes.

Paul Benfield, who came to South India as Civil Architect and Assistant Engineer in 1764, was contracted for building part of the ramparts of Black Town. It is said that he introduced the use of the inverted arch into India, thereby economising on masonry. He employed foundation-wells to support the heavy works, a method which he is said to have copied from the natives of

[103] Robert E. Frykenberg, The Socio-Political Moophology of Madras.

Madras.[104] It is not clear what an inverted arch means, but there is no evidence to sustain this claim, especially in a region with a long tradition of massive masonry construction in building and irrigation works. After all Benfield did not build the ramparts himself, even if he did 'copy from the natives'. He had to employ Indians to supervise, design and execute the work. For this he had to enter into local partnerships.

There are few details as to the precise Indo-British structure of business partnerships in a construction industry where building contracts covered a variety of activities, besides straightforward building. Enterprising new 'science men' like Benfield, John Goldingham, appointed Civil Engineer in 1800, and de Havilland served the Company state not only as designers, but also as contractors. De Havilland contracted for the sewers of Black Town and built the sea wall of Fort St. George. They were large, complicated engineering projects demanding knowledge of local conditions and materials. The contract details suggest that they were built with Indian partners. It is difficult to judge how equal such partnerships were. The fact that only Europeans appear in the records does not always mean that they were the principals.[105] However silent the records—collaboration, Indian institutions and personnel formed the bedrock of the Company state. When it came to building material production and construction there was only a single building world and it was indigenous.[106]

Subtle Transformations

De Havilland's predecessor in post, Paul Benfield, held the title 'civil architect and assistant engineer'.[107] The title 'civil architect' may have bestowed a certain superior rank or social status unavailable to the run-of-the-mill military engineer. By 1818 Calcutta had employed two civil architects: Richard Blechynden succeeded Edward Tiretta as the Company's architect in 1803.[108] De Havilland's artistic and technical success with St. Andrew's earned him another

[104] E.W. Sandes, *Military Engineer*, vol. 1, p. 80.

[105] Although Kerr discusses the later period of railway construction, where special conditions pertained, the extent of Indian agency at the contractual level is interesting. He regarded railway design as a European engineering affair. Ian Kerr, *Building the Railways of the Raj*.

[106] John Sullivan argued that Indian administrative usages were fully capable of providing the basis for British colonial institutions, with some minor modifications. Tipu Sultan's regulations, the *al Sirajiyya*, of 1786 or 1788, were known to Cornwallis by 1792. In 1802, Charles Harris, the first Collector of Tanjore, promulgated orders to revenue officials that were the same as those used by the Maratha Rajas of Tanjore. See John Sullivan, *Tracts Upon India; Written in the Years 1779, 1780 and 1788 with Subsequent Observations* (London, 1795) and Burton Stein, *Sir Thomas Munro*, pp. 33–35.

[107] E.W. Sandes, *Military Engineer*, vol. 1, p. 80.

[108] For Blechynden see the Blechynden Papers, Add MS 45,645: 45,646 and for Tiretta see, Sten Nilsson, *European Architecture*.

accolade. In August 1820 Major de Havilland was signing himself as 'civil architect'.[109] One could surmise that the special status accruing to the civil architect hinted at some learning to be attained by an educated cultivated gentleman, and that it had more of a novelty value than much else. It is unlikely that the social status of the architect surpassed that of the military engineer in colonial India. The title makes sense in the context of several other appointments also held by de Havilland. As mentioned earlier, he was Inspector of Estimates for the Repair of Tanks and Water Courses under the Board of Revenue and Assessor and Civil Engineer for the Town Assessment. The state rewarded its military engineers with coveted civil titles. The absence of private professional institutions allowed the state to control standards of taste and regulate the professional status of the architect in British India.

The eighteenth-century civil building programme of the Company was minimal and possessed little 'art' content, but burgeoning civil responsibility and new building, increasingly forced it to address the artistic component of even its minor buildings. In discussions pertaining to de Havilland's design submissions for a new market, the government was pleased that the 'east side towards the fort is given a neat and respectable appearance as it must always be desirable, in public edifices under a liberal and great government to combine taste and elegance with convenience and utility'.[110] The specialist division of tasks within the state sector of the construction industry was fluid. It made professional reputation-building arduous. The vulnerability of technocratic status compelled the aspiring professional to don many hats and move from one activity to another. De Havilland's account of the building of the Kirk was doubtless written as a promotional brochure.

In the *Account* he made several favourable comparisons between his work, the Great Masters, and the strict rules of architecture. St. Andrew's was unblushingly grander than or almost as grand as his chosen European masterpieces. The steeple at St. Andrew's was 11 feet taller than that of St. Martin-in-the-Fields, in London. At St. Andrew's, having made the link between the circular main body and the rectangular portions using bent pilasters, he opined that bent pilasters should, 'as much as possible', be avoided as 'defective in taste and elegance' although they were to be met with in many buildings and occurred frequently in the Cathedral of St. Pauls, 'that chef d'oeuvre of the Great Wren and of British architecture'.[111] De Havilland alluded to a Mr. Rondelet's table which compared the ratio of wall to column, and the interior area of the body of the building to the section of the columns supporting the whole roof in

[109] 11 August 1820, P/245/14, No. 16, MPPC.

[110] 8 January 1819, P/444/77, p.163, MPPC.

[111] T.F. de Havilland, *An Account*, p. 5.

several church buildings. The former ratio for St. Andrew's was nearly the same as that calculated by Mr. Rondelet for the Church of St. Sulpice, at Paris, but greater than that for St. Paul's, in London. The latter ratio showed that St. Joseph's at Palermo was the lightest and St. Andrew's was within a small fraction of it. From an outside reckoning, the only useful function Mr. Rondelet's table of scientific information served was to rank new churches against selected masterpieces. By expressing awareness of the table and espousing its classification for St. Andrew's, de Havilland staked an international claim for himself and his work. Though his artistic and technical measure remained aligned toward Europe, it was a synthesis of Company state sponsorship and an Indo-European knowledge and skill that made the contemplation of such a stupendous imperial bid remotely possible for an aspiring engineer in a colonial outpost. De Havilland's gaze at Indian building was not neutral. As he appropriated Indian knowledge he disempowered his Indian counterpart. In this instance, if there was an Indian contribution to universal knowledge, it was channelled through professional agents like de Havilland.

Exciting Spaces

In the hurly burly of promoting science in early nineteenth-century India, the concept of building as art did not lag too far behind. The Company had established the India Museum in the metropolis in 1801. It was also supporting antiquarian archaeology in search of a glorious Indian past. Under the initiative of the Governor-General, Lord Minto, who was also a fellow of the Royal Society and one of the few scientific men of his class involved in India, the government appointed a Taj Committee in 1808. Governor-General, Lord Hastings, ordered repairs to Fatehpur Sikri and Sikandra in 1815.[112] In the South, powerful officials like Lionel Place, Collector of the Jagir from 1794–98, had been active in the restoration of temples and tanks.[113] None of this interest in Indian architecture was actually reflected in prestigious Company buildings for which classical was the favoured style in India and at home.

Neo-classicism in England passed through several phases. In tune with late eighteenth-century trends, the East India Company Head Offices, in Leadenhall Street, were remodelled in a loosely Roman mode (see Fig. 39). The same sense of Roman grandeur was aimed for in the Kirk. It expressed the expanding power and coherence of the new 'British' national and imperial identity. Experientially the most impressive and imposing parts of the church were the raised portico of double Ionic columns, approached by a generous series of steps and

[112] Ray Desmond, *The India Museum*, p. 111.

[113] Eugene Irschick, *Dialogue and History: Constructing South India 1795–1895* (Berkeley, 1994), p. 83.

Figure 39: East India House, Leadenhall Street, 1817

the interior domed space. The portico and the vault speak of a powerful earthly empire rather than a heavenly one. The dome in this design was made shallow in order not to detract from the steeple, which was the principal object. A circle of ponderous, closely spaced columns and a shallow corridor further suffocated the interior domed space. Wooden shutters covered the openings on the external wall of the corridor, removing the opportunity for spatially extended vistas.

Large Indian domical spaces exhibited considerable regional variation. The spatial resonance of the Kirk dome is akin to the dark, flat domes found in Delhi and the Deccan up to the fourteenth century. Despite close inter-columniation the Madurai vaults were rendered insubstantial and spacious in two ways. The windows at the base of the dome lifted it off its structural supports, creating the illusion of floating.[114] Laterally the eye was led away along a series of interpenetrating columned vistas where light and shade were used to shift the boundaries of space. This quality is absent in the static space of St. Andrew's. In England, John Soane discovered the potential excitement of chiaroscuro and vaulted space and went on to deploy

[114] The practice of piercing the drum with windows is said to have arisen in Iran in 1322. It was rare in the Deccan. Elizabeth Merklinger, *Indian Islamic Architecture in the Deccan 1437–1686* (Warminster, 1981).

them so successfully that they became his architectural trademark. It is believed that during travels in Italy, in 1779, Soane was struck by the quality of light of the mirrored vaulted ceilings of the Palazzo Palagonia at Bagheria, outside Palermo, and the double ceilings of the Biscari Palace in Catania, Sicily, with their 'stolen light effect'; features which continued to fascinate him all his life.[115] De Havilland's play with South Indian dome construction methods, paralleled Soane's experiments with Byzantine/Islamic dome building traditions of the greater Mediterranean.

Taylor Munro felt that St. Andrew's had too great a proportion of plaster inside (see Fig. 40) and that:

> if its principal end was not to gratify the vanity of the architect but to be, a sacred edifice in which the ritual devotion and the doctrines of the Church of Scotland should be HEARD by an auditory, then this end was missed to a lamentable degree and architectural skill seriously counterbalanced by ignorance in the science of Acoustics.

Figure 40: St. Andrew's, the interior

[115] Gillain Darley, *John Soane*, pp. 45–48.

This criticism was levelled against the chief evil, the dome, because a considerable echo muffled the voice of the Reverend Dr. Allan. The architect attributed the echo not to faulty acoustics in the dome but to the advancing age of the 'good reverend' and the newness of the interior plaster. He was confident that as the plaster 'exsiccated' the problem would cease. It is probable that there was an element of truth in both explanations. Like the Gola, which was never put to practical use, the experimental nature of the dome design lends weight to the accusation that the science of acoustics and the design of domes was not well understood by the designer.

De Havilland tells us that the stucco that 'encrustrated' the walls externally and internally was 'put on with the greatest care, especially the columns which represent parian marble in whiteness and in polish. The Madras stucco [was] renowned for its superiority over every other, and this edifice offers a fine specimen of its elegance.'[116] Madras chunam was highly prized for its lustrous finish. The plasterwork of the ceiling was especially ornate and the *rayonned* [*sic*] tympanum of the pediment of the western portico was quite breathtaking; the sacred name JEHOVA appeared in Hebrew characters of gold, amid an explosion of rays of glory. The designs on the eastern pediment proclaimed this to be the church of The East India Company. It carried the Company's arms 'with two monsters *passant*, intended for lions: a figure that native artists somehow cannot hit'.[117] The Company motto was emblazoned on the frieze. The building, like St. George's Church, was coloured in pristine white inside and out (see Fig. 41). This was an aesthetic quite different from what the British had hitherto adopted for Government House and the Banqueting Hall where coloured chunam of all shades was used on the floors, walls and pillars, 'almost equal in splendour to marble itself'. The snow-white aesthetic was the 'product of the marble cult of neo-classicism'.[118] The floor at St. Andrew's was a spectacular black and white marble checkerboard, imported from England or Italy. It complemented the deep blue vault.

Although de Havilland's rhetoric may lead to the conclusion that he considered European building components and methods superior to Indian ones, his practice here proves otherwise. In this particular building he was pragmatic, blending European designs with the safety and skill of Indian design and construction modes. His relationship with his builders was such that he placed his reputation in their trust. The final form of the building evolved from an intimate collaboration and convergence of two different systems of design and construction. The potential grandeur of Indian domes merged with the ambitions to grandeur of

[116] T.F. de Havilland, *An Account*, p. 11.

[117] W.T. Munro, *Madrasiana*, p. 37.

[118] Sten Nilsson, *European Architecture*, p. 171.

Figure 41: St. Andrew's, east elevation

the Scottish Church and its patron—the Company state in Madras. The transformation of ideas into material form was achieved by an Indian construction industry, Indian knowledge, drawing, design, building and management skills. Seated at the centre of the site the church was a pure white rounded form with a tall slim spire shooting upwards, outward looking and commanding attention—designed to be seen. In its heyday the building celebrated the alliance between the Company and a Scottish merchant class in Madras. Today it serves the Church of South India.

The Hidden Pleasures of Imperial Conversations

The Indo-British dialogue which led to the conception and erection of this church was layered. Distant imperial patrons represented by members of the Home Government and the Company state made up one level. Soldiers made up another. They mediated demands, made by imperial patrons, of Indian construction personnel.[119]

Although Indo-Britons might have conversed as technical equals in terms of knowledge and practical skill on building sites; their multi-lingual conversations entered British records in English, as those conducted between superior and inferior. Indians were denied personal names and no named Indian, equal to a British engineer, appears in colonial records. Most Britons were unwilling to admit engineering and scientific knowledge-sharing with Indian intellectuals. They pretended that knowledge only passed from West to East; a view current as late as 1996.[120] Colonial literature only admitted an undifferentiated Indian workforce of subordinate builders, craftsmen or labour. The contest for knowledge was so bitter that the upper ranks of the engineer establishment remained the preserve of the European, until the advent of Indians trained by the British in the new 'science'.

Similar knowledge-sharing was common in the professional spheres of law, medicine, art and education. It was not peculiar to the building world. Indian indegenous knowledge was simply subsumed into factual statements and colonial histories.[121] Indo-British knowledge reached the European scientific community folded within scientific papers and specialist journals, where its Indian component was easily diffused or erased. The hidden process has given longevity to the myth that Europeans were the exclusive creators of the universal knowledge of modern science. This project shows the key role played by the Company state in this transformation, when it slowly began to commandeer patronage that combined exciting prospects for scientific innovation and social advancement. However, despite these observations, it is important to recognise that knowledge exchange on building sites combined a popular tradition of knowledge-sharing as well as a more formal one. It serves as a reminder that indigenous building knowledge was a fluid and evolving mixture of superstition, ritual and empirical and theoretical knowledge systems.

De Havilland's perception of the status of science and his bid to secure greater power for engineers brought him into another zone of conflict, this time inside the army. Some inkling of this is apparent in the contest between the ardent reformer Major de Havilland, Chief Engineer

[119] The Society of Civil Engineers in England was almost purely a social institution in 1818. The Institution of Civil Engineers was formed in January 1820, with Thomas Telford as its President. L.T.C. Rolt, *Thomas Telford* (London, 1958), p. 190.

[120] John Weiler discussed a one way transfer of building knowledge from Britons to Indians using three examples from Madras, 'Colonial Connections'.

[121] Matthew E. Edney noted that Indians were named in Buchanan's survey only when they acted like the British or entered territory outside British control. Edney, *Mapping an Empire*, p. 81.

Madras, and the Quartermaster General (QMG). In November 1821 de Havilland submitted a gigantic report on his ideas of the status, duties and organisation of engineers, pioneers, sappers and miners. He proposed shifting control of the pioneers, then under the QMG, to the chief engineer and remarked among other things that the QMG was always interfering in engineering matters. The astute QMG, giving voice to a commonplace prejudice, noted that it was farcical to talk of science when speaking about road construction since it was well known that the best road maker in England, J.L. McAdam, was, in fact, a ship's purser. He wittily mocked professional scientific aspirations.

> These lofty pretensions of the Corps of engineers are nothing new; and when they assumed in the French service the proud title of the Corps of Genius, they showed the extent to which they were inclined to push their exclusive aims to all scientific requirements. In general they are ignorant of the manner in which troops manoeuvre; they even object to [attaining] that knowledge. Considering their own as the first of all arts, they look down with disdain on every other branch of the service. If this prejudice is kept alive amongst them by the fine name of Genius, I beg leave to inform them that the word 'Engineer' is derived, not from Genius, but from the word 'Engine'.[122]

In the domain of art, design and new knowledge British professionals held the advantage of access to a European tradition of aesthetics and alleged 'modern', 'scientific' methods and materials; but due to their small numbers and internal competition it is unlikely that early nineteenth-century European professionals posed a substantial threat to the Indian designer. However, Indians increasingly had to compete with more exclusive European notions of taste in the private sector as well. A military ethos leaked into the civil space of building material production and management of the construction industry. 'New science' began to demand changes in the social and technical life of Indian construction personnel. De Havilland's career in India elegantly demonstrates the range of pleasure accessible through building. The pleasure of creating architectural space and aesthetics was just a part of the story. The pleasure of power, of control and the physical and intellectual thrill of scrutinising the life and work of others, without reciprocity, permission or censure was the bonus received by imperial professionals. De Havilland returned to Guernsey a rich man. In 1828 he built himself a large elegant mansion in the Palladian manner called Havilland Hall in the parish of St. Andrews.

[122] E.W. Sandes, *Military Engineer*, vol. 1, p. 228.

3

Excited by Athenian Antiquities

The Pachaiyappa School 1846–50

The Trustees of the Pachaiyappa Trust commissioned a design for the Pachaiyappa School building on 7 June 1846. The patrons—a group of élite Indians and the Company state—settled on the Greek architectural style as the one best suited to convey their perception of the convergence of Indian and European culture. The aim of the institution was to provide free education to poor 'Hindu' boys in the elementary branches of English literature and science, with instruction in Tamil and Telugu. The Trustees, who were also closely allied to the colonial state's institutions of higher learning, had also intended to sponsor the further education of some of the more gifted boys. From the school's inception, the state upheld it as a 'Hindu' institution. But it was emphatically a joint Indo-British venture; the patron of the Board of Trustees was George Norton, Advocate General of Madras. Norton in the role of *eminence grise* discreetly exercised state control behind the scenes.

Pachaiyappa Mudaliar

Pachaiyappa Mudaliar 'the most munificent patron of learning and religion in modern South India' was born in 1754, to a poor family near Madras. The archetypal *dubash*, he went on to amass fame and fortune as a financier and merchant prince.[1] He was an intimate of the royal

[1] N.S. Ramaswami, *Pachaiyappa and His Institutions* (Madras, 1986), p. 1. The only account on *dubashes* is Neild-Basu's article 'The Dubashes of Madras'.

courts of the Carnatic Nawab, the Rajah of Thanjavur and several private Britons then tampering with the typical Indo-Muslim system of fiscal state-building and military entrepreneurship, activities that colonial administrators conveniently dubbed the ' Debts of the Nawab of Arcot'. Pachaiyappa died in 1794, a very rich man. His will left an estate of 116,300 star pagodas with a further 120,214 as outstanding dues. There is little evidence to suggest that Pachaiyappa especially endowed institutions of learning, although the range of his court contacts indicates that he spoke English, Tamil, Persian, Marathi and Telugu and probably was learned. The reasons as to why his name, in modern South India, is associated with an institution of learning, lie in events that occurred after his death.

The executor of Pachaiyappa's will, Narayana Pillai, was unable to fully execute his duties since the beneficiaries were in dispute. In February 1826, the Madras Supreme Court passed the first of its four decrees on the will. Our story in some ways really begins with George Norton, Advocate General of Madras, and 'second founder of the Pachaiyappa's Charities': the man who would 'live long in the affectionate memory of many of the most highly educated natives of India'.[2] The diversion of a part of the estate, in the service of the state, was achieved by irregular practice of the law and paternalistic manoeuvring.

It has been sometimes said that it is a curious comment on Pachaiyappa Mudaliar's foundations that from his gifts have sprung into existence institutions which he never contemplated, and that his funds were diverted from the objects to which he intended to apply them in favour of objects which—unquestionably deserving of endowment and goodwill—are as unquestionably called into existence by a pure fiction of the law.[3]

In 1839, a large number of native inhabitants, around 70,000, petitioned the government to establish institutions of higher learning in the Presidency. Robert Frykenberg, the only modern scholar to have discussed the subject, opines that neither the Education Petition nor the Pachaiyappa's Charities can be understood without reference to the alarm stirred up by conversion in Anderson's School: a Scottish Free Church school, set up by John Anderson, in Madras, in 1837.[4] Anderson's School epitomised a new brand of missionary education deriving from the Scottish Enlightenment and St. Andrew's University. But, prior to turning to this subject, it is useful for the reader to have an overview of indigenous education practice

[2] N.S. Ramaswami, *Pachaiyappa*, p. 48.

[3] Krishnama Chariar, *Select Papers, Speeches and Poems Connected with Pachaiyappa Mudaliar* (Madras, 1892), p. xxv. George Norton, *Speech at the Fourteenth Anniversary Meeting of the Patcheapah Moodelliar's Institution in Madras on Thursday April 23, 1857* (London, 1857), p. 26, defends the Supreme Court decision as reflecting the 'general intention of the will'.

[4] Robert E. Frykenberg, 'Modern Education in South India, 1754–1854: Its Roots and Its Role as a Vehicle of Integration Under Company Raj', *American Historical Review,* 96, 1 (1986), pp. 37–65.

encountered by Europeans arriving in the South. The indigenous system of education and the educational ideas developed by Indian intellectuals in the nineteenth century were, in some ways, distinct from the colonial system of education.[5]

Multi-cultural Education in the Eighteenth Century

Education in eighteenth-century South India contained two skeins of different origin—the indigenous and the European. Though indigenous education was starkly divided along lines of wealth and social stratification, the aristocracy and the common man held scholars and teachers in high esteem:

> The teachers and students of Sanskrit schools constitute the cultivated intellect of the Hindu people and they command that respect and exert that influence which cultivated intellect always enjoys. There is no class of persons that exercise a greater degree of influence in giving native society the tone, the form and the character which it actually possesses than the body of the learned.[6]

Rulers and nobles extensively patronised the arts and letters. The wealthy had private domestic teaching arrangements and endowed public schools for elementary education as well as prestigious institutions of higher learning. The southern aristocracy was also active in promoting European mission and civil teaching during this time. Though Brahmins constituted the learned class in South Indian society, there existed a substantial non-Brahmin learned class as well. Thanjavur, Kanchipuram, Trichinopoly and Madurai were among the centres of learning where the exclusive upper echelons of the scribal sects were trained as scholars: either as *Vaidic*, who had the role of teaching the Vedas, performing and superintending sacrifice and preserving moral principles; or as *Laukic*, who served as secular diplomats and advisors to kings and statesmen. Colleges were maintained for Hindu scholars where sectarian divisions appeared to have been surmounted. The *madrasas* forged a parallel tradition of Islamic scholarship, promoted by the Nawabi court at Arcot and later at Chepauk. The court patronised Islamic scholars, Sufi mystics and poets from all over India, encouraging scholarship and poetry in Arabic, Persian and Dakhni.

High-born Saivaite Brahmins were exposed to European thought via the Jesuits in the seventeenth century.[7] The Brahmins who came into contact with Protestant missionaries in

[5] Panikkar avers that modern discussion of this issue is almost non-existent, see K.N. Panikkar, *Culture, Ideology and Hegemony: Intellectuals and Social Consciousness in Colonial India* (New Delhi, 1995), p. 47.

[6] Ibid., p. 48.

[7] Brijraj Singh, *The First Protestant Missionary in India* (Delhi, 1999), p. 49.

the eighteenth century were the *pandarams*, neither exalted nor learned; they pursued worldly tasks and were not rich. The Jesuit Father Nobili was taught Sanskrit by Sivadharma, a Saivaite temple Brahmin in 1608. In return, Nobili is said to have introduced Italian science to Madurai.[8] But habits of secrecy were not easily abandoned. Brahmins practising astronomy at the Chandragiri court, for example, refused to divulge their modes of calculation to the Jesuits. It was forbidden to share knowledge of the Vedas; the power of the Brahmins was believed to flow from them. Similar southern Indo-European intellectual exchanges had occurred long before the celebrated British Orientalist projects in Bengal.

The common man received education in elementary schools funded by wealthy patrons, by pupils and by village communities. It is estimated that in 1823 there was one student for every three males of school age. The facilities were unevenly distributed with fewer schools in the Telugu than the Tamil districts where Vellalar teachers predominated and older non-Brahmanical learning patterns prevailed.[9] Brahmins did not, however, enjoy a monopoly of learning as they did in the North. A significant feature of the system was the virtual exclusion of untouchable communities.

Even during the nineteenth century the wealthy studied at home and employed scholars in their establishments for this purpose. Scholars, like craftsmen, used secret methods to safeguard and retain control of their knowledge. The power of the hereditary system of sacred-and-secret lore learning, personal patronage and kinship influences kept western knowledge exclusive. The British became employers of such families and they developed mutual obligations. Prior to the 1850s the Company drew its native servants mainly from the Maharashtra-descended Desastha Brahmins.[10] It is also possible that these Brahmins (chiefly from the Tanjore Maratha court) may actually have studied in some of the early mission schools, spreading inland from Danish Tranquebar (450 kilometres south of Madras, where the Danes had a coastal fort and settlement from 1620), as well as north to Madras and south to Palamcottah. Some Indian intellectuals explored European culture and were conversant with one or several European languages. The Portuguese, German, French, Italian, Danish, Dutch and English were all present in the region and the services of translators and interpreters were indispensable for affairs of state and commerce. In recognition of the value of this service, the Company began to give

[8] Vincent Cronin, *A Pearl to India*, p. 81.

[9] Robert E. Frykenberg believes that the non-Brahmanical heritage stimulated creativity and was hinted at in the works of Nobili, Beschi and the early Tranquebar scholars. See Frykenberg, 'Modern Education', p. 45.

[10] Tamil Brahmins in the towns were so ignorant that the records were kept in Marathi, see W. Francis, *Madras District Gazetteer, Madura* (Madras, 1906), p. 175.

grants to mission schools because 'the training they [the Indians] received, especially their command of English, became so valuable'.[11] During the political struggles of the nineteenth century this group of savants manoeuvred to protect the advantages they had secured.

More Multi-cultural Education

The Coromandel coast possesses a rich Indo-European heritage of education, which pre-dates Company efforts. Eighteenth-century European schools owed their origins to northern Europe where new techniques for building radically new social institutions and for releasing unknown social energies were under way. German Pietist ideas of 'mass', 'national' or even 'public' education arrived in India via the auspices of the Danish in Tranquebar and the Society for Promoting Christian Knowledge (SPCK). These radical impulses had the support of the royal houses of Denmark and Hanover and the Court of St. James. In 1717, the Company supported the Danish missionaries' desire to establish schools in Madras, with German and Danish as the mediums of instruction. This event has been identified as the 'beginning of the great system of Anglo-Vernacular education maintained under the patronage of Government in this Presidency'.[12]

Schooling for the poor, a mingling of the high-born with the low, equal opportunity for deserving students of any means and a broad curriculum, including practical sciences and skilled trades, were the goals of the Germanic Protestant missionary schools begun by Bartholomaeus Ziegenbalg, in Tranquebar, in 1706. The Vepery School in Madras opened under the missionary Schultze in 1726. The school served many purposes. In 1750, Schultze's protégé, Christian Friederich Schwartz, was sailing from Germany to India. He had learnt Greek, Latin, Hebrew, and a little Tamil from Schultze at the University of Halle, after the latter's return from the Madurai Mission. On arrival in India, Schwartz knew little English, but learnt Tamil from a German-speaking native catechist and Portuguese from a native merchant who spoke English, Danish and French.[13]

The service Schwartz performed for the Company at the siege of Madurai earned him a great deal of money and the unofficial role of Company servant and Regent of Tanjore. In this capacity he undertook the audacious 'rescue' of the young Rajah Serfoji from the clutches of his family and sent him to Vepery in Madras. There, Serfoji was educated under the Missionary

[11] Robert E. Frykenberg, 'Modern Education', p. 4.

[12] S. Satthianadhan, *History of Education in the Madras Presidency* (Madras, 1894), appendix J.

[13] Jesse Page, *Schwartz of Tanjore* (London, 1921), p. 46.

Gericke from 1793 to 1797. He was expected to become an exemplary young ruler, loyal to his masters. Serfoji belonged to an enlightened dynasty of sophisticated cultural innovators and modernisers. Though he lacked economic and political power, interestingly he remained 'a strange hybrid of Indian and British manners' and one might add cultural worlds.[14] He stayed a Hindu all his life and was an enthusiastic patron of a hybrid occidentalist strain of art and architecture, and was learned in the European classics as well as philosophy, mathematics and astronomy.

A less public feature of the alleged 'British government' patronage of missionary schools was that the government and the Indian aristocracy shared patronage of such establishments. In 1786 the Company aided the founding of the Military Female Orphan Asylum and the Nawab of Carnatic presented the buildings. The philanthropic character of Indo-Britons in Madras was well attested to by the many excellent institutions they founded.[15] The opening of the Military Male Orphan Asylum in 1788 marked an era in the history of elementary education, not only in Madras but in Britain as well. Dr. Bell, placed in charge of the Asylum, experimented with native teaching methods and devised the Madras System that subsequently became the basis of the modern in elementary education system in Britain until the middle of the century.

Bell was given the honour of having 'invented' the Madras System which originated in the Military Male Orphan Asylum. The Madras System was 'transplanted to England in 1797' and established at 'the parochial schools of White Chapel and of Lambeth, and at the Royal Military Asylum, Chelsea'.[16] Missionaries induced the rajas of Thanjavur, Ramnad and Sivaganga and other petty princes to fund similar schools in every province. Hence, a shared, mutually beneficial and reasonably broad-based Indo-European education system evolved in the South, with a well-publicised exchange component travelling from India back to Europe.

With the Tamil printing press at Tranquebar churning out basic material, Indian kings and missionaries united to produce in South India, an education system to satisfy the Company, ever reluctant to spend money. The Orientalist-Anglicist controversy which took centre-stage in northern Indian education debates, focusing on whether emphasis should be placed on western or Indian subjects and knowledge, passed by Madras. Some have even said that British education in the North was aimed at remedying the damage done to Indians by depredation, dereliction of duty and abuse of power by nabobs and other leaders.[17] The trajectory of the

[14] Mildred Archer, 'Serfogee An Enlightened'.

[15] As late as 1794 the Male Asylum was seeking endowments to run 'independent of public liberality', *Madras Courier*, 31 January 1794. See *A Gazetteer of Southern India with the Tenasserim Provinces and Singapore* (Madras, 1855), p. 185.

[16] Andrew Bell, *The Madras School or Elements of Tuition* (London, 1808, reprint 2000), p. 1.

[17] Gauri Viswanathan, *Masks of Conquest* (London, 1990), p. 26.

Madras debate was turned by Thomas Munro's Minute of 1826, conceived jointly with Indian intellectuals.[18] It anticipated a long-term policy of complete state-supported education with a pivotal role assigned to the creation of a teacher-training school whence teachers would spill out to lead the proposed 40 Collectorate and 300 Tahsildari schools. The protracted struggle to implement these policies endured through the century.

The general impoverishment of the country came frequently to the notice of the authorities in those days. They often remarked on the inability of the middling and lower classes to defray the cost of education, especially as families relied on the labour of children in order to survive.[19] It is well-known that during the period 1825–54 the Madras Presidency suffered from a severe economic depression; revenue assessments were high and the Ryotwari revenue settlement did not yield increased production.[20] In this context the safest, most influential and prestigious employment was increasingly to be found within the state sector.

The Court was particularly interested in the promotion of education of the higher classes and the Supreme Government had taken measures to this end in Bengal. The object was to provide instruction for candidates in the higher branches of European literature and science, with a view chiefly to fit them for employment in the various departments. However, in Madras, by the 1830s an estimated 500 'school' signboards, claiming to offer the 'best' training in English had sprung up along Mount Road alone, to cater to the desire for access to advanced scientific and technical education.[21] But they posed little threat to the established hereditary sacred-secret teaching given to the wealthy high-born, who were further cocooned by family influence when seeking state employment.

The demands of the poor high-born, coupled with those of the middling groups unable to find secure employment, generated a forceful demand for education in Madras and resulted in the Education Petition of 1839. In 1837 John Anderson's Scottish Free Church School, promulgating a Calvinist brand of higher learning, proved so attractive because it offered a completely English curriculum where teachers, books and laboratory equipment were all imported. The school taught a range of subjects including sciences, political economy, mathematics and theology.

[18] Robert E. Frykenberg, 'Modern Education', p. 47, claims that the like of it was not seen again for another century.

[19] S. Satthianadhan, *History of Education*, p. 7.

[20] Rev. P. Thomas, 'The Catholic Mission in Madras', in Madras Tercentenary Celebration Committee (ed.), *Madras Tercentenary Commemoration Volume,* 3rd revised edn. (New Delhi, 1999).

[21] Quoted in Robert E. Frykenberg, 'Modern Education', p. 46.

The presence of Anderson's School fanned the flames of an already prevailing desire for more such modern schools, increasingly and rightly regarded by Indians as 'the only means by which advancement in political stations and the higher walks of life is to be gained'.[22] The Petition also prayed that his 'Lordship [would] not impose as a condition of National Education that the people should act as if they renounced the religious faith in which they [had] been brought up. It [was] no toleration of the religion of a people to visit it with the pains of ignorance.'[23] Thus, while Anderson's school is relevant for an understanding of Pachaiyappa's Charities, it is likely that the School, 'exclusively under Hindu control', was initiated less for religious and more for economic and political reasons. The Indian demand was for modern, non-sectarian, broad-based education.

The Company State's Stealthy Multi-culturalism

Pachaiyappa had bequeathed his wealth for the performance of sacred service at temples and charities. In kingly fashion his most lavish gift, a lofty *gopuram*, was bequeathed to the famous Saivite shrine at Chidambaram. His munificence ranged across many southern temples, reaching as far north as Benares.[24] Robust state intervention diverted his wealth to service colonial education. The Supreme Court directed that funds, surplus to the performance of the charities, be used to set up institutions for the education of 'Hindu' youths. In October 1832, the Supreme Court appointed the Hindu Trustees of the estate. They were to function under the general supervision of the Board of Revenue, entitled to exercise this right under Regulation VII, of 1817.

George Norton, despite a shady past in racy Bombay, succeeded in securing the lucrative appointment of Advocate of the Supreme Court in Madras, in 1828. It was here that he affected the paternalistic pose of teacher and friend of the native. This pose coloured his speeches and writing on education and attracted ridicule in some English circles. Norton began a scheme of education for the 'better class of natives', developed through conversations held in his home. Julia Maitland, wife of a senior civil servant, pilloried the scheme in print. The Madras Gazette objected to Norton's announcement of law lectures for Indians, 'open to all respectable persons'. The paper argued that if the lectures were to be public, they should be open to all classes without distinction.[25] Norton's pretensions to respectability, perhaps best explain his

[22] Petition to the Governor of 11 November 1839. Cited in N.S. Ramaswami, *Pachaiyappa*, p. 55.

[23] Ibid., p. 57.

[24] Chariar, *Select Papers*, *Speeches*, gives a list of sacred places which immediately benefited from the bequest, p. xxvi.

[25] See G.S. White. 'The Norton Family', pp. 89–95.

condescension to Indians, who were, doubtless, well attuned to fissures in English society. They understood his political utility in furthering their own causes, even as they assisted him in securing some status in society.

The first Board of Trustees was comprised of V. Raghavachari (President), Srinivasa Pillai, Arumugam Mudali, Raghava Chetty, Ramanjulu Naidu, Ekambara Mudaliar, Chokkappa Chetty and W. Adinarayana Ayya. The patrons of the school were Indo-British and colonial law commanded the pupils to be 'Hindu' boys. The Trustees held their first meeting in 1841. They chose the house, formerly occupied by the Hindu Literary Society, for their office. The Trustees were invested with powers and funds to establish more schools, in appointed spots, throughout the Presidency. Ostensibly, they had a free hand, but Parliament, through the Court in London, whilst warmly approving measures to permit the Trustees to set up schools, warned that 'the government should exercise a real control and supervision of them'.[26] State control, unspoken in Madras, was unmasked in London.

New Friends

The Company's involvement with the Vaishnava sect of the Sri Parthasarathy Temple began in 1676, when the temple was under the charge of the Company's chief merchant. Social overlap and deep mutual obligation tied the Company into a cohesive plural cultural network of many segments. It explains why the Company had its own temple, 'The Company Temple', in Black Town. The school project reveals Indo-Britons cultivating new sources of loyalty among each other. The fact that the *Aiyangar*-Vaishnavite sect was 'by far the most industrious, thrifty and intelligent: [and were] at present the most rising and prosperous' may have proved useful to the Company.[27] The Pachaiyappa School Trustees represented a mainly non-Brahmin sub-Vaishnavite faction of articulate city magnates and intellectuals. In supporting them, the Company was expressing its desire to reduce its historical dependence on the Saiva Brahmins. After all, those heaven-born Desastha Brahmins, convinced of their cosmic superiority and secure in their private access to European knowledge, were hardly seeking state-sponsored egalitarian education. It may have even posed some slight future threat to their delicate traditional arrangements with the state.

The Company, Indian merchant houses and the *nattar*, had jointly administered Madras in the seventeenth and eighteenth centuries. It was in continuation of these associations that

[26] Parliamentary Papers, East India—Lords Second Report (25) 1852–53, p. 91.

[27] T. Venkasami Row, *Manual of the District of Tanjore in the Madras Presidency* (Madras, 1883), p. 170.

their nineteenth-century descendants believed that the state should play a significant role in effecting social change in India. They disagreed as to what form it should take. The Madras Native Association, established in 1852, was sharply critical of Company rule, but a lack of unanimity regarding goals led to an early split. The Srinivasapillai faction, for instance, envisaged far closer ties with the colonial state than a merchant prince like Lakshmanarasu Chetty would espouse. The more conservative elements called for an entire identification of European and native interests to bring about the regeneration of India. A more radical strain pushed for greater independence.[28] The politics of the shadowy city magnates and merchant princes who backed the Pachaiyappa School oscillated in both directions. They were ambivalent and inconsistent in their support of the British and at times they were in part the state.

If the Trustees did not uniformly represent 'Indians' and had no affinity with the Saivite leaning of their benefactor,[29] then the egotistical Norton barely represented the uniform opinion of the Company at large, or for that matter of parliament. Indo-British opinion was fractured along lines of power, religion and education policy, as well as personal rivalry. Norton was so conscious of his unpopularity that in his speech, at the ceremony for the laying of the foundation stone of the Pachaiyappa Hall, on 2 October 1846, he bemoaned the 'obloquy of a large and influential portion of my fellow countrymen of this place', which he endured on account of the efforts he had made in service of the Indian community.[30] In his witness statement to parliament Norton observed that 'those [natives] who are highly educated are remarkable for their loyal feelings towards the British government.' But there also existed a strong spirit of disloyalty, particularly amongst those natives who were not his influential friends. Some of his native friends, who were governors of the school and the university, even opposed power-sharing, because they felt the natives were not 'sufficiently educated to share government'.[31] A commingling of paternalism and dominance was evident on the part of the state.

Where Intellectuals Gather

The Pachaiyappa School grew from an already established scene of Indo-European loyalty and cultural exchange at the centre of which was the College of Fort St. George, modelled partly on Fort William College, in Calcutta, and on Haileybury College: it was the premier Indo-European scholastic centre in the city. Established in 1812, its main function was the

[28] R. Suntheralingam, *Politics and Nationalist Awakening*, p. 51.

[29] Bequests also serviced Vaishnava shrines like those at Srirangam and Triplicane.

[30] Chariar, *Select Papers*, *Speeches*, p. 22.

[31] PP East India, 1852–53, p. 105.

training of English civil servants. It attracted Brahmin and other scholars and fostered a 'distinctive Madras School of Orientalism, seeking to challenge the Orientalist establishment of Calcutta and the Asiatic Society'.[32]

At the behest of senior Board member, F.W. Ellis, Muttasami Pillai, Manager of the College of Fort St. George wrote an article on the life of the Italian Jesuit Father Joseph Beschi. Pillai had conducted his research in 1822, under the direction of Richard Clarke—skilled in both dialects of Tamil and a distinguished ornament to the Board—and Benjamin Guy Babington who possessed a profound knowledge of Tamil and Sanskrit. Guy Babington had many of Beschi's works sent to England. Beschi, who knew Tamil, Telugu, Sanskrit, Hindustani and Persian, had lived in the luxurious style of a Hindu guru. Early eighteenth-century luminaries of the prestigious Madura Academy had conferred the title of *Viramuniver*, learned sage, upon Father Beschi, impressed by the excellence of his work *Tembavani*.[33] Pillai believed that by encouraging the study of native languages, the Madras College was coveting the distinguished mantle of the Madurai College.[34] The Madras School Book Society, a voluntary organisation promoted by Governor Munro, and the Hindu Literary Society were other sites where fruitful Indo-European intellectual exchanges occurred. The constellations of South Indian intellectuals, deprived employment under impoverished native chiefs, sought work with new patrons like the Company, city magnates and the Madras College. New patrons opened up an exciting world of universal knowledge and the Pachaiyappa School project was attractive precisely because it upheld that promise.

Notwithstanding its libertarian tenor the school's education policy masked discriminatory gender and religious agendas. It consolidated a pioneering Indo-European image by appointing a European headmaster, P.J. McNee. A building in Black Town was rented to accommodate 300 boys and the first teachers were V. Venkatesa Sastry, T. Audenarayana Moodaliar, C. Arumooga Moodaliar, N. Casavaloo, P. Chinaiah, C. Sabapaty and C. Luchmanah Charloo. The school was popular from the beginning. In 1849 there were so many pupils—between 400 and 500—that it was decided to collect fees from those who could pay. A sum of one lakh of rupees was available for the support of the charities and the surplus revenue was to be used

[32] He traces a conversation on linguistics where Indians and Britons brought their own preoccupation to the discussion. See T.R. Trautmann, 'Hullabaloo about Telugu'.

[33] K. Rajayyan, *Administration and Society in the Carnatic 1701–1801* (Tirupati, 1969), p. 150.

[34] A. Muttasami Pillai, 'A Brief Sketch of the Life and Writings of Father C.J. Beschi, or Viramuni', *Madras Journal of Literature and Science,* XI, January–June (1840), pp. 250–301. The original was in Tamil. Father Beschi, who arrived in Goa in 1700, lived in Arcot and Trichinopoly. His patron was the Nawab Chanda Saib who showered him with gifts and appointed him to the office of *diwan*.

to defray the salaries and expenses of the professors and the eight schools to be maintained outside Madras.[35]

In April 1841 the formal inauguration of the so-called High School of the Madras University, better known as the 'Madras High School', was celebrated. It was to have important consequences not only for the metropolis but for South India as a whole. It heralded the 'birth of an élite school' whose role was to train a new administrative élite in the new learning.[36] At its inception, Madras High School charged a fee of Rs. 4 per month, which most students could not afford.[37] Consequently, during the 1840s, there was never at any time more than 182 boys on the roll. The Pachaiyappa School functioned as a feeder to the Madras High School. Although the two schools were strongly connected, with overlapping governing personnel, there were significant differences. The High School was the explicit flagship school of the Company state.

The opening ceremony of the High School was marked with pomp and grandeur; attended by the Nawab of Arcot and principal members of Presidency society, both European and native. No such aristocratic cosmopolitan ceremony was accorded to the more sectarian establishment. The first president of the University Board, established by the Government in 1840, was George Norton himself. Four of the seven Indian governors of the university were Trustees of the Pachaiyappa institutions as well. The relationship between the state and the Pachaiyappa School was close. At the foundation laying ceremony Norton deftly overlooked the intimacy:

> No such example or precedent as this has ever occurred before in India—of a native body assembling amidst the shouts of thousands upon thousands of their fellow countrymen, to lay the foundation of a magnificent structure, out of funds of their own, the fruits of native benevolence, dedicated to the sole purpose of intellectual cultivation, justly so called. The means and the management are all your own; they have been supplied neither by Europeans, nor by Government; nor are they dependent upon them. We may look in vain throughout the vast Indian empire for an Institution of such a character—(though I have no doubt others are destined to arise) and it may well be source of pride to the people of this city, not only that such a spirit of charity as we now celebrate should have appeared amongst you, but there are not wanting, among those at the head of native society, and in their highest esteem, such as will devote their labour to the truest service of their countrymen by that effectual spread of education to which so large a portion of Pachaiyappa's Charities is devoted.[38]

[35] N.S. Ramaswami, *Pachiayappa*, p. 65.

[36] R. Suntheralingam, *Politics and Nationalist Awakening*, p. 59.

[37] By way of comparison regular agricultural labourers earned a maximum of Rs. 16–20 per annum. The great majority was much worse off. Artisans in Madras were more prosperous with an average rate of pay of 3 annas 9 pies per day. See J.D. Bourdillon, 'Description of the Madras Ryot', in Srinivasa S. Raghavaiyangar (ed.), *Memorandum on the Progress of the Madras Presidency During the Last Forty Years of British Administration* (Madras, 1892), p. 89.

[38] 'Speech by George Norton on the occasion of Laying the Foundation Stone of Pachaiyappa's Hall, on 2nd October 1846' in Chariar, *Select Papers, Speeches*, pp. 21–26.

Native leaders associated with the Pachaiyappa School were slightly different from the staunch conservatives placated in the case of the High School and University Board, who did not want their children to mix with inferior classes. The University Board, 'overzealous in respecting the susceptibilities of the high caste Hindus' had resisted attempts to reduce fees for almost a decade and denied admission to students from the 'polluting castes'.[39] By 1851, however, the Board was no longer prepared to compromise on avowed egalitarian principles. It allowed low-caste students to enter the portals of the High School. Despite the change the student body continued to be exclusive, drawn chiefly from Brahmin and high-born non-Brahmin families, with a small sprinkling of Christians, Eurasians and Muslims.

Conservatives and Liberals—
The Building Commission, 1846

The two schools adroitly implemented current official educational theory, delineated in the 1839 Minute of Lord Elphinstone. The Filtration Theory proposed the entailment of limited state resources to train an élite from the upper echelons of Indian society, in the literary culture of the west, through the medium of the English language. The resultant élite group was entrusted with the dual tasks of 'diffusing its enlightenment to the rest of the community and of shouldering the responsibilities of high office in the government'.[40] Only a superior minority was to be honoured with degrees. Indians, monitored by men like Norton, met the cost of elementary education. Higher education was to stay in the hands of the ruler. The special status of the High School was confirmed when Eyre Burton Powell was appointed headmaster. Powell, a recent BA graduate, with the highest grade of honour from Cambridge, was indefatigable in his dedication to the welfare of his students. His connection with the Pachaiyappa Institution was long and close. He took the most important share in organising its school in 1842.

The President of the Trustees, Raghvachariar, 'the very first in social station amongst you, and holding the highest native Magisterial offices'[41] was by now dead. He was succeeded by C. Srinivasapillai. The state had already honoured the latter in 1831 with the prestigious appointment as *dharmakarta,* chief executive, of the ancient and powerful Sri Parthsarathy Temple. In July 1832 he resigned the post on a point of honour, alleging excessive interference from the Collectorate. Srinivasapillai was a man of high status and honour and he maintained that

[39] R. Suntheralingam, *Politics and Nationalist Awakening*, p. 61.

[40] Ibid., p. 60.

[41] 'Speech by George Norton on the occasion' in Chariar, *Select Papers, Speeches.*

the Collector treated him like a 'mere Ameen in his service'. [42] He was not inclined to dispute the authority of the Collector of Madras for the sake of his honour.

Lord Elphinstone, the Governor, Sir Walter Elliot (his secretary and cousin) and Norton, alongside Powell and Peter Pope, secretary of the University Board, were part of the intellectual set associated with setting up the University Board. Elliot, in whose honour the fabulous Amaravati sculptures were known as the Elliot Marbles, was a leading light in what I have tentatively identified as a Madras school of art orientalism. Elliot, also a man with convictions, had resigned his place on the University Board during the pro-missionary Tweedale regime of the 1840s, as a protest against its dilatory tactics in setting up the university.[43] With the grand confidence of his station, in 1844 he wrote to Elphinstone that Srinivasapillai 'is a good for nothing fellow and an ass to boot'[44] and complained that the native governors were not exerting themselves by enrolling boys in the High School, consequently dwindling into a non-entity. Norton's view was rather different. With customary flamboyance he publicly praised Srinivasapillai's endeavours in the

> cause of native education and the social advancement of his countrymen, not only the hours of his leisure, but almost all the hours of his life; and he [was] not without his best reward, the abounding esteem and gratitude of all who know or hear of him. Happy as a native, in his lot, he lives amongst you, and will throughout his useful life, enjoy your constant affection.[45]

Srinivasapillai belonged to the older urban oligarchy that supported moderate reforms in Indian society, extending only so far as widow remarriage, education for women and the uplifting of depressed castes. Their attitude to modern ideas was commensurate with traditional cultural values. They explored European architecture with a confident and easy intellectual curiosity. Although the school was intended to be non-fee paying, filtration theories and Indian social values colluded to perpetuate discrimination even among poorer classes. Guarded views on social 'progress' and the patrons' long-proven attachment to the British Government and its enlightened institutions, expressed a happy convergence of ideas amongst some Indo-Britons.

[42] Quoted in Arjun Appadurai, *Worship and Conflict Under Colonial Rule* (Cambridge, 1981), p. 151.

[43] For an account of Elliot's involvement with the sculptures see 'The Government Museum in Madras' in B.S Baliga (ed.), *Studies in Madras Administration* (Madras, 1960), p. 184. Also see MSS Eur J684–705, Walter Elliot Collection. Elliot had close links with Brahmin intellectuals and had a circle of Indian collectors. His was a wide-ranging collection, like Mackenzie's, with whom he was in touch. He was in Madras from 1821 to 1860 as civil servant and later as council member. For more useful bio-data, see OIOC Manuscript hand-list, British Library.

[44] Quoted in Robert E. Frykenberg, 'Modern Education', p. 57.

[45] 'Speech by George Norton', in Chariar, *Select Papers, Speeches*, p. 21.

The famous Young Bengal group, a product of Adam Hare and Hindu College, Calcutta, disavowed traditional values in favour of a set of rationalist, atheist educational experiments. Its culture of conflict had no southern counterpart.[46] This does not mean that there were no extreme conservative factions who had nothing whatsoever to do with colonial rule and chose to turn their backs on the British.[47]

In 1846 the school had a new headmaster, R. Ewing, and enrolled over 600 students. This number far exceeded the limit anticipated. As a consequence, on 7 June 1846, the Trustees requested the President to 'prepare an estimate for the construction of a suitable structure for Pachaiyappa's School, and a spacious hall attached thereto'. The Trustees 'could have easily contented themselves with a mere school building. It is to their credit that they decided to build an architectural building.'[48]

The Site

In November 1844 the Trustees made an application to the government to purchase a plot of vacant land near the hospital, for the purposes of erecting a schoolroom and hall. Lieutenant Colonel Sim, the Chief Engineer, rejected the application on the grounds that the plot was very central and could add to the encroachment already noted on the Fort Esplanade.[49] The attempt to relocate the school in a more salubrious area, out of Black Town, failed and the original school building, on Popham's Broadway, was razed to accommodate the new. The site was located at the south end of Peddanaickpet, traditionally reserved for the 'powerful Tamil Vellalar caste and its Paraiyar dependents', and the Telugu commercial and martial castes who claimed social precedence over the Left Hand caste group. Extreme missionary groups regarded Black Town as the 'citadel of Satan, the centre of caste, pride and Brahminism'. The advantage of the

[46] There is little to suggest that they suffered the conflict of ideas displayed by the contemporary Young Bengal ferment centred on Hindu College. For some insight into the Calcutta Hindu College, whose junior division became the equivalent of the Madras High School and the senior division became Presidency College, see David Kopf, *The Brahmo Samaj* (Princeton, 1979). The Sadur Veda Siddhanta Sabha was an anti-Christian organisation, allegedly funded by wealthy Hindus: it was blamed for instigating the Tinnevelly riots of 1845, see R. Suntheralingam, *Politics and Nationalist Awakening*, p. 42.

[47] The famous singer and poet Thyagaraja refused the blandishments of the reformist court of the Rajah Serfoji. See Christopher Bayly, *Indian Soceity*, p. 115. In a discussion of Islamic leaders' response to the British, Francis Robinson notes that one group of ulama vigorously entered politics under colonial rule and that the Deoband turned inwards and ignored the state as far as was humanly possible. Francis Robinson (ed.), 'Problems in the History of the Farangi Mahall; Family of Learned and Holymen', *Oxford University Papers on India*, (New Delhi, 1987), pp. 1–25.

[48] N.S. Ramaswami, *Pachiyappa*, p. 75.

[49] 7 February 1845, P/248/18, p. 366, MPPC.

site was its convenience for students and its relationship to the fort. If the proposed building was suitably tall it would constitute a landmark when viewed from the fort.

On the east of the site was Anderson's Church and beyond it the Sailor's Home which became Anderson's School in 1846, the same year that building work on the Pachaiyappa School commenced. Anderson's School was the most prestigious modern private English school in Madras and it is appropriate that the two pioneering educational institutions were in Black Town. The erection of a purpose-built building, in the modern architectural style, would give the Indian school a status which no other school in the Presidency possessed.[50] The Pachaiyappa building proclaimed several ambivalent messages. On one level it upstaged and challenged the state which had yet to stake its claim in building for modern education. On the other, it would not be far wrong to regard it as a state building.

Due to the scarcity of land and high rents in colonial cities it was not unusual to find three-storey buildings, in the Italian classical style, in the fort and in Black Town. As I noted in Chapter 1, by the 1780s, the Madras sea-front, north of the fort, was lined with a series of white buildings with arched and rusticated basements and colonnaded upper floors, surmounted by a flat terrace roof with the standard Italian balustrade. Many domestic buildings in Black town and Mylapore too had classical façades, even though they were inward-looking and planned in the traditional manner around a courtyard. Indo-British merchant houses had long controlled city life and the classical style of Black Town reflected a 150-year shared genealogy.

The Designer—Captain Ludlow

Following the practice of the day it was only natural to have a military officer of the Madras Engineers design a building intended for Europeans, especially an official building. At first glance the building in question fits neither category. The appointment of a military-engineer to design the school confirms the suspicion that this was a joint venture between Indians and the state. The designs were made by a junior military-engineer, Captain Ludlow 'who although fully engaged in important public duties, has given his able and scientific attention (and that not a little) even to the details of the building'.[51] It is likely that since Captain Ludlow and his patrons copied the designs from a book, an Indian architect could have done much the same. Captain Ludlow could have had no experience in school designs any more than his Indian

[50] S. Muthiah, *Madras Discovered* (New Delhi, 1992), p. 233. The new buildings for Anderson's School began in 1876 when it was christened Madras Christian College.

[51] 'Speech by George Norton on the Occasion of Laying the Foundation' in Chariar, *Select Papers*, *Speeches*, p. 26.

counterparts. The authority modern science bestowed on the military-engineer in colonial society no doubt swayed the choice of designer. The Trustees were, after all, excited and aware of the aesthetic scope, experimental nature and technical innovation of the design.

'Taken from the Temple of Theseus'

The brief called for a school and a hall. The design as built provided for a three-storey school in two blocks. Our Reporter from the *Athenaeum* wrote that the edifice:

> if constructed after the plan and estimates, will be a lofty structure resembling in general appearance the Banqueting Room. It is to have a plain habitable basement fourteen feet high embracing a commodious hall subdivided into rooms to serve as repository for the records and to answer, as it is believed, the purpose of the lower classes.[52]

Figure 42: View of school hall from street

From conception it was intended that the building be powerful, lofty and resemble the Banqueting Hall—the most distinguished new, secular building erected by the state in Madras in 1801. The design was born of a convergence of Indo-British social and spatial ideologies—whereby the lower classes and the vernacular were appropriately consigned to the dark basement. The basement (ground floor) consisted of a central corridor with rooms on either side and a verandah on the east. The hall and teaching blocks together alluded to the older multi-purpose teaching patterns of indigenous systems. The front block was two storeys tall, with the hall on the upper level, intended for the superior classes and public meetings. 'A neat three storied building containing three sides of a quadrangle, in the rear of the principal edifice, [was]

[52] *Athenaeum*, 6 October 1846.

quite like it in India. Its famous predecessor, Hindu College in Calcutta, received its sprawling single-storey classical buildings when under state control in 1847. The 'schools' for orphans of military personnel in Madras had, as far as I can tell, no purpose-built edifices at the time.

Figure 48: Brahmin village dwelling, Dakshin Chitra, Chennai

Figure 49: Indian-style second courtyard, second floor

A Greek temple mounted on a podium intended as an educational building was not without precedent in Europe: the Royal High School, Edinburgh, designed by Thomas Hamilton in 1825, had a man-made acropolis exuding Egyptian monumentality.[54] It was a supreme essay in Doric architecture (see Fig. 51). Alexander Thomson, the great master of the Greek Revival, praised it as 'one of the two finest buildings in the kingdom'. William Wilkins' designs for London University, built in 1827, repeated the same tremendously grand theme, with the main block possessing a fine portico raised on a high podium with steps. The latter was a prestigious flagship institution marking the arrival of secular modern higher education in England. For those of the dissent persuasion, the scourge of the 'Greek revival' had well and truly begun.

The first truly Greek neo-classical buildings in England are reputedly those of Downing College, Cambridge, 1806–11. In 1806, at Haileybury College, Hertford, the Company opened its newly built Greek portals to the future bureaucrats of India. By building Haileybury College, in the style of Downing College, the Company was declaring a shift in how it wanted to be perceived in Britain. Through architecture it sought a new national and intellectual image and a place at the forefront of the stylistic revolution. The architect who designed Haileybury and Downing College was William Wilkins. His designs have been variously labelled as priggish, doctrinaire and 'intensely intellectual'; based as they were on a scholarly study of the classical

Figure 50: Tamil letters in a Greek frieze

[54] Gavin Stamp, *Alexander Greek Thomson* (London, 1999), p. 153.

antiquities of Athens.[55] In 1806 very few people had any direct experience of Greek architecture or knew of its existence. Wilkins, a 'Cambridge man', had many contacts with the Cambridge Graecophiles and his book, *Antiquities of Magna Graecia* was published in 1807. Company links with the Cambridge circle were cemented through Charles Grant, a member of the Court of Directors, an intellectual and avowed evangelist. He was influential in shifting the teaching of Company civil servants onto the shoulders of the Cambridge clergy, away from Calcutta, Haileybury and the orientalists.[56] Another factor common to the school design and the Cambridge élite was Powell.

The genesis of the Pachaiyappa Hall as an architectural space was a response to the expanding spatial needs of the Indo-British élite. The hall served them as a public meeting place. However, the massing of the building, with the hall seated on a lofty podium and the classrooms well concealed behind, was unambiguous in its reference to a building form firmly anchored to imperial power. The built form secured an immediate aura of power and internationalism for the patrons and the school, difficult to achieve in other ways.

For Indians, excluded from access to British monuments, the skill of the message lay in the way the columned portico (each column was four feet in diameter) was set against the bare walls of the hall and the austere base. The scale of the composition yielded a sense of power, a traditional preserve of high-walled temples and mosques. The large interior space of the hall is sparingly ornamented in Indo-European style. The pilasters around the interior have ornate capitals and an ornamented frieze and cornice in Indian-style stucco (see Figs. 56–58). Today the walls are painted blue and the decorated areas pink. The north, west and east sides have three timber doors of the Venetian type and rectangular windows above. The verandahs of the first block are protected from the elements by Venetian-type windows in the popular Indo-British way. The second block has a tile roof with low eaves over open verandahs secured with timber balcony rails (see Fig. 49). The frieze of the Tuscan

Figure 51: The Royal High School, Edinburgh, 1825

[55] Maria Sicca offers a view that Greek architecture was thought to 'embody with magnificent clarity the intellectual and moral values upheld by the academic community' at Cambridge. Cinzia Maria Sicca, *Committed to Classicism: The Building of Downing College Cambridge* (Cambridge, 1987), p. 57.

[56] David Kopf, *British Orientalism and the Bengal Renaissance: The Dynamics of Indian Modernization 1773–1835* (California, 1969), p. 135.

entablature has the name Pachaiyappan (in Tamil) set in granite (see Fig. 50). These letters, with the fluting and volutes on the columns and the circular windows (a Palladian note) in the pediment (see Figs. 42 and 47), were the only concessions to ornament in the otherwise spare, angular outlines. The entire building would have been covered in dazzling white chunam stark and stunning in the sun set against a blue sky with nothing challenging its undisputed command of space.[57]

A Guide to the City of Madras announced that 'the European population was indebted to the Trustees for giving the hall for scientific and social purposes.'[58] The hall gave certain Indo-Britons a large and novel environment for secular co-operative activities. Until this time the unofficial English held public functions in the Madras College hall, the Athenaeum and the Theatre. There is no evidence to confirm or deny that Indians were admitted to these venues. It is possible to guess that high-class Indians were accepted everywhere in the 1840s.

Figure 52: Eastern terrace, Pachaiyappa Hall

The wonderful eastern terrace of the hall (see Fig. 52) afforded a vantage point from which to gaze at friends or powerful rulers within the fort. Evening functions in the hall, with open doors bringing in sea breezes and sea views, must have been pleasant affairs.[59] An extract from the *Athenaeum* yields a flavour of how the hall was used in 1870: Professor and Madam Ruchwaldy (the celebrated Hungarian artistes) took much pleasure in informing the nobility, the officers and the gentry of a Charity Night for the Benefit of the Poor of Madras. It took the form of a grand magical musical entertainment. The hall watched the fort across the military esplanade. It was the first grand public Indo-British building to make a physical statement within the newly fashionable 'Greek revival' aesthetic mode of the ruler. The egalitarian mandate to serve poor boys was rather underplayed. It is unlikely that the subtleties of the Greek revival style struck a chord with the largely uneducated European or Indian population.

[57] Today the abacus of the columns, the ceiling of the portico and the doors and windows outside are painted blue. There is no way of knowing whether this differs from the original.

[58] *A Guide to the City of Madras and its Suburbs*, 2nd edn. (Madras, 1881), p. 51.

[59] *Athenaeum and Daily News*, 6 January 1870.

The Trustees, who were in the habit of submitting regular building reports to Norton, proudly stated in their full Report of 12 August 1850, that the design was of the Greek Ionic order and 'taken from the temple of Theseus, with the difference that it is erected on an elevated basement represented by the lower storey or 1st floor'.[60] The easy familiarity with Greek masterpieces and architectural terminology implies that the men who prepared the report were conversant with ideas pertaining to European design and aesthetics.

However, a cursory glance will confirm that there were, in fact, several other significant differences from the original. The Temple of Theseus was peripteral, had a ponderous Doric order and was described by Sir William Gell as 'perhaps the most beautiful and best preserved monument in antiquity', as cited by James Stuart and Nicholas Revett in their famous 1761 account of Athens (see Fig. 53). Stuart and Revett described the temple as 'the least dilapidated among the remaining structures of ancient Greece, [it] has in an especial manner excited the admiration of the most accomplished travellers'.[61] The Pachaiyappa Hall has only six free-

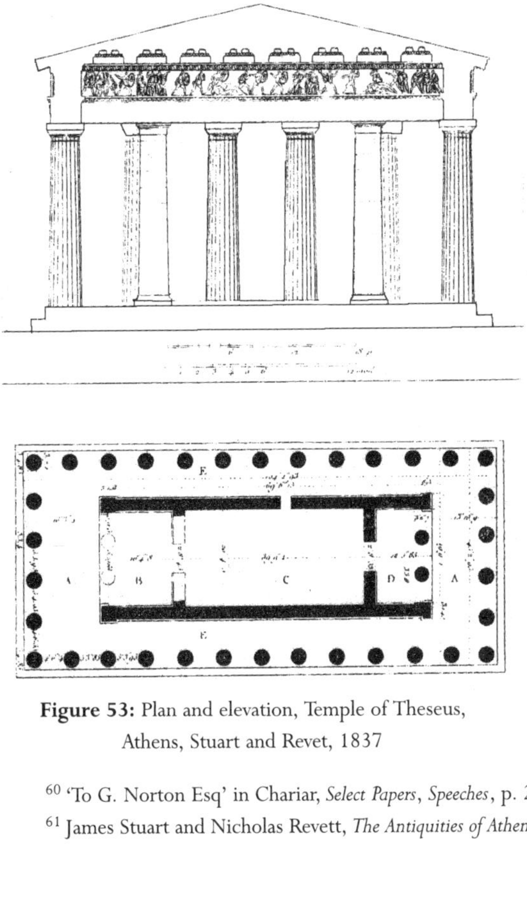

Figure 53: Plan and elevation, Temple of Theseus, Athens, Stuart and Revet, 1837

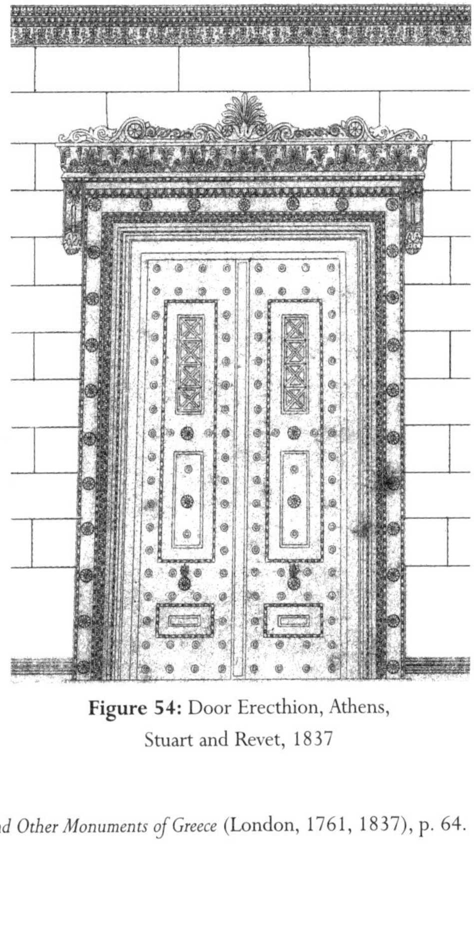

Figure 54: Door Erecthion, Athens, Stuart and Revet, 1837

[60] 'To G. Norton Esq' in Chariar, *Select Papers*, *Speeches*, p. 27.

[61] James Stuart and Nicholas Revett, *The Antiquities of Athens and Other Monuments of Greece* (London, 1761, 1837), p. 64.

Figure 55: Main entrance door, Pachaiyappa Hall

standing columns, of the Ionic order, comprising the southern portico (with an almost Tuscan entablature similar to that of Downing College) as compared to the 34 surrounding the Theseion. Absence of the pteromata, extra columns, triglyphs and sculptures of the Doric entablature deprived it of claims to sublime beauty and the 'inconceivable effect of majesty and grandeur' of the Theseion. In size, too, the latter was significantly longer, being 104 by 45 feet, as compared to the hall's overall 71 by 45 feet. The Trustees claim to classical authenticity was largely rhetorical. The capitals of the columns, the entablature and pediment were to be 'tastefully wrought in ornamental work' which, when finished, 'will present an imposing appearance'.[62] Sadly, it is not known why, but this was not to be.

Commitment to the Greek idiom was in jeopardy of some compromise since controversy clearly arose with regard to the introduction of Indian motifs. The main body of the superstructure was to be entered by three doors (see Fig. 55):

the centre one to be large and conspicuous for carved work in imitation, as it is said, of the doorways leading into some of the more tastefully decorated of the heathen temples. The principal hall, designed for the purpose of the superior classes and all public meetings, is a spacious entire whole about seventy eight feet in length and fifty three

[62] *Athenaeum*, 6 October 1846.

feet in width, having six lofty windows on each side and three at the back, which correspond with the front, has half-columns running up the whole height and supporting the entablature.[63]

The faction that supported a carved central door, in imitation of heathen temples, lost out because only one door was ever made. Carved from rosewood, this enormous door closely resembled the doors of the Erecthion, far away in Athens (see Fig. 54).[64] The controversy echoed the wider inconsistencies of crossing cultures and the dual loyalties of the patronage group as a whole. For the Pachaiyappa Hall is not a replica of the Theseion, or even the Banqueting Hall. Just as the school behind is hardly Greek.

The Greek style was the height of avant-garde architecture in the intellectual circles of England and Scotland. And it would be fair to suggest that for a very small, élite group of Indians, it possibly meant the same. The message was nonetheless explicit—this building represented the enlightened, modern Indian contribution to the Indo-British partnership. As the Tamil letters in granite, set into the front entablature proudly announced, this was an Indo-Greek building. A reading of the classical style in this context engages multiple meanings that place it beyond the ambit of simple power dichotomies of imposition and imitation. This is not to deny that in colonial India the classical style did also assume overtones of race and imperial power.

A Multi-cultural Event

George Norton laid the foundation stone for the building on 2 October 1846. The ceremony began when a large body of people assembled at the house of Kovur Ekambara Mudaliar, a prominent religious benefactor. The assembly included Powell, Srinivasapillai and other gentlemen both native and English, pupils of the school and several thousand men and women, with a preponderance of Brahmins. Several Tamil, Telugu and Sanskrit poets recited effusions in honour of Queen Victoria, Lord Hardinge, the Governor-General, and Lord Elphinstone, the Governor. They also recited songs praying that the Charity might endure long and a student read a long essay on the promotion of education. The procession which set out for the venue was gay and colourful, accompanied by musicians. Those in front carried flags imprinted with Pachaiyappa's name.[65]

[63] Ibid. The proceedings of the Trustees relating to the period of building were missing from the Pachaiyappa Trust record room in Madras.

[64] James Stuart and Nicholas Revett, *The Antiquities of Athens*.

[65] *Athenaeum*, 6 October 1846. Many distinguished families had their own flags. See V. Raghavan, 'The Sarva Deva Vilasaya', p. 109.

Figure 56: Detail of capital

Figure 57: Hall, interior

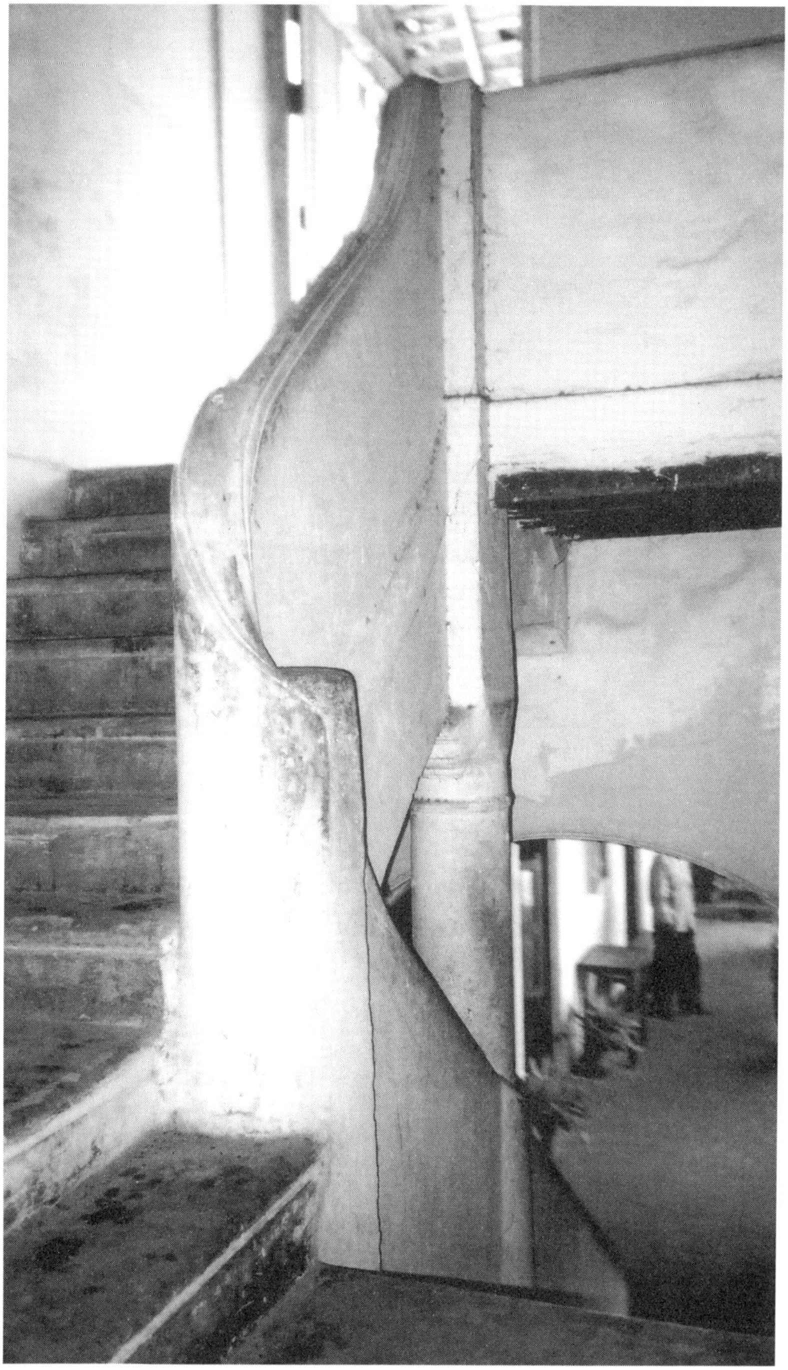

Figure 58: Staircase, Indian-style courtyard building

At the site, the band 'rather inappropriately, as it would seem, [struck up] the popular air known as the "British Grenadiers"'.[66] The scholars were paraded about the excavations which were 'beswamied [sic] by conspicuous stripes of chalk or chunam'. A few older students held poles at regular distances, surmounted by crimson banners fringed with orange. Norton made a speech for three-quarters of an hour and Srinivasapillai replied. 'Due to the general hum and buzz of the congregated mass' only few people, amongst the thousands, heard what was said and the ceremony ended with the band playing 'Roly O'More'. 'The Brahmins lived not to be disappointed for pieces of money were distributed among them to attach sanctity to the memorable event.'[67] Notwithstanding disaffection for Brahmins, Our Reporter succeeded in capturing the cosmopolitan atmosphere of the event. Hindu ritual, western military music, a heathen procession and multi-lingual poetry blended to celebrate the institutional progress of imported knowledge.

A Truss Roof

The Trustees were very proud of the roof of the hall. They described it as 'a curiosity of its kind and novel to this part of India'.[68] The main 'roof was to be made as usual of iron and wood and covered with plates of zinc instead of the ordinary slate'. The estimated cost of the building was around Rs. 30,000. The zinc sheets were ordered from England and would cost an additional Rs. 10,000.[69] The roof structure was made up of 14 wrought-iron trusses placed at six-foot intervals. They were connected by wind ties, fastened by bolts and nuts, and ran diagonally. Angular laths fastened to the principals by rivets completed the whole framework. The rest was constructed entirely of wrought-iron rafters, tie beams, king and queen bars, struts, bolts and nuts. The roof was 71 feet long and 50 feet wide. It covered the verandah in front, as well as the hall and extended 2½ feet on each side, over the walls. The ends of the rafters were attached to the walls by strong iron bolts, 12½ inches long and 1 inch in diameter, inserted into large granite blocks and secured by nuts. An extra covering of galvanised, corrugated or furrowed iron was fitted in between the iron rafters for the purpose of receiving zinc sheets.

The roof had three coverings made up of zinc, felt and slate successively. The report noted that corrugated sheets had a great advantage over 'a plain flat surface the strength of

[66] Ibid.

[67] This no doubt related to the traditional *bhumi puja* ritual to consecrate the earth, prior to building, although Our Reporter was more concerned with the venality of the Brahmins.

[68] This information is gathered chiefly from the 'Report made by the trustees to G. Norton on 12 August 1850', in Chariar, *Select Papers, Speeches*, pp. 27–30.

[69] *Athenaeum*, 6 October 1846.

which merely consists of the tenacity of the metal', whereas the ridged surface of the sheets gave an increased strength.

> The appearance of the external surface is extremely neat, elegant and in admirable keeping with the whole structure. In the description of the roof the immense span it covers is a distinguished feature, no building of like dimensions in Madras without intervening pillars being similarly supported.[70]

As the John Malcolm episode in Mysore demonstrated, high officials coveted vast uninterrupted space for prestigious southern buildings. Evidently the Trustees were conversant with the priorities of imperial engineering ideology. At the same time, the treatment of architectural space at Madurai, Thanjavur and Bijapur suggests that the command of uninterrupted space signified divinity and exalted status within certain indigenous ideologies. The Banqueting Hall, for example, had not resorted to daring technology and hence lacked large spans. The report thus made several important, technically innovative and ideological points. The use of wrought-iron roof trusses was new. The bolting or riveting of truss components was new and the triple roof covering was also new. Its structural component—corrugated zinc sheet—came entirely from England, at a third of the cost of the building.

From around 1837 manufacturers like Richard Walker were shipping a whole range of building products to the colonies that included entire cast and wrought-iron buildings clad with corrugated iron sheets. For the first time there was now available 'a large-scale, relatively lightweight, building element suitable for roofing and wall-cladding', notable for its economy, durability, portability, impermeability and resistance to termites.[71] The development of corrugated iron resulted in a quick and easy system far superior than that of wood since a roof could now be made entirely of corrugated iron without trusses or further covering.

In our example, however, the zinc sheets were used for structural purposes only. They were covered by felt and slates, the slates being attached to the laths by nails. Whatever the reason for the use of iron trusses, it may have been cheaper to use timber rafters instead of corrugated iron sheets, but the sources do not indicate that cost overrode the ideological power of technical novelty. This aside, in 1840s England or India, the roof structure described was state-of-the-art structural design. Its construction too required specialist knowledge and skill. In the view of some writers, iron roof trusses were first developed in France and used elsewhere

[70] 'To G. Norton Esq', p. 28.

[71] Changing economic and social relations in Europe and America had led to the emergence of new building types and materials. Wrought-iron roof trusses were used as early as 1776 in Paris. In America an iron chain suspension bridge was built in Newport in 1810. Export to the colonies featured in the development of new materials and is discussed by Gilbert Herbert, *Pioneers of Prefabrication* (Baltimore, 1978), p. 32 and chapters 3 and 4.

after Camille Polonceau patented a truss form in 1837. In Britain the iron-truss form was adopted for train-shed roofs at the railroad terminals of Euston Square, in London, and Curzon Street, in Birmingham. They were completed by 1839 and had spans of 40 and 57 feet respectively.[72]

The accepted view with regard to iron construction in India is that it began with railway construction in 1850, when iron was used extensively in bridge building and plate laying. Until the 1860s skilled workers were usually brought out from England. Ian Kerr who wrote the only detailed account of the subject mentions that skilled British workmen undertook the initial training of bridge specialists and riveting was identified as a 'new skill', although Indian technology was adapted on the Jubbulpore bridges for heating the rivets, in preference to English forges.[73] Sources are uninformative as to where iron components used in the railways were manufactured.

Figure 59: Cast-iron columns with stamp of manufacturer's name, C. Copaul Nayagar, rear extension, first floor

The methods used to produce the iron roof members and their provenance is not known. But, had they been imported, it seems likely that Our Reporter may have mentioned it, since he did so with pride in regard to the roof sheets. The techniques of iron-truss design and assembly in Madras are also unknown. The columns supporting the verandah stairs of the rear extension at the Pachaiyappa School are cast-iron and bear the stamp C.COPAUL. NAYAGAR & SON MADRAS. The date of construction of the extension is also uncertain (see Fig. 59).

[72] See D.A. Gasparini and Caterina Provost, 'Early Nineteenth Century Development in Truss Design in Britain, France and the United States', *Construction History*, 5 (1989), pp. 21–33.

[73] Ian J. Kerr, *Building the Railways of the Raj*, pp. 117 and 141–49.

Producing Iron

At the start of the century the Mint was maintained in FSG and 'was entirely under the management of natives'.[74] The Mint master was Mr. J.H. Cassamaijor and the coins were made by contract with Ling Chetty. In 1824 Lord Elphinstone, Governor of Madras, wrote to the Board on the progress of experimenting in iron casting at the Madras Mint; he said that the mint master could 'cast any article less than three tons' in a mint that was entirely managed by 'native servants'.[75] Heyne, in his *Tracts of India*, written in 1814, recorded that southern India possessed a steel manufacturing process which astonished Europeans[76] and J.M. Heath, in charge of the Porto Novo Iron Works (South of Madras), wrote that Indian methods of steel manufacture were much quicker than those patented in the UK, by 1825. Captain J. Campbell who wrote *On the Manufacture of Bar Iron in Southern India* posed the question of manufacturing India's own bar-iron needs at a cheaper rate than England's extensive exports to India, where Madras alone consumed 1,000 tons per annum. He criticised the use of the word 'scientific' to describe England's knowledge of iron manufacture, when in fact, 'the principles of the mode of operation are still totally unknown and it cannot be yet produced at pleasure'. He argued for a careful examination of 'the principles of the long-established, cheap, simple mode of manufacture of the natives of India'. Campbell believed that Indian methods might lead to improvements and modifications and be found to answer better than the 'operose' methods of English manufacture which require the construction of costly buildings and considerable trade to make it profitable.[77]

With the approval of the Supreme Government Campbell conducted 'experiments', presumably similar to those of the engineers encountered in Chapter 2, in the Salem district in 1841. He recounts that natives used natural steel for axes, bill hooks and tipping ploughshares

[74] *A Gazetteer of Southern India*, p. 21. During the late eighteenth century the Company was angling to take control of the Mint. It did so in 1807. See H.D. Love, *Vestiges of Old Madras*, vol. 3, part 1, p. 425.

[75] Minute of 19 Feb. 1824, MSS Eur F/87/33 Elphinstone Papers.

[76] Quoted in Edward Balfour, *Report on the Iron Ores and Iron and Steel of Southern India* (London, 1855), p. 4. This report appears to have been prepared in response to a request for information on the subject of *wootz* (Indian steel), made by The Royal Asiatic Society of Great Britain and Ireland in a letter sent to the Governor of Madras. I was unable to find any information on the Indian Iron and Steel Company in the nineteenth century. The Bengal Iron Works was set up in 1874.

According to Prasanna Parthasarathi, 'Iron Smelting the Indian Sub-continent', XIV International Economic History Congress, Helsinki, 2006, Session 38, pp. 1–9 (electronic). The Porto Novo Iron Works began as a private company, started by J.M. Heath in 1825, with permission from the Madras Council. He was given exclusive rights to produce steel in this way for the duration of the Company's charter. It exported substantial quantities of iron to Britain in the 1830s which was used in the Royal Arsenal at Woolwich. The Company actually loaned Heath money for capital investment. The Iron Works at Porto Novo quietly closed down in the 1860s because cheaper poor quality iron was imported from Britain. Colonial state policy did not offer protection for Indian industrial products.

[77] Edward Balfour, *Report*, p. 9.

and he offered to make iron at Rs. 30/ton, of exactly similar quality to the finest Swedish iron sold in Bombay at Rs. 160–200/ton. He even sent his samples to the Bombay government. It is telling that when in 1844 the Bombay Government offered to buy 20–30 tons of Campbell's iron, the Supreme Government confined Campbell's services to military duties.

Conflict between the Court, the Supreme Government and the Madras Government over the future of the Porto Novo Iron Works and the refusal to release Campbell from his military duties, to pursue research, meant that in the long run, Indian iron manufactures were abandoned in favour of European imports. The Minute of the Honourable H. Charmier of July 1844, Secretary to the Madras Government, records a Court of Directors' despatch which 'requires that several Governments of the Presidencies shall make use of Porto Novo Iron in preference to that of Europe'.[78] Charmier continued to say that the Madras Presidency would deserve the name 'benighted' if the Company withdrew its investment in this project. He wanted Madras to supply her wants from her own resources, for Campbell to be allowed to continue his work and for the East India Company to forego its claims on the Porto Novo Company altogether.

This episode suggests that South India had a promising state-controlled iron manufactory in the 1830s, and that Indians possessed independent knowledge in this field. It is thus entirely possible that iron building components were manufactured in the South, not simply by the state, but also by Indian and Indo-British entrepreneurs. Whether they manufactured components used for making wrought-iron roof trusses is a different matter, as is the question of the availability of skilled labour necessary to assemble such trusses. On the other hand, had labour been imported from England for this purpose, it is probable that the Trustees, Norton or Our Reporter would have made some capital out of it, simply for its novelty value. Since all three sources are silent and no contrary evidence is forthcoming, it seems reasonable to tentatively conclude that the building was constructed using Indian expertise and Indian building materials (except for the corrugated galvanised iron sheet roof), despite the modernity of the roofing system and the skill it entailed. Whatever the case may be, the patrons certainly enjoyed developing and using new technology that was partly western. They were also aware of the ideological impact of the new spaces, made possible by new knowledge.

Captains, Contracts and Labour

The sources are entirely silent, not only on the labour process, but in regard to the contract process too. What is known is that Lieutenant Hitchins and other gentlemen offered 'advice

[78] Ibid., p. 31.

and suggestions' during the progress of erection. At the opening of the new school, Lieutenant Hitchins read a report in connection with the erection of the building and its durability. The patrons took great pride in advertising, to a captive Madras élite, their daring classical building constructed according to the exacting standards of modern science.[79] The building was built of brick and finished with chunam. The Trustees provide a fairly detailed account of the construction of the foundation and the walls:

> Prior to laying the foundation, and in order to ensure as firm a basis for the walls as possible, the trenches having been dry to the depth of several feet, a large quantity of river sand was introduced, which having been moistened was well rammed down with iron crowbars until the whole became a perfectly solid mass three feet deep...over this stratum a layer of brick and mortar mixed (jelly) was laid.[80]

The six-feet-deep brick foundation was built on this base, each course being rammed and levelled to preclude failure from cracks. The walls of the superstructure were not allowed to advance unequally, but an entire course of bricks all round was completed, previous to the beginning of another. The scaffolding was erected independently of the walls and no holes were allowed in the walls to support it. In short, everything was done throughout construction to render the building permanently durable. It is a credit to the builders and managers that, despite severe neglect, the building is still standing and serving its original purpose.

Although there are no sources of any kind on the contractual procedure for the Pachaiyappa building, some insight into social relations in the construction industry is available. At this time, in Madras, the term 'contractor' encompassed a range of activities beyond that of construction. It was a normal practice for a contractor to be asked to tender for premises—in this case the Company asked the tenderer to 'find and maintain a suitable building [for a court-house] which shall afford the requisite accommodation and which shall be in a centrical [*sic*] situation relative to the great mass of the centrical population'. Major de Havilland (who was the contractor here) gave a detailed spatial breakdown of the accommodation required for a court house. He also asked to be paid 280 pagodas a month, 'until the agreement shall endure or the Company could buy the property'. The contract included payment of rent to the landlord, arranging suitable accommodation for the activities of the court and for the maintenance of the building. This form of contract was useful to a government which relied on Indian

[79] *Athenaeum*, 21 March 1850. The Lieutenant is called Hutchinson by the *Athenaeum*, although the Trustees refer to him as Hitchins. There was a Colonel Hitchins co-signing the acceptance of a tender for the Engineering Department of the Military Board alongside the Chief Engineer, Lt. Col. A. Lowe, 14 July 1846, No. 35, MPPC, TNA.

[80] 'To G. Norton' in Chariar, *Select Papers*, *Speeches*.

agency. It demanded a social knowledge and access to networks beyond the technical expertise of building contracts.[81] If the process of asking the contractor to tender a proposal for the design and construction of complex structural items, as shown below, was followed at the school, I conclude that the design and construction of the roof may well have been left to Indian contractors.

Sometime in early 1847 Moodokistna and Comarenchery Moodeliar tendered a plan, at a cost of Rs. 22,424–22,443, for the construction of the Coovum Bridge. Their tender to erect a complete bridge as per plan, delivered with good materials was approved by the Military Board in October 1847. On 11 February the contractor's solicitor signed an agreement with the Company's solicitor and received Rs. 5,000 to commence work. On 5 September 1850, Moodokistna Maistry [*sic*] and Comarenchery Veerabuthra Moodeliar, two of the surviving contractors of the Coovum Bridge, submitted a petition to the Governor-in-Council. The petition noted that the work was damaged and delayed due to heavy rain: the dams were washed away and the *pecottah*s' contrivance for drawing and carrying water, thrown down. The loss due to the floods was Rs. 1,832. As work progressed, the Superintending Engineer, Captain Reilly, directed work to be constructed 20 feet north of the old bridge. The contractors incurred extra time and money to execute Reilly's instructions but the Military Board refused to reply to their letters. Hence the petitioners accused the Superintending Engineer of being the cause of their ruin.

On 18 April, Reilly forwarded a memorandum to the petitioners saying he needed, in the space of seven days, '7 lacks [*sic*] of arch brick, 5 lacks [*sic*] of wall brick, 5000 parahs of choonam and 16000 parahs of sand'. They took no heed of it as it was an imposition, and informed the Military Board of their decision. On 27 April 1849 the petitioners received a letter from the Board instructing them to deliver charge of the work to the Superintending Engineer. On 28 April the petitioners and their workmen were 'with violence turned out of the place' by Captain Reilly with the assistance of the Military Board. Their materials were used to complete the structure and although the contract expiry time was 31 May, Reilly did not complete the work until September.

It would be inaccurate to consider this unresolved conflict as typical of social relations in the building industry. At the same time, it is interesting that despite the presence of a legal contract, the Military Board and its engineers were able to use violence and break the law

[81] 16 December 1816, P/244/58, page 4848, MPPC. Also see page 4848 for the tender made by Mr. Sherson for the same premises.

with some impunity, on a building site which was a civil concern. The intrinsically military nature of the colonial state and its policy of employing military-engineers for civil work made certain that the construction industry and the military remained linked throughout the nineteenth century.

As the traveller in 1811 observed: 'The people in power here seem wonderfully fond of smelling gunpowder; I suspect they never tried it in earnest. The saluting battery [was] scarcely at rest, for either news of the arrival or departure of men-of-war, or the visits of the Nabob.'[82] Although such comments poked fun at the effete and greedy Company government and a maliciously chuckling Frenchman claimed that it charged the Prince Rs. 3 for every gun fired, the preponderance of guns and accoutrements of war are indicators of a familiar military presence in daily life. Julia Maitland, wife of the Magistrate at Rajamundry gave a rare insight into the way the army was seen in English civil society, when she wrote of the frequency with which Indian chiefs challenged the Company's army. She was so unafraid of mini-rebellions as to describe them as '*petite drolerie*'. According to her, the little rajahs who mounted these little rebellions, succumbed as soon as they saw the red-coats and the sepoys.[83]

The Opening

'The opening ceremony for the Patcheapa's [*sic*] New School took place on 20 March 1850. The Governor, Sir Henry Pottinger, and the Commander in Chief, the Honourable D. Eliot, presided with a very large number of the elite of the Presidency and several ladies present.' On his Lordship entering the theatre where the ceremony took place a vocal band sang 'God Save the Queen' preceded by loud and continuous cheers. The Governor was shown to his seat placed on the platform on which also sat the other members of the assembly,

> Streenivasa Pilly called upon the secretary of the Patcheappa's Charities to read the address presented to his Lordship. Thandialoo one of the proficients of the High School followed with another address to the Secretary and the Directors, presented by himself and the other students, as well we believe of the High School, as of Patcheapa's and some of the native community in praise of their exertions and returning thanks for Streenivas Pilly's labours in their connection.[84]

The tone of the ceremony was decidedly European. Following Lieutenant Hitchin's talk, George Norton spoke in perusal of a request made of him to address the students on the use and

[82] *A Visit to Madras, Being a Sketch of the Local Characteristics and Peculiarities of that Presidency in the year 1811* (London, 1821), p. 16.

[83] Julia Maitland, *Letters from Madras*, p. 280.

[84] *Athenaeum*, 21 March 1850.

advantages of education, dwelling more particularly on its influence on 'enlarging and enriching the intellectual faculties' and of the 'substantive good' derivable from it. It is a testimony to the rhetoric of colonial education that a man with no educational credentials came to occupy such a pivotal position in modern South Indian education, when the cream of the pundits did not.

'Barbarian Ugliness'

I conclude this chapter by examining the building's place in the changing contours of indigenous architecture. The fact that there are no extant courtly buildings, pre-dating Hampi, capital of the Vijayanagara Empire, suggests that at least until the fourteenth century, royal abodes in the South were temporary structures, erected wherever the king's mobile retinue assembled.[85] Such an approach to royal residential accommodation may concur with the older Tamil country, Chola model of kingship emphasising virtue and simplicity. It is believed that the former faced competition from the Nayaka model, developed at Vijayanagara, which upheld wealth and consumption, although there is no firm evidence to conclude that the large civil structures at Hampi were, in fact, palaces. Likewise, the information available on pre-colonial domestic buildings of South Indian nobles and *nattar*s is scant. Aside from great tree-lined roads leading to sprawling and splendid temple complexes, and stone and mud forts surrounded by thick prickly hedges, as well as protected mercantile towns, visitors to the region did not describe substantial 'public' or private edifices in urban conurbations.[86] What they did describe were small houses inside mud forts or *pettah*s, which were walled production units containing around 400 persons. Outside *pettah*s, European forts and coastal towns, the 'public' buildings encountered by travellers were walled temples and *choultrie*s.

The latter were of several types, the simplest serving as inns. The more sophisticated were composed of four elements: a temple, a garden, a tank and a large service building which could have multiple functions, serving as school, hospital or hospice for the elderly, maternity unit and administrative unit to collect rents and dues.[87] The main building of the Orthanadu

[85] The point that South Indian kingship exercised a rigorous control on building is made by Jennifer Howes in her thesis 'Kings, Things', p. 150. Only the king and his retinue could live in impressive structures.

[86] The inadequacy of the term public/private, secular/religious for discussing Indian architectural space is to be noted. I use it in a limited sense. For an introduction to this problem see Jennifer Howes, 'Kings, Things', p. 96. The temple was a public space accommodating many 'secular' activities.

[87] This information was given to me by Dr. Raju Poundurai during a site visit made in January 2001. He believes this to be a Marathi built form since the buildings have multiple masonry vaults as a common roof form. Masonry vaults were not, in his view, a part of the mainstream South Indian tradition.

Chattram(Maratha period) in Thanjavur, possessed multiple courtyards. Some pavilions had three floors and the tiled, flat and vaulted roofs were supported on masonry piers and timber columns with elaborate carvings. The *chattram* was a royal endowment with an attached garden, purported to have been built for Rajah Serfoji's lover, Muthambal. In areas under royal jurisdiction, royal largesse endowed public facilities or granted permission for other notables to do the same. The parvenu royal houses of the new successor states of the sixteenth and seventeenth centuries, following the Vijayanagara kingship model, evolved static neo-traditional courts. The magnificent fort-palaces at Madurai, Ginjee, Thanjavur and Chandragiri, best exemplify their buildings. The large garrisoned forts contained other buildings to service the army such as a watch-tower, granary, barracks, stables and arsenal.

In areas where there was a Muslim presence since the fourteenth century, the situation appears to have been different. The town surrounding the Arcot fort, for instance, was said to have been extensive with good houses.[88] The eighteenth century also witnessed the merger of older hierarchical ritual and scribal groups, *nattar*s and new rich magnates into urban oligarchies, able and curious to experiment with exotic cultures on their own terms. As mentioned earlier, they enjoyed social mobility, wealth and a princely lifestyle.

And yet, it is puzzling that there are no records of any grand domestic structures attributed to them, either in Madras or in their renowned gardens. When they did build houses in the city, they were small and in the Indo-European manner (see Fig. 60). Contradictions between great wealth and austere surroundings were not uncommon in India; they featured in the lifestyles and beliefs of merchants, peasants and priests. Did the new ascendant oligarchies like Brahmins shun personal material display and husband their resources, closely emulating Jain and Vaishnava traditions, antithetical to the kingly? Or did they resemble the great peasant castes in their asceticism and frugality, espousing ideas usually associated with devotional Vaishnava sects that had softened hierarchical ritual practice and even evolved corporate monastic-type institutions? 'Their tenets of sobriety, orderly householding and commercial rectitude flourished in colonial India too, making as significant a contribution to the way the modern Indian middle class thinks as did the more spectacular borrowing from western rationalism and positivism.'[89]

Generally, public gatherings for educational and entertainment purposes were open-air events in the shade of large trees, in pavilions, besides the pools of temples, or in tents in the

[88] F. Buchanan, *A Journey from Madras through the Countries of Mysore, Canara and Malabar*, vol. 1 (3 vols., London, 1807), p. 17. Eighteenth-century Thanjavur must be seen as an exception on account of its link to major trade routes.

[89] Christopher Bayly, *Indian Society*, p. 160.

Figure 60: A European house: A group of bearers with a palanquin in the foreground, Madras, 1811, John Gantz, watercolour

gardens of magnates.[90] Moreover, Indian leaders maintained gardens outside the city which were frequently visited. They were probably furnished with simple, impermanent pavilions. As mentioned earlier, like the rulers of old, new leaders and their retinues appear to have relaxed in tents. During the hot season, in 1830, the Nawab Regent, Azim Jah, went on an excursion to the *Roshan Bagh*. The *sarkar baghs*, state gardens, were large tracts covered with trees, interspersed with small streams and springs. On this occasion an 'elegant bungalow covered with thatch' was put up in the garden. It was furnished with rugs and lanterns in all shades of colour.[91] The description indicates a modicum of luxury where shelter from the heat was sought under awnings in shaded groves, cooled by streams, and feasting and entertainment took place in the cool of the night.

Tents belonging to different magnates were identified by special colours and must have been elaborate affairs and yet, being temporary structures, they constituted little precedent for the erection of grand permanent edifices fixed to specific plots of land. Present knowledge of

[90] V. Raghavan, 'The Sarva Deva Vilasaya', pp. 50, 87, and 105. The nawabs too were constantly erecting temporary structures for entertainment.

[91] Muhammad Karim, *Swanihat*, vol. 2, p. 40.

eighteenth-century private building is too scarce to attempt any general conclusions with regard to houses or other 'public' structures. In the absence of serious study most modern writers have considered the garden-house to be a European invention, whereas a few believe that Europeans simply imitated 'local nobles'.[92]

Garden-houses on record are European-owned structures in the classical style (see Fig. 61). Early examples were plain, 'generally only of one storey, but of a pleasing stile of architecture'.[93] They had chunamed pillars, walls that were white or coloured, and floors were covered with rattan mats. These simple buildings had terraces/flat roofs and were hardly reminiscent of English country-houses. It was when garden-houses became symbols of extravagance, in the late eighteenth century, that the Company stepped in to restrict land acquisition. The plainness of the early garden-house may indicate that Europeans, in their desire to make permanent garden-houses, simply elaborated Indian pavilion models in more durable materials. In 1699 Thomas Salmon commented on Black Town as having a few brick houses; the rest were miserable cottages of clay and thatch, with no windows to the outside, or any furniture. The houses of the better sort were the same, with a little square courtyard in the middle. 'Notwithstanding all the appearance of poverty I never was in a place where wealth abounded more plentifully.'[94]

Figure 61: Garden House, Madras, c. 1780

[92] V. Raghavan, 'The Sarva Deva Vilasaya', p. 106. For the opposing view see, for instance, Norma Evenson, *The Indian Metropolis,* p. 6 or Susan Neild, 'Colonial Urbanism', p. 242. Neild believes that upper-class English country estates inspired suburban residences in Madras.

[93] Walter Hamilton, *The East India Gazetteer* (London, 1815), p. 505.

[94] Krishnaswami Nayudu, *Old Madras* (Madras, 1965), p. 76.

Central to an understanding of the Indian ideological contribution to the Pachaiyappa School building is recognition that freedom to build, untrammelled by religion and royal restrictions, may have been a fairly 'new' opportunity for urban oligarchies in European enclaves. They could experiment. The form and aesthetic of the Pachaiyappa hall was a free interpretation of the Greek original. Critics have usually associated the sparse classicism of the early years of Company building in India with parsimony and military engineering priorities. An Indian contribution has been at a discount. But in the example under discussion here, the Indian contribution was paramount. It is this that compels consideration of the conflicting undertones and complex ideological implications the building may embody.

Despite long links with the British, new urban oligarchies were staunch supporters of traditional culture and appear to have shunned any personal display of wealth, reserving ostentation and grand building for gods, or kings as divine by proxy.[95] With the gradual eclipse of the power of indigenous kings, temples acquired added importance as bastions for legitimising power. They now had to compete with the places and spaces accessible to the colonial state and its modes of legitimisation. The temple as an institution and architectural space became an intensely contested site, ever more fraught and sacrosanct. In this sense, the education theatre opened up a new civil space for the political activity of the oligarchs.

The hall posed several design problems. The patrons clearly envisaged a multiple use for it: as a school hall and a public assembly room. It hardly needed to make any grand statement to meet either requirement. I suggest that Indian patrons brought contradictory ideologies to the design conversations which created this building. On the one hand, the new 'public' political activity (the term 'public' used here does not mean that there was no public activity before this time, it simply means that the terms public, secular and religious were inseparable in the indigenous context) could gain prestige if it was conducted in a stately, modern building. On the other, the powerful strain of asceticism that infused the entire private world of the South Indian élite may have acted as a foil to any attempts towards undue ornament.[96]

Company parsimony and military engineering philistinism may not have to take the entire blame for variations of the style bearing the standard as the hallmark of public building in India. It held an undeniably deep allure for Indian engineers through the long twentieth century.

[95] An introduction to the subject can be found in Velcheru Narayana Rao, David Shulman and Sanjay Subrahmanyam, *Symbols of Substance: Court and State in Nayaka Period Tamil Nadu* (Delhi, 1992).

[96] Although the sources are silent, it is possible that the austerity of the building was also influenced by finance. The final cost of Rs. 85,624, more than doubled the original estimate of Rs. 40,000. 'To G. Norton' in Chariar, *Select Papers*, *Speechs*, p. 30.

The style has been vilified by many writers as the vulgar creation of military engineers and Public Works Department standardisation programmes, pursued under the central control of the Supreme Government. The idea that it was a product of Indo-European confluence has not been addressed.

This brings us to the theme of Indian pleasure seekers curious and enthusiastic about an ancient Greek architecture. I am surmising that southern Indo-Britons shared sources on European architecture available in colleges and private libraries. The evidence for this claim is the library of General Claude Martin, the nabob and French general, who built several flamboyant castle-style houses in Lucknow, in the 1780s. It contained a wealth of books on contemporary architecture, fine arts and gardening. Martin was a gifted amateur who used his wealth to create a strange and lavish Indo-European architecture, said to have had an enormous influence on the Indo-European architecture of Lucknow city.[97] The National Library of Calcutta also contains a whole collection of treatises and handbooks on architecture, in several European languages, ranging from James Gibbs, William Chambers and Stuart and Revett to the *Civil Engineers and Architect's Journal* from 1837. When nineteenth-century European intellectuals took the political decision to mythologise ancient Greece as the 'cradle of civilisation', classical aesthetics rapidly ascended the ladder of taste. It acquired a global imperial identity and became synonymous with imperial power in India. European architecture held enormous appeal for the Anglophile Indian élite but their pleasure posed no threat to Greeks, Romans or Britons. It had none of the aggression that transformed British orientalism into a double-edged sword. There always were dissenting viewpoints too! Rabindranath Tagore is said to have cried at the 'sheer "barbarian ugliness" of the ruins he saw on the Acropolis'.[98]

[97] Rosie Llewellyn Jones, *A Fatal Friendship*, p. 155.

[98] Mary Beard, *The Parthenon* (London, 2002), p. 11.

4

The 'Aesthetic Imperialists'

The Public Works Department (PWD)

Beginnings

It is impossible to study state building without some understanding of the PWD. The PWD was the premier building institution of the new crown state. Its formation links the story told so far, to the state buildings to be discussed in the next chapter. Between 1850 and 1858 civil public works departments were established across the three presidencies. They grew from an amalgamation of local Indian and British building and military organisations of the early nineteenth century and incorporated many regional differences. The term 'public works', not used in England, was most probably borrowed from eighteenth-century France where state presence in the building industry was pervasive and militaristic. The École Centrale des Travaux Public was set up in Paris in 1794 to unite all the various aspects of training in engineering science under one roof, and to provide a general scientific education for future mining engineers, geographers, civil architects, and eventually, teachers of mathematics and the physical sciences.[1]

Nineteenth-century administrative reformers in London greatly admired the Indian Civil Service which may have inspired the organisation of the PWD. The PWD was an Indo-British institution created to service a centralising, militarised territorial state. It had no counterpart

[1] Margaret Bradley, 'Scientific Education versus Military Training; The Influence of Napoleon Bonaparte on the Ecole Polytechnique', *Annals of Science*, 32 (1975), pp. 415–49. She claims the École Polytechnique became a prep school for the newly reorganised écoles d'applications which prepared students for various branches of the public services, both civil and military and that its influence was felt abroad in, for instance, Germany, Austria, Prague and St. Petersburg.

in Britain. The notion of training for 'public service' was not a new practice in some centralised European states. Robert Pyper believes that the modern civil service in Britain was indebted to India. The Northcote-Trevelyan *Report on the Organisation of the Permanent Civil Service*, prepared in 1854 in Britain, drew heavily on the Haileybury alumnus Charles Trevelyan's early experience in India.[2] In its mature phase, the now familiar all-India organisation known as the PWD had its own secretary to the government of India, based in Calcutta, with a counterpart in London. These subsequent national and global developments were not implicit or inevitable in the beginning.

The tussles between Calcutta and the provinces that plagued the consolidation of the organisation, and shaped its early evolution, have not interested historians. Even the PWD's own historian, G.W. MacGeorge, was guilty of this omission. In 1894 he published *Ways and Works in India: Being an Account of the Public Works in that Country from the Earliest Times upto the Present Day*. It drew a picture of the PWD as a cosy, white, male fraternity with a civilising mission—to execute 'the engineering works of general usefulness which bear directly on the material progress of the people'. MacGeorge gave the PWD a smooth narrative history and a comfortable all-India format. In comparison to its civil engineering sector the architectural component of the PWD's workload was small but influential. It left modern India with a building legacy very different from its pre-colonial one.[3]

In light of the formidable scope and reach of the PWD's building programme, this chapter has the limited objective of trying to uncover the interface at which the state intervened to absorb and transform older architectural practices. The establishment of the PWD was also a move to disengage building from military control; and this explains why the military/civil interplay appears here as a sub-theme. The present chapter is set out in four sections. The first section outlines a framework for approaching the study of the PWD. In it I explore the idea that the central task of the PWD was the building of a territorial state, commensurate with the political and engineering imaginings of imperial proconsuls and élite technocrats. The second part examines the relationship between the state and the designers who were placed in charge of this enormous material transformation. Section three looks at the education programmes developed to train the new designers. The final section expands the idea that imperial patrons

[2] Robert Pyper, *The British Civil Service* (London, 1995).

[3] G.W. MacGeorge, *Ways and Works in India: Being an Account of the Public Works in that Country from the Earliest Times upto the Present Day* (Westminster, 1894). Probably due to the enormity of the task, there is no modern overarching history of the PWD. Instead scholars have tended to look at specific aspects of PWD practice. Jean-Marie Lafont, *Chitra* gives a good visual idea of what the building landscape was like just before British intervention. He taps the unseen French archive of the Centre des Archives d'Outre-Mer.

used the range of facilities afforded by the PWD to make a new hybrid imperial architecture in the South.

A Territorial State

It is not usual practice to connect the PWD to the construction of the imperium and the Indian territorial superstate. But, because this connection is closely relevant to the themes of this book, I question the assumption that 'India'—as a recognisable territorial, political and cultural entity—was already in place when the PWD was set up. I am proposing that this was not the case and that, in fact, the ideology of the territorial nation-state was the underpinning for the PWD—they were inseparable. If ideologues conceived of an Indian territorial state and nation, then the Survey Department mapped it and drew it, and the PWD built it.

While this book is certainly not the place for too in depth a discussion of this question, it is however, useful to draw attention to two new studies that explore the role of public works in nation-building. The first looks at water, the US army corps of engineers and the uniting of states in America. The second explores land, culture and the gardens at Versailles, and the making of the territorial state in revolutionary France. In the United States great conduits of navigation were seen to bind the republic, 'fusing the States, making America'. In France, in a similar vein, building and war became potent tools for constructing a territorial state.[4]

By 1800, although 'India' had a cartographic identity, the politics of its boundaries and the identity of the colonial state were in dispute; as was the question of the 'national' identity of a people comprising a hugely diverse ethnicity. By the 1840s the British were using the term 'national' in an Indian context, but its meanings were understandably vague. It is interesting that Ian J. Kerr, in his diligent study of the railways of the Raj, failed to link that massive undertaking to any form of nation-building. But Lord Dalhousie, the Governor-General who initiated the programme of 'material improvement', unequivocally regarded railways as a 'national concern' even though they were private undertakings.[5]

Over the course of the nineteenth century British mapping framed 'India' as an actual if ambiguous geographical region and consolidated its modern image. In writing this, Matthew Edney adverted that the creation of an India that was a single political state, coincident with its

[4] The role of the United States Army Corps in nation-building is studied by Todd Shallat, *Structures in the Stream: Water and the Rise of the US Army Corps of Engineers* (Texas, 1994); the culture of land and the territorial state in France is examined by Chandra Mukerji, *Territorial Ambitions and the Gardens of Versailles* (Cambridge, 1997).

[5] See Ian Kerr, *Building the Railways*, and Suresh Chandra Ghosh, 'The Utilitarianism of Dalhousie and the Material Improvement of India', *MAS*, 12, 1 (1978), pp. 97–110.

cartographically defined geographical whole, was from the point of view of its imperial rulers, one of their greatest achievements.[6] In order to make sense of the material transformation launched by the state, through the PWD's centralised building programmes, it is necessary to connect the growth of the territorial state with colonial rule and middle-class government in Britain, all of which were shaped by an ethos of domination over nature. This ethos made Europeans believe that 'their vastly superior understandings of the workings of nature' and their ability to turn nature to human use, was a powerful justification for 'their monopolization of leadership and managerial roles in colonized societies'.[7]

A Big Idea

Before Lord Dalhousie appointed a Central Public Works Secretariat at Calcutta, with the object of general supervision, each presidency possessed its own system for conducting public works, each having an independent history of development. The key difference between the new and earlier forms of building organisation in north India was the status and reach of the army. Prior to 1854 the engineer department of the Military Board had executed public works in Bengal. In Madras, however, things were different. In addition to the engineer establishment of the Military, the Board of Revenue had its own engineer department. The latter maintained the extensive irrigation works scattered throughout the presidency. Put simply, by 1850 Madras already possessed well-developed military and civil engineering establishments designed to cater to its own needs. The initiative to establish the Madras PWD came from the Court of Directors, not from Calcutta.

Dissatisfaction with the prevailing structures of power forced the Court to set up a Commission to enquire into 'public works' in the Madras Presidency in 1851.[8] In 1852 the Commission gave a full account of the existing system of public works and 'reviewed at length the working of the *Maramut* Maintenance Department'. At the time, the term 'public works' referred to three main areas of civil building activity—roads, canals and irrigation, and associated civil buildings. The Madras PWD was eventually set up in 1858; six years after discussions on the subject first began between Madras and London. With crown rule Calcutta assumed the

[6] Matthew Edney, *Mapping an Empire*.

[7] Michael Adas, as cited in David Gilmartin. 'Models of the Hydraulic Environment: Colonial Irrigation, State Power and Community in the Indus Basin', in David Arnold (ed.), *Nature, Culture and Imperialism: Essays on the Environmental History of South Asia* (Delhi, 1996).

[8] For irrigation see Robert Buckley, *The Irrigation Works of India* (London, 1880).

burden of centralising and streamlining the different units and the creation of a homogenous, all-India identity for the PWD. The centralising process was fraught; the Madras and Bombay Governments challenged and regularly defied Calcutta's autocratic tendencies. The contest took material form in the civic building programmes of the emerging imperial state. The PWD, together with the army, was assigned the task of making a new material culture that configured a territorial identity for the new all-India state.

If early restoration work in Madras constituted a benchmark in British hydraulic engineering experience, the conquest of the Punjab, with its canals still in working order, and the construction of the totally new Ganges Canal (the longest in the world), begun in 1842, were the catalysts for the creation of a PWD. The Ganges Canal was the earliest major British initiative in the material development of India, and though built according to Indian methods, it attracted enthusiasm for British technical hubris. Such projects encouraged the aspirations of visionary technocrats—the military engineers and governors—keen to transform the Indian countryside through 'material improvement'. The completion of the Ganges Canal in 1854—a major international engineering feat—fuelled imperial pride and Lord Dalhousie's wish to expand public works and reform the way irrigation systems were funded and constructed. Accordingly, he abolished the Military Boards and placed engineering work under central civil control.[9] For Dalhousie the 'railways, electricity and the telegraph were the three great engines of social improvement'. What he could not achieve in England he achieved in India, through the absolute power of a military state. Dalhousie's vision was the expansion of unitary state power. He proposed that the new public works structure would have a two-fold function: construction and the routine maintenance needed for administration, and prosecution of work calculated to increase wealth and promote the prosperity of the country. The first set of tasks, which affected the well-being of the community, was to be executed by the government. This naturally gave British designers and contractors (in other words engineers) executive responsibility for massive building programmes that brought railways, telegraphs and new irrigation works to India; it was also intended that these building programmes would prove immensely profitable to certain commercial groups in Britain.

Dalhousie also instituted changes in funding: expenditure for construction and maintenance was classified as ordinary expenditure and set against the revenue of the year. Outlays on projects 'calculated to increase wealth like irrigation, harbours and railways, were to be met mainly with borrowed money'.[10] This move seemed to go against the noted reluctance of

[9] Ian Stone, *Canal Irrigation in British India* (Cambridge, 1984), p. 18.

[10] Ibid., p. 19.

colonial governments to promote cultural and economic unities that could threaten their control. The British did develop a limited national market and contribute to the standardisation of languages, but as yet we have little understanding of the creeping material cultural unity and physical fusion achieved by the building of railways, canals, roads and buildings that bound men and things together.

Dalhousie's proposals briefly led to Indian irrigation being promoted through private enterprise, in ways similar to the railways, i.e., by guaranteeing a return to private companies. The experiment lasted from 1858 to 1866. The 'driving force behind both the Madras Irrigation Company, and the East India (Orissa) Irrigation and Canal Company was Sir Arthur Cotton of the Madras Engineers, then at the height of his powers as a hydraulic engineer'. The private sector canal experiment proved immensely lucrative for the Canal Companies and a costly failure to the government. Irrigation became a branch of the PWD in 1867.[11] It is not surprising that Major Cotton was also one of the three Public Works Commissioners who reported to the Court on the reforms suitable for public work organisation in Madras, in 1852.[12]

'Englishmen who are not turned into Asiatics'

The development of public works in Madras owed much to the territorial and political landscape which succeeded the Poligar wars in 1801. Native rebellion was brutally quelled and a tenuous political stability was achieved by the new state. Local notables were experiencing a steady erosion of their old economic and political roles. They used new organisations like the Madras Native Association to appeal to Parliament against the seriously unjust conduct of the Company state in the 1850s;[13] but they remained, on the whole, loyal to the British. Liberal Britons sympathised with Indian aristocrats whose grievances they wanted redressed. John Bruce Norton, a leading legal luminary in Madras, for example, sympathised with the native princes 'who are now in London with their various petitions' carrying the charge of 'robbery and spoliation'

[11] The Madras Irrigation and Canal Company was bought out by the Government for £1.8million. It was unable to recover its loan of £ 1.5 million to the Company which had proved to be 'careless and inefficient', quoted in A. Sivasankaran, 'History of the Public Works Department of the Madras Presidency, 1858-1947' (University of Madras, Ph.D., 1985), p. 61.

[12] V/26/700/8, *Proceedings and Correspondence Connected with the late Public Works Commission for the Madras Presidency*, Madras, 1855. Also see V/26/700/6, *Views and Proceedings of the Madras Government on the First Report of the Commission of Public Works*, 1853.

[13] The best account of these conflicts is still to be found in R. Suntheralingam, *Politics and Nationalist Awakening*.

against the despotic Company government.[14] On the other hand, some reforming Britons wanted a change of government, bringing to an end existing modes of native agency, with a complete British monopoly of power. The culture of loyalism was strong in Madras, and it is seductively easy to dismiss it as 'greed and sycophancy'. However, a more sensitive reading would choose to depict it as a form of patriotism evolving from Indo-British ideas and practices of government. Indian leaders had offered a guarded support to the Company state in the form of private counsel and guidance, in return for just government. Addressing a subject seldom raised by historians, Christopher Bayly suggests that, loyalism combined 'genuine political ideas, ones which the British often proclaimed but usually did not themselves live up to'.[15] It also included ideas of power-sharing with mutual respect, drawn from traditional theories of governance and ethical practices.

The layered and shared sovereignty of the indigenous state systems comprised a decentralised network of mutual obligations mediated through sacro-royal centres.[16] Quotidian land management was carried out through local networks mediated by *sabha*s, village assemblies. The gradual dismantling of this social order saw indigenous building organisation being replaced by the Military and Revenue Boards, which shared responsibility for building and land control. Regulation VII of 1817 had, moreover, vastly increased the power and scope of the Revenue Board by placing under its management all *inam* tax-exempt lands, which included the extensive resources of the semi-urban temple complexes.[17] Of the two boards, the Military Board was the one more actively engaged in the material alteration of the Indian landscape. Military objectives caused the destruction of centres of rebellion such as forts and *pettah*s. They were replaced with new colonial building types: cantonments, barracks, hospitals, schools, jails and court-houses. The army executed civil building and siege works under European control. But as seen in Chapter 2, the Revenue Board left agency for building with Indians in the *Maramut* Department.

In South India the term 'public works' described the vast, irregular and dispersed irrigation schemes that the British inherited. For instance, in 1860, the Canal and Irrigation Company

[14] Long before the Rebellion, Norton pointed to the need to redress native grievance for the fear 'they would seek revenge for their injuries'. See John Bruce Norton, *A Letter to Sir Robert*, p. 124. And John Bruce Norton, *The Rebellion in India: How to Prevent Another* (London, 1857), p. 224.

[15] Christopher Bayly, *The Origins of Nationality in South Asia* (New Delhi, 1998), p. 123. For a new slant on old patriotisms see p. 75.

[16] Nicholas B. Dirks, *The Hollow Crown: Ethnohistory of an Indian Kingdom* (Cambridge, 1987).

[17] See Robert E. Frykenberg's chapter 'The Construction of Hinduism as a "Public" Religion: Looking Again at the Religious Roots of Company Raj in South India' in Keith Yandell and John Paul (eds.), *Religion and Public Culture: Encounters and Identities in Modern South India* (Surrey, 2000), pp. 3–26.

reported that it had 6,000 labourers ready to put to work on the first 14 miles of the canal from Kurnool.[18] In the rest of the subcontinent similar land management systems were found only in districts north of Delhi; the size and complexity of the existing irrigation and land management procedures discouraged state interference with land control and building in the south. The most impressive of the inherited schemes was the 1080-feet long Grand Anicut, a dam across the Cauvery river with its canal systems, built in the second century by Chola kings. The British acquired it in working order in 1801 and confined their role to managing repair and maintenance. Scholars have noted the existence of a 'tank supervision committee' for the purpose of monitoring irrigation facilities in medieval South India, though its precise functions are not clear. It is thought that the committee was appointed by the *sabha* village assembly, and handled finance, commissioned building, paid labour, organised repairs and collected taxes, amongst other duties.[19] It is possible to surmise that transitional forms of the *sabha*, the *nadu* or regional councils, and tank supervision committees continued to function until they were replaced by colonial institutions wherever the British began to intervene in material transformation.

Restoration of the Grand Anicut commenced in the 1830s and Cotton began the building of the lower dam in 1834. Work on the Godavari River began in 1846 and the Krishna River in 1851. It is occasionally possible to gain insight into British engineers' debt to Indian engineers. In 1859 Major Cotton solicited the government to confer free-hold tenure on a piece of land to sub-engineer T. Veeranna and his heirs, for having been the 'right-hand of all the officers who have been in charge of these [Godavari] works'.[20] The irony was that after 40 years of service in public works, Veeranna remained a sub-engineer. According to Peter Scriver, Indian hydraulic engineering systems were poorly understood in England. It seems likely that British engineers gained knowledge from working alongside the *jala-sutrala* Indian engineers specialised in tank and dam construction, on the extensive restoration carried out on irrigation works.[21] Government records for 1854 generously praised the 'judicious and economical work executed by the Native *Maramut* Superintendent Polony Vellur Moodelliar' in the construction of a 30-feet span bridge with six arches across the Goondaur and that built by Native *Maramut*

[18] Letters to the Secretary of State from the Madras PWD, 1860–61, Madras Collections, L/PWD/3/188, No. 44, 1860.

[19] T.M. Srinivasan, *Irrigation and Water Supply: South India 200BC–AD1600* (Madras, 1991), p. 207.

[20] Madras Collections, L/PWD/3/519, 16-No. 69, 1859.

[21] Peter Scriver, 'Rationalisation, Standardisation, and Control of Design: A Cognitive Historical Study of Architectural Design and Planning in the Public Works Department of British India 1855–1900' (University of Delft, Ph.D., 1994), p. 161. The reader should be warned that he only considers a British point of view.

Superintendent Vencataramiah across the Oopaur.[22] Native ascription ceased with the inception of formal PWD records.

The rewarding of science skills was ethnocentric. Engineers like Major Arthur Cotton of the Madras Army, came to be knighted for their hydraulic engineering services to empire. Cotton went on to advocate the necessity of anglicising the system of government in India, convinced that India was 'so depressed' because Englishmen in India, 'instead of teaching the Natives of India the things which make us what we are, sit down to learn of the Natives the things that make them what they are'. Believing that 'old Indian ideas' were the destruction of India, Cotton wanted 'untainted Englishmen to rule India. Englishmen who are not turned into Asiatics'.[23] Cotton's inconsistency was not unusual. Again, one is left to assume that some of the natives appearing in the earlier records, denoted as superintendents, were Indian engineers/architects whose practice relied on indigenous knowledge. By the 1850s indigenous knowledge shared with Britons had been transformed. Through the agency of men like Cotton it silently entered the ambit of 'science' available to the international community.

Regional Dissent

The forging of the territorial Company state was contested by Indo-Britons. The central organs of state were divided between England and Calcutta and its physical boundaries were far away, in regions controlled by often uncooperative provincial governments, accustomed to autonomy and commanding armies that could threaten the stability of the supreme government. Leading officials and private citizens in the south resented not having the same opportunities for development as in the north. It is in this vein that an old Madras hand tells us:

> when I came to Madras it was known as the 'benighted Presidency'. There were strong presidency jealousies and the Bengalees always affected to despise Madras. This was absurd even in those days, for as a matter of fact the Madras Presidency was in some respects in advance of any other part of India. The English language was spoken by natives in Madras very much more than was the case elsewhere.[24]

Even with crown rule, conflict over regional autonomy was a continuing thread of contention in the evolution of the territorial state. Criticism of the dominant tendency emanating from Calcutta was made by Madras Governor, Charles Trevelyan, in his Minute of 13 July 1859.[25]

[22] *Selections from the Records of the Madras Government No. XXV, Report on Important Public Works for 1854* (Madras, 1856), p. 29.

[23] Sir A.T. Cotton, *Public Works in India: Their Importance with Suggestions for Their Extension and Improvement,* 3rd edn. (London, Madras, 1885), p. 50.

[24] Alexander Arbuthnot, *Memories of Rugby*, p. 118.

[25] GO 218–24, 12 November 1863, MPPWD, TNA.

Trevelyan believed that 'it [was] physically impossible that the real government of the whole of India can be carried on by one set of men from one place' and argued that South India could not be governed from Calcutta because it needed men trained in 'the peculiar system of the south'.[26] He was responsible for instigating major reform in the PWD, overhauling its audit systems and securing skilled staff for laying out the scale, rules of admission, curriculum and scope of teaching of the Engineering College. Fourteen months into his term of office, Trevelyan was recalled for challenging the Supreme Government on its taxation policy, which the Madras council considered inimical to the interests of the Presidency.

Recalcitrant tendencies reached a high point in the 1863 discussion concerning re-organisation of the PWD. Lord Denison, Governor of Madras, sought clarification from the Secretary of State as to the relationship between the Governor-General and the governors of the different presidencies. He was criticising the practice which had 'gradually crept in' of 'referring everything to the governor-general'. He argued that the Government of India alone could deal with general matters, but the limit had been over-stepped when it made claims to interfere in local affairs. Denison drew on Madras PWD precedents such as the Trevelyan view that local decisions should be taken by those aware of local conditions and peculiarities of the country and was adamant that 'our system of public works does differ materially from that of any other part in India'.[27]

The autocratic and ever arrogant Colonel Strachey, Secretary to the PWD in the Supreme Government, and his brother, the even more powerful John Strachey, who sat on the Viceroy's Council and represented the so-called authoritarian liberal view, wanted the Indian PWD to accommodate Royal Engineers from Britain.[28] This strategy was resisted by Denison, himself an engineer, and the Madras Government; both wanted civil engineers trained in Madras.[29] The Madras PWD elders desired the creation of an engineering establishment dedicated to serve the peculiar material environment of the Presidency. They held that in Madras there were many more projects, scattered over very large and remote areas, whereas Bengal had only a few, concentrated in three or four divisions.[30]

[26] B.S. Baliga, 'Sir Charles Trevelyan'; Trevelyan was a zealous reformer responsible for initiating reform of the home Civil Service and the introduction of open exams in 1855.

[27] GO 218–24, 12 November 1863, MPPWD, TNA.

[28] He is considered a disciple of James Fitzjames Stephens but it would be misleading to seek essential differences between their views and say those of Napier who also advocated a strong imperial government. See Thomas Metcalf, *Ideologies of the Raj* , paperback edn. (Cambridge, 1997), p. 58.

[29] GO 490–92, 21 November 1863, MPPWD, TNA.

[30] P250/43, January–March 1861, MPPWD, p. 33. The projects were chiefly irrigation ones. They also resisted the imposition of an accounting and audit system developed in Bengal. See GO 58, 7 January 1861, MPPWD, TNA.

The crown state of 1858 did not initiate any fundamental change of direction in the approach to building from that of the Company state. Investment in the material arena remained limited and geared to the military and extractive impulses of colonialism. The construction of major engineering works such as railways, canals, roads, and the telegraph did nevertheless result in effecting substantial changes to the Indian landscape. Modest building activity was undertaken in line with reform of administration and improvements in health and education. Overall the production of a new material culture geared to colonial priorities was underway.

Native Agency

The project to transform the material environment matured with the merging of the political visions of imperial proconsuls and the engineering vision of environmental domination. It rapidly demanded well-trained men to design and manage it. The Company and crown states did not employ Indians to design buildings or engineering works. It is likely that the state's refusal to engage Indian designers[31] stemmed from a more general policy of excluding Indians from high office. David Gilmartin showed how in colonial India, the international ethos of irrigation science and state science colluded to define indigenous communities as 'parts of the natural environment to be modelled and controlled' and not as partners who shared in the definitions of water use policy.[32]

In 1859 Trevelyan called for a report on the reorganisation and improvement of the system of conducting public works in the Presidency because the Madras Departmental system was 'not open to competition'. It was held that the natives and subordinates who controlled the system, and made good money out of it were obstructing free competition.[33] Another lobby condoned state control of construction, especially where building materials production was concerned.[34] Moreover, it was also the case that Bengal did not face problems of native power in the Departmental construction sector, because the Governor-General and the Bengal PWD were doubtful as to the efficacy of the Madras Government's proposals. What was at

[31] I use the term designer inclusively to cover both engineering and architectural design because in British India there were very few designers who were actually trained as architects. In France, for instance, after the closure of the Academy of Architecture in 1793, the state was demanding engineers trained as architects. The nineteenth-century separation between the two only began after the establishment of the École des Beaux-Arts in 1819. See Antoine Picon, *French Architects*, p. 331.

[32] David Gilmartin, 'Models of the Hydraulic Environment'.

[33] GO 67, 31 August 1859, MPPWD, TNA.

[34] For a detailed report see GO 89–90, 6 March 1863, MPPWD, TNA.

issue in Madras was the desire on the part of the state to break the old guard Indo-British monopoly within the Department and the construction sector.

The problem of 'native agency' within the office of the civil architect came to the fore in 1859. Captain Winscom, who had recently been appointed acting-officer-in-charge, discovered a serious over-charge and breach of duty. A discrepancy amounting to Rs. 2,478 between the alleged cost and the actual value of work performed at Government House. The committee appointed by the chief engineer to enquire into the discrepancy reported that the fraud arose due to imperfect estimates, lack of checks and direction of work by an 'ignorant *Maistry* and Sub-Overseer'. Winscom observed that the civil architect, Colonel Atkinson, was sick and he named Soobaroyah *maistry*, Rungasawmy (a *conicopoly*, accountant, since discharged), Mr. Fitzgerald, the office manager, and sub-overseer Rackeappah, as the parties responsible for the work. 'Captain Winscom urge[d] the abolition of the situation of the manager and the addition of more European Superintendence, and in so doing oppose[d] the views of the late Colonel Atkinson who relied almost entirely on Native Agency.'[35]

Mr. Fitzgerald was a mixed-race builder and stone mason from Black Town. He came with impeccable testimonials from other engineers. The first assistant civil engineer H.W. Rawlins recommended that if it were contemplated appointing an East Indian assistant engineer, Fitzgerald would prove valuable because he had great experience in Madras. Colonel Atkinson had even presented him with a gold watch as a mark of esteem. Colonel Faber, the Chief Engineer, cautiously proffered the opinion that 'as an invariable rule it is undesirable to authorize important alterations that may be suggested by any other than the Officer permanently appointed to an office'. He was critical of 'the radical change of system proposed in the Civil Architect's Office'. The civil architect and garrison engineer's department in 1860 had the following staff: managers, accountants, estimate makers, draughtsmen, writers, *lascars*, storekeepers, auditors, *moochees* and overseers.[36]

Indo-European partnerships in the construction sector appeared in colonial records mainly in regard to fraud cases, where it was often the case that colonial law was deployed differently for Europeans and for Indians, notwithstanding joint embezzlement. In 1874 contractor Ragavacharry and Mr. Colquhoun contrived to cheat the government of a large sum of money. The government ordered that the latter be tried by Special Commission.[37] PWD reforms of

[35] GO 16–18, 9 February 1859, MPPWD, TNA.

[36] For details of civil architect's establishment see handwritten enlosure from chief engineer to secretary to government in PWD, GO 406–07, 26 June 1860, MPPWD, TNA.

[37] The records are replete with fraud cases involving Europeans and Indians. See for instance, GO 171–173, 7 February 1874, MPPWD, TNA.

the 1860s aimed at changing Indo-British alliances through the use of the law. Colonial law validated PWD Codes on contracts, labour and design and decreed which training certificate was valid for employment. The law colluded with the state in the demarcation of its material domain with even greater power accruing to the engineer.

In its social composition the Indian Engineering corps had a high percentage of aristocrats and landed gentry. It could therefore claim a degree of exclusivity not found in the Indian army or the Royal Engineers at home. This served to enhance the authority of engineers in India; the 'highly professional engineering and artillery corps was much admired'.[38] They were a new breed of scholar-soldiers. When the PWD was rationalised on para-military lines the state developed a special relationship with design professionals. It established a clear race and class hierarchy to contain conflict and competition, with ambitious *babus*, clerks, kept in place by mixed-race staff to transmit knowledge from above to the natives below. The yoke of bureaucratic authority was willingly accepted by engineers, as it was balanced by a modicum of power when the department embraced the view that 'their destiny was to dominate and control a timeless, unchanging India'.[39] Increasingly the British designer was drawn from a class different from that of the artisan. In the colonial situation this meant that a new group of Indo-British intermediaries, endowed with a scientific fluency to liaise between the new professionals and Indian builders, had to be trained.

The pupillage system by which the English civil engineer and architect was trained had no method of assessing competence and proved inadequate to cater to the specialist demands being made by the colonial state. It was in response to that demand that in March 1859, the India office in London placed an advertisement calling for engineering candidates to sit for an open examination for the Indian engineering establishment. As candidates were required to produce a certificate attesting to their training at an approved engineering college, the terms of eligibility set here, implicitly ranked engineering schools in Britain.[40] The Home and Madras Governments' correspondence indicates that all the prestigious engineering schools in London, Scotland and Ireland sought recognition from the India office to field candidates. Such widespread interest could only mean that engineering employment in India was keenly sought after by English gentlemen in the 1850s.[41] Men like Arthur Cotton and his north Indian

[38] P.J. Marshall, 'British Society in India Under the East India Company', *Modern Asian Studies*, 31, 1 (1997), pp. 89–108.

[39] Peter Scriver, 'Rationalisation', p. 208.

[40] Civil Engineers' Home Correspondence 1859–79, Minute Paper, 11 May 1860, L/PWD/2/222.

[41] King's College, London; University College, London; Queens College, Belfast; Trinity College, Dublin; Madras College, St. Andrew's, The Civil Engineering School, London, were some of them.

counterpart Proby Cautley—designer of the Ganges Canal—were graduates of the Company's Military Academy at Addiscombe. Civil engineering schools in Britain were new institutions, having begun in the early 1840s long after the military ones.[42]

Furthermore, the setting up of Cooper's Hill, the Royal Indian Training College, in London, in 1871, to train military engineers for the Indian Establishment, confirmed the value of the Indian service to the British middle classes. It ensured that engineering knowledge, for service in India, was made ever more exclusive and denied to Indians. High entry fees protected the sons of the well-heeled who were trained in seclusion to perform their management roles in the Indian building world. Distinctions of race and class were strongly guarded by a military hierarchy that aimed to forestall the advance of civil engineers by rationalising and strictly controlling entry standards to the PWD.[42] Springing from colonial social relations the PWD organisation was characterised by a layered conflict between European civil and military engineers and between them and locally trained European, East Indian and Indian engineers.[44]

Engineering Visions

By nature of the power devolving from an authoritarian state the engineer in India was to perform a far more influential role in the construction industry than his home counterpart. Salaried designers in England were regarded with some contempt in the profession of architecture, which most practitioners still regarded as a gentlemanly art. Architectural historian John Summerson found that the contractor, the developer and the architect were the prime movers in the London building world of the 1860s. He failed to mention a single salaried engineer. However, he offered a clue as to why the Indian engineers' functions overlapped that of a businessman: 'As building became more an industry than a trade, so architecture became more a business than a profession.'[45] The tendering system became the touchstone of change, not only in building, but also in architecture. Since no reputable builder would tender unless quantities were supplied by a recognised quantity surveyor, therefore, the architect was compelled to produce full working drawings for the making out of quantities. It created a lower deck of

[42] Mark Crinson and Jules Lubbock, *Architecture, Art or Profession? Three Hundred Years of Architectural Education in Britain* (Manchester, 1994), p. 49. The Chatham School was set up in 1812.

[43] Peter Scriver, 'Rationalisation', p. 265.

[44] 'Public Works Department in India' (From *The Builder*) in the *Bombay Builder*, 5 April 1866, p. 204. The author, signing himself as 'Another Victim', lamented that all the higher appointments were exclusively filled by military men.

[45] John Summerson (ed.), 'The London Building World of the 1860s', *The Unromantic Caste and Other Essarys* (London, 1990), pp. 175–92.

useful staff of limited competence. Indians suitably trained for the purpose filled this role in the PWD.

If Summerson's adage that mid-Victorian Britons had a 'hatred of official architecture' was true, it was also true that by the time they arrived in India, their mindset had undergone a radical reversal. Overall, colonial officials approved of the services of state-employed engineers for building design. It was a period where no clear distinctions prevailed between architectural and engineering activities, and professional bodies were in their infancy. As the workload of the public sector increased, the state—reluctant to pay the high cost of importing engineers from abroad—decided to train them locally. Dalhousie had declared that engineers were as scarce as 'freshly descended angels'.[46] Thomason College of Engineering at Roorkee, the pioneering colonial engineering science institute was opened in 1847. Civil engineering was the favoured subject where 'the courses were structured to serve the immediate requirements of the department'.[47] Roorkee was to serve the north where a dearth of engineers had arisen on account of the 'dominant preoccupation to guarantee soil fertility by creating material improvement' and the Sikh wars of 1845 in the Punjab. This exercise had engaged four Governor-Generals, Auckland, Ellenborough, Hardinge and Dalhousie. James Thomason, Lieutenant Governor of the North Western Provinces (NWP), was inspired to tackle irrigation after the famine of 1837 to 'advance the productive value of the soil, the comfort of the people, and their securities from the ravages of famine'.[48] Governors and military engineers were mutually dependent in the formulation and execution of ambitious programmes for material and social improvement.

Such a comprehensive state initiative in engineering education was not matched in Madras till later. Madras, however, pioneered private Western (science?) technical teaching with Michael Topping's Survey School, established in 1794, and Major Maitland's School for Ordnance Artificers, begun in 1840. It is possible that these early schools experimented with European and indigenous 'fusion' knowledge, especially as they were concerned more with practice than theory. Fusion knowledge and native teaching came to be dismissed as 'superstitious' and 'unscientific' with the emergence of the new knowledge.[49] The private technical schools in Madras had the added disqualification of a social engineering component, directed towards

[46] Quoted in Peter Penner, *The Patronage Bureaucracy in North India* (New Delhi, 1986), p. 187. This study provides an excellent account of the 'Rurki' debates.

[47] Arun Kumar. 'Colonial Requirements and Engineering Education: The Public Works Department, 1847–1947', in Roy MacLeod and Deepak Kumar (eds.), *Technology and the Raj* (New Delhi, 1995), pp. 217–32.

[48] Peter Penner, *The Patronage Bureaucracy*, p. 170.

[49] The Hindu College Medical School in Calcutta was closed in 1835 for this reason. See Deepak Kumar, *Science and the Raj 1857–1905* (Delhi, 1995), p. 51.

elevating the intellectual and moral fibre of poor whites and mixed-race boys. The aim was to raise them from 'utter moral and mental degradation' and offer a sound practical education to fit them for work as tradesmen, foremen and overseers. In 1855, F.J. Mouat, Secretary to the Indian Council of Education, deemed Maitland's achievement to be 'more creditable than that of any similar institution which I have ever seen in Europe or in India'.[50] Mouat observed that 'half-castes' were cheap to produce, had healthy muscle and firm hands and their minds, though they were the 'dregs of society', had been through the whole of Addiscombe and General Pasley's (Chatham) course and could make drawings and plan machines. He leaves us in no doubt that the students were taught engineering science knowledge. The Addiscombe/Chatham combination was the most prestigious education pedigree a Company-trained engineer could possess.

The Madras Public Works commissioners, however, were unimpressed by evangelical exhortations with a hidden agenda. In 1852 they had expressed the view that technical education could not be left in private hands and that the state should provide all the training needed to admit candidates to the service; to them, the idea of the upgrading of existing schools proved distinctly unappealing. They intended that new designers should constitute a socially privileged professional élite, distinct from the building trades and the 'unclean' poor. The Madras Civil Engineering College was finally opened in 1859, after a great deal of hostile exchange between the commissioners and the Government. It formalised the convergence of interests between the colonial state and a new middle class of soldier-engineer designers from England.

The contest between the centralising tendency issuing from Calcutta and the regions was keenly expressed within the PWD. Staff recruitment, design, accounts and contracting were all rationalised through a series of centrally monitored reforms. Knowledge was standardised by a system which absorbed challenge to military authority and devalued the intellectual agency of the professional in the process. Design and settlement plans were evolved on rationalised para-military lines. And yet, the Calcutta preference for the classical style and soldier-designers was ignored in Madras. The government proudly declared in 1885 that it had employed an architect for 15 years, with a view to improving its architectural and structural designs. 'The introduction of European taste is avoided, with the two-fold object of developing arts indigenous to the country, and of dispensing with European ornamental materials difficult to import or imitate.'[51]

[50] IOR.MF1/12297, Selections from the Records of the Madras Government, No. IV, Major Maitland's School for the Instruction of the Artificers and Pupils at the Gun Carriage Manufactory (Madras, 1855), p. 39.

[51] C.D. Mclean, *Manual of Administration*, p. 536.

In the light of these regional differences it is useful to know how the state set about having major public buildings designed. It had in fact several choices: it could turn to private architects in Britain, call on its own employees (the engineer/architects) or on private Indian architects. Only the Bombay Government, favoured with wealthy Indian benefactors, commissioned private British architects. Usually, official buildings were designed by salaried military or civil engineers and occasionally by designers from other backgrounds such as surveying or drawing.

Although the state was a major employer of the professions in Britain, it maintained a benign but low-key approach. Public building in Britain was subject to Treasury control. The Office of Works, created in 1851, was designed to function as a Ministry of Public Building, although it was not allowed to initiate and conduct major public works as did the *batiments civils* and parallel services in France. The powerlessness of the Office of Works arose from a deliberate policy to subordinate it to the Treasury. And, equally, the Minister of Public Works was chosen, not for his knowledge of the arts as in France, but for his political stance. In Britain the state was not overly concerned with building monuments of international artistic acclaim—an indifference attributed to the degree of provincial representation in parliament, which refused to vote money for major London projects until after the 1880s.[52]

There were, none the less, several 'art' lobbies of fluctuating power, advocating different and robust state intervention in architectural matters. Art connoisseur, politician, orientalist and trustee of the newly opened National Gallery, Austen Henry Layard, led one such faction, based in the Office of Works: in 1861, he was Under-Secretary of State for foreign affairs. He began as a covert operator for his patron, Stratford Canning, British ambassador to the Ottoman empire and was given the task of stealing Assyrian antiquities. Layard was responsible for the illegal digging and transportation to London, of the colossal Assyrian winged bulls and lions from Nimrud, in the 1840s. With heavy public fanfare, they were enshrined in purpose-built galleries in the British Museum by 1853. In 1847 the French had opened the Louvre's Musée Assyrien, with the first display of Near Eastern artefacts to be presented to European eyes. British ideologues, in keen competition with the French for the imperial mantle of a civilised nation, appropriated the artefacts in the name of civilisation, effacing the nationhood and country of the Mesopotamian Arabs in the process.[53] The monumentality of the buildings of the Mesopotamian region was inspiring the nationalist sentiments of the proconsular élite at

[52] M.H. Port, *Imperial London: Civil Government Buildings in London 1851–1915* (New Haven, 1995), p. 12.

[53] Frederick N. Bohrer, 'Monumental Nationalism: Layard's Assyrian Discoveries and the Formations of British National Identity' in Dana Arnold (ed.), *Cultural Identities: The Aesthetics of Britishness* (Manchester, 2004).

home. Layard took a personal interest in the design proposals for the British consulate in Alexandria, for which he seems to have advocated an 'overtly Islamicizing style'.[54]

Indo-Briton, James Fergusson, eminent critic and self-declared architectural historian, having made a fortune in India, was busy promoting himself as the expert on Indian architecture and was shortly to write the first history of world architecture.[55] He too was an admirer of the architecture of Babylon and Nineveh—recognised as the precursors to Islamic architecture. Leading art critic John Ruskin was also offering a hybrid as the model for imperial architecture in his choice of the faintly Islamic or, at least, the very cosmopolitan Gothic Ducal Palace in Venice as his 'central building of the world'. When Layard became the First Commissioner of Works in 1868, he installed James Fergusson as his architectural design adviser. The politically radical Layard's architectural ambitions were thwarted. He was bitterly attacked in parliament and replaced as First Commissioner in October 1869. A royal engineer-officer replaced Fergusson as director of works. The next chapter will trace how Layard's grandiose architectural visions came to fruition not in London but in Madras, through the aegis of the proconsular élite commanding the colonial state.[56]

The second 'art' faction clustered around the new Science and Art Department, a powerful body with royal links. Under the influence of Henry Cole, it cultivated an enthusiasm for soldier-engineers as designers. Cole had 'urged the value of employing royal engineers (available like tap water) to prepare preliminary plans for public buildings and watch over the execution of "the artistic completion" for which an architect would be employed, if possible, on a full-time engagement'.[57] Captain Douglas Galton was appointed Director of Works and Building. He monitored many prestigious building projects designed by private architects, including the Home and Colonial Office, the Law Courts and the Natural History Museum. It comes as no surprise to find that a military engineer held the highest state appointment in architecture in Britain in the 1870s. The Government of India briefly engaged Walter Granville, a civilian, as its Consulting Architect, from 1863–68, for the 'express purpose of designing public buildings in Calcutta'.[58] Bombay employed military engineers and purchased sophisticated architectural services of leading practitioners from London through the marketplace. The Madras Government

[54] Mark Crinson, *Empire Building*, p. 186.

[55] James Fergusson, *The Illustrated Handbook of Architecture* and *History of the Modern Styles of Architecture* (London, 1862).

[56] Layard Papers, Add. MS 39112, 39115, 39116. They corresponded during Layard's appointment as Under Secretary for Foreign Affairs during 1864–65.

[57] M.H. Port, *Imperial London*, p. 66.

[58] Philip Davies, *Splendours of the Raj*, p. 207.

extended the early Calcutta venture by setting up a separate establishment for the consulting architect in 1868.

There was little consensus as to what constituted a proper training for design. 'Art' architecture seldom rated a high priority in official colonial circles, packed with soldiers and Haileybury men, whose Haileybury certificate became compulsory for a Company writer in 1813. Haileybury aimed to make students, previously educated at inferior 'seminaries', more like 'English gentlemen educated at our great national schools and universities' and to be seen as 'scholars, gentlemen and men of principle'.[59] The lack of professional definition in the building world encouraged varying routes of entry into the practice of architecture. Patronage was the key to employment. There was little to discourage a gentleman of taste and an engineer from collaborating in the design of a major public building. Official patrons with taste and opinions on architectural style and their design advisers were the ultimate trendsetters in architecture.

By the 1860s the soldier-engineer was in charge of the state building sector. Their dominance accompanied the development of a particular kind of engineering education, where the measure of expertise by examination was instituted. The state groomed the engineer to perform the role of impresario to the construction industry.[60] The engineer was valued not simply for his mathematical flair, but also as a social engineer possessing the scientific expertise to materially improve the lives of the Indian people.

Only once did the Madras Government hold a competition to select designs for major public buildings. Robert Chisholm came to the notice of the government when his entry won first prize in the competition held for the Presidency College and Senate House projects in 1864. Chisholm joined the Bengal PWD on 8 February 1859, as an assistant engineer. His transformation into an architect took place in Madras and will be discussed in Chapter 6.

New Design Professionals

Colonial ideology buttressed the myth that the design and construction of new building types needed a new scientific knowledge. The upshot of this ideology was that the colonial model eschewed continuities with indigenous education. Indigenous education was marginalised and

[59] P.J. Marshall, 'British Society in India Under the East India Company', *MAS*, 31, 1 (1997), pp. 89–108.

[60] Skempton notes that the design and build contract was used in the early eighteenth century to a limited extent. Some engineers even financed their own work; see A.W. Skempton, *Civil Engineers and Engineering in Britain 1600–1830* (Aldershot, 1996), p. xvii. An overview of the range of engineer activity and the expanded commanding role visualised for them may be had from V/26/700/7, *The Second Report of the Commission Appointed to Enquire into and Report on the System of Superintending and Executing Public Works in the Madras Presidency*, Madras, 1853.

disparaged. Nevertheless, indigenous architecture continued under the patronage power of South Indian temples and though impoverished, continues to survive even today.

The Royal Engineers School at Chatham, begun in 1812, was the first school to train engineers in England. It developed an approach to architecture which was practical and utilitarian, with a low priority given to design, aesthetics and ornament. Design attitudes were guided by parsimony and efficiency and aptly reflected the military priorities of soldiers.[61] The Civil Engineering College for Preparing Young Gentlemen, established in 1847 in Russell Square, taught the following under the title of architecture: roofing, framing, brick laying, masonry, carpentry, ironwork, building construction, drawing plans, elevations, sections, making finished working drawings, preparing specifications, taking out quantities, measuring, working drawings of machinery, mechanical, geometrical, isometrical and perspective drawing and colouring.[62] In engineering schools the teaching of architecture was disassociated from design. As early as 1826, some military theorists were eager not to leave military engineers idle in times of peace. C.W. Pasley was adamant that they be used for superintendence of 'Public Buildings' and the execution of other public works. He did not pretend to lay down the rules for 'proportioning the various parts of the edifice' and for designing the decoration, which formed the terrain of study of 'professed architects'.[63] He expected the engineer to design common military buildings such as barracks, hospitals or store-houses. The ethos of soldier intervention in civil life, as design professionals, was common at the highest levels of thinking on Indian engineering education.

Colonial engineering education produced a new type of professional, the engineer/ architect, equipped with a new rationalised systematic technical knowledge, geared to the ambitious programmes of the PWD. Similar developments in the USA have been attributed to the influence of the alleged 'French model' in which military influence was predominant. The American Corps of Engineers leading the construction industry favoured 'a planned economy where the army guided construction and science was the methodical tool of a rational, centralised state'. It is believed that the ideals of the engineer-scholar left the new American Corps with 'French values: a talent for planning and applied mathematics, a flair for monumental construction that empowered the nation state'. [64]

[61] C.W. Pasley, *Outline Course of Architecture compiled for the use of Junior Officers of the Royal Engineers* (Chathama, 1826).

[62] Civil Engineers' Home Correspondence, 1859–79, Minute Paper, 4 May 1860, L/PWD/2/222. The Secretary of State refused to classify it as an engineering school because it did not have a certificate of approval issued by the Council of the London Institution of Civil Engineers.

[63] C.W. Pasley, *Outline Course*, p. 111.

[64] Todd Shallat, *Structures in the Stream*, p. 2.

In India, the impetus to train design professionals was British, official and had a military bias. But unlike in France or England, Indians were denied the intellectual forum to conduct an architectural discourse alongside the engineering one. This task was appropriated by British proconsuls, engineers and bureaucrats. Engineering ideologues also often sought to distance themselves from architectural discourse by developing their own engineering discourses. In England, as discussed previously, architectural design skills were gained through pupillage, coupled with a few lectures and formal drawing classes in an academy. Design education was completed with a period of travel abroad when drawing and personal observation of buildings in Italy, Greece and the Levant were made. The system grew partly from the middle-class desire to avoid contact with the building trades. It attained a certain professional and social exclusivity through the specialist division of labour in the construction industry. By the 1840s some lectures in engineering and architecture were offered at University College and King's College, London. They attracted those persons who wished to challenge the monopoly of the Royal Academy on art education, respond to changes in the construction industry and organise a centralised profession. In most schools, excepting the Architectural Association, no formal design training was offered till the next century.[65]

The education of engineers in Madras began with the opening of the Civil Engineering College in 1859. It was to stay under the grip of the military till 1907.[66] The broad aims of the school were to provide the technical staff needed by the PWD to develop the resources of the country. Every district engineer would contribute to the revenue of the country and to the wealth of the people. Policy makers emphasised theoretical and scientific training and took their ideas direct from Addiscombe and Chatham. The student intake was both military and civil and comprised four socially stratified divisions of which only the lower three were open to civilians.[67] The senior department was for commissioned army officers. The first department trained assistant engineers. The lower departments trained draughtsmen, estimators, overseers, surveyors, and accountants.

The course of studies was adapted to meet the requirements of the examination for the degree of the bachelor of civil engineering of Madras University. In 1881 the only student who presented for the degree exam failed. In 1881–82 there were no students in the first class and only nine in the second. Communal representation depicted a high proportion of Brahmin

[65] For a guide to the subject see Mark Crinson and Jules Lubbock, *Architecture, Art or Profession?*

[66] The link between British engineering education and military priorities has not been studied. See S. Ambirajan, 'Science and Technology Education in South India' in Roy MacLeod and Deepak Kumar (eds.), *Technology and the Raj*, pp. 112–33.

[67] S. Ambirajan, 'Science and Technology Education'. Separate architectural teaching began in the 1930s.

pupils followed by Hindus (non-Brahmin), Europeans and Eurasians. The Director of Public Instruction understood that until open competition for admission to the subordinate ranks of the PWD was a reality, engineering education would remain unattractive.[68]

The 1875 issue of the *Professional Papers on Indian Engineering* carried the first account of a building, a jail in Amritsar, designed by the new breed of Indian engineers, Rai Kunhya Lal, Executive Engineer, Assoc. Inst. C.E.[69] Rai Kunhya Lal was not employed by the British, but it shows that in the north, as early as 1875, Indian technocrats begin to appear on the lower rungs of the professional ladder. He was probably trained at Roorkee and was also a member of the professional institute, implying incipient social convergence amongst new Indo-Britons. It is interesting that the proposal Robert Chisholm made in 1869, to the senate of the Madras University, for the establishment of a chair in architecture, was lost 'with no hands raised in its defence'.[70] Chisholm's was a lone voice protesting against the equation of architecture with engineering. The crown state made no provisions for training architects as distinct from engineers.

An Art School?

Madras was also the place that pioneered a School of Industrial Art. The school, privately begun by Dr. Alexander Hunter in 1850, was self-funding from small student fees and the sale of drawings, engravings and other work. Dr. Hunter and his allies favoured enlarging its scope and scale and reducing its dependence on production.[71] It was taken over by the government in 1855. The director of public instruction was anxious that its practical bias be directed away from profit.[72] He advised Dr. Hunter to confine manufacture to fire-bricks and was prepared to permit the manufacture of items like telegraph-insulators 'as an exception in pressing circumstances', with the proviso that every encouragement be given to 'Native workmen and contractors to set up manufactories'. The exclusion of fine arts and academic

[68] SRPI, 1881–82, p. 56, TNA.

[69] PPIE, 2nd Series, vol. x, 1875, p. 31. Also featured was a station at Ulwar for the Maharao Rajahs, designed by Teekaram, head draughtsman, Engineer-in-Chief's office, Rajpootana State Railways.

[70] *The Builder*, 5 June 1868, p. 449.

[71] 'The Useful Arts in India', in *Athenaeum*, 21 March 1850. Also gives an idea of the range of experiments being carried out on local products such as the preparation of fibre from pineapple, plantain and aloe leaves, sugar from coconut, and fuel from guava, on which Hunter reported.

[72] There exists some discrepancy as to the date. 1853 is the date given by Marukh Tarapor. 'Art Education in Imperial India', in K. Ballhatchet (ed.), *Changing South Asia: City and Culture* (London, 1984), pp. 91–98, and 1855 is given by C.D. McLean, *Manual of Administration*, p. 536. Tarapor is also useful for a background to the art schools.

art in the curriculum led to a great deal of dissent amongst education policy-makers. The lack of resolve to follow either course left it unclear as to whether the school was training artisans or artists.[73]

Henry Cole was Secretary to the newly formed Home State Department of Science and Art, and Superintendent to the Government School of Design since 1852. He was responsible for the development of a national system of vocational art education in Britain and was a key figure in the imperial nexus of the Great Exhibition and the South Kensington Museum (SKM). The Museum went on to foster links with the imperial art world and earned a reputation as a leading centre for innovative theories in art and design, aimed at raising national standards of British art. Richard Redgrave, temporary headmaster of the Government School of Design in 1845 and Cole's ally, throughout his South Kensington career, advised the Court on matters related to the Madras Art School.[74]

When the British began teaching Indians both western and (by the 1880s) Indian art, Indian art objects were being shipped to Britain under the pejorative label, 'handicrafts'.[75] Nonetheless, their design principles were analysed and used to train the British industrial designer.[76] Some thinkers believed that art ideas, and objects, flowing in from the colonies could be transformed by industrial designers to give British products a keen competitive edge in the global market. The latter project was fuelled by the other function of the SKM which was to monitor and direct colonial art policy, on behalf of the metropolitan state. This was a symbiotic relationship; the museum's staff worked closely with colonial officials who supplied it with rare art material from the colonies. The influence of the Kensington Museum circle pushed the trajectory of the Madras school curriculum towards manual labour and industrial production and aped the conflicts in British art teaching.

The Madras Art School was not popular with Europeans and Eurasians. Most students belonged chiefly to the poorer class of artisans who knew little English. Few completed the

[73] The Bombay experience of the period was similar. See Partha Mitter 'The Formative Period c. 1856–1900: Sir JJ School of Art and the Raj' in Christopher London (ed.), *Architecture in Victorian and Edwardian India* (Bombay, 1994), pp. 1–14.

[74] Redgrave liaised on such matters between the Court and the Department. See SRPI, No. 89, p. 72. For Redgrave and Cole see John Physick, *The Victoria and Albert Museum: The History of its Building* (London, 1982), p. 15. For a general account of the period see Partha Mitter, *Much Maligned Monsters*, chapter V and *Art and Nationalism in Colonial India 1850–1922* (Cambridge, 1994).

[75] This refers to attempts by the British to teach native art. See, Report on Public Instruction 1871–72, MPPWD,TNA where Dr. Hunter reported that the Hindus were beginning to apply the ornaments of their own pagodas to building and house decoration.

[76] For example SRPI, 1871–72, p. 83, where copies of figures from the Vellore pagoda gateway were sent to the School of Design, Kensington.

course due to lack of funds.[77] Robert Chisholm relieved Major Hunt as Director in 1878.[78] His appointment diluted military ideas and suggests that London and the Madras Government were anxious to raise the profile of the school and link it to a high-art world which Chisholm may have had access to. It was also a conscious move away from teaching art as manufacture and towards a drawing academy with an art gallery that promoted western art ideology inspired by 'traditional' Indian art.[79]

Underscoring the colonial art education enterprise was the steady and unremarked upon process of knowledge-sharing. Indians were trained in drawing skills from Europe, of which only mechanical and perspective drawing were really 'new'. In contrast, the building materials industry was the scene of the greatest innovation because engineers were eager to blend Indian knowledge with European developments. Colonial art institutions were on the other hand centrally controlled receptacles of art and craft knowledge. Perhaps their core function was to supply information to art education theorists, students and industrialists in the metropolis and practising architects or manufacturers in the colonies. It is possibly more accurate to see them primarily as art reservoirs and feeders in the service of the metropolitan state, which sought a role in defining their aims and structures from the very start.[80] Institutions like the Government Museum and the Art School had multiple agendas where educating Indians was, arguably, a peripheral one.

The Government School of Design, in London, absorbing and transmuting art from the colonies, acquired a leading role in defining middle-class English taste and a wider British cultural identity. From Owen Jones to William Morris, India and the colonies were never far from the engines of imperial art institutions in Britain. Benedict Anderson has argued that the museum, census and map were three profoundly political institutions, which contributed to the making of the colonial state.[81] It is possible to say that colonial art schools had an added function; they silently contributed to shaping the aesthetic taste of the imperial nation-state in Britain. The limited educational functions performed by the art schools in India make better sense when viewed from this oblique angle.

[77] SRPI, 1882–83, p. 120.

[78] SRPI, 1877–78, p. 121.

[79] See Partha Mitter, *Art and Nationalism,* p. 38.

[80] The debts incurred by the school in 1869 were met by special grant by the Government of India. SRPI, 1870–71, p. 59. TNA.

[81] Benedict Anderson, *Imagined Communities*, revised edn. (London, 1983), chapter 10. He argues that archaeological restorations directed by museum officials and scholars had clear ideological dimensions.

The preservation and development of traditional Indian art industries in Bengal took place under British tutelage.[82] It was not for want of trying on the part of the British that the Madras school never became a school of fine art on the Bengal model. The struggle to control taste involved the state in sponsoring fine art exhibitions, making judgements about art and awarding prizes. Although students did put forward entries for state-sponsored fine-arts exhibitions and secured prizes and honourable mention in drawing, no fine-art tradition inspired by the school was supported by Indian patrons who set the standards of taste. Ravi Varma, for instance, hailed as the first great 'Indian' artist by the Indo-British establishment, had no connection with the school. He was privately taught by Indian artists in his home in Travancore. We can only conclude that indigenous art and architecture traversed an alternate trajectory, extensively patronised by Indians, outside the orbit of the colonial universe. In fact, it has been said that southern Indian court painting produced an independent stream of westernisation, quite distinct from that associated with the Art School.[83]

The art schools offered vocational training for those who lacked opportunity elsewhere, and they trained a new stratum of skilled, semi-clerical professionals for the burgeoning state sector. The Director of Public Instruction declared that the school of art 'opens out a field of employment to those who have not the means of securing an English education, and to those who have no inclination for it'.[84] The school served architecture more indirectly; Indian draughtsmen, who may have been trained by the school, prepared construction drawings for British buildings.[85] The Industrial Department experimented with new materials and ornamentation in enamelling glass, decorating in oil paint, metal work and wood-carving. Chisholm used this facility to ornament in several of the buildings he designed in Madras.[86]

By 1859 the government had ruled that all officers in the PWD, whether English or vernacular, must be drawn from persons who had passed at the half yearly uncovenanted civil service examination. Draughtsmen and estimate-makers needed to obtain certificates of proficiency from the Civil Engineering College. These harsh measures served to further exclude traditional architects from the lower tiers of public service. Men passing through the newly instituted colonial education process effectively displaced those lacking the pecuniary

[82] For this Bengali development see Tapati Guha-Thakurta, *The Making of a New Indian Art*.

[83] Tapati Guha-Thakurta, 'Westernisation and Tradition in South Indian Painting in the Nineteenth Century: The Case of Raja Ravi Varma (1848–1906)', *Studies in History*, 2, 2 (1986), pp. 165–95.

[84] SRPI 1882–83, p. 121.

[85] Pratapaditya Pal and Vidya Dehejiya, *From Merchants to Emperors: British Artists in India 1757–1930* (Ithaca, 1986), p. 159. Also see Mildred Archer, *Company Drawings in the India Office Library* (London, 1972).

[86] SRPI, 1877–78, p. 121.

means to attend college in Madras.[87] Lieutenant Colonel Roberts, Superintending Engineer, Tanjore, was seeking to employ the uncertificated [*sic*] head draughtsman Manicum Moodelliar whom he considered to be 'more capable for Overseer's duty than the greater number of certificated overseers in the service, [he] has no prospect whatever of promotion before him'.[88] Roberts also recorded that, in his experience, certificated overseers were 'incapable' of making plans or estimates.

Architecture as a new professional practice in India was confined to intellectual labour and to those classes that wished to direct the crafts, not to engage in them. Education was theoretical and gained in the classroom divorced from builders. The Military Board was firm in the conviction that:

> the Civil engineer has a craft of his own; his skill is in his science; his tools are his formulae and his surveying and mathematical instruments; his labours are for the most part those of the mind; his studies those of projecting and controlling; and he must therefore be one of a very different class and status in society as well as of totally different attainments from those of the mechanic whose labours he has to direct.[89]

Indian engineers-architects trained in new fee-paying schools were not sons of *maistries*, foremen, traditionally engaged in the building trades. They were drawn from more affluent sections of society, alien to indigenous knowledge and groomed to bridge the gap between Englishmen of the engineering corps and Indian builders. They became sub-leaders of the construction industry.

The new schools fostered an intellectually and socially exclusive Indian engineer who was almost a mirror image of the British military technocrat, with one essential difference: the Indian engineer had to endure the yoke of subordinacy. To him the acme of bureaucratic power was permanently unattainable. In 1871 only one Indian trained in the first department of the Civil Engineering College was assured of employment under the government.[90] In later years, they rose to occupy coveted and powerful positions of relative leadership across society. Within their ranks no alternative was indeed proposed to this so-called utilitarian model of professionalism. Tight state control of education and employment discouraged intellectual debate, making certain that the colonial model remained uncontested. In England, however,

[87] GO No. 7–8, 5 April 1859, MPPWD, TNA. This injustice was highlighted in the *Bombay Builder*, 5 October 1865.

[88] MPPWD, November 1874, No. 376. Roberts noted that youth with college certificates were unwilling to work in the Mofussil.

[89] Quoted in S. Ambirajan, 'Science and Technology', p. 120.

[90] RPI 1871–72, Appendix A. TNA.

resistance to the utilitarian model was widespread. It was conducted at several levels by gentlemen architects and the building fraternity throughout the century.[91]

What then was the nature of the new design education and practice configured under colonial rule? The British model of design education developed in India was similar to the French in the power and scope of its professional imagination and scholarly training, but its intellectual development was inhibited by military and imperial exigencies and design apartheid. In short, the colonial model suppressed the emergence of multiple Indo-European architectural discourses. The educational horizon extended only to cater to departmental needs. Teaching and employment were racially and socially tiered and civilians were prevented from competing with the soldier-engineer. The poor were trained specifically to occupy the lower tiers of the system. Colonial society redefined the social role of designers by providing them access to a formidable range of powers, otherwise outside the reach of conventional design activity. It was the unfamiliar pleasure and appeal of this power that seems to have more than compensated for any loss of intellectual or creative freedom.

'Conventional Aesthetic Imperialists'

But the story of imperial architecture hardly stops in the intellectual by-lanes of soldier-engineers, portrayed by Philip Davies as the

> conventional aesthetic imperialists who ran the PWD as an elite club [and] looked aghast upon the interfering civilian architects who wanted to go native and adopt indigenous architectural apparel. It was as if the inner, trousered sanctum of the Raj were under attack from men advocating the use of loin cloths—and not natives, but Englishmen. It was unheard of, dangerously seditious and damned un-English.[92]

Even more powerfully placed patrons like Sir Bartle Frere, Lord Mayo, Lord Napier and Lord Curzon, commanding the highest echelons of imperial service, and their Indian friends and allies had other ideological agendas that contributed unevenly and equally dramatically to the alteration of the material landscape. In his travels in the presidency Lord Napier had observed that the 'beautiful arts of this country' were falling into 'a pitiable state'. He rebuked unrefined official policy with the statement that: 'Art is not a capital interest, but it is an interest. A civilised Government cannot in the present time neglect any branch of human thought or

[91] In England, resistance to this model of utilitarian practice was conducted by the Pugin group and other splinter groups like the art faction in later years. See Mark Crinson and Jules Lubbock, *Architecture, Art or Profession?* p. 51.

[92] Philip Davies, *Splendours of the Raj*, p. 193.

culture with impunity. Even in a commercial point of view, beauty is becoming every day a larger element in value.'[93]

The implication of the system described above was portentous for architectural design. Amongst the Europeans who set the normative standards in the PWD, architectural design was a self-taught affair, usually from pattern books. It is easy to think that in the world of soldiers and Company men, who dominated the mainstream of Indian architecture, there was little room for the artistic niceties of the cosmopolitan world of European art academies and institutes. It is just as easy to forget that design was controlled by a tiny minority, of whom many were scholars, with élite roots.[94] If architectural design held no special place in the training of engineers, it is worth asking how they approached building design? The answer is that they used type plans.

As early as 1834 standard plans had been utilised for military barracks, with the Military Board advising that no departure could take place without sanction from the Governor-General.[95] In 1864 the Government of India promulgated a PWD code advising executive engineers that 'no variation of a standard plan ought, on any account to be carried out without previous departmental permission'.[96] The earliest PWD manuals were careful to delineate their own notions of 'beauty inherent in a utility conscious building design'. The official viewpoint warned against confusion of beauty with the mere presence of ornament. 'A building utterly devoid of ornament may possess great beauty architecturally from the perfection of its proportions generally; the variety of outline resulting from the projection of some of its parts and the difference of relief.'[97]

It was inevitable that the minimalist design theories of army and Company officials made up the core aesthetic and spatial patterns of PWD building. Artistic effect and technology were very highly rated in the departmental design world but they were driven by new forces, incubated and empowered in the colonial context. What was at stake in these debates was the very nature

[93] Minute No. 97, 18 November 1868, 'On Captain Lyon's Photographic Illustrations of National Art in Southern India, and the expediency of restoring the most interesting examples of Secular Architecture in the Madras Presidency', in *Minutes Recorded by the Rt. Hon. Francis Baron Lord Napier and Ettrick, K.T. During the Administration of the Government of the Madras Presidency from 1866–72* (Madras, 1872).

[94] The Bombay Government, for instance, bought the services of George Gilbert Scott, paid for by Sir Cowasjee Readymoney and Premchand Roychand. Scott's University Library is regarded as one of his most outstanding designs. See Philip Davies, *Splendours of the Raj*, p. 160.

[95] Peter Scriver, 'Rationalisation', p. 427. His is the only study of the subject but it lacks an Indian dimension.

[96] Code XIX, IV.17, P/250/56, 24 February 1864, MPPWD.

[97] Quoted in Peter Scriver, 'Rationalisation', p. 491.

of the departmental canon itself. Standard plans, technologies, and aesthetics, (lifted partly from pattern books used by PWD secretaries and the senior-most staff), and practical Indian experience were moulded into a homogenous aesthetic canon. Conventional professional ideals of autonomy and innovation were rejected in favour of a design method of conformity and order. The official record supports the view that standard designs had the more important function of serving to proscribe designs which were technically or canonically unacceptable.[98]

The bare PWD canon often led to 'oblong flat roofed structures with whitewashed walls and wooden architraves, defaced by being harnessed to Grecian porticoes'.[99] Political attitudes of Company officials were eloquently lampooned by satirists like John Norton, an eminent lawyer who declared that 'calculators compute them out of their senses. The jester and the buffoon shame them out of everything grand and elevated. Littleness in object and in means, to them appears soundness and sobriety.'[100] His caricature captured the frugal tenor of Company thinking. Such sentiments, coupled with military demand for precision and uniformity, constituted the intellectual well-spring of PWD design philosophy. But the military aesthetic was not without links to an avant-garde thirteenth-century European architecture with definite intellectual leanings. It bore affinities to the bare, severe styles generated in England by John Soane and the extravagant 'visionary' designs of Etienne-Louis Boullée and Claude-Nicolas Ledoux whose ideas entered the nineteenth century with the work of Jean-Nicolas-Louis Durand. From them, Durand developed a normative and economic building typology in the service of Republican France, disseminated by the influential I'scole Polytechnique.[101] James Curl believes that the French style and mode of building was free of overt clerical and aristocratic association and hence found favour with the avant-garde, many of whom were Freemasons who had lacked political clout in the previous century.[102]

Thus, almost beyond the reach of the mainstream military-technocratic intellectual fraternity, less mundane priorities choreographed the design of important public buildings. Influential governors, senior civil servants and high ecclesiasts formed another forum, dispensing

[98] Ibid., p. 509.

[99] Robert Chisholm, *Napier Museum, Trevandrum*, RIBA Pamphlet, 1873. The polemical attack on PWD architecture began in earnest when Purdon Clarke, Keeper of Indian Art at the SKM took up the defence of native architecture against the tyranny of the PWD in a lecture at the Royal Society of Arts in May 1884. The Indian Orientalists launched *The Journal of Indian Art* in 1886. For a recent account of this polemic, see Giles Tillotson, *The Tradition of Indian Architecture*, chapter 3.

[100] John Bruce Norton, *The Rebellion in India*, p. 222.

[101] For how the French twisted the authority of tradition see Werner Szambien, 'Durand and the Continuity of Tradition', in Robin Middleton (ed.), *The Beaux-Arts and Nineteenth-century French Architecture* (London, 1984).

[102] This view is mentioned by James Stevens Curl, *The Art and Architecture of Free Masonry* (London, 1991), p. 229.

patronage and espousing a different, more familiar architectural idiom. Due to their intimacy with local networks, the views of powerful civil servants, who briefed largely ignorant incoming governors, were often the most decisive lobby. They operated behind-the-scenes, using their knowledge to sway governors and implement vested interests.

Philip Davies identified two aesthetic trends in colonial architecture—'aesthetic imperialist' and 'native revivalist'.[103] At the simplest level the nomenclature makes the directions of the two schools obvious: one veered towards imperial Roman themes and the other wished to protect the living tradition of the Indian master craftsman, or revive the now dead 'Indian' tradition. It is usually assumed that the British led both tendencies, with no recorded Indian participation.

Unconventional 'Aesthetic Imperialists': The 'Native Revivalists'

As discussed earlier, the material presence of an intriguing Indo-European architecture of Indian royalty suggests that a dynamic Indian architectural discourse stood behind Ram Raz's *Essay on the Architecture of the Hindus*, published by the Royal Asiatic Society of Great Britain and Ireland in 1834. His book is a rare reminder of the hidden presence of an early regional patriotism woven into colonial and nationalist discourses.[104] As the first chapter showed, one agenda of the orientalist circle around the Madras College was to seek authority over the production of knowledge of southern India. The art wing of this tendency, self-consciously expressed itself with the 'rediscovery' of the Amaravati marbles. The genealogy of the sculptures, prior to their arrival for display in London, yields a potted history of the Madras art orientalists' ascendant interest in art. The period between 1857 and 1867 saw their intellectual contributions fêted in London and Paris. We can surmise that metropolitan colonial intellectuals participated in the competition within orientalist circles.

Governor Charles Trevelyan made significant inroads into the material culture of Madras. His life was officially eulogised in 1859 by J.D. Bourdillon, Secretary to the Government and by a more recent administrator, B.S. Baliga.[105] Trevelyan's fourteen-month reign could hardly have been regarded as successful unless he had excellent advisers, responsive to Indo-British

[103] Philip Davies, *Splendours of the Raj*, p. 192.

[104] Christopher Bayly, *The Origins of Nationality*, chapter 2.

[105] J.D. Bourdillon, *Trevelyan's Administration of Madras*, cited in B.S. Baliga, 'Sir Charles Trevelyan, Governor of Madras 1859–60'. Bourdillon was Secretary to the Government.

demands. Lord Napier, Governor of Madras from 1866 to 1872, took his cue from this zealous gubernatorial tradition. He acquired the aura of his illustrious predecessors by traversing Munrovian terrain, championing the theme of Indian agency and cultural revival.[106] Napier's stirring speech on 'Fine Arts of India', made in Travancore in 1871, exhorting Indians to return to their native arts, is almost canonical in art-historical writing, but little is known of the wider canvas of his views on Indian architecture.[107] Napier did not enter an art vacuum in Madras. His confident call for a 'revival of native art' and his vision of imperial architecture were the culmination of the intellectual traditions and international achievements of the Madras art orientalists. They drew upon a pre-colonial and colonial, shared, Indo-British interest in art.

The study of Indian architecture as an academic discipline, conducted by western art historians in European academies, had not begun in Napier's day. State backing for recording Indian architectural antiquities was an incipient phenomenon. Captain Gill, his Indian assistants and his Camera Lucida were recording the Ajanta caves in 1844.[108] In 1849, spurred by the Madras Literary Society, the government called for information on ancient buildings and cave temples.[109] More extensive interest in Indian monuments began in 1856 when Linnaeus Tripe was appointed official photographer to the presidency. Tripe confidently spelt out his primary aim as follows: 'to secure before they disappear the objects of the Presidency that are interesting to the Antiquary, Architect, Sculptor, Mythologist and Historian'.[110] Shortly thereafter, in 1857, the government commissioned a report on *Ancient Architectural Remains*,[111] and Captain Lyon and his wife were engaged to undertake a photographic record of southern Indian monuments.[112] Furthermore, the Supreme Government had liberally spent revenue on the repair of monuments at Mysore, Agra and Delhi 'without any view to utility whatever, merely for their historic association and artistic beauty'. Led by this precedent, in 1868 Lord

[106] See Alexander Arbuthnot, *Major General Sir Thomas Munro*. Arbuthnot was a dedicated admirer of Lord Napier. See Alexander Arbuthnot, *Memories of Rugby,* chapter xii.

[107] He made his speech on the 'Fine Arts of India' in Travancore in 1871, see Tapati Guha-Thakurta, *The Making of a New Indian Art*, p. 109.

[108] 14 January 1845, No. 789, MPPC, TNA.

[109] See Circular calling for Information on Ancient Buildings, Cave Temples etc., Madras, 1849, V/27/941/2.

[110] Janet Dewan, 'Linnaeus Tripe; Documenting South Indian Architecture', *History of Photography*, 13, 2 (April–June 1989), pp. 147–54. Tripe published his work in 1860 entitled *Photographic Views of Tanjore and Trivady*.

[111] A copy of the report for the year 1857–58 was requested by the Madras Literary Society in GO 1–2, 1 June 1860, MPPWD, TNA. The request implies that these were annual reports.

[112] British Library Photograph Catalogue, OIOC, Edmund David Lyon, 1868.

Napier requested the restoration of the most interesting examples of secular architecture in southern India.[113]

James Fergusson, returning to England after eight years of business and travel between 1835 and 1842, had laid open the virgin field of Indian architecture. A man of no false modesty, Fergusson advertised his self-perception as the supreme expert by announcing that he was studying the Ajanta Caves, not through inscriptions as Dr. Bird in Bombay was struggling to do, but instead:

> I had other advantages for prosecuting the inquiry that have fallen to the lot of few; for in the various journeys I undertook I was enabled to visit almost all the rock-cut Temples of India, from those of Cuttack and Mahavellipore on the east coast, to those of Ellora and Salsette on the western side; and there are few buildings or cities of importance in India which I have not at one time or other been able to visit and examine. I had besides the advantage, that as all my journies were undertaken for the sole purpose of antiquarian research, I was enabled to devote my whole and undivided attention to the subject, and all my notes and sketches were made with only one object in view,...and none that I know of, have been able to embrace so extensive a field of research as I have.[114]

The new architectural expert had to have visited the building and recorded aspects of its physical form. As we know, Fergusson's prodigious, pseudo-scientific endeavours gained him access to the high-art circles of the Home Government. As early as 1865 Fergusson claimed that 'the study of architecture may be raised from dry details of measurement to the dignity of a historical science'.[115] Apart from Fergusson's books, Gujarat and Bijapur were the very first Indian states whose architectural remains were photographed and published as 'detailed monographic studies'. *The Architectural Illustrations of the Principal Mahometan Buildings of Beejapore* appeared in 1859.[116] Further volumes on Bijapur, Ahmedabad, the capital of Gujarat, and the Mysore State, were published in the 1860s. These were Indo-British ventures; overseen by the Governor of Bombay, Sir Bartle Frere, funded by two 'native gentlemen' and written by British soldiers, Captain Meadows-Taylor and Captain Hart. The former wanted his countrymen to appreciate the intellect, taste and high power of art and execution of the Bijapur builders, who therefore could not be barbarians. For nineteenth-century Britons, Ahmedabad and Bijapur 'loomed above all the others'. Ahmedabad was special on account of its Hindu-Muslim fusion architecture, where Muslim rulers had adapted Hindu architecture to suit their own needs.

[113] GO No. 97, 18 November 1868, 'On Captain Lyon's '.

[114] James Fergusson, *On the Rock-Cut Temples of India* (London, 1845), p. 3.

[115] James Fergusson, *History of Architecture in All Countries from Earliest Times to the Present Day*, preface of first edn., p. xi.

[116] James Fergusson and P.D. Hart (eds.), *Architectural Illustrations of the Principal Mahometan Buildings of Beejapore* (London, 1859) and Philip Meadows-Taylor, *Architecture at Beejapore, Architectural Notes by James Fergusson* (London, 1866).

Bijapur impressed because of the consummate skill and scientific knowledge of the region's dome builders.

Imagine—An 'Indian' Architecture

Two ideas of far-ranging impact emerged from such studies. First, Fergusson imagined a delightfully neat, communal classification for 'Indian' architecture, founded on ethnology. It signalled a bid for leadership of knowledge in the history of architecture. Second, following Fergusson's categories, the British expressed affinity for something they called 'Indian Saracenic' architecture, incommensurable with something they called 'Hindu' architecture. Metcalf believed that for Europeans, 'Muslims were always, unlike Hindus, a people to be feared; and much Orientalist scholarship was directed to reducing this, "menacing orient" to manageable proportions.'[117] But Muslim architecture was nevertheless more familiar and aesthetically satisfying than the barbaric architecture of the Hindus. State backing for this peculiar, misinformed discourse on Indian architecture, reformulated as 'history', was not long in arriving. In the meantime, Sir Bartle Frere and his wealthy Indian patrons had set about the physical transformation of Bombay on a stunning scale. Financial independence secured for them the luxury of ignoring Calcutta and the Home Government. Indo-Britons set the standards of taste. In this way, Bombay developed its own tropical Gothic architecture closely modelled on monumental public building in London.

After the 1860s, colonial civic priorities produced a spate of new building types including the office, post office, railway station, school, law courts, university administration buildings, town hall and PWD headquarters. Imperial governors and PWD technocrats plunged into the material production of the politically created 'India' through its drains, parks, sanitation and water supply, harbours, light-houses, roads, bridges, railways, dams, canals, sluices and reservoirs, schools and post offices—all deemed as hallmarks of the modern. The new material intra-connections assured British India of a visually homogenous second-tier public architecture, accomplished with standard plans and, because of it, an almost palpable territorial identity.

Native leaders who had funded the building of eighteenth-century Madras were no longer active, but temples and mosques were well maintained and embellished throughout the period. The development of urban Madras was largely state-led and -funded and the PWD was the leading institution in its material transformation. Prestige and power were expressed not only via the modernity of utilitarian building but also through other highly visible signs of material

[117] Thomas Metcalf, *An Imperial Vision,* chapter 2 and p. 40.

prosperity. In Madras this process began in 1859, soon after the 'Rebellion', when Charles Trevelyan gave the order to tear down the ramparts of Black Town and with the making of the People's Park at the bend of the Cooum river. Such activity took place against a background where the Hyderabad, Mysore and Travancore royalty, encircling British South India, patronised an independent stream of political modernisation and hybrid western architecture rivalling British India.[118] Planned urban development in Madras was relatively limited. Nonetheless it was marked by an outstanding feature which made it politically and aesthetically unique and ideologically ambiguous. Madras officialdom, though anxious to follow other presidencies in fostering urban development, was disinclined to imitate their aesthetic precedents for prestigious civic building. They self-consciously and daringly abandoned a 200-year commitment to classical architecture by choosing to experiment with the indigenous architectural canon.

Lord Napier, a keen follower of artistic trends in European capitals and aware of Layard's and Fergusson's thwarted plans for a designer London, was sensitive to the power of architectural statement. The political and artistic currents from London, Egypt and the eastern empire converged in his thinking. He went so far as to advocate that the Supreme Government adopt the 'Mussulman' style as the 'official style of architecture'. Napier went on exploit his high office to build a southern Indian interpretation of such an official architecture in Madras.[119] Thomas Metcalf made the astute argument that by the time Fergusson published his *History of Indian and Eastern Architecture* in 1876,

> the British knew, or thought they knew what India's architecture consisted of. They had, they believed, brought India's past history almost fully to light and had discovered the categories to order that past. In so doing, its rulers [i.e. the British] found a way to control that past and hence India's present, for their own purposes.[120]

Napier used the authority of Fergusson's ethno-architectural assertions to incorporate ethnicity into the imperial discourse on the new southern architecture. Pivotal to Napier's decision was the counsel and support of the Madras intelligentsia and the Chepauk Palace. The exercise also revealed a new source of pleasure opening up to high-flying official Britons. The entire corpus of Indian architectural aesthetics was slowly but surely becoming their playground.

[118] Giles Tillotson, *The Tradition of Indian Architecture*, chapter 3. It is also interesting to see the building programmes of the South Indian zamindari nobility like the Rajas of Ramnad, Sivaganga, Pudukottai, Ettiyappuram and Udaiyarpalaiyam who built in mixed styles and maintained their own teams of building experts. See K. Rajayyan, *Administration and Society in the Carnatic 1701–1801* (Tirupati, 1969), p. 33; C. Vadivelu, *The Aristocracy of Southern India*, vol. 2 (2 vols., Delhi, 1984), and Pamela Price, *Kingship and Political Practice in Colonial India*, for some description of the subject.

[119] Lord Napier, 'Architecture for India', *The Builder*, 10 September 1870, pp. 722–23.

[120] Thomas Metcalf, *An Imperial Vision*, p. 24.

5

Coveting a Forbidden Palace

The Board of Revenue Building 1859–70

A Forgotten Palace

There are several reasons why the Chepauk court and Palace continue to remain in shadow, both in the colonial and modern histories of the presidency capital. A visitor to Madras in 1811, explains one of them:

> We saw the Nabob's or Chepaux palace, at a distance, but no Europeans, under any pretence, are admitted within its walls, without the express permission of the English governor. An officer's guard continually resides within the precincts, in order to prevent improper intrusion of any sort, designing natives having more than once endeavoured to promote dissatisfaction and intrigue against the Company's government.[1]

Other reasons for the neglect of the palace are more recent in origin. Together with nationalist politics there may exist a sectarian desire to mask a conspicuous reminder of Muslim rule and 'Islamicate' culture in the capital city of a modern state espousing a Tamil 'Hindu' identity.

To the gaze of the early nineteenth-century visitor, the palace was a forbidden, hidden landmark in the city. A 'retreat embosomed in trees',[2] enclosed by an imposing high wall, redolent of wealth, intrigue, durbars and lavish entertainment. A brooding sentinel, it stood in between FSG and Government House—with the imprisoned nawabs cocooned within.

[1] *A Visit to Madras*, p. 16. Also see fn. 6, chapter 1.

[2] James Wathen, *Journal of a Voyage*, p. 32.

Chepauk Palace was an inescapable reminder of contested power. Its aura of kingship was legitimised by an older Indian order inaccessible to the colonial state. The contrasting built forms of palace, fort and Government House locked in tight physical embrace, mocked British claims to supremacy.

British involvement with the palace, too, remains a forgotten chapter of imperial building. Under Napier's direction, the Madras Government destroyed the palace and all it stood for, not by razing the buildings, but by transforming them into offices for the Board of Revenue, where haughty imperial agents ran the most powerful state department in South India. The Board of Revenue Building came into being as a result of the state's decision to remodel the *diwan khana* audience hall of the nawab's palace, to serve its expanding spatial needs. It was also at Chepauk that the new state began a series of major alterations to the spatial configuration of the urban landscape. These transformations were inflected by the intellectual concerns of the Madras school of orientalists; who, in line with intellectuals in the sister capitals, were also negotiating the political and ideological contours of nation, culture and empire. But it was in the south that cultural sharing gave rise to a completely new official architecture. The pleasure and subtleties of this culture sharing, whilst self-evident in the built forms, are otherwise elusive, for the familiar reason that documentary evidence is sparse and entirely British.

This chapter tells the story of an architectural pleasure whose range was steadily expanding. Not only did Britons now have access to the intellectual pleasure of inventing a history and aesthetics of Indian architecture; they also developed an unfounded confidence in their mastery of this genre. It was this that encouraged some Britons to freely experiment with Indian aesthetics in built form. The first tentative foray in this direction can be tracked in two of the earliest imperial buildings to emerge on the Chepauk site: the Revenue Board Building and the Tower.

Betrayal

As has been mentioned earlier, a modern history of the place of the house of Carnatic in South Indian history is awaited. At present, the more popular view is that it was a client dynasty, first to the Nizams of Hyderabad and later to the British. By 1710 the Naviyat line of imperial Mughal office-holders, who had served Deccani sultans, began to control a line of fortresses in the Carnatic, beginning with Vellore, the most heavily fortified of these citadels. They were ambitious builders, investing heavily in fortifications, mosques and new towns. Muhammad Ali, Nawab of the Carnatic, ruled from his base at Arcot where he built a new fort with palaces, gardens and mosques. He received Mughal *sanad*s granting him the prestigious new titles of

Amir al-Hind and Walajah, in 1766. In 1767 he built himself a lavish new residence next door to FSG, in Madras.

I have chosen to place the eighteenth-century cultural response of the Carnatic house to the British, in the same mould as that of their royal neighbours in Mysore, Hyderabad and Travancore; who were themselves engaged in state-building activities that earned them a degree of distance and independence from British dominance. British sources recorded the mixed ethnic composition of Chepauk courtiers; the administration was headed by a mixture of Hindus, Muslims, Deccanis and north Indians, of whom the outstanding examples were Avanigadeli Venkatachellum, Abdul Rashid Khan and Sayid Asim Khan: three principal advisors to the nawab, present at all discussions.[3] In pursuance of southern legitimacy Muhammad Ali Walajah practised a statecraft and court culture that transcended ethnicity. He supplemented dynastic connections with the Islamic kingdoms of Lucknow and Hyderabad by forging links with the great South Indian temples at Tirupati, Chidambaram, and Srirangam; in doing so he was seeking a reputation as the 'ruler who fulfilled the standard dharmic obligation to protect and endow Hindu holy places'.[4] Contact with the British, however, brought to a head an altogether different set of challenges to existing modes of governance; never so apparent as when the nawab expressed bewilderment as to why the British refused to understand that although he gave them the right to enjoy the benefits from the land he gave them, it did not give them sovereignty over his subjects.[5] It was also true that as a code of honour, the nawab accepted responsibility for meeting the debts of his courtiers, if such agreements were made in his name.

East India Company servants, who had discovered that private sources of wealth and power were far more lucrative than their salaries, joined Muhammad Ali's state-building activities. It was this Indo-British state building that frightened parliament and led to the disbanding of subsequent British subsidiary alliances with native rulers. Muhammad Ali's son, titled Umdat-ul-Umara, was an unconcealed Anglophobe, but his reign was shortlived, from 1795 to 1801. His death gave the British the opportunity to end the farce of a dual government in the presidency. In order to secure law and order and protect the treasures of the palace, the British government, through the Governor- General, Lord Wellesley, (who was in residence in

[3] J.D. Gurney, 'The Debts of the Nawab of Arcot' (University of Oxford, D. Phil., 1968), p. 20.

[4] This argument is presented by Susan Bayly, *Saints, Goddesses and Kings: Muslims and Christians in South Indian Society 1700–1900* (Cambridge, 1989), p. 165.

[5] Paterson Diaries, MSS Eur. E 379/4, p. 87. Also see, C.S. Srinivasachari, *The Inwardness of British Annexations in India. Sir William Meyer Endowment Lectures 1948–49* (Madras, no date).

Madras) ordered Lord Clive, Governor of Madras, to assume control of the Carnatic. Clive personally led the troops who camped in the Chepauk parade ground to disarm the nawab's forces. Umdat-ul-Umara's son, Ali Hussain, rejected Clive's iniquitous offer of handing over the revenue and military and civil administration of the Carnatic. He was imprisoned, his forts sequestered, and the rebellion of the southern Carnatic was quelled. The nawab was targeted and vilified as a decadent and corrupt ruler whose court was rife with peculation.

The fate of the dynasty was sealed when the king-makers bestowed the title on a more pliant cousin, Azim-ud-daula. In return for the title he agreed to receive a mere one-fifth of the revenue of the Carnatic. The British had almost achieved what they had striven for so long: the Carnatic was annexed.[6] The Secretary of State, Lord Castlereagh, who orchestrated the crushing of the Irish Rebellion, despite confirming Wellesley's plan, had grave misgivings over it.[7] The final phase of the plan of 1801 to usurp the government of the Carnatic had to await Nawab Ghulam Muhammed's death, without issue, in 1855. Then the Government of India was quick to rule that the treaty, made with Nawab Azim-ud-daula in 1801 was of a personal character—it was only a matter of grace that its terms had been extended to his successors. Once again physical force removed the regent Prince Azim Jah from the palace; all it required was one British regiment, one native infantry and the governor's bodyguard. Lord Dalhousie, the Governor-General, and Lord Harris, Governor of Madras, were anxious to root out the pestilential threat to British interests.

> serious moral evil is caused by the continuance of the pageant of effete royalty.... And political inconvenience might at any time arise from the existence of a court at the Presidency which, though destitute of authority, must be inimical or at all events, discontented and capable of being made a nucleus of intrigue.[8]

From London, the Court of Directors ordered confiscation of the royal home. The property went into receivership, awaiting sale. Prince Azim Jah applied to the Calcutta Legislative Council to keep the property in reserve until parliament made a decision regarding his challenge to the Company's right to alienate his ancestral domains—'hereditary palaces and time honoured elements of pride and ancestral dignity belonging to the royal house'.[9] The Court peremptorily ordered the government to buy the palace.[10] The pile of abandoned buildings sold by public

[6] H.D. Love, *Vestiges of Old Madras*, vol. 3, p. 529.

[7] C.S. Srinivasachari, *The Inwardness*, p. 87.

[8] B.S. Baliga, 'British Relations'.

[9] *Madras Times*, 30 August 1858.

[10] *Madras Times*, 1 September 1858.

auction fell to the government for Rs. 5.5 lakh. The arms and historical pictures were also taken by the government. This act of aggression completely destroyed a repository of Indo-Islamic culture and an aristocratic way of life.

The Court and government desired to give a handsome allowance to the king and continue the salaries of the principal officers of his household for the rest of their lives. A reluctant nawab accepted a minor 15-gun salute and a bodyguard of 50 sepoys. It reduced his status below that of the rulers of Travancore, Mysore, Baroda and Hyderabad (the largest and wealthiest in the subcontinent). In 1866, Lord Napier, Governor of Madras, defended the action of the Home Government as 'just and benevolent'.[11] The family's campaign for restitution, conducted in India and London, failed; the title and assets were never returned. Bowing to pressure, in 1870 Her Majesty decreed that the Prince Regent Azim Jah be accorded the diminutive title, First Nobleman of the Carnatic and the Prince of Arcot.[12] The Carnatic Stipend was fixed at a paltry 1.5 lakh in 1876. An Indian paper denounced the sum as unjust and accused the Company of 'demolish[ing] the House of Carnatic, which had been granted the title of Amir-al-Hind by the Delhi Emperor'. It pointed out that on the eve of Her Majesty's assumption of the title, the Empress of India, the first well-wisher of the British government was the Carnatic family 'by whose instrumentality the foundation of their rule in this part of the empire was strengthened and consolidated'.[13] The famous Arcot diamonds, including five brilliants—three of which are mounted on the Westminster tiara in London—were 'gifted' to Queen Charlotte, wife of George III, of England, by the nawab in 1777. The diamonds presaged the drift of unequal political relationships.

The Madras Government now moved to deny the king a physical presence in Triplicane—his ancestral domain in the city. It insisted that the Shadhi Mahal, another of the king's Triplicane palaces, favoured by him as his new home, was 'not a place fit for the residence of the Prince of Arcot'.[14] Unable to completely suppress the royal house, in 1867, the government agreed to provide a personal residence for the king, in Royapettah, also in Triplicane. Against the king's wishes, however, government architect Robert Chisholm, was given the task of converting the Royapettah police building into a palace, Amir Mahal. Chisholm provided the government

[11] Letter from Napier to Lord Cranborne, 15 August 1866, IOR Negative 11672, Salisbury Collection. An introduction to the subject is given by Barbara Ramusack, *TNCHI, 111.6, The Indian Princes and their States* (Cambridge, 2004) and Ian Copland, *The British Raj and the Indian Princes: Paramountcy in Western India 1857–1930* (Bombay, 1982).

[12] B.S. Baliga, 'British Relations'. This account is marred by an anti-Muslim undercurrent.

[13] *Jaridai-i-Rozgar*, 16 September 1876, and 7 October 1876, Report on Native Newspapers in the Madras Presidency, L/R/5/103.

[14] *Athenaeum*, 19 June 1870. The Nawab was born and bred in Triplicane.

with a set of revised plans in 1873 and building work was underway in 1874.[15] The Amir Mahal design copied Queen Victoria's Italian villa-style home, Osborne House, on the Isle of Wight (see Figs. 62–65).

Following the great Rebellion, the Supreme Government had enacted a policy of conciliating princes and bolstering traditional values. The extensive southern kingdoms of Travancore, Mysore, Hyderabad, and Baroda, notwithstanding internal political turmoil, were not annexed. Instead, royal lineages were actively created, reinstated and protected by the British. Napier's views on the long unsettled and thorny question of the reinstatement of the Rajah of Mysore are telling. He wanted a real sovereign on the Mysore throne, not 'a bogus royal' and one as free as at Travancore.[16] In this case the king-makers, anxious to erase the memory of their vanquished foe Tipu Sultan, were seeking to reinstate a Hindu king. Tipu's sons were ignored in favour of the allegedly legitimate, pre-Tipu, Wodeyar dynasty. It was duly installed. The *parvenu* royals were brought to order under the tutelage of immensely powerful British Residents. In fact, in princely and British India, under the guise of supporting traditional mores, the government nurtured a new tradition of royalty and an Indian Civil Service loyal to its own ideas. David Cannadine has recently suggested that the British Empire of Disraeli,

Figure 62: Amir Mahal Palace, front entrance

[15] See GO 67, 10 July 1873, and for zenana drawings GO 160, 20 November 1874, MPPWD, TNA.

[16] Napier to Lord Cranborne, 24 January 1867, No. 23, Salisbury Collection.

Figure 63: Zenana from palace garden

like that of Wellesley, was built around 'innovation disguised as antiquity'.[17]

The punitive anti-royalist policy favoured in Madras contradicted this general trend, lending credence to the view that despite claims to the contrary, the state still regarded the house of Carnatic as a major threat to the consolidation of its presence in the south. The physical proximity of the palace to the centre of southern British power made its survival untenable. Lord Napier strove to deprive the nawab of all royal etiquette 'hitherto shown him by the governors and curb the royal presence in Madras'. He wanted to 'scatter the Carnatic Tribe in districts where they [had] no interests or considerations whatever connected with the past, they [were] a plague here at Madras'.[18]

Spoils of War

Charles Trevelyan landed in Madras on 28 March 1859. In August he was touring the country as was the fashion.[19] He visited nine districts and was most impressed by the natural and architectural beauty of Trichinopoly (Tiruchirapalli). This prompted him to record that justice had not been done to the architecture of the Hindus; he proposed to redress the neglect by acquiring and preserving the palace of the nawabs. Trevelyan further recommended the

Figure 64: Zenana courtyard, Amir Mahal

[17] David Cannadine, *Ornamentalism: How the British saw their Empire* (London, 2001), p. 148.

[18] Napier to Lord de Grey, 8 May 1866, and Napier to Cranborne, 15 August 1866, Salisbury Collection.

[19] Napier noted this fashion and the government allowance for it in his letter to Lord Cranborne, 14 August 1866, No. 5, Salisbury Collection.

removal of dilapidated fortifications and the laying out of parks and gardens for recreation.[20] Trevelyan was an ardent advocate of state intrusion in the Indian built fabric. Under his auspices several palaces in the south were transformed into office space. By October 1860 the Arcot North Palace at Chandragiri, the Madurai Palace and the Suraj Mahal at Thanjavur had joined the list. With the approval of the Government of India, engineers transformed the palaces for practical use.[21] Throughout the region, forts and palaces abandoned or damaged by war were acquired by decree, or purchased by local governments.

Figure 65: Entrance gateway, Amir Mahal

The Chepauk Palace consisted of a variety of buildings, scattered over a 117-acre site adorned with lakes and parkland. The main entrance was a massive triple arched gateway accommodating guard-rooms, storage for arms and musicians. Colonial records tell us that the ground to the west was taken up by tanks, sepoys' barracks and elephant and slave lines. The saluting battery was on the east. In July 1859 the government considered the repair and alteration of Chepauk Palace for the reception of certain public offices. The largest of the existing structures were two blocks—the northern Humayun Mahal and the southern Khalsa Mahal; the *mahkana* court of justice was adapted for the residence of the Principal of the engineering college. The *toshakhana* treasury, close to the sea, was repaired to accommodate soldier-students and the *diwan khana* audience hall, of the Humayun Mahal received an upper storey, to house the offices of the police commissioner, the consulting engineer and the director of public instruction. In 1860 it was decided to include the Revenue Board in the *diwan khana* of the Humayun Mahal.[22] The Secretary of State and the Government of India

[20] B.S. Baliga, 'Sir Charles Trevelyan'.

[21] See for instance the appropriation of Tirumal Nayaka's Palace for a *zillah* school GO 104–05, 10 November 1859, MPPWD, TNA, or the Chepauk Palace for the engineers' office, GO 93–94, 16 September 1859, MPPWD, TNA.

[22] GO 140–41, 1 June and GO 285–86, 20 October 1860, MPPWD, TNA. It is possible to gain a clear idea of the change of use proposed for the spaces. Court houses were the priority.

were both informed of the Madras Government's anxiety to speed up building 'to avoid the continuance of the heavy expense of providing separate offices in private houses in different parts of the town'.[23]

'Fantastic but Agreeable Native style'—Chepauk Palace

The PWD plans and sections of 1859 (see Fig. 67) show the *diwan khana* as a single-storey building, where rooms are arranged on three sides (or four), around a central space, similar to a courtyard. It is impossible to say with any certainty what the building looked like prior to alteration, but it is possible that the central space was the usual double height durbar hall surrounded by galleries and multi-storeyed corner pavilions. The alterations proposed by the government architect added an entire upper floor surrounding the central space. The new floor was given a classical façade of Tuscan pilasters, and a flat roof with a parapet (see Fig. 72). The drawings depict both floors with similar façades. A tiled roof verandah was proposed for the inside of the new courtyard at the upper level.[24] Today this building lacks a double height durbar hall. It contains several rows of large brick columns 20 feet high, 5 feet wide, and placed at 30-feet intervals. It is likely that iron columns and wood beams were introduced to support the new upper floors in 1859. In 1862 the government laid out Rs. 2,200 for levelling and laying out the grounds surrounding the Chepauk Palace and *diwan khana* and for deepening and cleaning the tanks and defining the roads. Earthworks were undertaken to turf or level the sides of the tanks and Casserania and other seeds were planted on the sides of the road.[25]

The architectural aesthetic of the two-storey Khalsa Mahal (see Fig. 66) which the British now called the palace, served as the stylistic inspiration for the extensive remodelling of the *diwan khana* of the Humayun Mahal, undertaken during Napier's regime which, together with a palatial new entrance block on the eastern side, became the Revenue Board building (see Fig. 79). Unfortunately, since English sources have not yet yielded a clear account of the architectural character of the palace as a whole; it remains surrounded in controversy. In order to clarify this issue, I have tried to recover the physical form of the palace on the eve of its transfer to the British. Colonial historian H.D. Love (1913) and modern anthropologist Susan Bayly (1989) assigned the designs of the buildings of the Walajah period of 1768, to Company

[23] GO 18–19, 1 December 1859, MPPWD, TNA.

[24] GO 18–19, 10 December 1859, MPPWD, TNA. This is a rare instance where the drawings are attached to the text. A colour code differentiates the old from the new in the original drawings.

[25] GO 190, 13 August 1862, MPPWD, TNA.

Figure 66: Palace of the Nawab of Carnatic in Madras, c. 1851, showing dome in the distance

Architect, Paul Benfield.[26] They assumed the designs were in classical mode.[27] George Willison's portrait of *Muhammad Ali Khan, Nawab of Arcot, with attendants*, c. 1775, affirms their contention. The Nawab was shown standing inside the palace:

he is virtually enveloped in a large drape or curtain that cascades down in sluggish folds. A rounded pillar soars upwards and beside it is the half semi-circle of a huge archway. Two servants, watched by a major domo bend low and beyond the archway is a hint of palm trees.[28]

Willison repeated many of the conventions used by Tilly Kettle, in his portrait of the nawab done a few years earlier. This raises doubts as to whether the grand setting of Willison's portrait was an exaggeration of the standard fare of architectural motifs, deployed by the portrait painter, rather than an accurate rendering of the palace (see Figure 1, for Willison's later portrait of the Nawab). George Chinnery, however, was eyewitness to the durbar of 1805. His sketch, *The Durbar of Azim-ud-Daula, 'Feby. 18. 1805'* is probably a more accurate rendering of one of the durbar halls of the palace (see Fig. 68). Chinnery drew plain lofty round archways, but made no definite identification of the room.[29]

[26] Benfield's financial dealings were unscrupulous and the durbar wanted to break all contact with him. J.D. Gurney, 'Debts of the Nawab', p. 252.

[27] H.D. Love said of the palace, 'the architect [was] not known' but speculated that it was Benfield, *Vestiges*, vol. 2, p. 612. For Bayly's views see fn. 38.

[28] Mildred Archer, *India and British Portraiture 1770–1825* (London, 1979), col. plate II.

[29] Patrick Conner, *George Chinnery 1774–1852 : Artist of India and the China Coast* (Suffolk, 1993), p. 80.

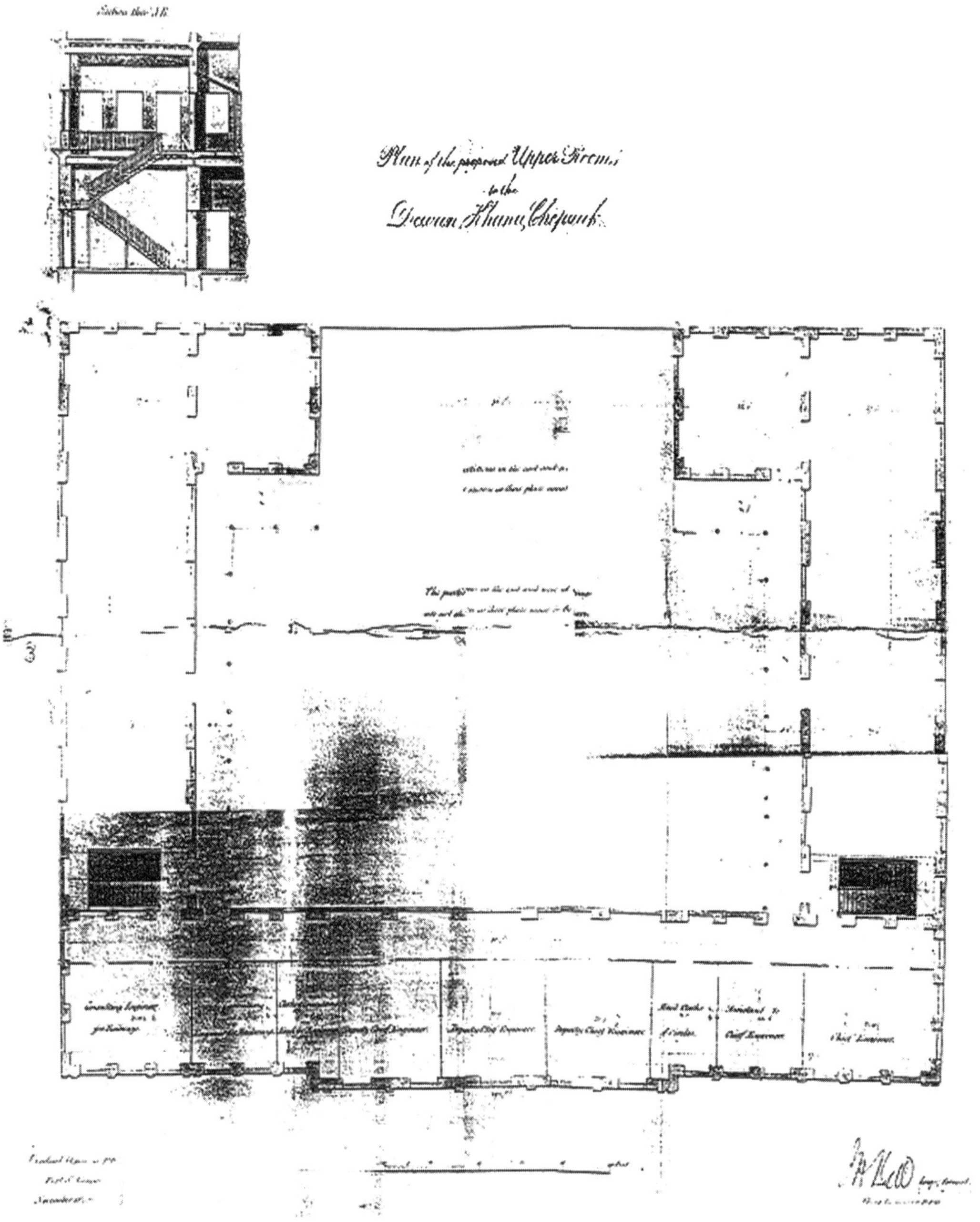

Figure 67: Plan of proposed upper rooms to the *diwan khana*, Chepauk, Central Office PWD, Fort St. George, 1859

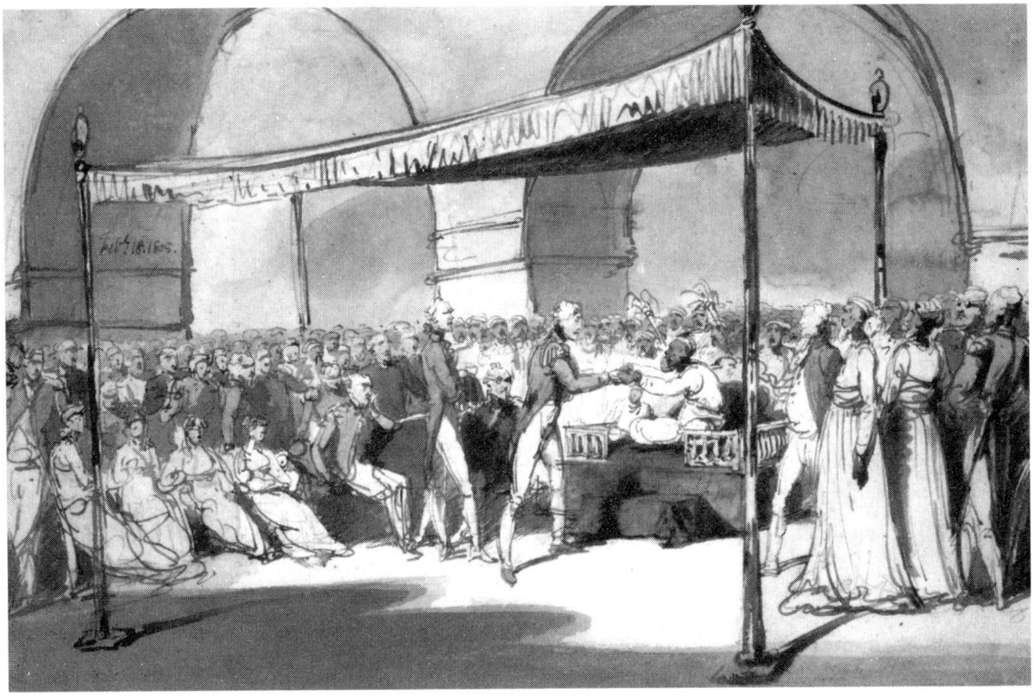

Figure 68: Major General Arthur Wellesley being received in durbar at Chepauk Palace by Azim-ud-Daula, Nawab of the Carnatic, 18 February 1805, George Chinnery, watercolour

The pompous and opinionated aristocratic traveller, Lord Valentia, peeved that he was not invited to Chepauk, had to engineer a meeting with the Nawab Azim-ud-Daula, around the time the latter was placed on the *musnud* throne by Wellesley and simultaneously made a virtual prisoner of the British. Valentia recorded a muted European presence. The nawab and his courtiers were very handsomely dressed, and the nawab used an interpreter, though he spoke English well. He enquired after the King and Queen, and a picture of the Prince of Wales by Hopner adorned one side of the durbar hall. Valentia speculated that a British officer designed the hall. He gave no clue as to the building style. It was, he said, 'extremely handsome, of large dimension and divided by pillars' though unfinished and if it was ever finished 'it will be the handsomest durbar I have seen in India'.[30] And Valentia, mindful of status and not easily given to praise, noticed such things.

Henry Love, in his description of Frederick Christian Lewis' picture of the *Installation of Nawab Ghulam Muhammad Ghaus Khan by Lord Elphinstone in 1842*, wrote that it took place in

[30] Viscount Valentia, *Voyages*, vol. 3, p. 384.

Figure 69: Stone columns behind entrance number 2 in the former Old Palace

the 'Durbar Hall' of the nawab's palace at Chepauk: 'The hall is of great size and height and displays crenellated Saracenic arches carried on massive stone columns grouped in fours...through an open archway on the right are seen the Beach, the Fort, and the ships in the roads dressed with flags.'[31] He continued that 'the artist must have drawn largely on his imagination for his architectural details' because the hall, at the time of installation, was probably in much the same condition as when Valentia visited it in 1804. Love implies that Lewis was not present and drew from descriptions, although Lewis's was the later version. Lewis may have known of crenellated arches in South Indian palaces from Daniells' published drawings of the Madurai Palace.

It is mysterious that there is no extant building with which to reconcile class-conscious Valentia's generous claim, or Lewis's crenellated arches. There are extant, twelve massive two-feet square stone columns (see Fig. 69), with lightly

Figure 70: Roof of Old Palace

[31] H.D. Love, *Descriptive List of Pictures in Government House and the Banqueting Hall Madras* (Madras, 1903). The picture was in Government House, Lower Hall, North Side, p. 90. A print can be seen in the Fort Museum, Chennai.

carved stone capitals, rising to a height of around twelve feet, in one of the buildings adjacent to the domed Khalsa Mahal—the structure denoted as the Chepauk Palace in the 1860s (see Figs. 66 and 70). The grandeur of the pillars and the fact that they are of an expensive material like stone, not used for structural purposes elsewhere in the complex, raises the possibility that this may be the building Lewis drew, from a description of it. And it could have been the building Valentia saw, although it had been 'finished' by 1842. There remains a less likely possibility that this was a pavilion erected solely to receive Europeans, as found in the Padmanabhapuram Palace, in Trevandrum.

On the other hand, there is no good reason to doubt the existence of several halls of audience, of different sizes, materials and styles. In fact, it is certain that Umdat-ul-Umara held audience in different halls at different times in the day.[32] John Murray's *Handbook for India*, 1859, noted that the palace was 'formerly visited by those who wished to see a specimen of a Muhammadan *chieftain's* [italics added] court in India'. The 'Darba' or reception room was described as 'large and handsome and adorned with pillars.' I suspect this note was lifted from Valentia, except of course that Valentia would never have paid much attention to a mere 'chieftain'.

Susan Bayly wrote in 1989 that Muhammad Ali accepted the view that 'an Italianate neo-classicism—or at least an exuberant approximation of the neo-classical —was the proper style for a princely residence'. He apparently filled the 'vast neo-Palladian mahals of the palace with English furniture'.[33] Thomas Metcalf, writing in the same year as Bayly, was unconcerned with her sources. He wrote that the palace, 'a massive structure prominently placed in Madras, was of "Saracenic" design, which remained until 1855, the focus of a continuing Islamic court'.[34] According to Metcalf, in 1795 the most impressive parts of the palace comprised the large single storey *diwan khana*, and a two storey *Kalsa* (elsewhere Khalsa) *Mahal*. Other distinctive features were the massive triple-arched gateway at the end of the Walajah road, an octagonal bathing pavilion, and the *Hasht Bangla,* Marine Villa. Only the Marine Villa was built in a clear Indo-European style. Metcalf attributes its design to Paul Benfield whose style 'did not involve a self-conscious "revival" of "native art"', unlike the Indian 'revival' the British were to shortly

[32] This sense of the multi-purpose space where the king, prince and princesses held different courts is present throughout the *Swanihat*. See for instance Muhammad Karim, *Swanihat-I-Mumtaz*, vol. 1 (2 vols., Madras, 1940–44), p. 50 or p. 88.

[33] Her argument that Muhammad Ali accepted the Italianate neo-classicism as the proper style for a palace is based on the example of the Lucknow nawabs. It is possible that she overstates the case for European architectural influence at the Chepauk court. Susan Bayly, *Saints, Goddesses and Kings*, p. 169.

[34] Thomas Metcalf, *An Imperial Vision*, p. 59.

invent in architecture.[35] In balance, the cumulative evidence supports the idea that several architectural styles and designers were used by successive nawabs, who constructed the palace complex over a period of 80 years.

According to the Nawab Umdat-ul-Umara's chronicle *Swanihat-i-Mumtaz,* he assumed the *musnud* in 1795. Prior to this he held his audience in the *Fatah-chowki* where he had his own suite of rooms and retainers. He also had an alchemy house, with a tile roof, built nearby. When he decided to demolish the *Fatah-chowki* and build a new residence for himself in the big garden, he instructed Haji Hafiz Maghribi sahib to collect 'masons, carpenters and delvers of the *sarkar* [government]' to carry out his wishes. He chose a plot near the vine-arbour and the sweet-water pond. His advisers accorded it 'an excellent decision', but advised that 'a large number of cocoanut [*sic*] trees have to be cut down'. They thought it preferable 'if the plot behind the sweet-water pond [was] chosen, for it [was] empty of trees and also nearer to the Kalas Mahall'.[36]

There was no mention here of a European presence in the Chepauk building establishment. The nawab had several tents pitched near the site which he visited daily to discuss his ideas with the workmen. He also built the two-storey Nusrat-mahall for his own *dar-ul-amara,* government house. The nawab built a thatched house on the seashore, contiguous with the house of his younger sister, for use during his excursions to the sea. It was a lofty building with a brick floor, straw roof and walls painted with pink-colour lime. 'The rooms were devised in a manner pretty to look at, with extensive court yards in an enclosed compound, with bamboo tatty fitted in an elegant style.'[37] Iftikhar-ud-Daula Bahadur was given the task of supervising the building and the furnishings. The carpets were to be obtained from the *farrash-khana* carpet workshop, and the lights from the *tablur-khana* storehouse.

The nawab also ordered Sayyid Ibrahim and the Pulcheri *maistry* head workman, to build a wooden building near the pool, behind the *diwan khana* of the *Kalas Mahal* and explained to them the plan of the building. It was called the *Mubarak-chawk* and he intended that it should excel the *diwan khana* of the *Kalas Mahal.*[38] He listened to vina-singers in the *Hasht bangla* and held tamashas of 'tigers, bears, elephants, camels and horses and wrestling matches among *pahlawans* [wrestlers]' in his own *bagh* (garden), and watched with the family from the terrace.[39]

[35] Ibid., p. 61.

[36] Muhammad Karim, *Swanihat-I-Mumtaz*, vol. 1, p. 67.

[37] Ibid., p. 129.

[38] Ibid., p. 88.

[39] Ibid., p. 33.

Some nights he held moonlight tamashas at the Nungambakkam or Sayidabad lakes, on the sea-shore or in the *baghs*, and enjoyed the nautch and singing girls.[40] The *Swanihat-i-Mumtaz* mentioned several audience halls and yielded a sense of Indian gardens and buildings. It animated architectural spaces, aesthetics and lifestyles of a very different order from the picture drawn by Bayly. It was the objective of the chronicle to portray the nawab as a devout king who refused to succumb to British pressure, designed to curtail his sovereignty—a defiant streak that cost his son the *musnud*.

Since the Chepauk Palace contained several phases of building under the rule of different nawabs, each responding differently to European powers, I tread a middle ground between Bayly and Metcalf and offer the hypothesis that the palace was an agglomerate of several architectural forms and spaces (of which some were classical pavilions like the durbar hall), arranged in the indigenous manner—an organic, honeycomb spatial syntax of enclosed, interlinked spaces catering to extended family networks and royal and state functions. The plan of the Padmanabhapuram Palace in Kerala, dating from 1500 to the present, with many accretions, offers a good example of this type of planning (see Fig. 71).[41] The spaces were sometimes multi-functional and some buildings were semi-permanent structures readily demolished and relocated. The quality of semi-permanence ties the built fabric of the palace to ancient patterns of royal life conducted around mobile courts. Aristocratic families moved amongst their many palaces and gardens and visited holy places as a matter of exercising sovereignty and in search of comfort and pleasure. The constant erection and demolition of temporary pavilions such as luxury marquees or tented enclosures, for travel, feasting, entertainment and privacy was a way of life with the ruling classes.[42]

In 1804, Francis Blagdon published a book on Indian history. The drawing titled *The Palace of the Late Nabob of Arcot in Madras* appears in the section, '24 Views of Hindostan',

[40] Ibid., vol. 1, p. 26.

[41] Raj Rewal, K.T. Ravindran and the Architectural Research Cell, 'Padmanabhapuram Palace' in *Mimar Architecture in Development*, July–September 1986, pp. 61–68. This organic, haphazard, honeycombed spatial syntax, with modest façades, may be gleaned from Dirks' description of what was a much smaller palace at Pudukottai. He contrasted this with the single free-standing new palace with impressive façades, built by the British for the Rajah, later in the century. See Nicholas B. Dirks, *The Hollow Crown*, p. 390.

[42] As seen in the *Sarva Deva Vilasaya*. The factor of purdah required the erection of temporary screens and structures every time women moved outside their zones. The nawab was often making 'arrangements for purdah' for his sisters when they travelled within the compound from their houses to the *Fatah-chawk* (elsewhere chawki). It is said that he pitched tents on the sea-side or in the *baghs* and achieved seclusion by the use of the *qannat* marquee and the *saracha* tent-enclosure; see Muhammad Karim, *Swanihat-I-Mumtaz*, vol. 1, p. 145.

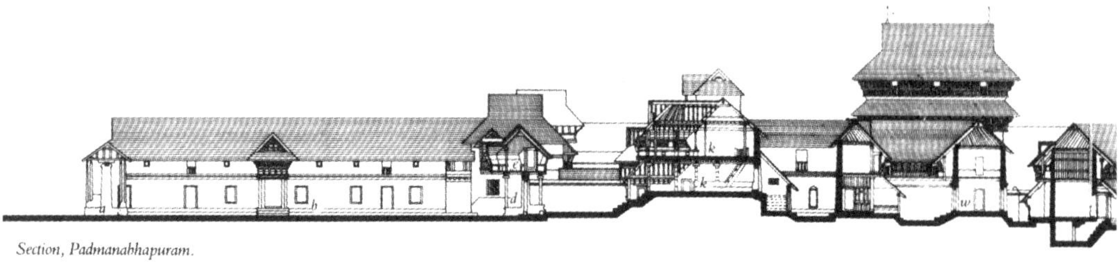

Section, Padmanabhapuram.

- a Gate
- b Court for ceremonies
- c The old mint
- d Entrance porch
- e Weapon store
- f Kitchen
- g Temple
- h Dance hall
- j Audience hall for Europeans
- k Ministerial audience hall
- m Hall for performing arts
- n Large feeding hall
- p Mother palace
- q Small feeding hall
- r Bath houses
- tt Tank
- u Residence
- v King's residence
- w Woman's residence
- y Well
- z Palace offices

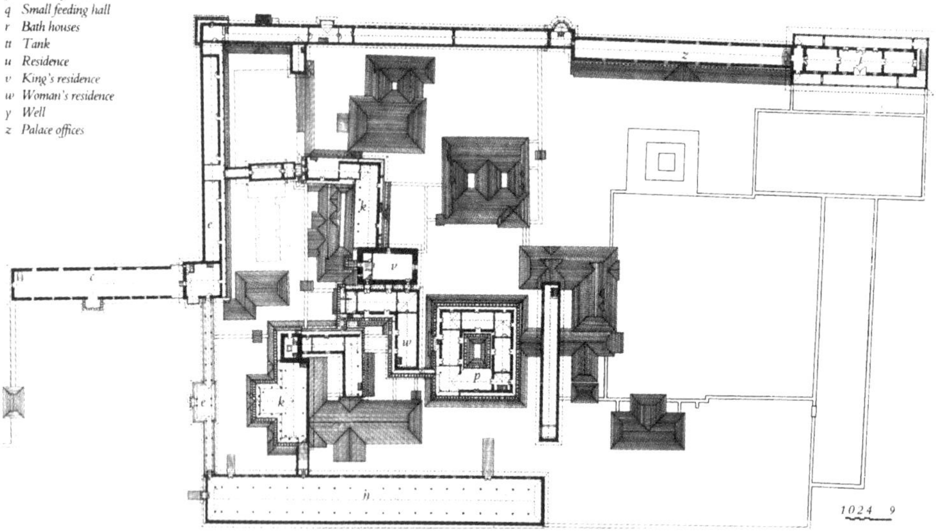

Figure 71: Plan, Padmanabhapuram Palace, c. 1400

drawn by William Orme (see Fig. 73).[43] The palace is shown on the left of a mosque in the foreground. A similar mosque is extant at Trichinopoly. Since the accompanying text claims the palace to be the Trichinopoly Palace, I am inclined to believe that the 'Madras' in the title must refer to the Presidency and not the city. I include it here because it is a rare illustration of late eighteenth-century nawabi domestic building.

[43] The volume comprises one of the three volumes by Francis Blagdon, see Francis Blagdon, *A Brief History of Ancient and Modern India* (3 vols., London, 1804).

My decision to weight the balance in favour of the Chepauk Palace architecture being a mixed one is based on three sources. The only pre-1855 illustration of the palace I have located is a photograph (see Fig. 66), taken outside the ten-feet high wall, entitled

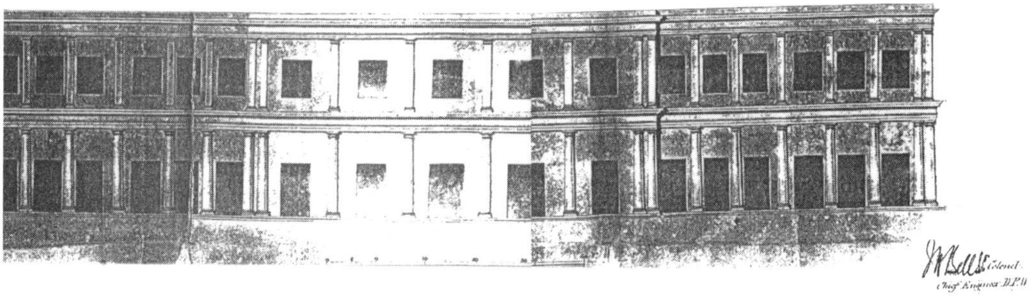

Figure 72: Elevation of proposed upper rooms to the *diwan khana*, Chepauk, Central Office PWD, Fort St. George, 1859

Figure 73: The Palace of the late Nabob of Arcot in Madras—Trichinopoly, c. 1804, with mosque in foreground, William Orme

Palace of the Nawab of the Carnatic, c. 1851.[44] It shows a view mostly of a high boundary wall and beyond it is a distant, wispy, domed pavilion on a terrace roof. (For a view of the dome today, see Fig. 70). The more conclusive evidence however comes from Lord Napier who, as a connoisseur of architecture, made the observation that the 'whole of the new façades' proposed for the Revenue Board buildings 'might be harmonized with the fantastic but agreeable style of the old Native palace'.[45] He makes it clear that he was not referring to western classical architecture.

Lord Napier made his remarks in May 1868, but the PWD drawings made in 1859 showed the *diwan khana* as having a spare classical-style façade. I suggest that when Lord Napier saw the palace, the *diwan khana* (which may have been a Palladian pavilion to start with) had already been transformed—through nine years of colonial intervention—into the Revenue Board, now clad in the spare classical Indo-European architectural style fashionable in PWD circles. Napier was proposing that the latter be altered to match the remaining pavilions of the Khalsa Mahal palace, which were in the Indian style. The more robust state intervention during Napier's regime completely transformed the mixed Indo-European architecture of the eighteenth-century palace. He commanded that the remaining palace buildings and the Revenue Board be given a matching facelift to accord with his personal predilection for a 'fantastic' and 'revived' Indian style based on the 'old Native palace'.

Figure 74: Chowmahalla Palace, courtyard with durbar hall, prior to restoration, c. 1750s

My third source is the Chowmahalla Palace of the Nizams of Hyderabad (see Fig. 74): it is likely that Nawab Muhammad Ali was familiar with at least parts of this palace, built from around the 1750s. The palace seems to be laid out as a series of interconnected courtyards originally spread over a 45-acre site. The courtyard containing one durbar hall *khilwat mubarak*, comprises mainly single-storey structures, in the Deccani style, surrounding a large garden in the centre of which is a long raised rectangular pool with fountains (see Fig. 75). The durbar

[44] No. 27, *Fiebig Collection*, Photographs Catalogue, OIOC.

[45] Minute No. 76, 29 May 1868, 'Suggesting certain improvements with a view to clearing the sea-front of the Chepauk Palace and to the Development of the Revenue Board Building', in *Minutes Recorded by the Rt. Honble. Francis Baron Napier and Ettrick during the Administration of the Government of the Madras Presidency* (Madras, 1872).

hall is multi-storeyed and embellished with octagonal corner pavilions to denote its special status. Subsidiary courtyards contain buildings with some European motifs (see Fig. 76). The structures in the second large courtyard (in the process of refurbishment) are said to be in the neo-classical style. The Chepauk Palace, built slightly later than the Chowmahalla Palace, may be seen as its Madras counterpart. It is a reasonable guess that the Chepauk Palace, too, would have had buildings in various Indo-European styles, with courtyards and gardens of similar scale and layout to those in Hyderabad. Like the Carnatic nawabs, the Nizams had several other palaces some of which, such as the imposing Falaknuma, were of European design.

Figure 75: Chowmahalla Palace, courtyard after restoration, showing raised central pool

Lord Napier—Enthralled by Indian Art

Strung between the gubernatorial regimes of the paternalistic Charles Trevelyan and Napier was that of William Denison, from 1860 to 1866. It was founded on the view that 'we must look upon ourselves as holding the country by the sword'. He regarded Indians as semi-savages incapable of self-government for another 2,000 years.[46] Denison also viewed as unjust, government treatment of the South Indian royal houses of Thanjavur and Arcot, declaring that the British had treated the 'great men of this land nefariously', but he could not reconcile a sympathy for aristocrats, with the vulnerability of empire. He opposed Governor-General Lord Canning's reforms which strove to make political space for the native gentry. The Government cry of 'India for Indians' held no appeal for him.

Napier inherited the task of placating and neutralising Indian and official grievances ignored by a series of unpopular predecessors. Born in 1819 in Thirlstane, Selkirkshire, Sir Francis Napier was Ninth Baron in the Scottish peerage, and eleventh baronet of Scott of

[46] William Denison, *Varieties of Vice-Regal Life*, vol. 2, p. 38.

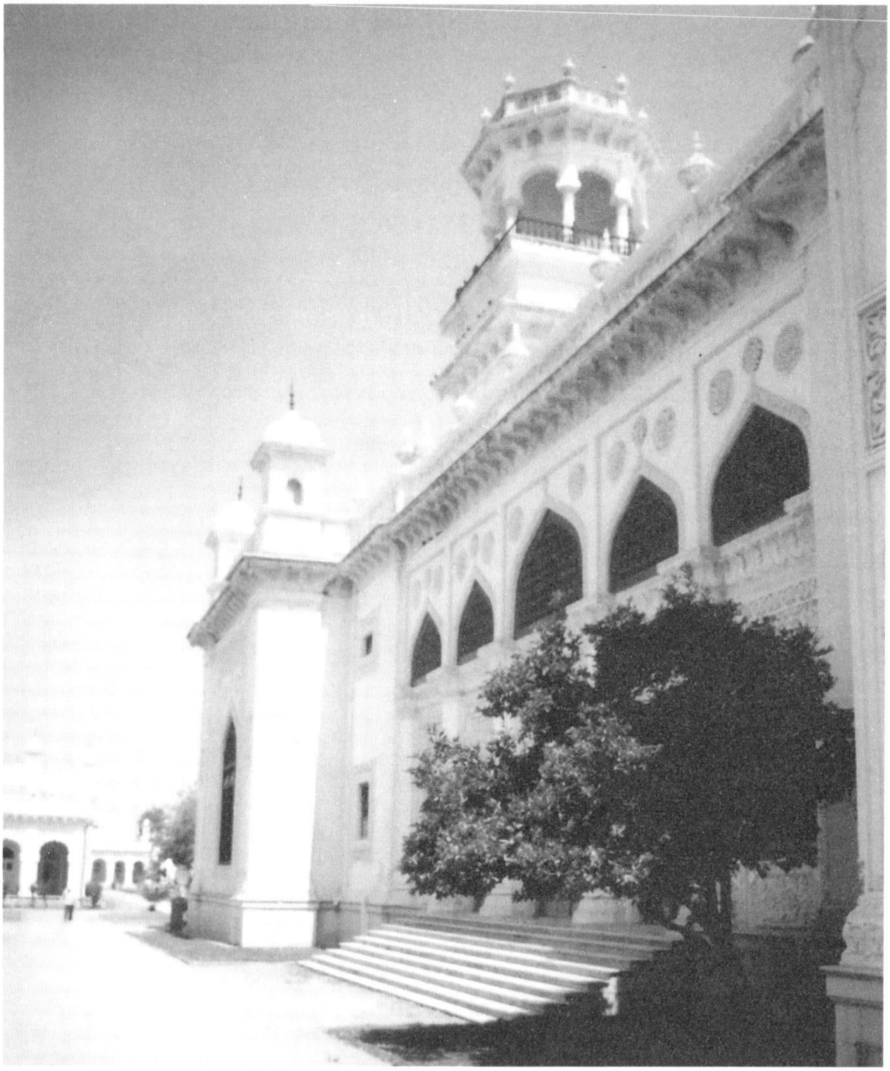

Figure 76: Chowmahalla Palace, durbar hall after restoration

Thirlstane. Following his imperial service, he was created first Baron Ettrick, in the peerage of the UK, in 1872. He entered Trinity College, Cambridge in 1835 and is known to have studied languages in Geneva. In 1842 he importuned Lord Aberdeen (foreign secretary) to sponsor him for the post of second paid attaché, to Her Majesty's Embassy, at the Court of Vienna.[47] Financial need drove him to diplomatic service in Washington, The Hague, and Constantinople.

[47] Napier to Lord Aberdeen, 22 December 1842, Add. MS 43240, Aberdeen Papers.

He was later appointed ambassador to St. Petersburg, then Berlin and finally to India. Napier was a well-educated and widely travelled Scottish aristocrat, regarded as the most distinguished career diplomat in the service. But his ambitions hardly matched the straitened finances that were to plague him all his life and rob him of the parliamentary career he coveted.

When the India offer came in 1864, Napier was attached to Berlin, which had its compensations as a centre of culture and learning and afforded him the delightful opportunity to meet learned men. 'I intend to cultivate them with the greatest pleasure that I have been so long almost excluded from literary society.'[48] In 1865 he wrote to Layard, in the Foreign Office, that 'the truth is the little fortune I possess was always growing less, the boys were growing up and the employment offered to me was more lucrative than an embassy and invested with some patronage.'[49] The Madras governor was paid around £14,000 per annum: more than three times the English prime minister: a bonus for the hardship of enduring a harsh climate.[50] Napier's sights had in fact been set on Europe and he had for many years cherished the hope of serving as ambassador to Constantinople: 'The more I reflect on it the more I mourn for the loss of the Constantinople Embassy which I always hoped to make my official grave.'[51]

In 1866 Napier accepted the Madras appointment for money, prestige and also due to sheer lack of choice. His connection with South India was tenuous—in the late eighteenth century his aunt and her group of Brahmin intellectuals had succoured Colin Mackenzie during his days in Madurai. She was married to a colonial official in Madurai and was using Brahmins to collect information on mathematics for the book she was writing on their ancestor, the Scottish mathematician John Napier, born in 1550. (John Napier was credited with having invented logarithms and simplifying the decimal system.) Francis Napier brought to his Indian posting a rare cosmopolitan erudition and aesthetic flair, nurtured at Cambridge, the cultural capitals of Europe and America, and more significantly, Istanbul and St. Petersburg, and a certain raw ambition. Despite his lack of money, there is little doubt that once in imperial service, he set his sights on the glittering viceregal prize. Napier was to be disappointed. His highest appointment was as temporary viceroy, after the assassination of Lord Mayo, in 1872. His ardent admirer Alexander Arbuthnot, a long-standing Madras high-official, 'never could

[48] Napier to Layard, December 1864, Add. MS 39112, Layard Papers, ff. 295.

[49] Napier to Layard, 27 December 1865, Add. MS 39117, Layard Papers, f. 356.

[50] *Madras Times*, 11 October 1873.

[51] Napier to Layard, 24 September 1865, Add. MS 39116, Layard Papers, ff. 371and ff. 384. Austen Henry Layard was Parliamentary Under-Secretary for Foreign Affairs. Also see *Concise Dictionary of National Biography*, vol. 1 to 1900 (Oxford, 1948), p. 927 and the *Dictionary of National Biography*, vol. xxii, Supplement (Oxford, 1885–1901), p. 1090, for further details of Lord Napier's career.

understand why Napier was passed over for the vice-royalty.' Arbuthnot blamed the *Athenaeum's* attack on Napier for this omission.[52]

In Madras, Napier's mix of snobbery, learning and fine aesthetic sensibilities found fertile ground in the intellectual circles of the orientalists and embryonic state-building programmes. The scale of the latter afforded his ambition a unique avenue to negotiate and materialise a specific vision of empire. There is nothing to suggest that Napier knew or cared about India prior to his appointment. As noted in the last chapter, it would appear that Napier's dream of empire arose in consonance with the intellectual and political aspirations of the Madras intelligentsia. He came to share the Indo-British vision held by a select team of senior officials who effectively governed the presidency. It was this shared historical and political vision that led to the maturing of a different approach to imperial architectural design.

It is as well to remind ourselves that Indo-European architecture was commonplace in the princely states and elsewhere in British India. However, experiments in Indian architecture were not undertaken by the state at the other presidency capitals. Napier's northern counterpart in this exercise was Sir Richard Temple, successively Governor of Bengal and Bombay and one of the most powerful officials of his day. Temple was busy overseeing princely Indo-British experiments in Indian architecture.[53] These were not developments confined to India alone. The appointment of Napier's mentor in the foreign office, Henry Layard, as First Commissioner of Works in 1868, suggests that for a brief interlude, more cosmopolitan aesthetics may have penetrated the official architectural discourses of the metropolis.

Trevelyan had already set a precedent for change in building use, executed at Chepauk and especially at Trichinopoly Palace where he had admired the raja's audience hall and the nawab's hall, the *Jahan-numa* (world exhibitor). He unhesitatingly recommended that the urban feature of 'remarkably high walls that stagnate[s] air should be removed'. In a populist vein he even resurrected the memory of 'the wise and good Sir Thomas Munro who visited Madura' 30 years earlier.[54] Continuing the tradition, Napier appropriated the Munro-Trevelyan

[52] Alexander Arbuthnot, *Memories of Rugby*, p. 179. The *Athenaeum*'s editors included John Norton. I have not been able to trace the nature of the attack, although it is clear that Napier antagonised a powerful faction of Madras officials. Gossip and keen discussion was conducted in the press about the pending appointment of the Lt. Governorship of Bengal, one of the richest prizes to fall to the civil service. As a rule, civil servants were not sent to Madras as governor. Interestingly, the appointment was from outside India, *Athenaeum*, 18 September 1870.

[53] For a discussion of Temple's association with Charles Mant and Indo-Saracenic architecture, see Thomas Metcalf, *An Imperial Vision*, p. 67. Mant built in princely India, and Emerson in British Allahabad for Indo-British patrons.

[54] *Minute by the Governor of Madras Relating to his Tour in the South of India Between* 5th *January and* 6th *March 1860*. V/27/246/4.

mantle by touring the districts and recording his own set of minutes. It was no accident that political, historical and aesthetic knowledge combined smoothly in the new generation of proconsuls. The scenario was directed behind the scenes by a powerful Madras élite who informed, educated and manoeuvred Napier and his 'distribution of patronage, in perfect accord with his avowed determination to advance the interests of the people of the country, native and Eurasian'.[55] An aim he conveniently disavowed with regard to the future of the Carnatic house, at the mercy of his recommendation to the Home Government.[56]

The Home Government's desire to 'secure substantial and comprehensive records of the religious and historical monuments of this extensive and diversified region' was interpreted by Napier as licence to restore the most interesting examples of secular architecture in the presidency. Already conversant with Fergusson, Napier had come to regard the arts of southern India as a 'mighty maze in which there is scarcely a glimmer of light or understanding'.[57] He was convinced that given the correct information, the true art history of the land could be 'deciphered and composed in England', with the benefit of 'direction from South Kensington'. The right person to collect the data needed for the undertaking was not to be found in India—for the obvious reason that he had to be 'perfectly versed in comparative aesthetics, the science which the Kensington Museum teaches'. The duty of this gentleman would be to 'select and describe the fabric or monument and compose its history'.[58]

Napier roundly asserted that Dr. Hunter, Head of the Art School, could hardly possess 'the recent critical culture' required. And PWD officers were 'out of the question. They [knew] little or nothing of these matters.' Napier who did know such things, equated art with archaeology and boldly launched a criticism of Captain Lyon's survey of *National Art in Southern India* because it included mediocre and modern monuments. To legitimise his preference for 'tradition' he appealed to the authority of the Secretary of State saying it would be 'unworthy of our government, and unjust to the natives of the country to permit the historical monuments of ancient native power to be obliterated'.[59] To build the new vision of empire Napier would have to rely on the advice and cooperation of a cosmopolitan Indian élite whose interest in European culture predated the arrival of the colonial state. The men ready to serve governors of Napier's

[55] *Athenaeum*, 20 September 1870.

[56] Napier to Lord Cranborne, 15 August 1866, *Salisbury Collection*.

[57] Minute No. 97, 18 November 1868. On Captain Lyons' Photographic Illustrations of National Art in Southern India, and the expediency of restoring the most interesting examples of Secular Architecture in the Madras Presidency, p. 22, *Minutes Recorded*.

[58] Ibid.

[59] Ibid.

persuasion had received a more formal training by colonial state intervention in education, also begun well before Napier's arrival.

Indian Mandarins

The aim of the Madras High School, in 1841 was to educate a privileged set of Indian mandarins. Most of the students were carefully selected Brahmin protégés of Cambridge-educated E.B. Powell, the headmaster. Its élite status was assured when, in 1855, Sir Charles Wood, head of the Board of Control, in London and his choice of Governor, Lord Harris, presided over its transformation into Presidency College; a feeder school for the University of Madras. The college served as an intellectual forum where Indo-British ideas and personnel mingled. The inauguration of the school was described as the arrival of 'the new learning and the advent of the administrative élite'.[60] Its ambitious sponsor was the colonial state. And it intended that the school ultimately surpass all that had been done or attempted before in India.

Madras officials and Sir Wood planned to educate a new cadre of loyal civil servants through Presidency College and the University. Under this scheme, state appointment was to be based on state-controlled educational qualifications and competitive examinations. The proposal endangered existing patterns of patronage employment. It allowed room for new power-brokers to seize control of recruitment. The University Board was established in 1840. Political opposition delayed its proper constitution until 1857. George Norton was appointed Governor and seven of the 15 seats on the Board were reserved for Indians. In view of their strongly voiced political demands, cooperation of Indians was deemed vital to the success of the enterprise. The university epitomised the long tradition of shared culture.

Crown rule in 1858 ushered in an altered political climate and the arrival of a new class of governors. Moreover, senior officials of liberal persuasion like John Bruce Norton, Powell, Walter Ellis, Christopher Rawlinson and Alexander Arbuthnot, who directed policy during this period, were anxious to push forward the delayed higher education programme. They made sure that education remained central to any political agenda in the early years of crown rule. Historian Robert Frykenberg, commenting on the establishment of modern education in the south observed that:

> Madras University became the major recruiting ground for successive generations of ever more highly trained officials. This exclusive and select leadership, almost entirely 'clean-caste' and mainly Brahaman, held sway within

[60] S. Suntheralingam, *Politics*, p. 63.

the imperial administration and within princely governments in the south. The position of this mandarin class was never seriously challenged until well into the twentieth century.[61]

In 1861 the Most Exalted Order of the Star of India was established. It drew the British proconsular and indigenous élites into a unified and ranked body. Outside British India royals such as the maharajahs of Travancore, Vizianagaram and the Nizam of Hyderabad were invited to join this privileged set. In British India the invitation was extended to members of royal houses and the new mandarins. Early celebrities of the High School were Brahmins from poor backgrounds; men like Pundi Runganada Mudaliyar, Runganada Sastri and Muthuswamy Iyer were lauded with imperial baubles and especially groomed to share power and forge the colonial state.[62] They came to constitute a select layer of cultured polymaths, steeped in eastern and western learning, who gathered in their homes pundits and students in the traditional manner.

As mentioned in Chapter 1, foremost amongst them was the high-born statesman and scholar Sir Madava Rao, typical of a transcultural élite that never abandoned its own culture and offered a guarded political support to the colonial regime. He stalled the annexation of Travancore and directed its modernisation on behalf of and in competition with the colonial state. Sir Madava Rao was also a Fellow of the University. It was no accident that the British elevated his status. Lord Napier spoke of him in eulogistic terms and he was awarded the KCSI (Knight Commander of the Star of India) at the same time as the maharaja of Travancore.[63] High School alumnus, Sir Seshiya Sastri, followed Madava Rao as *diwan* to Travancore and later went on to become *diwan* at Pudukottai. Pundi Runganada Mudaliyar became the Indian whose opinions on university questions were most appreciated and C. Runga Charlu became *diwan* of Mysore. British-educated Indians of the era are receiving more nuanced and sympathetic treatment by historians who are beginning to recognise that they tried to establish 'a social and political site for themselves, and in the process applied orientalist stereotypes to subalterns, or even to the British themselves, to serve their own fluctuating political ends'.[64] In short they were never uniformly loyal to the British; they assumed ambiguous multiple identities which supported, challenged, competed with and manipulated the British as well.

[61] Robert E. Frykenberg, *Modern Education*, p. 65.

[62] Parameswaran Pillai, *Representative Indians* (London, 1902), p. 104.

[63] See Nagam Aiya, *The Travancore State Manual*, vol. 1 (3 vols., Trivandrum, 1906), for the political entanglements between Sir Madava Rao, the British and the Raja. Madava Rao fell foul of the Raja and was dismissed in 1872.

[64] Julie F. Codell, 'Resistance and Performance: Native Informant Discourse in the Biographies of Maharajah Sayaji Rao III (1863–1939)', J.F. Codell and D.S. MacLeod (eds.) *Orientalism Transposed: The Impact of Colonialism on British Culture* (Aldershot, 1998), pp. 13–45.

'A Civilised Administration'

As the last chapter demonstrated, Madras officials were constantly at odds with the Supreme Government, forever cutting their public works allotments. Lack of building funds made palace conversion an attractive low budget alternative for gaining new office space.[65] At Madurai, Napier advocated a plan to 'repair a native palace, and make it the machine of *civilized administration* [italics added]'. In order to achieve this all he needed was a single Englishman with 'competent knowledge' to instruct native artificers. As everyone knew, 'We possess that Englishman in Mr. Chisholm'. In one skilful stroke Napier merged historical and artistic knowledge to distinguish the architect from amateur engineer and art educator. He justified state intervention in the Indian cultural domain, for which he knew precedent was rare, by promoting its efficiency value. Napier pressed home the view that it was only the colonial state that could now conduct a 'civilised administration'. If there was no precedent for the useful course of action of using Indian buildings to serve the new government, he remarked that 'this would be a good opportunity for creating one'.[66]

The project to comprehensively remodel the Revenue Board Building and the Chepauk Palace was not proposed for utilitarian reasons. The prestige accruing to the Revenue Board Building and the pride it aroused in the British came from its consanguinity with the Chepauk Palace. The other presidency capitals did not possess the unique feature of a native palace proximal to the core of British power. Napier was quick to exploit this unique feature. The clearing of the land between the palace and the sea was begun as early as 1862 and the land was purchased in 1864.[67] In 1863 a part of the Chepauk grounds was annexed to the gardens of Government House. Permission and funding was granted to the municipal commissioners to break down the western wall of the palace.[68] The ground between Government House and the palace was levelled and a new thoroughfare to Pycroft road added. A five-feet high iron railing replaced the solid brick boundary wall. The municipal commissioners insisted that the railing would permit sea breezes to reach congested areas beyond the palace (i.e., access to the sea and its breezes was gained for Government House). Open to imperial and public gaze, the compound was no longer mysterious and inaccessible in the old manner. Demolition of the wall

[65] *Athenaeum,* 18 January 1870 noted Napier's intense disgust that the Government of India had cribbed four and three quarter lakhs from the allotted sum.

[66] Minute No. 97, *Minutes Recorded.* It made sense for, after all, the revenues of the Supreme Government had been liberally expended at Delhi and Agra and Seringapatam without any utility value in view.

[67] 16 February 1863, Z/P/2544, MPPWD and GO 531–32, 29 July 1864, MPPWD, TNA.

[68] GO 474–75, 27 April 1863, MPPWD, TNA.

symbolised the destruction of a cultural memory of Indian kingship. It was the end of an era. The high visibility afforded by the low open railing fundamentally altered the spatial relationship between the palace, Government House and the city. It registered the triumph of a new colonial spatial order.

The palace compound housed a variety of buildings, including shelter for the nawab's personal army and arsenal. There were several parks, a lake large enough to have boating parties, a vine-arbour and fruit gardens. It was also a place of pleasure: music and bird-song filled the gardens and palaces; fruit trees such as the mango, palm and spreading tamarind, and various flowering trees provided shady walks; Jasmine blossoms scented the air cooled by fountains and pools. Beyond the eastern wall lay soft sandy beaches soothed by cool breezes, carrying the distant sound of the breaking surf. The ocean backdrop was often one of gaily decked, majestic, sailing ships from all over the world. The many buildings set amongst the pools and parks were airy, ephemeral pavilions where interior and exterior spaces merged. Some Britons were unhappy to simply destroy the cultural memory lingering in the abandoned buildings. Their aim was to destroy the original and capture its symbolic essence to enhance their own legitimacy—a delicate blend of innovation and antiquity. Official Britons were beginning to play with Indian architectural forms and aesthetics to serve their own ends. This was a game that was to prove deeply appealing to imperial patrons both in London and India.

Three new buildings were linked with the project: the Tower, built between the Revenue Board and the north face of the old palace; Presidency College, built south of the palace; and Senate House to the north (see Frontispiece and Fig. 77). The combined ensemble would radically transform the home of the nawabs long coveted by British governors. Presidency College and Senate House were the most prestigious new public buildings to be attempted by the crown state (they form the subject of Chapter 6). It was Napier's fancy that after their completion, the Revenue Board and the palace could not be left 'in the present condition of meanness and disorder. Those buildings must be placed in harmony with the others.' In 1868 Napier proposed that 'the [refurbishment] work be taken up at once and spread over the same time period as the construction of Senate House'.[69] The eastern side of the palace pavilion facing the sea, which eventually became a double storey façade introduced on three sides of the quadrangle, was now designated the 'front'. The Revenue Board Building made up the north side of the quadrangle (see Fig. 79). A new block was added to its east side with an impressive

[69] For a detailed list of the buildings to be removed, see Minute No. 76, 29 May 1868, 'Suggesting certain improvements with a view to clearing the sea-front of the Chepauk Palace and to the development of the Revenue Board Buildings', *Minutes Recorded*, p. 176.

double-height ceremonial entrance (see Figs. 82 and 83); possibly modelled on the Char Minar at Hyderabad whose design and political symbolism will be addressed a little later (see Fig. 89). The new structure was connected to the old building by an upper level bridge.

As noted earlier, piecemeal alterations to the palace buildings and the location of the Revenue Board among them were begun by the PWD in 1859. A vast conceptual gulf separated the latter from Lord Napier's comprehensive recommendations of 1868. His plan was to develop the entire area surrounding the palace, with its rather special sea-front, into a public space worthy of an imperial city. The new colonial urban space was intended to strike a note in the grand liberal manner by becoming a public zone for promenade with road access (see Fig. 78).[70] The official account for the year 1869–70 recorded that a part of the palace was

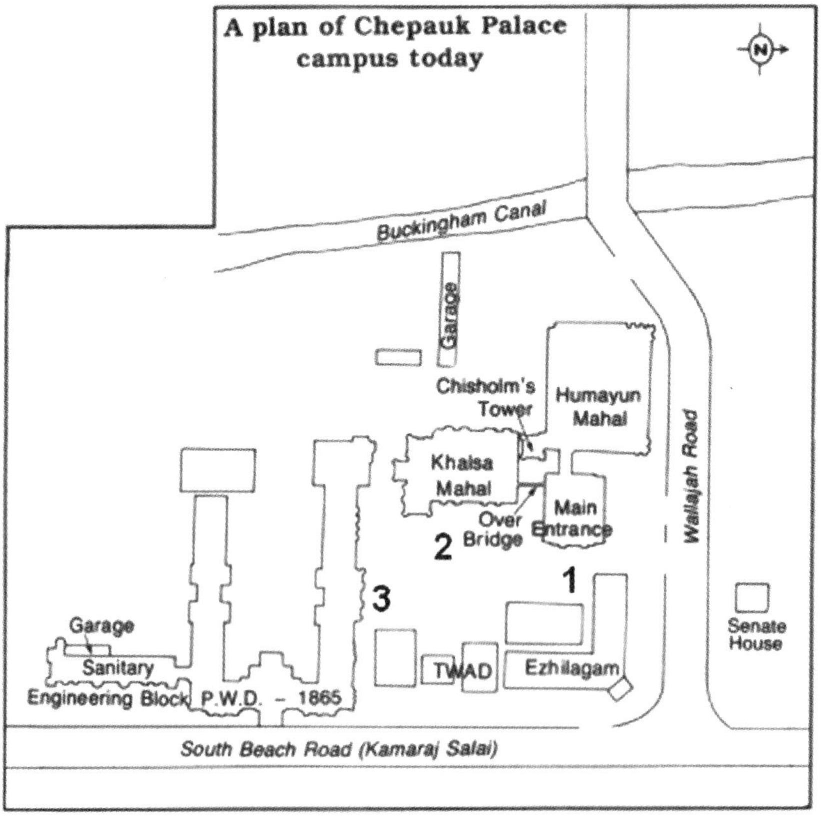

Figure 77: Plan of Chepauk site today

[70] The seventeenth-century Company Garden was the earliest of such colonial public urban spatial ventures. It was followed by the People's Park under Trevelyan's aegis.

Figure 78: Visions of an imperial marina—PWD building and Senate House from the beach, c. 1880—the palace is set between the two, behind the trees. The road between the beach and the buildings was developed in the 1990s.

transformed into the Revenue Board by the addition of a lower and an upper storey, and verandahs on all sides. 'The entire building will present a striking appearance when finished. It is in the Hindoo-Muhammadan style, a style it would have been impossible to carry out in any material more costly than stucco, which is so easily moulded to any form. It harmonizes well with the landscape, affords great variety of colour, and appeals particularly to the sympathies of the people (see Figs. 2 and 79).[71] Napier's artistic ensemble was an elaborate gesture of 'façadism'. Transformation of the existing buildings took place through the addition of a palatial façade, designed to tie together disparate extant units. A guidebook of 30 years later confirmed the importance of the building and the urban space in British eyes. It described the Revenue Board as: 'the most distinctly Moorish style of the architecture in Madras

Figure 79: The Revenue Board building, c. 1870, view from the north-east

[71] *Report on the Administration of the Madras Presidency* 1869–70, 1870–71, p. 66, V/10/201. For an early view of the Marina without road access from the beach, see Fig. 78.

Figure 80: Entrance 3, north façade, PWD building

[see Figs. 84 and 85] and in the opinion of many with its fine surroundings, it is the most beautiful building in Madras. It is surmounted by a fine Tower which gives the whole building a very striking appearance from the Marina.'[72]

The Revenue Board Building was featured in *The Builder* (1870) and *Indian Papers on Professional Engineering* (1872).[73] *The Builder* noted that the exterior of the palace was coloured dark red and white; a treatment regarded as 'more pleasing than that of many buildings subsequently erected by Anglo-Indians'. The main idea was to assimilate 'the buildings of the older structure'. Mr. Chisholm, while keeping to the general lines of the old structure, had taken his 'details and many forms from purer types of the style, and superior materials have enabled him to adopt a much lighter form of construction'.[74] The material used was the fine polished chunam of this coast.

Figure 81: Entrance 2, Old Palace

Today, the quadrangle of the remodelled palace and Revenue Board comprises a double storey façade of pointed-arched verandahs, punctuated by three lofty, arched ceremonial entrances, flanked by turrets with oriel windows. The north façade of the existing PWD building was incorporated to form the south side of the new quadrangle (see Fig. 80). It is generally accepted that the eastern elevation of the PWD, which faced the Marina, was also

[72] *A Guide to Madras (Higginbothams)* (Madras, 1903), p. 76.

[73] *PPIE*, vol. 1, Roorkee, 1872. Photograph only, inside front page.

[74] *The Builder*, 31 December 1870.

given a face-lift by Chisholm (see Fig. 78).[75] Oddly enough this was done in a red-brick Scottish Baronial style and is probably of an earlier date than its northern façade. The entire Old Palace and Revenue Board received Napier's façade treatment of pointed-arched verandahs (see Figs. 81 and 86). The terraced roofs were enlivened with a few small token domes. The façade had a parapet with finials, edging a roof that was mostly flat, with a few small domes. The style was an eclectic jumble of Deccani architectural motifs. The feature that unified the whole may have been the irregular red and white bands of paint, or coloured chunam, (today only to be seen in the Tower) (see Figs. 71 and 88). Overall the design may have replicated the spirit of the original aesthetic of the palace as its patron intended. The grandiose façade concealed a typical Indo-British public service spatial arrangement—the new ubiquitous perimeter verandah leading to a central core of office rooms.

Figure 82: Entrance 1, archway

Figure 83: Entrance 1, view through archway

Figure 84: Revenue Board, window detail of the bridge connecting the entrance block to the main building

[75] K. Kalpana and Frank Schiffer, *Madras the Architectural Heritage, An INTACH Guide* (Chennai, 2003), p. 162. The original PWD Head Office was built in the spare elegant military style common to many of the buildings in FSG, and is still visible in the rear.

Designated office space was not by any means a new phenomenon. David Rudner observed that agents of the South Indian banking community, the Nakarattar, conducted their international financial business out of modest offices called *kitangi* or *arai*: normally located in a communal building housing both the offices of other Nakarattar bankers and a temple or rest-house (*vituti*, *chattiram*, or *choultry*).[76] Colonial design fragmented the large inward looking multi-purpose spaces of indigenous communal buildings supplanting them with outward looking forms with showcase façades and spaces serving dedicated functions. Equally different was the open urban fabric created by imperial mandate. Its spatial arrangement laid emphasis on immediate visibility and readability of buildings that stood out as objects in space in contrast to the inward, interconnected indigenous spatial orientation. The catholic approach to style was common to the cosmopolitan aesthetic of Indian royalty as it was to the eclectic Euro-centric modes of England.

Figure 85: Revenue Board, roof of the entrance building

Napier's ambition was, 'with the advice of an accomplished architect, to exhibit in the improvements at the Revenue Board an example of the adoption of the Mussulman style to contemporaneous use'. As Napier saw it in 1870, the joint team of Napier and his engineer had paid 'the first tribute to the genius of the past; he [Chisholm had] set the first example of a *revival in native art* [italics added] which I hope will not remain unappreciated and unfruitful'.[77] A cherished aspect of the exercise was that the 'building [found] favour in the locality; both Europeans and natives seem to take a general interest in its progress'. Napier's announcement that official remodelling of the palace was 'a revival in native art' was based on the British decree that native art was already dead. It also implied the death of the native architect and British intent to launch control over the trajectory of architectural design.

[76] David Rudner, *Caste and Capitalism in Colonial India: The Nattukottai Chettiars* (Berkeley, 1994), p. 118.

[77] *The Builder*, 31 December 1870.

Figure 86: Old Palace, north façade, after restoration

Figure 87: Victory Tower at Manora (65 km. from Thanjavur), 1814, built by Rajah Serfoji to celebrate his British friends' victory over the French at Waterloo

A Tower

The least discussed today, but certainly the most enigmatic and prominent edifice in the remodelling exercise was the entirely new, domed and turreted 'record tower' (see Figs. 88, 90 and 91). All the sources I consulted are peculiarly reticent in their allusion to the Tower. The only contemporary reference was made in the administrative report of 1870; it stated that the Tower had been built to a height of 75 feet.[78] Lacking firm evidence to the contrary, I follow other modern writers in the assumption that Chisholm was the designer; the reason being that the distinctive balconies of the Tower were repeated in the later Senate House. There is a slim likelihood that it was an existing part of the palace; in which case Chisholm merely lifted, for Senate House, the motifs he fancied. The Tower is a square edifice with four corner turrets and a central dome. It was conspicuous due to its delicate form and the red and white striped painted surface. Its overall shape unerringly referred to the Char Minar, in Hyderabad, built in 1589 (see Fig. 89). British political rivalry with the Nizams of the princely state of Hyderabad was made physically explicit in two building projects: the extravagant Palladian Residency, second only to Calcutta, and at Secunderabad, the largest cantonment in India. Major James Kirkpatrick, the incumbent Resident, commissioned the Residency in 1803. It was a powerful reminder of the continuing power contest between native kings and British India. The desire to appropriate the unique urban icon of Hyderabad, renowned as the 'largest and most original architectural conception of the Qutb Shahis, and indeed of any of the Deccani sultans'[79] for Madras, southern capital of the British empire, was equally telling.

The eclectic proportions and aesthetics of the Tower drew on architectural specimens at Bijapur.[80] Especially the Mihtar Mahal whose outstanding features were cantilevered stone balconies with wide eaves (see Fig. 92). The eaves rested on carved brackets and were topped by a carved parapet and slim minarets. Similar motifs appeared in the tomb of Ibrahim Rauza, also at Bijapur; admired by the British as a structure 'achieving perfection as near as is humanly possible' (see Fig. 93).[81] One can only speculate that in addition to using Indian designers, Chisholm consulted Fergusson's and Captain Meadows Taylor's books on Deccani architecture to develop his design. A hollow brick cone supporting a spiral iron staircase, occupied almost all the space inside the Tower. It led to a terrace roof suitable for enjoying the view and

[78] *Report on the Administration of the Madras Presidency* 1870–71, p. 97, V/10/201.

[79] George Michell and Mark Zebrowski, *NCHI, I.7, Architecture and Art of the Deccan Sultanates* (Cambridge, 1999), p. 51.

[80] Philip Meadows Taylor, *Architecture at Beejapore*, p. 87. Chisholm never acknowledged Indian assistance in his designs.

[81] Percy Brown, *Indian Architecture*, p. 75 and Plates L and LIII.

sea-breeze. The limited storage space inside the Tower imputes that 'storage' was possibly a ruse to cover the funds being expended on its construction.[82] Napier's building programmes were not without critics and his Minutes record a sensitivity to 'some who have expressed an apprehension that the Government in prosecuting aesthetic designs, may be led to neglect the solid interests of the country'.[83]

Metcalf argued that the British built towers as a mark of conquest, heralding the new era of their progressive rule. From the Clock Tower in London to the early revolt-linked towers in Delhi and Lucknow, they embodied progress and conquest.[84] In the north, Tower building at this time may have celebrated suppression of revolt. But the Madras Tower had no clock of progress, nor was there a question of conquest or revolt. This makes the decision to build a Tower in this context evermore puzzling. It behoves asking the question—what momentous event was the southern colonial state celebrating by building a Tower? It is possible to make a reasonable guess that Madras Indo-Britons were celebrating not suppression but escape from

Figure 88: Chepauk Tower, west elevation, Revenue Board on left

[82] The interior of the Record Tower of the Revenue Board was fitted with teakwood racks, supported on wrought iron girders. GO 825, 24 March 1874, MPPWD, TNA. I am assuming this is the Tower standing today which has no sign of racks. The Revenue Board has a record room with elaborate timber shelving.

[83] Minute No. 170, 20 November 1871. On the restorations of Tirumala Naik's Palace at Madura and the manner in which the works should be conducted in future, *Minutes Recorded*.

[84] Thomas Metcalf, *An Imperial Vision*, p. 78.

Figure 89: Char Minar, Hyderabad, c. 1589

Figure 90: Tower, balcony details

Figure 91: Tower, from palace roof

revolt. Thus, although the purported function of the Chepauk Tower was record storage, its overarching inspiration, closely allied to Hyderabadi urban iconography, was unquestionably one of southern imperial power. Furthermore, towers were a standard element in South Indian palace architecture, readily visible at Thanjavur (see Fig. 26), Ginjee and Madurai, where they were used as armouries and for surveillance. Perhaps it is possible that by building a Tower the British (and the South Indian élite) intended to celebrate a victory. Were they imitating Rajah Serfoji of Thanjavur who, in 1814, built a Tower at Manora to affirm his friendship with the British by celebrating their victory over the French at Waterloo (see Fig. 87)?

Figure 92: Bijapur, Mihtar Mahal

The built form of the Tower imparts a royal/imperial resonance to the newly created public space. I suggest that the Tower was an ideal prototype for this imperial purpose because it was extremely conspicuous and equally ambiguous. It was an urban and royal built form in India and celebrated modernity in Britain; a cultural hybrid, perfect for simultaneously symbolising power, victory and an alternate modern southern empire. It could perhaps even symbolise progress without

Figure 93: Ibrahim Rauza, Bijapur

Figure 94: The Memorial Hall

a clock. At Chepauk, it indirectly and surreptitiously celebrated an Indo-British community of interests, reflected in economic and political progress, and a power-sharing that prevented a southern rebellion. This hypothesis complements and illuminates the steps taken by private Indo-Britons and the church, to make a ceremonial thanksgiving celebration through architecture, for being spared the horrors of the nortern 'Rebellion'. The unusual thanksgiving to God took shape as an ornately classical hall, built around 1860 (see Fig. 94).[85] The hall was designed by Captain Winscom. The committee for raising funds for the hall was made up of Christian religious bodies. It was erected through public subscription, 'To the Glory of God' and as a 'memorial of the goodness and forbearance of the almighty God in sparing this Presidency from partaking of the Sepoy Mutiny which devastated the sister Presidency of Bengal in the year 1857.'[86] Appropriately, a large proportion of the money needed for its completion was donated by wealthy Indians.

[85] 'To the Glory of God', *Athenaeum,* 1 September 1858. *Athenaeum*, 17 January 1859 noted the subscriptions had run dry with a shortfall of Rs. 25,000 of the estimated cost of Rs. 50,000.

[86] *Asylum Press Almanac*, 1869, p. 601.

Both buildings are fine examples of Indo-British culture sharing, marking the beginning of a design trend that would continue unabated till the end of empire. The remodelled royal structures, along with the new buildings at Chepauk, also signalled a British intent to capture the leadership of Indo-European architecture in the subcontinent.

6

The Lure of Indian Aesthetics

Presidency College 1864–67 and Senate House, University of Madras 1869–78

Architectural Propaganda—A Competition

In 1863, for the first time in the history of the presidency, the government organised an architectural competition to select designs for two buildings—Presidency College (an expanded version of the former Madras High School) and Senate House—asserting the importance accorded to higher education in the thinking of the new government. What prompted this unprecedented piece of architectural propaganda? And why select education? In the immediate aftermath of the 1857 Rebellion, parliament and the newly established crown state were naturally anxious to placate any major incidence of discontent that threatened imperial stability. Against this wider backdrop of uncertainty and vulnerability the Madras Government began searching for openings to make conspicuous statements of its renewed commitment to progressive government in India; architecture and education comfortably married these dual aims. The prevailing climate of political conciliation afforded those Indo-Britons, who had unsuccessfully agitated for greater investment in education under Company rule, another chance to press home their demands—given Madras' loyalty during the Rebellion, London was probably rather more sensitive towards appeasing and rewarding her Madras officials.

London approved a generous budget to launch the building project in South India and advertisements for the competition were placed in 12 issues of the *Fort St. George Gazette*. The

Madras Government went as far as to request the Secretary of State (in London) to advertise the competition as he thought desirable.[1] A prize of Rs. 3,000 was offered for the best plans and estimates for the erection of the proposed buildings.[2] The Madras Government's direct access to London suggests that it still retained a fair degree of political independence from the Supreme Government in Calcutta. All the same, the willingness of the imperial élite to completely fund the Madras project implies that there were other forces at work as well.

The governing élite in London was doubtless aware of the nascent competition posed by building programmes in Bombay where wealthy Indians had joined dynamic governors to construct a common vision of the new India; the Bombay University hall was funded by Sir Cowasjee Jehangir Readymoney, one of a number of Parsee benefactors with strong British loyalties. The library was endowed by a 'Hindu' banker, Premchand Roy. The financial independence of these Indo-Britons allowed them to sever links with military engineers and purchase designs from one of England's most renowned architects, Sir George Gilbert Scott, who never visited India. Even Calcutta had a government architect. Walter Granville was the first consulting architect to be appointed by the new Government of India; his brief tenure in Calcutta lasted from 1863 to 1868. The post was next filled by James Ransome in 1902.[3]

In concession to the political importance of the project it was proper that the site chosen for the College was the sea-front at Chepauk; immediately south of the PWD building (see Fig. 2). The latter made up the southern flank of the three sides of the Chepauk Palace quadrangle discussed in the previous chapter. Presidency College was the first of the new buildings to contribute to the marine vista destined to be comprehensively redeveloped with the improvements to the palace and the addition of Senate House in the Napier era. Land for the College was purchased in 1865 signifying the intention that it was to be built prior to Senate House.[4] In 1865, the man who would raise the stakes of the new Senate House building of the university by making certain it became the flagship building of the Madras Government, had not yet reached the shores of the subcontinent.

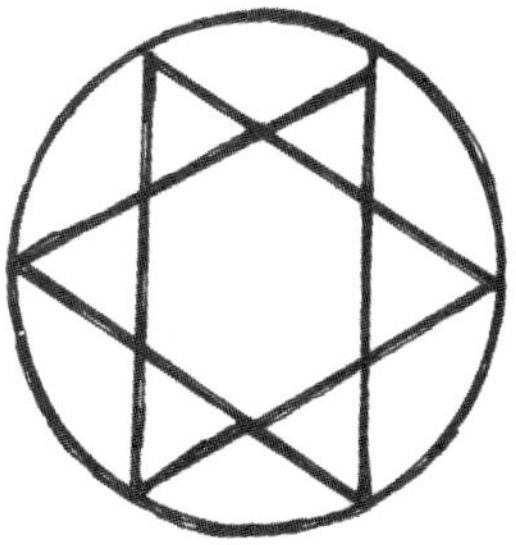

Figure 95: Hexalpha symbol used by Chisholm

[1] Letter No.107 from Fort St. George to Secretary of State, Letters from Madras, 1864, L/PWD/3/190. The Bombay Senate House was commenced in 1869. Presidency College, Calcutta was completed in 1872.

[2] GO 210–11, 9 December 1863, Z/P/2544, MPPWD, BL.

[3] James Ransome, 'European Architecture in India', *Journal of the RIBA,* 28 January 1905, pp. 185–204.

[4] 10 August 1865, Z/P/2545A, MPPWD, BL.

The committee appointed to judge the competition designs consisted of Colonel Orr, R.E., Secretary to the Government in the PWD, E.B. Powell, Director of Public Instruction and W.G. Smart, a member of the Institute of Civil Engineers. The views of senior civil servants were well represented in the committee by Colonel Orr and Powell. Seventeen designs of 'more or less merit' were received. The unanimous choice fell on the designs of Mr. Chisholm, an Executive Engineer, Pooree Division, Bengal Department of Public Works. Chisholm signed his work with a Hexalpha inscribed in a circle (the Hexalpha with Triple Tau was the Freemason symbol for the Temple of Jerusalem; see Fig. 95). There is little modern writing on the subject of Freemasonry in colonial India, but it was an activity known to the Madras élite. The Nawab, Umdat-ul-Umara, was 'the first native of India to be initiated to Freemasonry, having been initiated by Dr. Terence Gahagan at Trichinopoly, in 1775'.[5]

The judges had doubts as to 'the style of the domed cupola, by which the centre of the roof of the College was crowned, being in harmony with the Mansard roofing with which it was associated'.[6] But, when they approached Chisholm with their misgivings, they were informed that the dome could easily be changed to a tower; Chisholm went further and even sent a photograph of the proposed alteration. The judges decided that they preferred the original submission. They were not, however, entirely satisfied in regard to the designs for Senate House, remarking that:

> it may be doubted whether the style of the Senate House is in consonance with the received views but looking at the climate in which the structure is to be erected, and the different ends it is intended to fulfil, it is believed the design is decidedly the best of those which have been finished.[7]

The committee gave no indication as to what this 'style' or the 'received view' was. Chisholm's estimates were as follows: Rs. 142, 695 for the College (government estimate was Rs. 250,000) and Rs. 146,698 for Senate House (the government estimate was Rs. 150,000). Following the judges' decision, on 21 March 1865 an application was made for the services of Mr. Chisholm to superintend the erection of the building. The Government of India sanctioned Chisholm's transfer in June.[8] Contractors were invited to tender for the construction of the college and on 21 March 1866 the tender of Messrs. Barnett and Bonycastle Contractors, amounting

[5] James Stevens Curl, *The Art and Architecture*, p. 216. Quoted in H.D. Love, *Vestiges of Old Madras*, vol. 3, p. 529.

[6] Letter from Committee appointed to examine and select the best design of a Presidency College and Senate House, Madras, to the Honble. A.L. Arbuthnot, Chief Secretary to the Government, FSG, 7 March 1865, P/250/5, MPED, BL.

[7] Ibid.

[8] 6 June 1865, p. 229, P/250/5, MPED, BL.

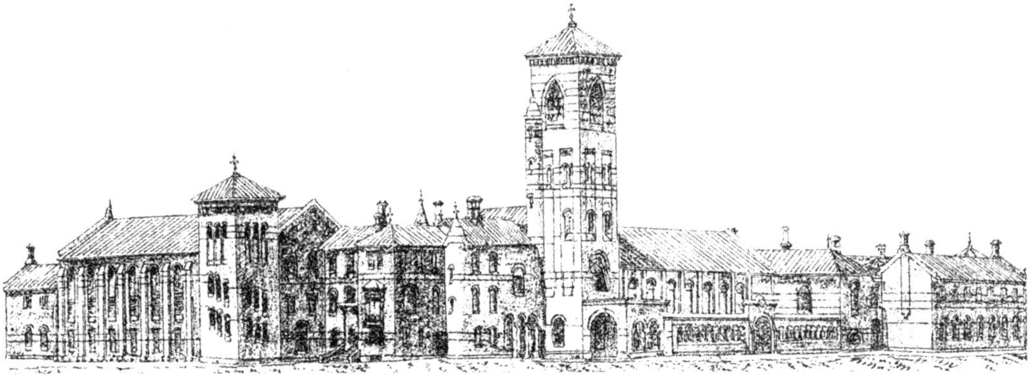

Figure 96: Lawrence Asylum, Ootacamund, c. 1872

to Rs. 239,851, was accepted in the PWD.[9] Lord Napier arrived in Madras on 27 March 1866.

Robert Chisholm—Favoured Status

Despite Lord Napier's presence in Madras, it appears that the College was built according to plans agreed on contract, with little input from him. He was understandably preoccupied with another design project of considerable political weight, located in Ootacamund: the building of the Military Male Orphan Asylum, now renamed the 'Lawrence Asylum', in honour of its new benefactor, John Lawrence, the Viceroy (see Fig. 96). The delay in the building, proposed to accommodate 400 boys, was causing much vexation to the viceroy, recuperating from illness in Simla. Lawrence apologised to Napier for being too busy to visit Madras.[10] Napier took command and stopped all work until he could visit the site with the architect. He wanted to make sure the building would be adapted internally to its object and be 'of good and grave proportion and of substantial materials appropriate to the climate'—aspects based on which he judged the current design to be faulty. 'I will set my face against all extravagance on useless ornament but I wish to see it made worthy of its purpose and of the name it will bear.'[11]

[9] 21 March 1866, P/439/11, MPED, BL. The construction time was extended from 24 to 30 months. The contract was originally given to Mr. Sowerby in February, he was asked to withdraw his tender on 28 March.

[10] Lawrence to Napier, 23 June and 21 September 1866, MSS Eur F 90/44, Letters to the Governors of Madras, John Lawrence Collection.

[11] Napier to Lawrence, 25 April 1866, MSS Eur F 90/43, Letters from the Governors of Madras, John Lawrence Collection.

Moreover, having discovered the designs for the asylum which happily were 'unsanctioned', he wrote that the architect Mr. Chisholm 'now engaged on them was hampered by the plans of his predecessors and had never even seen the site'. This was not quite true. Chisholm had in fact discussed the plans made by the PWD engineers, with Governor Denison, during a private interview. He then scuttled the engineers' proposal with one of his own, based on plans for a military hospital to be erected in Malta. His proposed design, in the Lombardy style, was to be executed in exposed bricks because 'it looks much better'; the many arches it included were to 'contain a ring of moulded brick and a ring of coloured brick, say red and black tuck pointed carefully'.[12] In May, Napier made a quick visit to the site. He confidently assured the viceroy that, 'the designs were in the hands of Mr. Chisholm a young architect of considerable taste and skill who came to this government, I think from Bengal. He was very much needed. We have excellent engineers but no artists.'[13] It was in this letter that Napier revealed his hostility to useless ornament, as well as some of his other design preferences that were to leave a mark on the architecture of Madras. Chief of course, á la Chisholm, was his antipathy to plastered brick walls.

> The bricks up there are very bad that it will be impossible to make a fair well cemented brick wall capable of standing the weather without the use of chunam. There will therefore be an external coating of chunam to my great vexation. I am satisfied however, having now seen the materials and enquired into the climate [that] this is unavoidable.[14]

Napier wrote to Lawrence that it was his intention to keep the architecture very simple with 'no small ornamentation susceptible of decay'. The roof was to project overall and the only decoration allowed was the introduction of terracotta pillars in the windows and bands of coloured tiles which could be cheaply prepared at Madras and sent up.

In the meantime, Chisholm had become so indispensable to Napier that in October 1866 Napier requested the Government of India to have him appointed consulting architect to the Madras Government (with the appointment treated as a special case).[15] Napier also requested that Chisholm receive the emolument of a first class executive engineer. The Government of India's response was to temporarily approve the grade of executive engineer, but in February 1867 it declined the request for the special designation of 'Consulting Architect'.[16] Undeterred by the obstructive tactics of Bengal civil servants Napier wrote directly

[12] GO 1275, 4 April 1866, MPPWD, TNA.

[13] Napier to Lawrence, 24 May 1866, John Lawrence Collection.

[14] Ibid.

[15] GO 269, 30 October 1866, p. 192, Z/P/2546, MPPWD, BL.

[16] GO 56–59, 4 February 1867, p. 194, Z/P/2547, MPPWD, BL.

to the viceroy in September 1868, informing him that he would shortly receive an official letter:

asking again [for it was refused before] to appoint Mr. Chisholm, a Bengal engineer given to this presidency, consulting architect to the Madras government, with an exceptional salary of Rs. 1200–1500 per mensem. Mr. Chisholm is a man of remarkable ability and taste. His assistance is quite indispensable to this government; at least while important works are going on.[17]

Napier listed several important works—the College, Senate House, Library, Art School—in the interests of which 'we have been obliged to forbid him to practise privately for his practice is becoming extensive and lucrative more than seemed consistent with his public duty'.[18] Having noted that members of government agreed it would save government money to employ Chisholm, he enjoined the viceroy to exercise his 'private judgement on the question when it [came] up'.[19] Two weeks later Lawrence replied that because Napier had 'set his heart on the proposal', he was glad to say that Chisholm's special designation appointment was approved, but the financial increase would require 'the sanction of the Secretary of State'.[20]

Chisholm's professional status was changing rapidly; it was his value as an artist that set him apart from other engineers. This assessment, made by senior Madras officials and Lord Napier, was corroborated by a demand for his artistic talents in the architectural market place. The government sent him to Madurai, to inspect the palace, and he was asked to prepare designs for the addition of a public library to the museum in Madras; he was further ordered to contact the University Syndicate to prepare plans for the new building. In 1868 the Archdeacon of Madras sought permission for Chisholm to prepare designs for the church at Shoolay, in Bangalore.[21] The Municipal Commissioners, too, had a preference for Chisholm to design the new General Market for Madras, rather than their own executive-engineer. They felt their engineer had other duties and 'has not had the time to work at these designs, and which, moreover, come more strictly within the province of the Architect'. The secretary to the commissioners pleaded that since the new market was to be built 'in a conspicuous place', it was very desirable that it 'should combine utility with an ornamental appearance. There is nobody in Madras who can render any assistance in this matter but the Government Architect, and I shall therefore feel very much obliged if the Government would be pleased to permit of

[17] Napier to Lawrence, 9 September 1868, John Lawrence Collection.

[18] Ibid.

[19] Ibid.

[20] Lawrence to Napier, 24 September 1868, John Lawrence Collection.

[21] 15 October 1868, Z/P/2548, Index MPPWD, BL.

Mr. Chisholm preparing a design.'[22] Even the Government of India was not immune to his fame. In 1871 it forwarded drawings and papers requesting him to design a façade for the Imperial Museum, under construction in Calcutta.[23]

By 1870 Chisholm was working on several projects including the museum, telegraph office, jail, *cutcherry* offices and a school. His reputation as an architect blossomed between 1866 and 1869. He was acquiring a new status as a design professional with the backing of the state, but without professional institutional support. It is possible that Freemason lodges provided institutional support and intellectual links to men of science and engineering, in the days of empire, before professional institutes replaced them. Chisholm's colonial experience differed from that of his peers in London who made their reputations chiefly in the private sector. In 1871 Chisholm was appointed a Fellow of the RIBA. His nomination was recommended by Lord Napier; three Fellows signed the nomination papers. In support of his nominee, Napier wrote that Chisholm held responsible office and was 'equally acquainted with the mechanical and artistic branches of his profession'.[24] In Lord Napier's view, engineer-officers were excellent men, 'devoid of style' but full of 'practical mechanical knowledge', who showed 'no jealousy of Mr. Chisholm who is a little, clever cockney crammed with high-art to Ruskin level'.[25] Over the 40 years of his career in India, Chisholm spoke many times at the RIBA, earning a reputation as an expert on Indian architecture, especially as a dome builder. His systematic pursuit of recognition from architectural peers at the RIBA, over that of the Indo-British engineering fraternity in the country where he lived and worked, demonstrates how the imbalance in political power was creating an institutional imbalance; recognition by western institutions became a sought after validation of professional status in the colony.

It is interesting that senior London bureaucrats meticulously tracked what was seemingly a minor appointment in the colonies. The Secretary of State approved the appointment of Mr. Chisholm, Consulting Architect, on a salary of Rs. 1,200 per mensem, from 1 April 1869, but he warned the Government of India of his 'considerable doubt as to the expediency of the new appointment of Consulting Architect to the Government of Madras'. He did not, he said, wish to:

[22] GO 189–90, 9 August 1869, MPPWD, TNA.

[23] GO 291, 291A, 18 July 1871, MPPWD, TNA.

[24] Letter from Napier to Thomas Donaldson, Professor and Honorary Secretary to the RIBA, 18 October 1870, RIBA Fellows Nomination Papers 4 (4 December 1865–9 June 1873), p. 104.

[25] Napier to Lord de Grey, 8 March 1866, no. 9, Salisbury Collection.

disturb the arrangements which you have made as regards the present incumbent; but having regard to the large staff of highly paid engineers now in the employment of Government, I do not consider that the separate appointment of Consulting Architect at Madras is really necessary, and I request that, on the retirement of Mr. Chisholm, the office may be abolished.[26]

A letter from the India Office to Lord Napier, written in 1872, pointed out that the Secretary of State's opinion was 'to some extent confirmed by the circumstance that the appointment of consulting architect has not been found necessary at either of the other Presidencies'.[27] Viewed in the context of the strong opposition from London and Calcutta, Chisholm's appointment was something of a coup for Madras. It implies that London did regard Madras as a special case.

The sources are silent on Chisholm's private life. The closest we can get to the life of an Englishman practising architecture in a presidency capital is through the diaries of Richard Blechynden. Blechynden arrived in India in 1782, at the age of 22. He had had some education in mathematics at Christ's Hospital School and first worked as a surveyor's assistant to Edward Tiretta, the surveyor of Calcutta roads; although this did not preclude him accepting private commissions. For design inspiration Blechynden studied the manuals of architecture and poured over Chamber's *Civil Architecture*. He was rather contemptuous of what he called the 'Blackey's' skills in building, but he used Indian workers, and foremen. At the root of his contempt for Indian builders was the fact that he competed with them. He lost work to them because they soon learnt the European style expected by the client, and undercut his price. 'Blechynden feared the Indian contractors because they could do what he did, but were less restricted than he was, as to costs and clients. Truly this was a colonial dilemma.'[28] It is very probable that Chisholm and his engineer colleagues, searching for lucrative private work, faced similar competition in the Madras of the 1860s. Lord Napier's sneering remarks about engineers and Chisholm evoke the sharply stratified social world of colonial Madras. We have to assume that Chisholm conversed with Indian architects and builders in the south in Tamil, Telugu and English.

Blechynden moved in the lower-middle circles of Calcutta society, had many trustworthy Indian friends and kept Indian bibis. Bibis were many things at once, not only were they paid

[26] GO 223, 12 December 1871, MPPWD, TNA.

[27] Letter from Secretary of State to His Excellency the Governor in Council, FSG, 15 February 1872, GO 460–61, MPPWD, TNA.

[28] Peter Robb, *Clash of Cultures? An Englishman in Calcutta*, pamphlet (London, 1988). Also see Blechynden Papers, Add MS 45,645, 45,646, 45,647.

servants, 'slaves and concubines' but they were also an important conduit between the European official and native culture. His principal bibi resided in his town house and the other in his garden house. They had their own servants, never accompanied him in public and only visited with him in the absence of European women. Blechynden had several children, none of whom were legitimate, although they were baptised Arthur, Sydney and Sally and treated very like legitimate offspring. He often went swimming with friends, in the tank in his garden house and was comfortable in a little known Indo-British social world. It is difficult to know whether the private lives of the two men had much in common, although, at a guess, it is unlikely.

In 1872, Lord Napier sent Chisholm to Trevandrum (Thiruvananthapuram) in the princely state of Travancore (Kerala), to design a museum for the Maharajah. Travancore was a state with a powerful tradition of independence. It rivalled British India in cultivating a liberal and progressive political and cultural image. It was against this canvas and against the preference of officials (who evidently wanted the classical style for new state buildings), that Chisholm attempted to promote 'native art' in architecture. He found himself in the incongruous position of having to instruct an erudite Travancore élite on how best to foster and extend their own art. In the short space of a few months, Chisholm 'thoroughly acquainted [himself] with all that had been done in an Architectural way, both by Europeans and Natives'.[29] His extremely idiosyncratic design for the museum was based on 'a very beautiful form of domestic art' seen in the numerous palaces of the rajahs (see Fig. 97). His architectural conversations in Trevandrum

Figure 97: Napier Museum, Trevandrum (Thiruvananthapuram) by Chisholm, 1872

[29] Robert Chisholm, *The Napier Museum, Trevandrum*, RIBA pamphlet (1873).

Figure 98: Padmanabhapuram Palace, elevation with clock-tower

have come down to us through his drawings and his records of the work of the 'native architects of Travancore', revealed in his watercolour details of the exquisite Padmanabhapuram Palace (see Figs. 71 and 98).[30] But, it is in writing about his favourite building, the Madurai Palace, that he offers us a real glimpse of the pleasures of his experience of cultural sharing as an imperial architect:

[This is] but a royal palace in which kings have lived and revelled. This great pillared hall, with its open court-yard covering an unbroken area of more than two acres has actually witnessed the barbaric splendour of the Great Tiroomal naik, and re-echoed with the roar of wild beasts and the shouts of the approving multitudes, or the more peaceful trumpeting of the elephants, and the chant and jangle of the Nautch girls. Whether it is that the mind instinctively depicts such scenes as these; whether it is from the effect of tropical sun—the flood of fierce light which pours down vertically into this courtyard and reflects in subdued brilliance through the long pillared aisles of the interior; or whether it is that the very memories of history itself, lend age to a building within historical times, I am unable to say, but whatever the cause I must confess that I feel, in common with most people who visit the place, those emotional sensations usually called into existence by the contemplation of a great work.[31]

In this extract he conveys the sensual delight of space and place and his appreciation of it. Although British efforts to understand Indian art were deeply flawed and often self-delusory, it is churlish not to recognise that the orientalist art enterprise included moments of genuine

[30] He gifted the paintings to the RIBA. For his paintings see Y 16/13–20 and for sketch plans of the museum see W 11/2, 1/2, RIBA British Architectural Library.

[31] Robert Chisholm, 'Tiroomal Naik's Palace'.

and sincere admiration across cultures. Chisholm's work is an example of a kind of cultural sharing; its bricks and mortar embody that insuperable contradiction of attempting humane cultural sharing in colonial society.

Napier's attraction to Chisholm combined art with politics; Chisholm was an essential tool in the bid to execute an innovative provincial building programme with its sights set on the Indian territorial state and the larger empire. Without strong state patronage, however, Chisholm's professional status was always vulnerable to challenge from military engineers. Napier left Madras in 1872. Thereafter Chisholm enjoyed the patronage of his successor, His Grace the Duke of Buckingham and Chandos, for some years to come.[32] Having fallen foul of high officials, Chisholm resigned in 1886. He alleged that he had been unjustly refused promotion to the lucrative grade of superintending engineer and he 'fearlessly assert[ed] himself to be the best qualified officer in the Presidency' to do the job. Government held the view that Chisholm lacked the experience of 'general work' to justify the promotion.

It was no secret that Chisholm's privileged position and overall earnings had been systematically monitored by the engineering fraternity. The government pointed out that since Chisholm, who was on a special salary of Rs. 1,200 per month had earned Rs. 30,000 in excess of what he would have, had he been an ordinary executive engineer (maximum salary Rs. 900), he was not being deprived of income.[33] Colonel Morant succeeded Chisholm who left British India to work in princely Baroda.

After Chisholm's retirement the Government of Madras sought permission from the Government of India to continue the post and to request the Secretary of State to send a gentleman from England. J.W. Brassington followed Colonel Morant and was in post by July 1887.[34] Brassington's appointment marked the end of an overt military presence in the architectural establishment, but the early experiments in Indo-European architecture continued unabated in Madras with Henry Irwin succeeding Brassington. Madras civil servants had developed a taste for Indo-European architecture. Under their patronage Irwin designed the famous law courts, and the National Art Gallery in the same style.

It is fitting that in his last major design commission Chisholm received an opportunity to revisit the themes of Senate House and the Madurai Palace that had excited his young imagination

[32] Under His Grace, a grateful Chisholm enjoyed the fullest confidence of the government and the freedom to remodel and develop the Madras School of Art according to his own ideas; he held charge of the Institution from 1878. See Robert Chisholm, *Notes on Technical Education Addressed to His Highness Sir Syaji Rao Gaekwar of Baroda* (Bombay, 1880), p. 17.

[33] GO 869, 21 March 1887, MPPWD, TNA.

[34] GO 1960 MW, 22 July 1887, MPPWD, TNA.

in Madras. It implies that they were close to his heart and appreciated by his new European patrons. It is also appropriate that this commission—the First Church of Christ Scientist—was built in Wilbraham Place, Chelsea, London in 1904. The church was in the Byzantine style and could accommodate a congregation of 1350. It was built from Portland stone with a stylish Art Deco interior whose defining feature was the steep barrel vaulted roof which rose on sheer walls. The building is now owned by the Cadogan Estate. It was completely refurbished and opened to the public as London's newest chic art venue Cadogan Hall, 5 Sloane Terrace, in June 2004. The Hall contains an auditorium seating 900 and is home to the Royal Philharmonic Orchestra.

From Presidency College to the South Kensington Museum (SKM)

Chisholm's designs for Presidency College have not attracted modern interest. Whilst in 1866 Chisholm casually revealed to Lord Denison that his source for the Lawrence Asylum design was a design prepared for a hospital in Malta; he proved far more secretive as to the design sources for the College. These he never revealed. By 1868 he appears to have realised that his reputation as an architect depended on being artistically exclusive and possessive, about the individual authorship of design. There is little reason to doubt his claim that he designed both the College and Senate House in the 'French Renaissance' manner.[35] It is significant that the College bears a resemblance to designs made by the military engineer, Colonel Francis Fowke, for the completion of the SKM (now the Victoria and Albert Museum) buildings in London (see Figs. 99 and 100).

Figure 99: Francis Fowke, proposal for the South Kensington Museum, c. 1860

[35] 8 May 1868, p. 1825, P/439/36, MPPWD, BL.

Figure 100: Presidency College, c. 1871

The Presidency College was built of red-brick. Its original 350-feet long main façade was faced in rusticated stone bands at the lower level. The similarities with Fowke's design included the overall massing of the blocks with projecting end wings, hip-roofed shallow towers, the red-brick façade with round arches and the stone rustication. A red-brick façade was added to the PWD building, intervening between the College and the palace along the sea-front, in order to connect the style of the College to the palace complex, when the latter's refurbishment began in 1869 (Fig. 78).[36] The reasons why this may have been Chisholm's main choice for imitation have to be looked for in the museum's burgeoning reputation as the foremost centre of art and art education in London.

The House of Commons committee that investigated the promotion of art in Britain in 1836 was aware that Britain lacked design instruction and public art galleries in the French manner. Artistic and commercial rivalry with other European powers fuelled the desire to improve the quality of British manufacturing design. Design was to be improved by studying and refining global art, which would now be collected and displayed in a new museum whose central function was didactic. The SKM would make the hitherto inaccessible art of empire and Europe, readily accessible to British art teachers and students.[37] The purchasing committee comprised leading art intellectuals like Henry Cole, Owen Jones, Richard Redgrave and A.W. Pugin: they advocated the study of Indian textiles because the formal qualities of Indian designs illustrated the correct principles of ornament in contrast to the naturalistic ornament of British designs.

[36] The PWD façade was another stylistic anomaly; it had an imposing double height round arched entrance with round towers surmounted by cupolas. Round arched verandahs ran along the façade. Its overall forms were of the same proportions as the new entrance to the Revenue Board but the round arches and towers imparted a Scottish baronial feel.

[37] Tim Barringer and Tom Flynn (eds.), *Colonialism and the Object: Empire, Material Culture and the Museum* (London, 1997).

The single most important factor in the formation of the museum was Henry Cole: the driving force behind the School of Design and the Great Exhibition of industrial art of 1851. The birth of the museum coalesced Prince Albert's ideas for a National Institute of the Arts, with Henry Cole's thinking on art education. The prince's vision was to centralise the existing learned and artistic societies in Britain in one institution that would form the nucleus of an imperial cultural centre in London. The new institution merged museum and art school. The museum was constituted with an imperial awareness that 'links should be maintained with India and the colonies by scholarship and other means'.[38] From the museum's inception India held a special place in the intellectual traditions that were to shape it.

The SKM opened at the Kensington site, in temporary structures, in 1857. Fowke presented his earliest version, of the second stage of the museum development plans to the Parliamentary Select Committee of 1860. The plan was only partly realised. According to John Physick, Fowke's museum designs were not French Renaissance: 'Flying in the face of the then current fashion for Gothic, Fowke proposed to continue to use the north Italian Renaissance style already adumbrated on the Sheepshank Gallery.'[39] It should be added that there were several European buildings in the same style which could have influenced the designs of both Fowke and Chisholm and this explains Chisholm's description of the designs as 'French Renaissance'; the massing of F. Duban's prestigious Parisian, Palais des Etudes, of 1833, and the arched façades of Henri Labrouste's designs for the Bibliotheque Ste-Genevieve, of 1838–43, also in Paris, are two of them. The north Italian style, however, had other more deep-seated political implications in Britain; it was the focal point in debates on architectural aesthetics, nation and empire.

Perhaps the most decisive link between architectural style, nation and empire in Britain occurred in 1861 when the House of Commons voted that the new Foreign and India Office buildings, located side by side in Whitehall, near Parliament, should be in the classical 'Italianate' style and not the Gothic. It was the style 'widely employed in gubernatorial buildings throughout the capitals of Britain's colonial empire and was the chosen language of civic architecture in the capital cities of Britain's major continental rivals, especially Paris'.[40] It comes as no surprise that Sir Charles Trevelyan, assistant secretary to the treasury in 1856, was called upon to expound his vision of architecture for London to a government select committee. Having

[38] John Physick, *The Victoria and Albert Museum, A History of its Building* (London, 1982), p. 20.

[39] Ibid., p. 99.

[40] G. Alex Bremner, 'Nation and Empire in the Government Architecture of Mid-Victorian London: The Foreign and India Office Reconsidered', *The Historical Journal*, 48, 3 (2005), pp. 703–42.

been exposed to some of north India's building traditions and the monumental colonial architecture of Calcutta, it was natural that Trevelyan wanted something of the same scale for London—grand buildings of national distinction, which reflected its central place as 'the mother of nations', in the act of 'civilising large portions of two ancient continents, Africa and Asia'. Venetian splendour was decided upon as the most appropriate of the Italian styles to impress foreign dignitaries of Britain's imperial success, represented in two prominent buildings in Whitehall completed in 1868: Gilbert Scott designed the Foreign Office and East India Company architect, Matthew Digby Wyatt, the India Office. Like the Foreign Office and India Office, the SKM served a vital national and imperial purpose; it was appropriate that it too should be built in a grand manner, similar to its sister buildings but with the difference that it was faced in red brick.

The London 'Art' Set and India

The artistic team designing the interior of the museum was drawn from the exclusive 'art' set of London designers; it included William Morris and the firm, Morris, Marshall and Faulkner, Philip Webb, Sir Edward Burne-Jones, Frank Moody, George Frederic Watts, and Lockwood Kipling. In a very practical way the interior decoration of the museum buildings offered commercial success to the 'art' set; it was also the official site where the 'art' set met empire through the impersonal medium of the museum's collections. The 'art' set had a more personal access to Indian art in the form of Lockwood Kipling whose expertise was garnered during his tenure as an art teacher in India. More covert access to India came through the artist George F. Watts, regarded by some as England's Michelangelo and the greatest painter of his age, best known for his epic, allegorical paintings. Watts was also a popular portrait painter whose clients included patrician statesmen and men of arts and letters. A selection of his portraits, from his *Hall of Fame* series, appeared in the National Portrait Gallery in 1895.[41] Among his list of 64 sitters were two of the Pattle sisters (to be introduced shortly), Lord Lytton, Sir Austen Henry Layard, Dante Gabriel Rossetti and William Morris. Morris' formal association with the museum began in 1865 when Cole asked the firm to prepare designs for the Green Dining Room.

From 1850 Little Holland House, in Holland Park, was the home of Indo-Britons Sara Pattle and her husband Thoby Prinsep; they took care of Watts and provided him with a home and a studio for 25 years. Sara and Thoby belonged to wealthy Anglo-Indian civil-service

[41] Colin Trodd and Stephanie Brown (eds.), *Representations of G.F. Watts: Art Making in Victorian Culture* (Aldershot, 2004).

families from Calcutta. Thoby retired in 1843 as chief secretary to the Government of India. In London he became a director of the East India Company and was appointed one of the seven members of the newly formed Council of India. Sara's sisters married into the upper echelons of society in Britain and Calcutta: Sophia married William Dalrymple of the Bengal Civil Service, Virginia married the Earl Somers and Julia Margaret (the now famous photographer) married Charles Hay Cameron, a lawyer and the first legal member of the Supreme Council of India, a post that out-ranked almost everyone else in British India.

The seven Pattle sisters received a cosmopolitan education in France (their mother was French), spoke in Hindustani, wore strange flowing dresses made of rare Indian fabrics and 'cultivated the exotic by exploiting their Anglo-Indian upbringing and parentage'. They are thought to have inspired English artists and writers such as Watts, Burne-Jones, Thackeray, Tennyson and Trollope. Sara's home was the venue for a cosmopolitan liberal salon where artists, politicians, scientists, civil servants and land-owners gathered in a 'breezy Bohemian' and 'highly civilised'[42] pursuit of culture.

Val Prinsep, Sara and Thoby's second son was being trained as an artist by Watts. He met Edward Burne-Jones and William Morris when they were decorating the Oxford University Union Debating Room in 1857. John Ruskin too was a friend of Sara Prinsep and supervised her son's training as an artist. When Burne-Jones fell seriously ill in 1858 he stayed at Little Holland House. Caroline Dakers suggests that Burne-Jones was in love with Sophia Pattle (Dalrymple) who lived most of the time with her sister Sara, until her husband retired from India in 1873. Burne-Jones' drawing, *The King's Daughters,* done in 1858, is an idealised vision of Sara with her sisters in the enchanted garden of Little Holland House. According to Burne-Jones' wife, he was starved of visible beauty in his early years and the artistic surroundings at Little Holland House, where he watched Watts and Tennyson at work, immersed in wonderful music, exerted a profound impression on him. It was during this stay with Val that Watts secured, for the young painter Burne-Jones, his first commission.

Little Holland House was an old farmhouse with irregular additions, and low large rooms unexpectedly placed, with long corridors. One visitor saw the house as an 'earthly paradise', with its blue painted ceilings with gold and silver stars; Georgiana Burne-Jones recorded her husband's impression of its 'low, dimly lighted, richly coloured rooms, dark passages opening into lofty studios filled with the noble works of Watts'. An anonymous visitor described how refreshing, to eyes accustomed to early Victorian wallpapers and carpets, was the delight of the

[42] Caroline Dakers, *The Holland Park Circle: Artists and Victorian Society* (New Haven, London, 1999), p. 30. The information on Little Holland House and the Pattle sisters is from Dakers.

matted rooms, with cool green walls against which hung paintings glowing with Venetian colour, deep blue ceilings with a gold planetary system traced on it, lattice windows, framed by creepers, through which were seen waving trees.[43]

The Little Holland House (dower house of Holland House), developed into a home under Caroline Fox. She supervised the joining of farm buildings to the main house and the creation of the enchanted garden that separated it from other places. She bequeathed it to her nephew Baron Holland (Watts' patron) in 1845. The combined effect of the organically evolved domestic spaces, Watts' luminous paintings and Sara's French and colonial Indo-British decorative themes from Calcutta, was to produce a new type of house and garden with an aesthetic wholeness unfamiliar in London. I suggest that it accidentally fused Gothic revival ideas about spatial layout and the 'common tradition of honest building', with a completely new, spare yet lustrous, decorative scheme for domestic architecture that could inspire the 'art' set.

William Morris—Imperial Designer?

The artist Edward Burne-Jones and William Morris maintained a lifelong friendship; ever since they met while attending Oxford University to study theology, in 1854. William Morris' Red House, designed in the 1850s by his friend, the reclusive architect Philip Webb, is accepted as a piece of Gothic revival domestic architecture that subscribed to the rules laid out by Pugin. The house was hailed as a revolutionary design on account of its 'modern Gothic' brick style,[44] informal layout, and art and crafts decoration. The design came about when the 'art' set made a decision to break with the,

> pedantic imitation of classical architecture of the most revolting ugliness, and ridiculous travesties of Gothic buildings, not quite so ugly, but meaner and sillier; and on the other hand, the utilitarian brick-box with a slate lid which the Anglo-Saxon generally in modern times considers as a good and sensible house with no nonsense about it.[45]

Burne-Jones declared that Morris was making it 'the beautifullest place on earth'. The Red House set the precedent for Webb's house designs for the 'art' set; houses that were not mere buildings but artistic ensembles. Around 1865 Philip Webb designed several houses in the Holland Park area; amongst others for Val Prinsep and the artist George Howard, 9th Earl of Carlisle.

[43] Ibid., p. 27.

[44] Mark Swenarton, *Artisans and Architects: The Ruskinian Tradition in Architectural Thought* (London, 1989), p. 42.

[45] Cited in E.P. Thompson, *William Morris: Romantic to Revolutionary* (New York, 1976), p. 90.

It is beyond the scope of this book to discuss whether it is simple coincidence that descriptions of the Red House are redolent of the spirit, volumes, decoration and gardens of Little Holland House, or whether Little Holland House, especially its decorative theme, was the living prototype for the arts and crafts decorations of the Red House. Nonetheless, it is important to raise this question, even in passing, because it is the case that (albeit for very understandable reasons) modern literature maintains a stoic distance between Morris' art and empire. Morris made his first contact with English socialists in 1882 and it is recognised that Morris' 'encounter with socialism (and particularly historical materialism) had no substantial effect on his architectural thought, which to the end of his life remained substantially as formed in the 1850s'[46]—that of the Romantics.

William Morris has been called John Ruskin's greatest disciple (the 'Master' to whom Morris looked back with gratitude to the end of his life). Ruskin's attitude to Indian art offers an appropriate starting point for understanding how art intellectuals in general approached Indian art. Ruskin is accepted as one of the most influential and original thinkers and writers on nineteenth-century art, and his assessment of Indian art in relation to global art would have been absorbed by the young Morris, aged 24 when, early in the year 1858, Ruskin delivered a talk at the SKM. His topic was supposedly aesthetic but he chose to discuss 'the effect of art on the human mind' and proceeded to subject a rather bemused audience to a hysterical outburst against Indian behaviour towards 'gentle and unoffending' Britons during the Rebellion of 1857. He generously added that 'among the models set before you in this institution and in others established throughout the kingdom for the teaching of design, there are, I suppose, none in their kind more admirable than the decorated works of India'. He lavished praise on the 'almost inimitable', delicate application of many colours and the 'fine arrangement of fantastic line' visible in the samples.[47]

Ruskin placed his disciples in a quandary with his suggestion that the Indian is 'bestial, degraded, abominable, and corrupt not despite his subtle art, but, at least in part, because of it'. Ruskin was hardly consistent; on occasion he also expressed utopian, quasi-socialist and at times anti-imperialist sentiments. We will never know whether Ruskin's rhetoric may have dampened Morris' desire to take the 'good' out of Indian art, even though it was the most admired source of global art for decorated works. Morris seldom mentioned India.

[46] Mark Swenarton, *Artisans and Architects*, p. 95.

[47] The information and citations from Ruskin are from Ian Baucom, *Out of Place: Englishness, Identity and Empire* (Princeton, 1999), p. 75.

Before we consider Morris' art, a brief digression is necessary to present the political background to his approach to empire. There exists no dispute amongst scholars that Morris was, in general, an anti-imperialist; the problem arises only in the case of India.[48] When Morris wrote 'On the Eastern Question' in 1876, he was an enthusiastic defender of empire:

> If England were to go to war in a righteous cause . . . a cause that concerned her liberty, her independence, or her empire, her resources would prove inexhaustible. She is not a country that, when she enters into a campaign, has to ask herself whether she can support a second or third campaign. If she enters a campaign she will not terminate it until right is done.

These lofty sentiments were soon put into rhyme, and became the popular song of the war party.

> 'We don't want to fight, but by jingo if we do,
> We've got the ships, we've got the men, we've got the money too!'[49]

Morris' position on the Eastern Question, in the early years, was confused and supportive of the oppressed peoples of the Balkans. He wanted Britain to annexe the Ottoman Empire and rule Turkey as it was ruling India.[50] Although Morris did strongly denounce the impact of empire and industrialisation elsewhere, his attitude to India has been called 'preservationist'. Where empire already existed, as in India, it could 'preserve' the existing medieval society from the encroaching horrors of industrialisation and capitalism. Thomas Metcalf has observed that historians have failed to take note of Morris' views being more sympathetic to empire.[51]

Morris once said that they talk of building museums for the public, 'but South Kensington Museum was really got together for about six people—I am one, and another is a comrade [Philip Webb] in the room', adding that 'Perhaps I have used it as much as any man living'. E.P. Thompson observed that Morris' design work was inspired by 'a close study of ancient Egyptian, Byzantine, Persian, Indian and Northern European and English traditions in particular'. Morris was careful to note that, 'it takes a man of considerable originality to deal with old examples and to get what is good out of them, without making a design which lays itself open distinctly to the charge of plagiarism'.[52]

[48] For this discussion refer to Patrick Brantlinger, 'A Post-industrial Prelude to Post-colonialism: John Ruskin, William Morris and Colonialism', *Critical Inquiry*, 22, 3 (Spring 1996), pp. 466–85.

[49] Cited in E.P. Thompson, *William Morris*, p. 208.

[50] E.P. Thompson, *William Morris*, p. 210. Marx was diametrically opposed to Morris on this question, p. 224.

[51] Thomas Metcalf, *An Imperial Vision*, p. 271, n. 29.

[52] E.P. Thompson, *William Morris*, pp. 102–4.

Judging by the felicity with which many Britons adopted the Gothic and the classical architectural styles as their own, plagiarism was accepted practice in the art world. The fact that Morris chose to explain how to avoid plagiarism suggests it was a matter of some importance to him as a thinker and designer. His comments, made in 1882, were solely with reference to imitating 'old' examples of unspecified provenance. Despite this safeguard, some of his textile designs are known to bear explicit resemblance to pieces in the museum's collections, many of which were not all that 'old', and to examples of contemporary Indian textiles widely available in fashionable London shops.

Such a veiled, surreptitious approach to dealing with non-European art connects all too easily with the dilemmas of imitation and borrowing that became a particularly acute contradiction for Indo-Britons like Chisholm, who were expected to ostensibly design in 'native' styles without copying. The difference was that Morris acquired his astonishing knowledge of global art by studying objects in a museum, from books and contemporary samples; a method that allowed his non-European sources to remain obscure and undisclosed. Sir Thomas Wardle, who had textile factories in Staffordshire, began collaborations with Morris in 1873. Wardle imported Indian fabrics and copied Indian patterns in his own work. Chisholm on the other hand learned 'native' art from living teachers and from specimens in situ.

Morris and his circle are regarded as radical transformers of the decorative arts in Britain and the museum's role in this transformation is well known. But Thompson's assessment of Morris' genius as 'peculiarly English', made almost 30 years ago, survives largely unrevised in relation to India.[53] Linda Parry in her study of Morris' textiles claims that he had an interest in contemporary Indian patterns around 1875 but 'this was soon forgotten'. His later work showed his appreciation of designs from Italy, Persia, China and Turkey; this, despite the fact that he was producing Indian patterns with an unequivocal attribution of Indian origin such as *Madras Muslin* in 1881.[54] In 1996 Patrick Brantlinger discussed Morris' few passages on Indian art and concluded that Morris found it superior to most western equivalents.[55] Tim Barringer went much further. In 2005 he argued that:

> Brantlinger missed the most compelling evidence: Morris's own work as a designer. It is here that we find a utopian conflation of Indian textile patterns and the Gothic. Almost all of Morris's designs for both woven and printed textiles betray both medieval and Islamic influences; the extent to which Indian design influenced his

[53] Ibid., p. 728.

[54] Linda Parry, *William Morris Textiles* (London, 1983), pp. 45–47.

[55] Patrick Brantlinger, 'A Post-industrial Prelude to Post-colonialism'.

work has been underestimated, though it is sometimes explicitly acknowledged as in the *Indian Diaper* pattern of 1877 to the *Madras Muslin* of 1880–81.[56]

It is unlikely that Barringer meant to reduce Indian textile designs to Islamic ones; all the same, the point he makes is an important one. Indian art gave Morris deep pleasure. It was a pleasure readily revealed in his work, but as a truly imperial pleasure it stayed hidden in his writing. Today his rich oêuvre is shared by Euro-Americans.

Cultural historians have discussed how empire dislocated, destabilised and reformed English identity in a variety of locales. The 'Englishness' of Morris' art is as much European as it is global—it is an art of empire. The lure of Indian aesthetics was an imperial conundrum for 'English' intellectuals and artists wherever they were and it is pertinent to the theme of this story that the study of the design of Presidency College in Madras raised unexpected questions about Indo-British cultural sharing in the production of 'English' art and architecture.

'Improving' Native Architecture

As early as 1868 Napier had admired the Mussulman architecture of the Chepauk Palace; sometime after November of that year he sent Chisholm to undertake an experimental restoration programme of another far grander seventeenth-century palace; that of Tirumala Nayaka at Madurai. When Chisholm presented his Senate House designs to the university, in May 1869, it is fair to assume that he had at least seen the Madurai Palace and was familiarising himself with its design and construction techniques. Of these he spoke eloquently a few years later at the RIBA. Chisholm's devotion to the project was so complete that Napier, who also attended the talk, instructed the audience that Chisholm's name 'ought forever to be associated with that of the sovereign Tiroomal Naik—they ought never to be divided'. Ironically, it is Napier's name that is carved on the new entrance gateway to the palace designed by the hapless Chisholm. Local native merchants gifted the sum of £500 for building the gateway, as 'a graceful recognition' of Napier's contribution to the restoration of the palace.[57]

The RIBA possesses an amazing set of drawings prepared for the refurbishment of parts of the Madurai Palace. The main quadrangle of the palace is a 405 feet by 235 feet rectangle where the central courtyard is surrounded by domed and columned halls. The adjoining

[56] Tim Barringer, *Men at Work: Art and Labour in Mid-Victorian Britain* (New Haven, London, 2005), p. 294.

[57] Robert Chisholm, 'Tiroomal Naik's Palace', pp. 159–78.

dance hall is covered with an enormous wagon vault. The drawings, made on sheets 10 feet long and 4 feet wide were signed by J.M. Lewis and drawn by Chisholm's office in 1872. It is unlikely that they were intended for accurate estimates. Chisholm wrote of many 'weary days of jolting in bullock *bandies* carts, and [the] vexation of spirit' of his three-day journeys from his headquarters to the palace.[58] This was the price he had to pay for pursuing a crash course in seventeenth-century South Indian architecture. A late eighteenth-century drawing, by the Daniells, of the lofty dance hall of the palace, showed it in a poor state of repair, shorn of its profuse decoration. The dance hall was extensively rebuilt under Chisholm's supervision and furnished with a new polychrome covering of rich, intricate plaster sculptures and ornamental decoration both inside and out in what was presumed to be the spirit of the original.

The refurbishments are still regarded as a British interpretation of Indian architecture.[59] Considering that Chisholm did not execute the work and could not have gained the knowledge required to design or draw it, except in rudimentary fashion, it was more likely done by Indians. Whatever knowledge he did acquire of the design traditions and building techniques he had to have gained from Indians. At the RIBA, in 1875, based on his own observations of the extant ruin, Chisholm challenged an old description of the palace written by a contemporary in native handwriting, asserting its lack of accuracy. He was happy to judge which of the remaining sculptures were 'full of life and vigorous action' and which were 'deformities'. In his long Indian career Chisholm acknowledged the assistance of only one person by name. In 1883 he wrote that the illustrations accompanying his article on the Chandragiri Palace were prepared by Mr. Lewis, 'my assistant'.[60] He gives no clue as to Mr. Lewis's origins.

Talking at the RIBA in 1896 of his work at the enormous Lakshmivilasa Palace at Baroda—the largest of its kind in India—Chisholm claimed that he climbed the scaffolding and personally drew with charcoal, on the first coat of dry plaster, all the details of the ornament of the walls and ceilings of several apartments; 'the workmen then traced my drawings, and the work was executed from these tracings'.[61] Taking Chisholm's statements at face-value, it is easy to accuse him of denying the artisan design freedom.[62] But, if we read Chisholm's writings

[58] Robert Chisholm, 'Tiroomal Naik's Palace'. See the two rolls of stunningly detailed, 4 × 10 feet, drawings of Tiroomal Naik's Palace, signed by J.M. Lewis of the architect's office, RIBA British Architectural Library, 3–4 cupboards, lower mezzanine, roll 2.

[59] Andrea Volwahsen, *Splendours of Imperial India: British Architecture in the 18th and 19th Centuries* (Munich, 2004).

[60] Robert Chisholm, 'The Old Palace of Chandragiri', *Indian Antiquary* (November 1883), pp. 295–96.

[61] Robert Chisholm, 'Baroda Palace: The Town Residence of H.H. Sir Syaji Rao', *JRIBA Third Series*, vol. 3 (1896), pp. 421–33. The palace was designed by Major Mant, on whose death Chisholm took over.

[62] See Giles Tillotson, *The Tradition of Indian Architecture*, chapter 3.

carefully, we find him admitting to a different practice in the early years. During the erection of the Napier Museum, at Trevandrum, in 1872, his objective was to control the main forms of the building 'but in all else, in finishing, in elaboration, and in ornamentation, I would leave the native artizan entirely unfettered'.[63] It was then that he also thanked Colonel Jacob for having published a series of details of Indian architecture in the six-volume *Jeypore Portfolio of Architectural Details* that he hoped the natives would copy as examples of good ornament, instead of the 'atrocious' details they usually resorted to.

Certainly, at least during the early part of his career, Chisholm was dependent on and competing with Indian architects. To build in India, even within a British interpretation of Indian aesthetic traditions, he was compelled to acquire some Indian knowledge through a few books and hands-on experience at site. Although Chisholm's buildings are products of Indo-British collaboration, he refused to discuss this except in relation to the preparation of drawings and ornament. The point I wish to make here is that he did not need to; the point of the necessary collaboration was clearly understood.

In India, Chisholm was expected to copy Indian architecture and pretend that he did not. His English peers thought differently. Public exposure of Indian involvement with Indo-British architectural design came about at the RIBA in 1881 when R. Phene Spiers read a paper on the late Major Mant's designs in India. Before 1872 Mant had designed in the Gothic style, but somehow, by 1874, he prepared drawings for two buildings in the Hindu-Saracenic style (Mant's chosen name for his style of work). Spiers commented that:

> It could scarcely be expected that in so short a period Major Mant could have mastered so complicated and ornate a style as that in which these buildings were designed, if he had not had the good sense to avail himself of the native talent of the country. Fairly conversant with the Hindustani and Urdu dialects in which he had passed examinations in the higher standard of proficiency in 1868, he engaged and trained native draughtsmen to work out his designs.[64]

All the same, some of Chisholm's silences and boastful claims have to be attributed to the difficulty that his brief was not merely to modify but also to 'improve' 'native' architecture. This made him predictably inconsistent in his attitudes to Indian architecture: he praised and deprecated it in equal measure and relied on it to further his career. As an imperial architect he enjoyed a peculiar pleasure, tinged with hesitancy, anxiety and uncertainty.

[63] Robert Chisholm, *The Napier Museum, Trevandrum*, RIBA Pamphlet (1873).

[64] R. Phene Spiers, 'The Late Major Mant, Fellow', *TRIBA*, *1st Series* (1881–82), pp. 100–111.

Robbing the People of their 'Architectural Art'

In 1869 the Senate of the University of Madras discussed the establishment of professorships. *The Builder* reported that Mr. Chisholm proposed that architecture should be added to the list of subjects. In his address to the Senate, Chisholm respectfully protested against the view 'that architecture [was] a branch of civil engineering'. He commented that 'In the race of construction the artist has unfortunately been left behind the man of science' and pleaded earnestly that a chair in architecture was desirable because 'I conceive it to be a duty we owe to the natives of the country'. He gallantly accepted the conqueror's duty to 'engraft art' on to the 'dormant art' of the natives because 'We like all conquering nations have robbed the people of the architectural art they once possessed'—this was not unlike James Fergusson. Chisolm struck a more sophisticated didactic note when speaking of the 'advantages likely to follow a mere cultivation of taste among the natives'; they could, he said, learn the 'morality of art' by studying the science of aesthetics—a new branch of philosophy. But the worthiest grounds for the chair was the urgent question of a suitable style for the country:

> I would advocate the endowment of a chair of architecture on still graver grounds. We have arrived at a most important period in the history of architecture in this country, and it will be decided in the course of the next five or ten years whether we are to have a style suited to this country, or whether we are to be mere copyists of every bubble which breaks on the surface of European art, and import our architecture with our beer.[65]

For the post of professor, Chisholm advised that a man with the qualities of 'fearless critic' be imported from England.

Chisholm's views on architectural education echoed the politics and rhetoric of empire; an awareness of the great burden of the task of nation-building inflated the role of the architect in India to that of ideologue for empire. It was in developing this overarching imperial theme that Lord Napier outlined the technical and aesthetic superiority of 'Muslim' over 'Hindu' architecture. Matching ethnicity to architecture, and with breathless élan, Napier announced to his Indian audience that, 'From Granada to Constantinople, from Samarcand to Bejapore the earth is adorned with the masterpieces of Mussulman piety and taste and too often strewed with their remains.'[66] The redeeming 'capital features' of the style were the arch and the dome inherited from Rome and Byzantium. He did not miss its associations with gardens, water and all manner of natural scenery either. From Delhi to Seringapatam he extolled the virtues of the

[65] *The Builder*, 5 June 1869.

[66] *The Builder*, 10 September 1870.

building tradition but waxed most lyrical further south: 'go to the grove of tamarind trees and palms' he said,

> beneath the rocks of Vellore where the funereal repose is accompanied by the muttered Koran and the murmur of waters from the well: there you will still feel how the voices of nature and art, of beauty and divinity and death are blended by the Mussulman builders.[67]

Napier advised the Government of India that it would, in his 'humble judgement, do well to consider whether the Mussulman forms might not be adopted generally as the *official style* [italics added] of architecture'. In Napier's imperial polity architecture was invested with new meanings for the India the British were creating. His project presented an alternate 'imperial' style to the classic and Gothic offerings of Calcutta and Bombay. It was a superior vision, without question, because it was tempered with the unique ingredient of native appeal. His trump card to deflect potential critics was the definition of the new style in the appealing language of a 'revival of native art'.

The rigour with which London pursued the question of the Supreme Government's intervention in the minor presidencies suggests that the relationship between the presidencies was fraught and unsettled. Napier and his officials resisted the creeping centralisation issuing from Calcutta. They informed London that the Supreme Government should be Supreme; with the viceroy residing at Simla, 'and as little identified with local Bengal interests as possible'.[68] Above all they resented Bengal interference in local public works, where a great deal of pedantry had been introduced. 'There is a system of standard plans which comes from Calcutta for all sorts of public buildings which if strictly enforced would be injudicious.' On the grounds that 'in a vast country like India a considerable diversity of style and construction should be allowed', Napier endorsed selective defiance of the standard plan whose positive points he gladly admitted.

Ideally, the political principle Napier advocated for governing India was the decentralised 'federal system', with some Madras and Bombay men in the viceroy's council; to create a fusion of feeling which 'did not now exist'. He wrote to London that he was 'a little afraid of Colonel Strachey of the Irrigation Department. The Viceroy ought to keep a tight hand on him and I will take the liberty of saying so when I get to Calcutta.'[69] Colonel Strachey's brother John was a very powerful civil servant, and already a member of the viceroy's council. Thus, a year into his

[67] Ibid.

[68] Napier to Cranborne, 24 February 1867, Salisbury Collection.

[69] Napier to Cranborne, 15 February 1867, Salisbury Collection.

arrival in Madras, Napier was fully embroiled in the PWD irrigation conflict. The Madras Government wanted Colonel Orr or Anderson (from Madras) not Strachey (from Calcutta) appointed as the Irrigation Secretary on the viceroy's council, since 'The Madras men know most about irrigation.' Following his predecessors, Napier wrote disapprovingly and disparagingly to the Secretary of State for India, Sir Stafford Northcote, that 'Madras irrigation works are very peculiar and with all the respect due to R. Strachey he cannot understand them. The lower kind of civil engineers here are not to be trusted.'[70]

Napier's all-India perspective supported a degree of financial and political decentralisation but with certain safeguards. Contrary to the sentiments he had expressed to Lord Cranborne four months earlier, he wrote to Sir Stafford Northcote that he discountenanced 'any approach to the federal system' if it was under the control of men like Massey and Strachey. In this event he supported a 'powerful and searching imperial government'.[71] He boasted of his contribution to Madras—'In short I have proposals out now for museums, sanitation, hospitals, for sanitariness [*sic*], for university education, schools, Art schools—I have gone the whole round of the modern social scheme. Money is the great want.'[72]

Napier's self-perception, then, was that of a social and artistic visionary, armed with a superior moral rectitude. It flourished in a paternal world where social benevolence and engineering mingled with the science of aesthetics, to make room for the self-expressions of a powerful Indo-British lobby. He was widely regarded as a benefactor of the sick, the suffering, and 'those who are too weak or poor to help themselves'. The Napier Park was created in 1872, as a memorial and a stimulus for 'succeeding governors to walk in his steps'.[73] Far from the orthodox stranglehold of the Supreme Government and its Bengal civil servants, Napier and his coterie developed their vision of another architecture for empire.

'Really Very Handsome Designs'

In 1864 the government intended to place the Senate House in juxtaposition to the College; the University Syndicate opposed this siting on the grounds that 'such a conjunction might confound the two institutions'; appearing to identify the independent university with the College of subordinate status. Although the validity of this argument was not apparent to the

[70] Napier to Sir Stafford Northcote, June 18 1867, Add. Ms. 50,027 Iddelsleigh Papers, ff. 125–51. Sir Stafford Northcote became Secretary of State for India in 1866.

[71] Napier to Sir Stafford Northcote, 9 November 1867, Iddelsleigh Papers.

[72] Napier to Florence Nightingale, 24 June 1868, Add. Ms. 45779 Nightingale Papers, ff. 215.

[73] *Asylum Press Almanac*, Madras 1873, p. 579.

government, the opinion of the university authorities was ratified by the Secretary of State in 1864. He ordered that no steps should be taken to 'give an appearance of identity or even special connexion between the University and Presidency College'. Accordingly, it was decided to build the Senate House on land near Marshall's Road. Three years later Lord Napier intervened in the dispute:

It forms no part of my purpose to oppose the wishes of the University authorities or the determination of Sir Charles Wood. There is, no doubt some force in the opinion of the Syndicate, and the decision of the Secretary of State is not likely to be altered. But because the buildings of the University and the buildings of the College are to be distinct, it does not follow that they should be distant, and I strongly object to placing the University on the piece of land near Marshall's Road.[74]

He proposed an alternate site between the Marine Villa and the Revenue Board Office commenting that between the site he was proposing and the College:

three public buildings intervene—the Revenue Board, the Chepauk Palace and the PWD. All these three structures belong to different orders of architecture, and if any apprehension should survive that the University might be confounded with the College in consequence of some similarity in the design, I do not doubt that the versatility of Mr. Chisholm could produce a fifth variety of style, which would be different from all the rest and more ornamental than any of them.[75]

The project lay in abeyance until March 1868 when the Government of India's financial department released the sum of Rs. 2,00,000, out of the capital of the local education building fund towards the cost of Senate House.[76] Lord Napier wrote to Sir Stafford Northcote that 'Its foundation in a conspicuous position on the shore is an event in the history of the university... the two buildings, Presidency College and the University building are really very handsome designs. I will send you photographs of them bye and bye' (see Fig. 2).[77]

The 60-member University Senate of 1869 included 12 Indians: among them were the First Prince of Travancore, Sir Madava Rao, Hyder Jung Bahadur, Shesiya Sastri, Ranganadam Sastri and V. Rama Aiyengar.[78] The composition of the Syndicate is not known but Sir Muthusamy Aiyer, a great lover of the fine arts, was appointed in 1877. In April 1868 the Syndicate was

[74] Minute No. 47, 28 November 1867, 'On the question of the most appropriate site for the new University Buildings and the source from which the funds for their construction should be provided'. *Minutes Recorded by the Rt. Honble. Francis Baron Napier and Ettrick during the Administration of the Government of the Madras Presidency*.

[75] Minute No. 47, *Minutes Recorded*.

[76] GO 4, 2 March 1868, MPED, TNA.

[77] Napier to Stafford Northcote, 7 April 1868, Iddelsleigh Papers.

[78] *Asylum Press Almanac*, 1869, p. 564 and Pillai, *Representative Indians*, p. 162.

asked to contact Mr. Chisholm, with a view to preparing plans for the new building.[79] The following month it unanimously accepted the change of site proposed by His Excellency the Governor-General.[80] In May, Chisholm put before the government a ground plan for his design, stating that he was in a position to start work with the laying of the foundation stone. He noted his intention to align the 'general face of the building in line with the new College'.[81] With the Governor presiding, the Syndicate approved the design; it resolved to direct the superintending engineer of the 4th Division to authorise Chisholm to take measurements for commencement of the work.[82] The foundation stone was laid on 30 May 1869.

The Design

Lord Napier's presence injected new life into the Senate House project. Chisholm had by now been asked to alter the original design whose style the judges had doubted would be in consonance with the 'received view'. Chisholm told the Syndicate that the new design was different in three ways: extent of accommodation, the arrangement of parts and in style. In the first alteration he merged the two requested small lecture rooms into one; guided by the 'latest English example of such buildings the London University Building executed last year in which there is but one large lecture hall'. In the original plan the building was kept cool by closing the lower portion entirely and sending a draught of air from below by artificial means. But now that he had gained some experience of the sea-coast, Chisholm was convinced 'in the almost universal opinion that a building on the beach should be as open as possible' (see Fig. 101).

He said that though the points of support collectively were a small area, he had endeavoured to subdue as far as practicable, the 'consequent flood of light'. The double wall on the exterior was meant to help keep the walls cool. It allowed the doors to slide back on wheels in place of folding hinges. Demurring to Mr. Powell, he had placed the great hall on a basement of store-rooms, the floor of which was 3 feet below the ground surface. Lastly, with regard to style, he asserted that the original was in 'what is called the French Renaissance', which to be

[79] 31 March 1868, p. 53, Z/P/2548, BL.

[80] GO 65, 24 April 1868, MPED, TNA. This research was done without the benefit of access to the University of Madras archive. The University's Public Relations Officer, Mr. Ramalingam, informed me that records of university proceedings were available only after 1968. Building access too was curtailed due to the uncertain state of repair. The basement and upper levels were out of bounds.

[81] GO 52, 2 May 1868, MPED, TNA.

[82] GO 12, 7 May 1868, MPED,TNA.

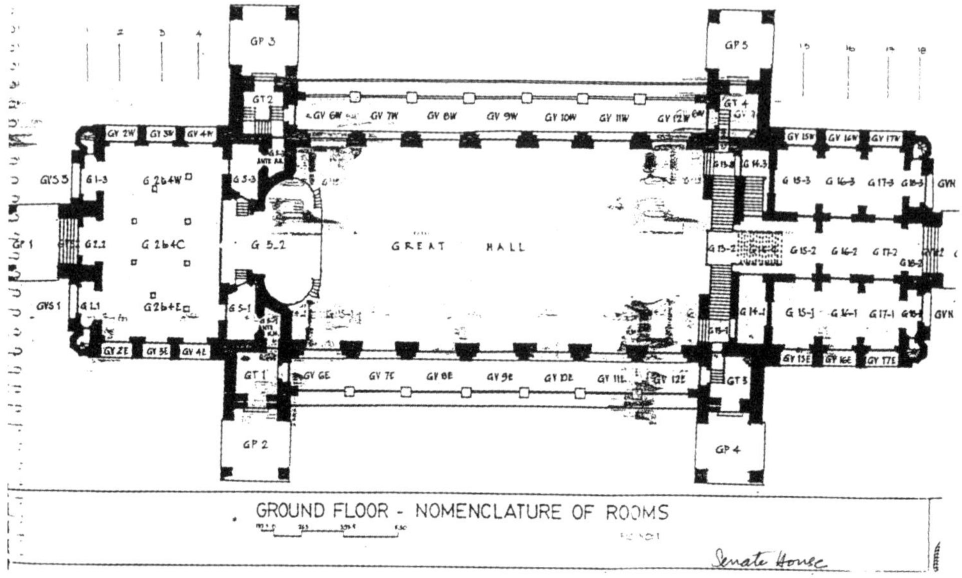

Figure 101: Senate House, ground floor plan

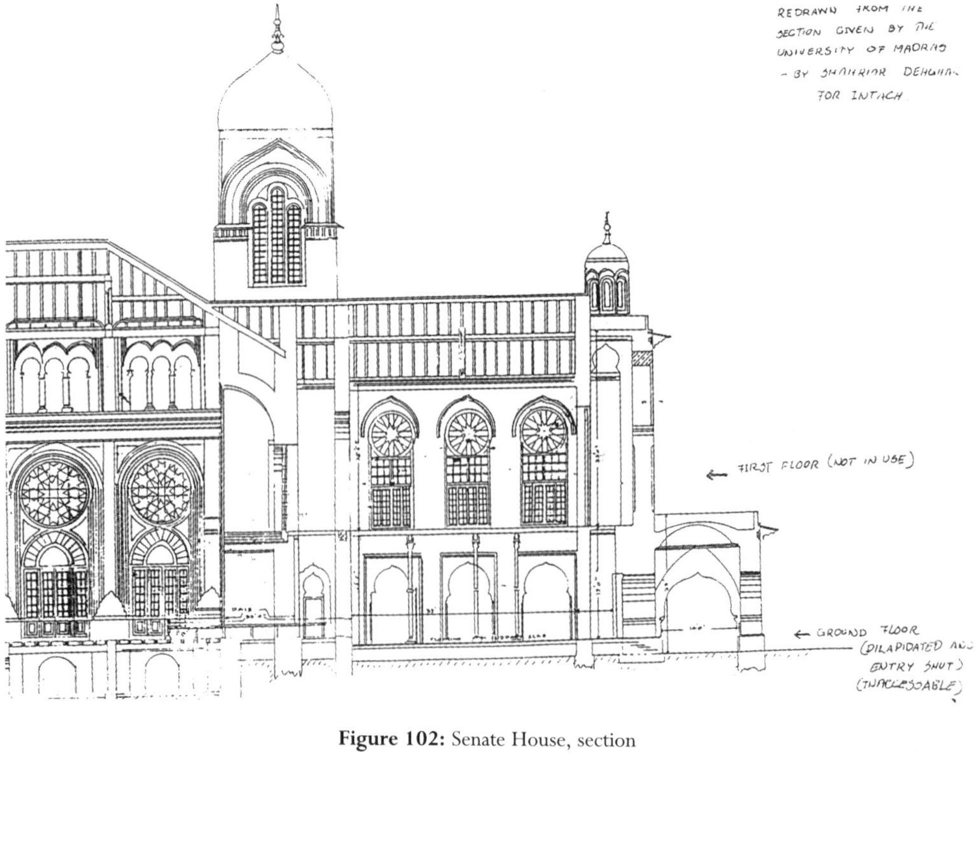

Figure 102: Senate House, section

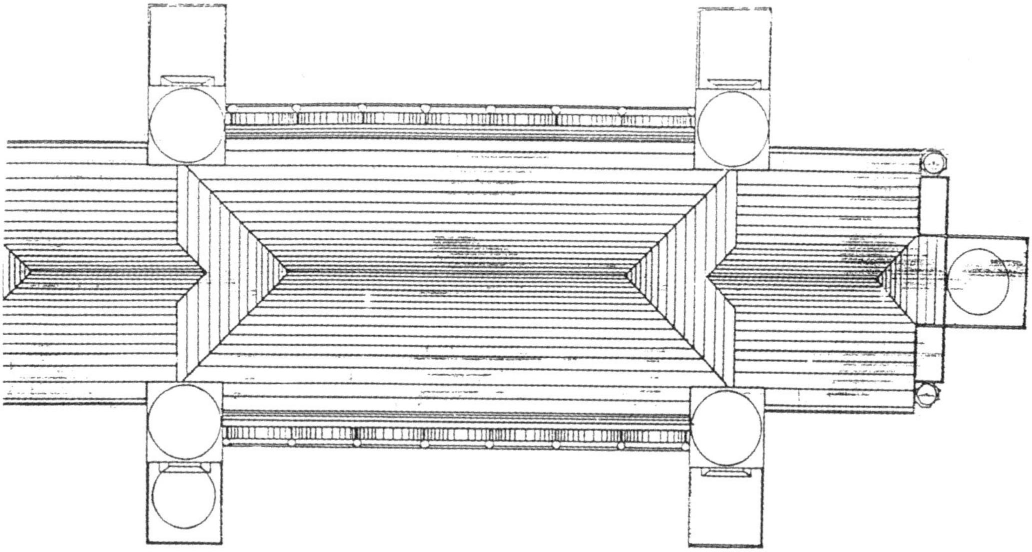

Figure 103: Senate House, roof plan

done properly, needed a large amount of stone-cutting. Stone was abandoned because of the difficulty of getting good labour and the high cost, Rs. 60–70/yard.

There is little doubt that Chisholm was subject to some pressure to alter the design. We can detect more than a touch of coercion in his description of the event:

> I have gladly altered the expression of the original into a style more in keeping with the internal arrangements; a round arched Gothic, of a simple and early type, in which stone is used only when absolutely required for strength; the material generally being moulded brick in natural colours.[83]

The estimated cost was two and a half lakhs with decoration amounting to ten thousand rupees.

In May 1869, Chisholm submitted a detailed estimate which exceeded the original because of the 'extra depth at which the foundations [were] laid, the cost of the spacious vault beneath the great hall, and the increased accommodation provided generally'.[84] In the accompanying design submission he claimed 'to some originality, both regards arrangement and details'. In most modern buildings he said, the 'admission of air is accompanied by the admission of an equal amount of glare, and on the other hand, the light cannot be excluded except by obstructing

[83] 8 May 1868, p.1825, P/439/36, MPPWD, BL. The drawings were not found.

[84] GO 585, 27 May 1869, MPPWD, TNA.

free ventilation'. His new design was glare-free but with adequate light and ventilation. He borrowed from late thirteenth-century Gothic, the practice of making walls with piers which acted simply as frameworks for glass paintings. Moreover, the buttresses ran up like piers and turned a series of deep arches round the windows; such elaborate soffits would give adequate weather protection. The building as constructed deployed the radically different solution of a verandah with vaulted roofs (see Fig. 102).

With regard to the style Chisholm went on to explain that

> although the building is in no particular style, it has a decided expression of Byzantine. It seemed to me that the very beautiful geometrical windows of Byzantine architecture would be the best suited for the system of top lighting, I adopted, and these features have given the keynote to the style of the whole building.[85]

He was convinced that this solution avoided the 'slavish copying of known forms'. He then compared the ratio, of the points of support to the entire floor area, of St. Peter's, Santa Maria del Fiore, St. Paul's and the Ste. Genevieve Pantheon, with that of Senate House and found the latter was the smallest; in the Convocation Hall, the ratio was even smaller. This clever table of comparison ranked Senate House above the most famous domed churches in Europe. His Excellency the Governor was 'not quite satisfied with the effect of the domes surmounting the turrets, and would wish to have laid before him for consideration of Government, one or two modified designs showing alternative modes of crowning turrets' (see Fig. 103).[86] Presumably, this was in reference to the domed turrets of the parapet that imitated those of the Jami Masjid of the Bijapur Sultans.

The discussion on style sheds light on social relations governing architectural design. Chisholm's dedicated self-promotion, recalling de Havilland before him, is a reminder of the harsh competition faced by designers. Modesty was not a prized commodity in the colonial building world. In 1868 Chisholm was freely admitting to altering the Senate House design to 'accord with universal opinion' and went as far as to record the contributions of Syndicate members like Powell. The tone of the 1869 report is that of a more self-assured designer possessive of his ideas. The design was evolving through consultation with the Senate and Napier, but Chisholm too was beginning to emphasise his own expertise in interpreting Gothic and Byzantine architecture.

[85] Ibid.

[86] His building for the Baroda College had a 70-foot diameter dome built of brick in the Indian style, whose construction he described at length. See Robert Chisholm, 'New College for the Gaekwar of Baroda,with Notes on Style and Domical Construction in India', *TRIBA* (1882–83), pp. 141–46.

The Perfect Style for Christianity in India—Deccani Byzantine?

It is certain that the Byzantine inspiration for the Senate House design came from Lord Napier and not Chisholm, although Chisholm knew his Ruskin. Ruskin was infatuated with Byzantine Venice and had argued that the Byzantine style could also be employed in the present. 'Located mainly in the East and yet born of Rome, Byzantine architecture presented especially acute problems for Victorian architects and historians.'[87] In the 1850s, Byzantine revivalists in Britain often ignored its oriental overtones in their efforts to make it serve their own needs.

Napier, having lived in Istanbul, was familiar with ancient Byzantine and Ottoman architecture and contemporary British experiments in hybrid architectural styles in Istanbul. In his opinion it was the perfect style for 'Christianity in India'.[88] Any association Byzantine art had with Islam and the Ottomans was deftly circumvented in this formula. Moreover, it allowed Napier to smoothly appropriate Indian-Islamic architectural forms into the new architecture for a Christian empire, divesting them of their Islamic content by hinting that they were in fact originally Byzantine.

Figure 104: Senate House, painted glass window

Thomas Metcalf identified Senate House as Chisholm's major work, incorporating Byzantine elements; a design both 'extravagant and idiosyncratic'.[89] One Indian assessment described it as 'admirable' in the Deccani style of Moslem architecture.[90] Tillotson thought it drew on sources as far apart as Moorish Spain and Mughal India.[91] Chisholm allowed that it veered to the Byzantine but claimed it was actually in 'no particular style' at all. The building defies comfortable classification within the norms of western and oriental design traditions offering few concessions to the seeker of precedent.

[87] For Europe's complex response to Byzantine architecture in the period, especially the difficulty surrounding its slippery western/oriental nature see Mark Crinson, *Empire Building*, p. 72.

[88] *The Builder*, 27 August 1870. For contemporary British architecture in Istanbul see Mark Crinson, *Empire Building*, chapter 5.

[89] Thomas Metcalf, *An Imperial Vision*, p. 63.

[90] *History of Higher Education in South India* (2 vols., Madras, 1957), p. 138.

[91] Giles Tillotson, 'Orientalising the Raj', in Christopher London (ed.), *Architecture in Victorian and Edwardian London* (London, 1994), pp. 15–34.

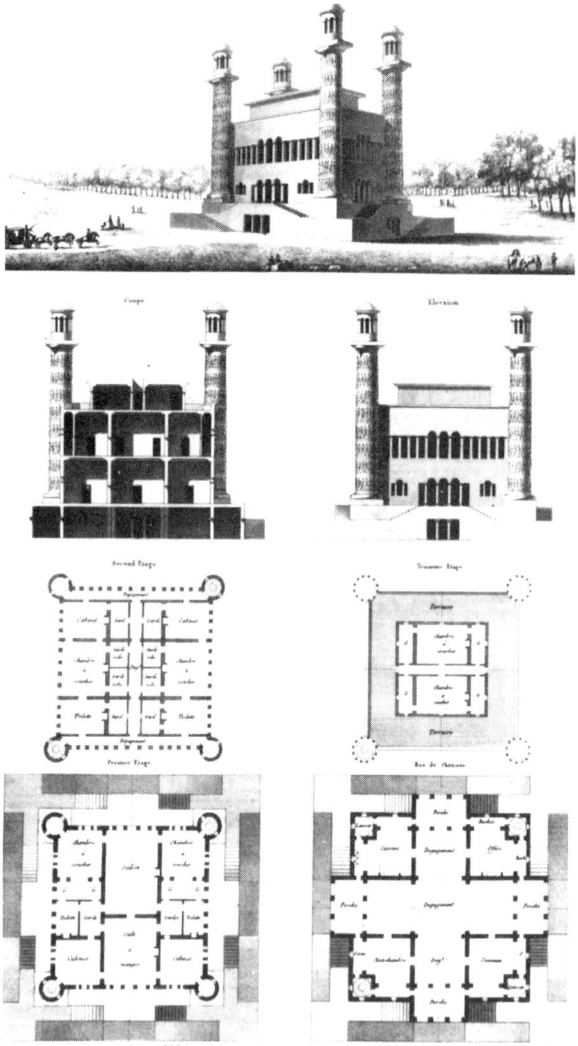

Figure 105: Plans and elevations, House in the Country or Temple of Memory, 1804

Senate House is a free-standing, outward facing rectangular block with four corner towers; each surmounted by a small dome. The overall form of the building sets it simultaneously within a general European and Islamic design tradition. The strongest claim to inspiration comes from the tombs and mosques of the Deccan, the stuff of dreams,[92] or the Dilkusha Palace in Lucknow, based on the baroque Northumberland country house, Seaton Delaval, designed by John Vanbrugh in 1718.[93] But other sources crop up too. The most insistent is the French Freemason design for a House in the Country, or Temple of Memory, featured in the neo-classical designer Claude-Nicolas Ledoux's treatise *L'Architecture* of 1804 (see Fig. 105). James Curl thought the extraordinary design recalled a fortress of:

> Trajanic columns, Palladian architecture, Greek, Roman, and Moresque Islamic themes, and much else. It can therefore be interpreted as a mnemonic of form, Architecture, and civilization, for Ledoux himself referred to the desirability of making the different characters of works of Architecture from various civilizations known to all. The Temple of Memory was intended to be free from the prejudices of Classically-trained Architects, and suggested a wider culture, taking elements from many centuries, languages of design, and civilizations.[94]

[92] George Michell, *Architecture and Art of the Deccan Sultanates,* p. 1.

[93] For a discussion of the Dilkusha Palace see Neeta Das, *Indian Architecture: Problems in the Interpretation of 18th and 19th Century Architecture, A Study of Dilkusha Palace Lucknow* (New Delhi, 1998).

[94] James Stevens Curl, *The Art and Architecture*, p. 175.

Figure 106: Senate House colonnade, arch details

The Temple of Memory design links the local élite's and Chisholm's association with Freemasonry, Chisholm's taste for French design and his desire to be free of the prejudices of those trained in the classical tradition. On the other hand, a form mnemonic of multiple civilisations was an ideal model for a Senate House in the multi-culture of South India.

Whilst it is impossible to be certain of the origin of the plan forms, it is simpler to identify several design themes originating in the Madurai Palace of which the key items are those of scale and spatial order (see Figs. 106–108). Napier was very conscious of the great size of the Palace. At the RIBA in 1876 he expansively described it as 'greatly [exceeding] in dimensions most of the Mussulman and Hindoo buildings. I believe it exceeds in dimensions the largest structures in the north of India' (see Fig. 21).[95] Madurai was also noted for its majestic halls covered with large masonry wagon-vaults. The seventeenth- century Madurai hall is 125 feet long, 69 feet wide and 56 feet high. The main hall of Senate House is 130 feet long, 58 feet wide and 54 feet high and could seat up to 1,600 people.[96]

When describing the palace at the RIBA Chisholm drew the listeners' attention:

to the extreme beauty and flexibility of the general form of the arches. The principal line rises vertically or with a slight backward curvature until a certain point is reached when the curve commences, slowly at first, then increasing to a steady curvature then decreasing again until it meets and reposes against its fellow from the opposite side. These lines so admirably expressive of increasing and decreasing momentum are highly suggestive

[95] Robert Chisholm, 'Tiroomal Naik's Palace', p. 173.

[96] Senate House Bombay was commenced in March 1869. The hall is 104 × 44 feet, it was designed by Sir Gilbert Scott in the Gothic style, see *Education Buildings in India, Department of Education Occasional Papers No. 6* (Calcutta, 1911), p. 17.

Figure 107: Madurai Palace, colonnade

Figure 108: Senate House, colonnade

of that concealment of effort which is one of the chief attributes of great art. The slight reflex curve at the apex is often beautifully introduced.[97]

It was, he said, a 'Saracenic arcade with a Hindoo cornice and entablature upwards of 60 feet high'. The central dome at Madurai rests on a square plan, 64 feet across. Its drum, pierced by a clerestory, rose in octagonal form through the roof. The clerestory is protected from the weather by double verandahs. Chisholm was inclined to argue that the palace was more Hindu than Saracenic. Lord Napier disagreed. Challenging Chisholm from the audience Napier suggested that it was first built as a mosque by a Muslim dynasty, basing his claim on the knowledge that Madurai was ruled by the Delhi Sultans from 1323, for 48 years, and nominally by the Carnatic Nawabs from 1739. Mr. Morris from the audience expressed the view that the

Figure 109: Detail of dome over turret

[97] Robert Chisholm, 'Tiroomal Naik's Palace', p. 166.

Figure 110: Senate House, parapet

men who directed it must have had European training of some kind, since a part of the building 'remind[s] us of Byzantine examples'.[98] The manifestly hybrid Deccani regional tradition, to which the palace designs belong, could not validate the rigid ethno-aesthetic classifications being developed by colonial intellectuals to understand Indian architecture; the result was a muddle.

Aside from Madurai there are other buildings in South India that contributed to the overall forms of Senate House. The prominent external colonnade is surmounted by an entablature with elaborate cornice above which is a parapet, with mini-turrets and finials (see Fig. 110); the ensemble is a variation of the cornice and parapet of the tomb of Ibrahim Rauza of Bijapur (see Fig. 93). The domed and turreted corner towers echo the forms of the Chepauk Tower, even to the extent of repeating the oriel windows (see Fig. 91). Four large pointed arches set immediately below the domes of the towers competed with the domes in scale and attention—an arrangement unseen in India (see Fig. 109). The clumsy juxtaposition of arch and dome exposed the designer's unfamiliarity with such motifs. The pointed arches of the towers were further distinguished by having set in them a round arch. This arrangement, whose early origins lay in Buddhist architecture, was seen closer to Madras in the Rathas of Mahabalipuram (see Fig. 111). Chisholm, familiar with both, observed that the pointed arch in India pre-dated 'the first Mohammedan invasion'.[99] The banded arch rings may refer to

[98] Ibid., p. 174.

[99] See Percy Brown, *Hindu Architecture*, Plate LX . Chisholm spoke of pointed arches seen on the Rathas in 'New College', p. 143.

early Byzantine architecture in Istanbul or to the mixed oriental and occidental designs for the Crimean Memorial Church, also in Istanbul, submitted for the architectural design competition by William Burges, in 1857.[100] The painted domes of the four corner towers recall the Deccan as well as the vaults of the Thanjavur Palace.

Figure 111: Rathas at Mahabalipuram showing pointed arches at the ends of shala roof, c. seventh century

The load bearing elements of the structure were a series of recessed brick piers. Set between the piers were 14 lofty painted-glass windows with round arches (see Fig. 104). The hall sat on a vaulted cellar. To the north and south of the hall were two-storey wings with the main entry porches. Arched double-height colonnaded verandahs flanked the main hall on the east and west. The latter, with their characteristic entablature, repeated the proportions of the colonnades at Madurai Palace on a slightly lesser scale; reaching a height of around 54 feet they afforded protection to the main walls. The extended eaves of the main roof protected the clerestory. The eaves themselves were supported by columns that sat on the narrow vaulted roof of the verandah below. The clerestory openings were small round arches with painted glass, harking back to Byzantine shapes, though the idea of a clerestory derived as much from the Madurai domes as from Istanbul.

The great hall had a tiled hip roof. Painted domes with finials surmounted the corner towers. The senate hall, which could accommodate over 300 people, was placed at the southern end of the first floor and the syndicate room was originally at the northern end. Round

[100] For the Memorial Church see Mark Crinson, *Empire Building*, chapter 5.

arched colonnades in the wings continued the external colonnade theme of the hall. Together they formed a line of 13 arches stretching across the façades producing the building's floating feel. Four additional porches, contiguous with the towers afforded entry on the eastern and western sides. Four small turrets with cupola roofs, containing spiral stairs, marked the corners of the two wings. The stylistic confusion that dogged British interpretations of the architecture at Madurai was compounded in the design for Senate House.

One modern Indian report described the great hall of Senate House as 'having the splendour of a historical royal court room *durbar* designed in the Mughal style'.[101] The scale of the space and external colonnades of the Senate House great hall were reminiscent of the durbar halls and courts at Madurai but the spatial arrangement was static. The block plan confined the space within a fixed rectangle of glazed windows and a flat ceiling. The three-dimensional depth and indeterminacy of colonnades surrounding courtyards, endless dark vistas and floating vaults, pierced by pin-points of high-level light were absent (see Fig. 13). The verandahs were too narrow and isolated to produce the shifting patterns of light and welcome relief between interior gloom and tropical glare. The spatial order shifted from the open to the closed abandoning in the process the sense of mystery that accompanied spatial indeterminacy at the palace.

The hall was completed in 1873 and occupied the same year.[102] A mere decade later Chisholm, now bolstered by an almost impregnable reputation as an 'Indian' architect, authoritatively informed his peers at the RIBA that: 'an architect practising in India should unhesitatingly elect to practise in the native styles of art—indeed, the natural art expression of these men is the *only* art to be obtained in the country.'[103] Napier and Chisholm had manufactured a Byzantine/Deccani style which was daringly new but masquerading as a 'native' style. I shall discuss the British aesthetic contribution to the design a little later.

Sharing Knowledge about Domes

Napier regarded the dome as a 'capital feature' in the Muslim tradition. Keeping in mind the European-style dome Chisholm introduced at Presidency College and the weight he accorded

[101] Undated PWD report, INTACH, p. 4.

[102] *History of Higher Education in South India*, vol. 1 (2 vols., Madras, 1957), p.138. A great deal of discrepancy surrounds these dates. Thomas Metcalf says it was begun in 1874 and completed in 1879, see *An Imperial Vision*, p. 63. The sparse PWD records certainly suggest that building carried on until 1878.

[103] Robert Chisholm, 'New College', p. 141. In the next few sentences Chisholm was adamant that the 'native arts' had no 'position amongst the matured arts of other countries'.

domes at Baroda in the 1880s, it is indeed curious that Senate House had no wagon vault or central dome over the main hall—the perfect place in which to boast a large vaulted roof. I suggest that Chisholm's lack of experience of Indian vault construction discouraged him from attempting to reproduce the lofty Madurai vaults or domes at Senate House; a move that would entail risking his reputation through a reliance on unknown native builders. But by 1875 he had gathered, or was in the process of gathering, sufficient information on the modes of construction and decoration of the domes and wagon vaults at Madurai to allow him to commence supervision of the restoration work.[104] And it is likely that he had come to know and trust a few local builders.

The omission of the dome in Madras becomes significant when set against events eight years later. Having mastered and improved Indian methods of dome building in Madurai and Baroda, Chisholm spoke confidently at the RIBA in 1882 on the practical aspects of his dome construction in Baroda.[105] His detailed report on arch and dome construction displayed a meticulous devotion to the task of acquiring Indian knowledge. Also at the RIBA, in 1884, Emerson commented on the fact that architects practising in England rarely had an opportunity to build a dome. He admired domes because they were the grandest and most impressive method of covering large areas; in 'all great architecture there should be mysteriousness' and 'there is mystery about the gloom of the interior of a vast dome that well suits the imagination of the Oriental'. His own dome at Muir College, Allahabad, 34 feet in diameter was only half the size of Chisholm's at Baroda.[106]

Chisholm, speaking from the audience, adverted to the abundance of material on 'dead' or archaeological sites and the difficulty in gaining knowledge about 'living' architecture in India. 'It is both difficult and expensive to learn anything about Indian art in India, and many journeys must be taken and much time expended ere one obtains that connected idea of the subject necessary to work in native styles.' Of his 74-feet diameter Baroda dome he noted 'it is simply an example of a modern dome constructed of brick without the aid of centering of any kind'. I suggest that in the early years in Madras both Chisholm and Napier lacked the knowledge and the confidence to experiment with the unfamiliar technology of vault construction in the Senate House design. Much as they admired domes there was too much at stake to risk structural failure. The project was, moreover, too prestigious to hand over to 'native' engineers.

[104] Robert Chisholm, 'Tiroomal Naik's Palace'.

[105] Robert Chisholm, 'New College'.

[106] William Emerson, 'A Description'.

'Constructive Expedient Unknown to the Native Workmen'

In 1870 Chisholm reported that when the trenches for the foundations for Senate House were cut, the ground was found to be 'irregular and soft'.[107] It was then decided that the foundation should go deeper, incurring extra cost. He gave no details of the design of the foundation other than that it supported a vaulted cellar. The foundations were probably similar in construction to those of St. Andrew's Church. The masonry in the foundations and rendered interior walls of the College were of country brick, in ordinary use in Madras.[108] Sixteen brick piers, resting on the vaulted cellar, carried the hall roof made of clay tiles on zinc sheets. The drawings imply that six roof trusses around 9 feet deep and 58 feet wide spanned the hall, affording support for purlins which in turn supported the rafters. The rafters and the reapers were probably made of wood. Chisholm explained that the work was over-budget due to the large excess quantities spent on the iron work. 'In the examination hall, owing to practical difficulties experienced in raising the girders as designed, it was found advisable to have eight plate girders made and rivetted on to the ends of the main girders.'[109] The trusses of the main hall were made of timber.[110] Elsewhere, iron columns supported the wooden floor of the south wing, and possibly the eaves of the main roof. Iron beams may have also supported the barrel vaults of the colonnades. The hall had a wooden floor and the verandah floors were of stone or cement. The upper floors were either constructed in 'Madras Terrace' mode, or with timber.

The towers were made of brick and surmounted by brick domes plastered and painted on the outside; probably constructed in the South Indian fashion. Chisholm was fascinated by the famous Madras plasterwork or 'bulpum'. He described it enthusiastically. It was applied in three coats, the first consisting of three parts river sand to two parts of shell lime laid on roughly by trowel and hand float. The second coat was composed of ground quartz sand and shell lime in equal proportions, 'brought to a surface by Derby floats, in the ordinary European manner'. The third coat was a similar mixture ground very fine to a consistency of cream which was trowelled on and polished with agate. After applying the creamy mixture,

[107] GO 300, 22 June 1870, MPPWD, TNA. The main sources for this information are a series of conservation reports held by the Indian National Trust for Art and Cultural Heritage (INTACH) Tamil Nadu. Shariar Deghan prepared the first undated report. It contains excellent drawings and photographs. The second undated report is by the PWD. The third report is by INTACH, directed by Benny Kuriakose, March 1990. None of the reports are comprehensive. The teams had limited access to the building and primary sources, for reasons unknown.

[108] GO 835, 13 March 1866, MPPWD, TNA.

[109] GO 300, 22 June 1870, MPPWD, TNA.

[110] I was given partial, carefully monitored access only to the ground-floor. I am indebted to Dr. Srivathsan, Faculty of Architecture, Anna University, for this information.

'the workman continually rubs the surface with fine dry powdered quartz contained in a small linen bag'.[111] It was said that ground egg-shells were used in the finishing coat of superior old work.

The columns, capitals, arch surrounds and the projecting cornice of the colonnades were made of stone. The main windows, doors, staircase and grilles were wooden and sometimes elaborately carved. When asked to explain the discrepancy between his estimates and costs, Chisholm justified it with the claim that, 'In a building so entirely new of its kind and full of constructive expedient unknown to the native workmen, I scarcely think that a closer result could be anticipated.'[112]

The 'constructive' novelty he was alluding to could only have been the iron roof. Except for minor items such as the pointing required for the unplastered brick, and the extensive glazing, the main structure appears to belong in the conventional regional tradition. Lord Napier described it as a rude, coarse tradition of stone, brick and plaster, without the refinement of 'curious sculpture', marble or precious metal. It ideally suited his purpose of making political statements through the ordering of urban and architectural space; he had realised rather early on that by using Indian labour and materials he could initiate remarkable building programmes without excessive expenditure. It was a rare luxury.

Modernising the Construction Industry

Public works buildings were built departmentally or by contract. Chapter 4 showed how Charles Trevelyan, during his brief tenure as Governor of Madras in 1859, had unsuccessfully endeavoured to introduce the lump sum contract in Madras, having declared that it was 'successfully used in Great Britain and all her forty colonies'. Senate House, unlike Presidency College, was built within the PWD system. In 1859 the departmental system employed one supplier for all articles except brick and chunam. The supplier had to 'enter into a legal arrangement to supply all articles at a fixed rate, sufficiently remunerative to him, depositing sealed samples of all articles he binds himself to supply, and failing in his contract to be bound to heavy penalties fixed in the bond'.[113]

[111] Robert Chisholm, 'Tiroomal Naik's Palace'.

[112] GO 300, 22 June 1878, MPPWD, TNA. *Athenaeum*, 18 January 1870, reported that Chisholm was to contact the General Superintendent of the PWD Workshop for the manufacture of the heavy pieces of iron, for the repair of Madurai Palace; it shows that local manufacture of iron building components was not new to Madras. GO 635A, 25 August 1874, MPPWD, TNA, says the iron ties came from England.

[113] GO 63–67, 31 August 1859, MPPWD, TNA.

As soon as the work was sanctioned the estimate worker would 'draw an indent' for all materials needed and have it signed by the architect. Chunam was obtained from the government factory, which had rented quarries near Pulicat, through the civil architect. Following the success of the lime-works, the government established a brick factory under Chisholm's control, which supplied the bricks for building Senate House.[114] The supplier made issues to the overseers who were furnished with estimates, and details of rates, and they were answerable for full work being carried out by the workmen. They kept a daily account of work done; these were checked fortnightly. Overseers were also responsible for the expenditure of materials, checked twice a week by the architect.

A report on the use of contracts in the PWD noted that because the PWD rates were low, 'the superior classes of workmen were employed by the railway'. Bricks, tiles, stones, sand and clay and cart hire, as well as 'English minor articles'—iron, brass, screws, locks and country minor articles—oils, palmirah, bamboos, nails and hinges were furnished by a general supplier on a yearly contract. Paint work was executed on contract at 'so much per square' and teakwood was purchased in the market, in lots, as required. The civil architect declared the preparation of estimates to be 'tedious and labour intensive' and 'if made for all works' would require two or more estimate makers in the office.[115]

To break the monopoly system of a single supplier Trevelyan had proposed abandoning fixing the prices for materials and labour; contracts were to be entered into after public competition. He also wanted the full current market rate of wages to be given to the workmen. Senior officials believed that the most serious obstacle to the introduction of the contract system was the 'general dishonesty of natives as a class'. Minor obstacles ranged from the want of capitalists, the ignorance of contractors and the stringency of the contract bonds. The chief engineer advised the government to do away with the 'whole body of Lower Subordinates' who practised petty espionage and preyed upon the contractors 'like harpies' and deprived them of their fair profits.[116]

The state's aim was to open the construction industry as a whole to the free competition of the market. From Chisholm we gather that there was a flourishing market for classical and Gothic architectural artefacts in the south. He was disparaging of bazaar production of building components such as wooden tracery, painted brickwork, quoins, and pottery

[114] GO 442, 19 September 1874. This order mobilised the Land Acquisition Act to acquire land for the brick kiln needed by Chisholm because the owner was charging too high a rate! The kiln was a semi-commercial venture selling bricks to other projects; it is not clear whether they were sold on the open market.

[115] GO 63–67, 31 August 1859, MPPWD, TNA.

[116] GO 46, 6 January 1863, MPPWD, TNA.

brattishing.[117] Nonetheless, the range of building components produced for the bazaar implied that European style buildings were popular and a healthy native design service, offering expertise in European aesthetics, was available outside the state sector. In recognition of Chisholm's special work, the PWD established a consulting architect's range in 1873, under his control.[118] The Controller of Accounts recorded that Chisholm 'had a peculiar position to fill in supervising the construction of buildings in addition to attending to his own more legitimate work' which was why his office accounts were not up to scratch.[119] He had failed to produce vouchers connected with expenditure for a period of over 16 months. His office comprised an estimator, two clerks, two draughtsmen, three peons and an accountant. The highest pay of Rs. 145 per month was given to the estimator. The draughtsmen received Rs. 30.

Chisholm's was an architectural practice in transition where efforts were being made to introduce imported practices into an essentially local construction industry. We can infer that the use of drawings to prepare detailed estimates, and the rigorous use of estimates to check expenditure, were fairly new practices. It was also regarded as unusual that Chisholm should supervise the construction of buildings. The architect's serious contribution to the building process appears to have been confined to the 'art' of design. Chisholm, after all, was the only person making the claim of being a professional architect. Any other work he did carried the potential threat of encroaching on the well-established territory of the military engineer. For example: Chisholm found his power on the Madurai site curtailed when, in 1877, he was deprived of authority to issue orders, except through the chief engineer. This prompted him to request the government to make explicit, the range of his authority on sites where his designs were being built.[120] Even so late in the century most engineers were military men; Chisholm's experience indicates that military control in the construction industry was the norm and that military influence in the civil branches of the colonial state was still a factor to be reckoned with.

Living Indian Architecture and the 'Light of Heaven and Reason and Freedom'

Lord Napier was nothing less than persuasive on the question of interior and exterior decoration (see Fig. 112). Here he is instructing a rich Indian on how to build a 'national house but

[117] Robert Chisholm, *The Napier Museum, Trevandrum*, RIBA Pamphlet (1873).

[118] This may have also been a concession to his civil status since the civil architect's office encountered in the last chapter was manned by soldiers. GO 29, 1 August 1874, MPPWD, TNA.

[119] GO 29, 1 August 1874, MPPWD, TNA.

[120] GO 152, 15 October 1877, MPPWD, TNA.

such a house as an Indian gentleman should inhabit under an honest Government in an age of peace, justice and learning'. A house in which the 'light of heaven and reason and freedom can penetrate':

> I say to him discharge your Madras architect and take a maistry from a remote part of the mofussil.... Adhere in general to the ancient plan especially to court and colonnade; collect the best models and patterns of native mouldings and sculpture, use brick of the finest quality, from the School of Arts, for the exposed surfaces, employ Cuddapah stone for the pillars without, glazed tiles for the floors and make liberal use of ornamental stucco and painting where rain cannot penetrate.[121]

For glazed openings where authentic 'models may be wanting' he asked the client to seek the advice of the government architect to 'treat them in the spirit of the style'. The carpets were to be got from Vellore and 'your stuffs from Madura and Tanjore. Where Hindu patterns fail you borrow from the Mussulmans.'

This peculiar orientalist decorative theme can easily be traced in the interior decoration of Senate House. It is also possible, that under Napier's aegis, the Government Art School, on the South Kensington model, was organised as a workshop to lead in the manufacture of items catering to British taste; whose range included glazed tiles, painted glass and terracotta mouldings. The government brick factory fulfilled this role by producing the exterior quality bricks specified for Senate House. When Chisholm became director of the school of art in 1878, he turned its industrial wing into a workshop for his buildings. It was using this method that the Post and Telegraph Office became his 'best piece of work yet executed in Madras, a result

Figure 112: Senate House, hall

[121] *The Builder*, 27 August 1870.

which could not have been achieved in any other way except at enormous outlay'.[122] In the construction of the latter he recorded the use of glass staining, painting and leading and employed skilled iron workers, carpenters, moulders, turners, throwers and painters to make all the articles he could not get outside.

Figure 113: Senate House, staircase detail

The carved wood-work on the stairs and grilles (see Fig. 113), the tall, coloured glass windows and the ornamental plaster covering the walls created a sumptuous interior; with the glare marginally reduced by the verandah. Two intensities of speckled light filtered through the main windows and the clerestory. The hall was dominated by an arched recess, framing the dais, on the southern wall. The twin balconies at high-level on either side of the arch, and the horse-shoe shaped grille accentuated the durbar effect. The central feature of the north wall was a finely carved double staircase. The floors were laid in a mixture of glazed tiles and *cuddapah* stone. Almost all of Lord Napier's decorative prescriptions for a revived South Indian domestic architecture were dutifully incorporated in Senate House. The interior of the hall was encrusted with ornamental plasterwork; a muted example of the exuberant stucco decoration common in South India. Internally the building is thus a curious mixture of the palatial and the domestic.

The external surfaces of grand buildings in Madurai and Bijapur were usually rendered in ornamental stucco painted and embellished with gold.[123] The dream quality of Deccani architecture is attributed to its singular blend of Persian, Arabic, Turkish, and South Indian traditions. Deccani art too 'was filled with a somewhat unearthly spirit quite different from the more realistic Mughal illustrations'. Annemarie Schimmel records that when the sun was about to set, it is said that the walls of the Ibrahim Rauza, 'the finest symbol of the iridescence of the

[122] Robert Chisholm, *Notes on Technical Education*.

[123] Polished stone, carved wood and coloured tiles were also widely used in architectural decoration, see George Michell and Mark Zebrowski, *Architecture and Art*, chapter 4.

sultans of the Deccan', revealed traces of the paintings that once covered the whole building.[124] It offered a glimpse into the 'world of fantasy and joy' created by the sultans.

The exterior finishes of Senate House were a stern reminder of another civilisation. It was clad in plain, Gothic revival red-brick, fashionable with the 'art' set in London. The exterior decoration of Fowke's Lecture Theatre building at the SKM, for example, was similarly clad in red brick, with stone columns and arches and terracotta ornamentation. Senate House was an architectural rhapsody; alien and unfamiliar in its irreverent mix of eastern and western aesthetics. Its appeal lay in the sharp, contrasting volumes, the red-colour of the bricks and lightness of the Gothic glazing, the floating colonnades, and the delicate detailing of its towers, parapets and painted domes. It was meant to contrast with the regular formal classical volumes and polished chunam, pastel finishes of august Company buildings. Senate House had to be a sensational building. It was the first imperial British answer to Indian-led Indo-European architecture; it announced British intentions to seize leadership of the Indo-European design tradition in India.

The manner in which the building related to public space and the public gaze was as new as its lack of association with nature and the environment. At Madurai the outer palace wall, over 400 feet in length, rose in one solid mass of unbroken walling to a height of 40 feet.[125] Senate House was surrounded by a low wall. It had to be seen. Colonial records made minimal reference to natural features such as trees and water, so important in the Indian sources. Napier's fascination with South Indian landscape architecture was subsumed beneath the more pressing political desire to consolidate the grand imperial marine vista begun with the Revenue Board building, the Tower and Presidency College.

The collision of two approaches to civic and architectural space resulted in a total reordering of the pre-colonial spatial order. Colonial rhetoric may have boasted of a revival of Indian architecture, but the truth was rather different.

Britain, Empire and the Aesthetics of 'European Supremacy'

From the early seventeenth century the classical style gradually became the chosen architectural language of the capital cities of Europe, America and Britain's colonial empire. But, until the Foreign Office and India Office designs in the Italian Renaissance style were approved by

[124] Annemarie Schimmel wrote that Muslim intellectuals of Delhi or Lucknow would be astonished to discover that one of the most beautiful monuments of the subcontinent is situated in the Bahmani capital, Gulbarga. See Annemarie Schimmel, 'Introduction' in George Michell (ed.), *Islamic Heritage of the Deccan* (Bombay, 1986), p. 6.

[125] Robert Chisholm, 'Tiroomal Naik's Palace'.

the government in 1861, it had to compete with the Gothic as the preferred 'national' style for London. The 1861 decision announced the triumph of those who held the view that if Britain was to stamp its authority on the world stage, as the first imperial power—then London had to copy Rome—the classical style (denounced by its British critics for being foreign) had to become another 'national' which it duly did. It is only recently that historians have been able to look beyond European rivalry to understand the place of empire in this critical aesthetic decision. The decision had as much to do with Paris as it did with the ostentatious classical building projects of British colonial capitals and the threatened loss of India, through Rebellion, that so engaged and inflamed British art-intellectuals (see fn. 40).

It is indeed ironic that imperial Britons, with their exclusive access to most of the world's culture, did not generate a dynamic new architecture in the nineteenth century. The dreary insularity of imperial Europe's monumental architecture reinforces the argument for the relocation of modernity away from the core of industrialising Europe to the vast and complex spaces of the colonies where the 'first globally multi-racial, multi-cultural, multi-continental societies of any substantial scale were formed'.[126] It may be argued that the idea of 'European supremacy' manifested in nineteenth-century Britain as a parochial, backward-looking, authoritarian tendency, marshalling and circumscribing the creative imagination of imperial patrons and their architects and belying the SKM's tangled didactic efforts to enrich and transform British design by absorbing the splendour and diversity of global art.

The few British grandees who marginally escaped the design stranglehold built country houses and leisure pavilions in Indian styles in their private domain. The Royal Pavilion at Brighton—John Nash's 1803 extravaganza designed for King George III with the help of the Daniells' illustrations, Indian outside and mostly Chinese inside—is the best known of such oddities.[127] But it was the proconsular British élite that really broke the shackles of Eurocentric design, not in Britain but in distant India. There, the intriguing architecture of the colonised beckoned with the irresistible promise of freedom of design.

The Senate House design opened a new sphere of experiment for assured high-imperialists; for the first time they began toying with the idea of commissioning new public buildings in Indo-European styles that blurred and glossed over Indo-British difference. Along with the privilege of a private dabble with Indian aesthetics came the opportunity

[126] Anthony King (ed.), *Culture, Globalisation and the World System* (Binghampton, 1991), p. 8.

[127] Also Sezincote, Gloucestershire, the country house built by Samuel Pepys Cockerell (Surveyor to the East India House), with Thomas Daniell as consultant, in the 1820s. John MacKenzie gives a different interpretation of 'Orientalism in Architecture', John MacKenzie, *Orientalism: History, Theory and the Arts* (Manchester, New York, 1995), chapter 4.

to experience the rare delights of commissioning state-funded monumental buildings in a completely new style.

The gubernatorial élites of Bombay and Calcutta remained intractably wedded to European forms: for their contemporary university senate house buildings they chose the Gothic and classical styles respectively (see Figs. 114 and 115). The aesthetic language chosen for the Madras Senate House was the deliberately ambiguous Indo-European (see Fig. 116); it alluded to India and the international in the same breath. For the first time a showpiece imperial building was to give public exposure to an Indo-European architectural aesthetic. In a sense the Madras élite was emulating the architectural patronage of Indian rulers, but with a difference. Lord Napier's articulation of the British view of the political context that led to the building may be part rhetoric, but it was also a reminder of the terms of power sharing as he saw it: 'the natives of India must be made to recognize that the English are the dominant race, and are determined to maintain their ascendancy in every department of government.'[128]

Figure 114: Senate House, University of Bombay, c. 1874, designed by G.G. Scott

[128] Minute No. 77, 31 May 1868, On the expediency of employing Natives of India in the Higher Offices of the Administration, *Minutes Recorded*.

Figure 115: Senate House, University of Calcutta, c. 1872, designed by Walter Granville

Figure 116: Senate House, University of Madras

The politics of Indian agitation surrounding education reform during the Company era were reflected in the Crown state's decision to select educational buildings with which to make political statements. The unmasking of an Indian contribution to the design of the building is less easy. To the extent that Lord Napier did not enter a cultural vacuum and was advised by high-ranking old Madras hands, the designs gave physical shape to the cultural legacy of a Madras school of orientalism, where a select group of Indo-Britons collectively formulated southern intellectual trajectories. The same conversations that decided to retain the aesthetics of the Chepauk Palace and extend them to the Revenue Board building defined the Senate House design. Ambitious Indo-Britons intended that the project enhance the civic beauty of the marine vista and give Madras a unique identity. Although official records cannot reflect those Indo-British conversations, the more influential personalities delineating taste and style in art, in the south, were Indian. Thus, notwithstanding Napier's passionate outpourings on art, I am leaving room for the reality of an unspoken, unacknowledged Indian participation in the official architectural discourse.

Indo-Britons and Indo-Saracenic Architecture in Madras

The term Indo-Saracenic owed much to Indo-Briton James Fergusson's problematic application of the fashionable science of ethnology to classify the architecture of the entire subcontinent. Borrowing the 'ethnologists' approach of grouping people, in 1867 Fergusson coined the phrase 'Indian Saracenic architecture' to label buildings he imagined were built by/for 'Muslims'.[129] As a self-proclaimed historian of world architecture Fergusson had already, in 1855, used the term in *An Illustrated Handbook of Architecture: Being a Concise and Popular Account of the Different Styles of Architecture Prevailing in All Ages and Countries*.[130] According to Fergusson 'Indian Saracenic architecture' included 'Muslim' buildings of places as far apart as Bijapur, Gujarat, and Bengal, as well as the Mughal and Pathan styles. Fergusson's taxonomy did not accommodate Indian building in European styles. He simply mocked Indian attempts to copy European architecture. Lucknow was dismissed as a 'jumble of vulgarity and bad taste'. Tanjore as 'inexpressibly ludicrous' and Delhi and Calcutta got more of the same treatment.[131]

[129] James Fergusson, *History of Architecture in All Countries from the Earliest Times to the Present Day*, vol. 2 (3 vols., London 1865–67), Book V, Indian Saracenic.

[130] Here he used the term 'Saracenic' to describe the architecture of Syria, Persia, India, Spain and Turkey. James Fergusson, *Illustrated Handbook of Architecture: Being a Concise and Popular Account of the Different Styles of Architecture Prevailing in All Ages and Countries*, (2 vols., London, 1855).

[131] James Fergusson, *History of Modern Style*, pp. 419–21.

Unconcerned by such denouncements the Indian aristocracy continued in their attempts to promote socially 'modern' progressive regimes whose aims were also expressed through building. Accomplished statesmen of the likes of the Maharajah of Travancore, the Gaekwad of Baroda and the occidentalist Sir Madava Rao were just some of the Indian rulers who unhesitatingly used native and European designers to adorn their states with an eclectic modern architecture that was at least Indo-European, if not more international, in reach. When Chisholm left Madras he went to the princely state of Baroda where Sir Madava Rao was chief minister. Chisholm's employer was the Gaekwad, for whom he continued building in hybrid styles for a further 16 years. Vikram Menon viewed the actions of men such as the Maharajah of Travancore and Sir Madava Rao as 'nationalism of an early kind'. He regarded them not as British puppets but as rulers who competed with the British to prove their skills of governance.[132]

Thomas Metcalf has argued that the British creation of their version of the Saracenic style (which they preferred to the 'Hindu'), was a matter of inventing a past for India, which was made available for appropriation by the Raj.

> They at once created a past for India and asserted British mastery of that past... these structures proclaimed the supremacy of the British as they sought to reshape India. At the same time they asserted a claim to knowledge, and hence to power, from within. Britain not only ruled, as the Romans had done, but had mastered the Orient. Far more than classical forms, Indo-Saracenic architecture expressed as it helped shape, the self-confident Age of Imperialism.[133]

I would like to build on to Metcalf's thesis the idea that the British were also doing something else: they were competing with and challenging the 'modern' politics and the innovative architecture of their simultaneously traditional and cosmopolitan princely neighbours.[134] I am suggesting that contending Indo-British visions of the new society were enacted in the politics and aesthetics of the Senate House design.

Metcalf's thesis rendered Indians into passive audiences for imperial architecture, providing no place for the Indo-British conversations on architecture that this story has tried to animate. In recognition of this omission he made a rare reference to material factors, implying that his analysis was possibly more true for later (national and global) developments in Indo-Saracenic architecture, than it was for the early phase in Madras.

[132] Vikram Menon, 'Popular Princes: Kingship and Social Change in Travancore and Cochin 1870–1930' (University of Oxford, D. Phil., 1998), p. 265.

[133] Thomas Metcalf, *An Imperial Vision*, p. 250.

[134] Metcalf's view on the matter of the princes is that they patronised this architecture because 'the British expected it of them, and they accommodated their ruler's wishes'. Thomas Metcalf, *An Imperial Vision*, p. 129.

> The construction of public buildings in a 'Saracenic' or any other Indian style was not easily accomplished. The British had to first come to terms with the structural forms of Indic architecture and then devise ways of accommodating those forms to the novel purposes of British Indian buildings. This was a long-drawn-out process, whose objectives were not fully realized until the 1880s and 1890s. It began however, in Madras....[135]

If Metcalf's theory lacked the breadth to fully explore architectural experiments in Madras, it is also true that no alternate explanation satisfies easily either. Those historians who took the opposing view argued that some Britons felt the policy of constructing in the classical style was now out of date. The time had come to present an image 'more amenable to' Indians.[136] The received view is that the Indo-Saracenic is an intensely political imperial architecture created by Britons for India.

Nonetheless, we are still left with having to explain why official architecture assumed a new and hybrid profile in Madras in the 1860s. Why, for instance, was it so different from the resolutely European orientations of the architecture of Bombay and Calcutta, where the same British proconsular élite was ostensibly wielding the reins of power? My hypothesis is that the search for the roots of the state-initiated Indo-European architectural endeavour in South India should begin in the shadowy, uncharted depths of seventeenth- and eighteenth-century Indo-British economic and socio-political exchange where the British never really dominated. Southern Indo-British relations betray evidence of a shared tradition of culture and governance that arguably forestalled the fires of rebellion in 1857. As this study has shown, the army held a central yet profoundly ambiguous place in the civil society of the South. Its civil role remains little understood even today. Carina Montgomery, in the first study of the social history of the Madras army, shows how its greater embeddedness in society and more progressive social policies than those of Bengal may help explain why the Madras army did not join the Rebellion of 1857.[137]

David Washbrook has argued that the post-Cornwallis (1793) generation of colonial rulers outside Bengal such as Thomas Munro, Charles Metcalf, John Malcolm and Mountstuart Elphinstone pursued the Clive-Hastings (Orientalist) model of state-building expounded in the period between 1750 and the 1770s. According to this model British rule could only be established through 'inherited Indian institutions—most notably those of "Oriental despotism" which would give the state (and its rapacious officials virtually unlimited authority'. Late eighteenth-century statesmen pursued an aggressive policy of expansion and domination

[135] Thomas Metcalf, *An Imperial Vision*, p. 58.

[136] Giles Tilltson, 'Orientalising the Raj' and Jon Lang, Madhavi Desai and Miki Desai, *Architecture and Independence*, p. 99.

[137] Carina Montgomery, 'The Sepoy Army in Colonial Madras'.

in the regions outside Bengal. The conquest of Mysore and the victory over the Marathas in 1801 brought about the consolidation of a despotic military state in control of the largest military force in Asia.[138] The Orientalist (as opposed to the Cornwallis style Anglicist) model of governance led Indian society backwards towards 'traditionalisation'. British rule, until the Rebellion of 1857, changed India, leaving it with 'a vast legacy of "backwardness" subsequently to undo'.

It is possible that the shared model of empire outlined by Munro and his circle of South Indian intellectuals, in the early years of the century, reflected the long history of a shared past between the two communities. Bonds, allegiances and mutual loyalties continued an unbroken shadowy existence in the intellectual traditions that prevailed in the South, in spite of the extreme militarisation of the state and the authoritarianism inherent in the Orientalist model. Old cross-community loyalties surfaced, for instance, in the policies of proconsuls of Napier's persuasion committing him to offer the natives of India the prospect of occupying a few really important state appointments:

> As far as this Presidency is concerned I see no danger to the stability of the English Government by the employment of natives in a greater number of the higher civil offices. Among the classes eligible to such functions there are no elements of conspiracy or resistance, hardly any disaffection. There are no aspirations to independence.... I am disposed to believe that in raising the natives with prudence, we shall identify them in a greater degree, with the English rule. As long as one fourth of the armed force is English, as long as the fortresses, the artillery, and the Military Commands are in the hands of Englishmen, the material interests of England are safe.... I would offer to the natives of India the prospect of attaining to a few really important appointments in the state, which would touch their pride, and give them the consciousness of being something in their country.[139]

Even as late as 1870 Madras civil servants were resisting centralisation emanating from Calcutta; stressing their economic ability to sustain regional autonomy. Such activities were discreetly watched by London grandees who understood that Madras had upstaged Bengal, intellectually and practically on two vital economic fronts: revenue and irrigation. Madras papers confidently jeered Colonel Strachey and:

> Bengal animus against the ryotwari system and us, impracticable Southerners. Bengal can never forgive Madras for the crime of accidentally having hit upon the form of land tenure which bids fair to be the model adopted by political and economical science when brought to perfection and for making its irrigation schemes pay.[140]

[138] The information about the Orientalist model is from David Washbrook, 'India, 1818–1860: The Two Faces of Colonialism' in Andrew Porter (ed.), *Oxford History of the British Empire, vol. III, the 19th Century* (Oxford, 1999), pp. 394–421.

[139] Minute No. 77, 31 May 1868, *Minutes Recorded*.

[140] *Athenaeum*, 15 October 1870.

Yet these ideas were not new or revolutionary. The absence of demands for major political or social reform in the period suggests that the Indo-British élites in the south were jointly defining their new empire. The ambiguity of the architectural forms of Senate House imply, if not a sincere will on the part of the British, then at least the rhetoric of a promise to share power; born out of deference to a shared past where it was understood and accepted that the terms of power sharing were constantly renegotiable. This is what the South Indian élite expected.

Viewed in this light Indians appear not as recipients of a British architecture but as invisible unequal partners in the joint manufacture of Indo-British architecture. Madras statesmen announced their distance from northern dissonance and rebellion through a cultural statement of Indo-European unity that was a new architecture; charged with alternate meanings for region and empire. Indo-Saracenic architecture in Madras takes its place within the older and wider programme of governance imagined by a southern Indo-British intelligentsia when they embarked on a tacit search for consensual values. The reading offered here does not diminish other political agendas served by this aesthetic, nor does it deny that Britons did want to present themselves as masters of Indian architecture.

The enigmatic symbolism of the style resonated outside the presidency. Senate House was an exuberant Indo-British durbar hall, built six years prior to Queen Victoria becoming empress of India, and 30 years before Viceroy Lord Curzon's eloquent speech on protecting 'Ancient Monuments in India'. Curzon, dubbed the 'ceremonial impresario', was noted as the 'grandest and most caparisoned statesman of his day'. The ritual and romance of the 'gorgeous east' made Britain seem 'dingy and unimaginative' to him.[141] His viceroyalty was a by-word for splendour and its high-point was the opulent Indian-style Delhi Durbar of 1903, wholly anticipated in the flamboyant designs of the Madras intelligentsia.

In recent years cultural historians have identified a 'central deliriousness in the workings of imperial history'.[142] The Victoria Terminus building at Bombay, designed in a tropicalised Gothic hybrid style has been described as a 'deeply schizophrenic artifact'—whose nature it is to produce 'unstable meanings and crises of reading for the viewer'. Ian Baucom argues that 'the confusion that such objects both locate and produce are their most salient feature. That confusion is, finally, the one thing that typifies the narratives of empire and Englishness.' The spaces and forms of architecture, like all cultural artefacts, he says, have an 'irremediable uncertainty and instability'.[143]

[141] David Cannadine, *Aspects of Aristocracy* (London, 1995), pp. 77–108.

[142] Ian Baucom, *Out of Place*. This information is mostly from the Introduction and chapter 2.

[143] Ibid., p. 74.

The indefinable allure of the Indo-Saracenic may lie in the paradox that it was, among other things, an Indian interpretation of a universal architecture.[144] Perhaps this is precisely why its powerful images proved irresistible to the high-imperialists imagining New Delhi in the next century. The ponderous forms and stylistic nuances of New Delhi also elude easy explanation.

Non-imperial Conversations?

This story has tried to shed light on a vibrant Indian architecture whose boundaries were shifting and expanding. Patrons, architects and builders built in many ways at once; traditional, as well as cosmopolitan. They were willing to experiment with new spatial arrangements, materials, construction techniques and exotic aesthetics, sometimes deployed with verve and ingenuity. For the Indian protagonists, European architecture was a source of great excitement and pleasure. They engaged with this architecture with and without the involvement of colonial Britons, enjoying the freedom of absorbing and transmuting new ideas on their own terms. Put simply, change was the hallmark of Indian architecture.

Indo-European architecture, at its finest, began to pose a threat and a challenge to the cultural ascendance of imperial Britons. It was to neutralise this threat that Britons intervened in the domain of architectural aesthetics, putting forth an imagined view of an 'Indian tradition' in 'decline'. However, a more nuanced reading of even a straightforward European building such as St. Andrew's Church, uncovered Indo-European conversations across almost the entire spectrum of building activities, even in the unexpected areas of structural design and construction methods. Indeed, sharing knowledge was unavoidable in the construction industry. The Pachaiyappa School is just one among the large number of austere, elegantly proportioned and detailed eighteenth- and nineteenth-century classical Indo-European buildings to be found in Madras. It could be argued that these buildings are evidence of wider Indo-European conversations about architecture which engaged southern intellectuals not solely with British experiments with European architecture, but more directly with French engineering and architectural developments (due to the proximity of Pondicherry), and the classical architecture of the Portuguese, the Dutch, the Italians, the Germans and the Danes. Even as Britons attempted to mediate Indian access to European architecture, they found themselves

[144] For the idea of a 'benign universalism' and problems in the relationship between universal culture and cultural imperialism see John Tomlinson, *Globalisation and Culture*, p. 69.

undermining those very same objectives by training Indians, as engineers, in advanced new institutions.

But, it was neither inevitable nor indeed predictable that this particular colonial model for training engineers would train Indians as 'architects'. Instead, the historical circumstances of the new century gave rise to a new colonial model of architectural education where the 'Indian Tradition' and the idea of mutually respectful Indo-European architectural conversations were actively discouraged, if not suppressed. This is a history that still needs to be told. For the present it can be said that after 1947 the intellectual orientations of the new schools matched the political desire to disown reminders of colonial occupation; as a consequence, the architects of independent India largely forsook the early collaborative endeavours that make up this story. It was only natural that they turned to the International style as the leading architectural aesthetic for modern India.

Britons' dalliance with Indian architecture in India, and Indian art in Britain, was plagued by concerns of possession, power, and 'forbidden' pleasure. The Indian dalliance with European architecture was equally concerned with power and pleasure but of another order. The power imbalances of empire gave rise to many different forms of architectural exchange and yet it is not too difficult to imagine other less aggressive, more open-minded cultural dialogues. It is still entirely possible that a new generation of Indo-Britons, like those early pleasure seekers, may yet open a door to that mysterious world of architecture that so beguiled their ancestors.

Glossary

bagh	garden
Bagh-i-Kunha	old garden
baoli	stepped well
banyan/bania	Indian agents of the British in Calcutta/merchant
baradari	garden pavilion
brahmaharam	brahmin village
brattishing	a decorative cresting which is found at the top of a cornice or screen, panel or parapet. The design often includes leaves or flowers, and the term is particularly associated with Tudor architecture
circar/sircar/sarkar	government or state as distinct from lands governed by zamindars or poligars
conicopoly/kanakapillai	auditor/accountant
cowle	a lease or grant in writing
chattram/choultry	inn/administrative/welfare house
chunam	lime mortar
darul-amara	government house
dharmakarta	chief executive
diwan khana	audience hall
dubash	one who speaks two languages
farsh	carpet

farrash khana	carpet workshop or store house
fatah chawki	victory court
gange	market town
ghat	landing place or river pier
gopuram	tower over temple gateway
hasht bangla	octagonal pavilion
inam/mirasi	tax-free grant by ruler
jaggery	palm or cane sugar
jahan numa	sky touching
jala-sutrala	irrigation (tank or dam) engineer
jati	kinship/collective bargaining/welfare body
jivan-nyasa	inspiration of life breath
kaniyatchi	dominion over land
katra	market belonging to town
kitangi	office
komati	Telugu merchant caste
lascar	an Indian serving the British as a sailor
mahal	palace/place
maistry	head workman
makhana	hall of justice
mamoty	digging tool
mandalam	socio-cultural zone in ancient Tamil country
mandapa	hall
mangalaropana	ground purification ritual
maramut	mend, repair
math/mutt	a species of college where a celibate Hindu priest lives with disciples
moochy	leather worker
mubarak	blessed
munshi	writer or secretary
musnud	throne of cushions
nadu	regional council
nattar	representatives of the jati at the nadu
Nusrat-mahal	palace of victory

pagoda	gold coin used in South India
pahlawan	wrestler
palaiyakkaran/poligar	holder of palayam—armed camp
pandaram	officiating priest at Shiva temple
panchayat	council
paracheri	area where parayars live
parrah	measure
peccottah	contrivance for drawing water from well
peon	armed man in palaiyakkarans' service
pettah	walled suburb or town, may be attached to a fort
purohita	high priest
qalin	rug
qandil	lamp
qannat	marquee
rasika	connoisseur of art
Roshan Bagh	illuminated garden
ruaz	mason expert in the orders of European architecture
ryotwari	form of land revenue settlement in which tax is levied on fields of individual owners
sabah	village assembly
sampradayika	supporter of traditional culture
saracha	tent-enclosure
sarai	inn
silpi	craftsman, artisan
silpa sastra	technical treatise on building/material hierarchy
sthapathi	architect/designer
sutragrahin	architect's disciple
Swanihat-i-Mumtaz	Events of the Illustrious
tablur khana	store house
taksaka	stone cutter
tahsildar	a revenue official
toshakhana	treasury or store house
Tuzak-i-Walajahi	Chronicle of the Walajahs
vardaki	assembler of cut stones

vimana	tower over sanctuary
walajah	of elevated dignity
zamindar	a landlord under British rule, or little king
zilla	district

Picture Credits

Frontispiece Map of Madras today, showing buildings discussed in the book, TTK Pharma Ltd., 1999, Chennai

CHAPTER 1

1 Muhammad Ali Khan, Nawab of Arcot, George Willison, oil on canvas, 1795, F 12, by permission of the BL

2 Map of Madras, 1798, H.D. Love, vol. 3, shelf mark 20647 d.31–34, The Boldeian Library, University of Oxford

3 Map of Madras 1859, John Murray, shelf mark 2064 e.157 (I, 1), vol. 1, p. 18, The Bodleian Library, University of Oxford

4 Beach of Madras, William Simpson, 1867, © Victoria Memorial Kolkata

5 Map of British Expansion in South India, from Christopher Bayly, *Indian Society and the Making of the British Empire*, 1990, Cambridge University Press

6 Map of British Expansion in north India, from Christopher Bayly, *Indian Society and the Making of the British Empire*, 1990, Cambridge University Press

7 Tottik-k-kalai Vedacal Mudaliar, V. Raghavan, *Adayar Library Bulletin*, 21.3–4 (Madras, 1958)

8 Sir Madava Rao, shelfmark 2133 3.8, p. 100; Lord Napier shelf mark 24617 e. 65, p. 265, The Bodleian Library, University of Oxford

9 A view of part of St. Thome Street, Fort St. George, 1803, Henri Merke, aquatint, X768/2(3), © BL

10 Map showing principal monuments and sites of South India, with permission from George Michell, drawn by Graham Reed
11 Insets for Map 10, with permission from George Michell, drawn by Graham Reed
12 Trichinopoly Palace, top-lit wagon vault, eighteenth century (author's collection)
13 Madurai Palace, top-lit dome (author's collection)
14 Chandragiri Palace, Tirupati, Chisholm, 1883, shelf mark Per. gen. d.20, p. 296, The Bodleian Library, University of Oxford

Chapter 2

15 Zion Church, Tranquebar, c. 1717, Official church of the Danish East India Company, shelf mark 100 d.49, p. 251
16 St. George's Church, Madras, side elevation (author's collection)
17 Tank on the Shiva Temple at Chidambaram, showing standard use of barrel vault over *gopuram* and wagon vault elsewhere, by Francis Swain Ward, oil on canvas, c. 1782, P 952, © BL
18 Banqueting Hall, Madras, c. 1800, © VV
19 Government House, Madras, c. 1800, © VV
20 Ruins of the Palace, Madura, Thomas and William Daniell, showing vaulted chamber, aquatint, c. 1798, P 952, © BL
21 Bara Imambara, Lucknow, eighteenth century, © Archaeological Survey of India
22 Gol Gumbaz, Bijapur, c. 1660, cross section, Percy Brown, *Indian Architecture: Islamic Period*, 4th edn. (Bombay, 1964, pl. LII)
23 Gol Gumbaz, Bijapur (author's collection)
24 Thanjavur Palace, seventeenth century, interior view of wagon vault over throne (author's collection)
25 Thanjavur Palace, domes over throne area (author's collection)
26 Thanjavur Palace, stepped vault and flat roof, with tower on the right (author's collection)
27 Thanjavur Palace, tower over throne, note European details (author's collection)
28 James Gibbs' circular design for St. Martin-in-the-Fields, London, section, James Gibbs, *A Book of Architecture*, 1728, plate 12, 62.i.12, by permission of the BL

29 James Gibbs' circular design for St. Martin-in-the-Fields, plan, London, James Gibbs, *A Book of Architecture*, 1728, plate 8, 62.i.12, by permission of the BL

30 St. Andrew's, south-west elevation (author's collection)

31 St. Andrew's, ground floor plan (de Havilland), X381, by permission of the BL

32 St. Andrew's, section (de Havilland), X381, by permission of the BL

33 St. Andrew's, roof, arches in the pediment (author's collection)

34 St. Andrew's, stepped dome and arches (author's collection)

35 Mahabodhi shrine, c. second century, conjectural reconstruction, Percy Brown, *Indian Architecture: Buddhist and Hindu*, 3rd revised edn. (Bombay, 1983), pl. XL

36 Bhitargaon shrine, c. fifth century, conjectural reconstruction, Percy Brown, *Indian Architecture: Buddhist and Hindu*, 3rd revised edn. (Bombay, 1983), pl. XL1

37 The Gola, Bankipur, designed by John Garstin, 1786, Sten Nilsson, *European Architecture in India 1750–1850* (London, 1968), fig. 24a, by permission of Sten Nilsson

38 St. Andrew's, foundation plan showing 150 brick and pottery wells (de Havilland), St. Andrew's, Madras

39 East India House, Leadenhall Street, 1817 Joseph Stadler, after Thomas Sheperd, aquatint, P 1389, © BL

40 St. Andrew's, the interior (de Havilland), St. Andrew's, Madras

41 St. Andrew's, east elevation, Madras, Sten Nilsson, *European Architecture in India 1750-1850* (London, 1968), fig. 50b, by permission of Sten Nilsson

Chapter 3

42 View of school hall from street (author's collection)

43 Hall, front verandah (author's collection)

44 Plan, first floor, Pachaiyappa School (author's collection)

45 Aerial view, Pachaiyappa School (author's collection)

46 European-style first courtyard (author's collection)

47 Hall, rear view (author's collection)

48 Brahmin village dwelling, Dakshin Chitra, Chennai (author's collection)

49 Indian-style second courtyard, second floor (author's collection)

50 Tamil letters in a Greek frieze (author's collection)

51 The Royal High School, Edinburgh, 1825, picture by Thomas Annan

CHAPTER 6

Bibliography

PRIMARY SOURCES

Printed

British Library: Oriental and India Office Collections.

Official

Balfour, Edward, *Report on the Iron Ores and Iron and Steel of Southern India* (London, 1855).

————, *Report on the Government Central Museum and the Local Museums in the Provinces 1855–56* (Madras, 1857).

Board's Collections 1796–1858, F series.

British India Administration Reports, V/10.

Index of Civil Engineers Appointed to Indian PWD, L/PWD/8/3 (1859–66).

Madras Collections, L/PWD/3/519.

Madras Proceedings Education Department.

Madras Proceedings Military Consultations.

Madras Proceedings Public Consultations.

Madras Proceedings Public Works Department.

Military Despatches, E series.

Military Department Records, L/MIL/series.

Minute by the Governor of Madras Relating to his Tour in the South of India Between 5th January and 6th March 1860, V 27/246/4.

Official Publications, V/27.

Professional Papers of the Madras Engineers (Private circulation).

Proceedings and Correspondence Connected with the late Public Works Commission for the Madras Presidency (Madras, 1855), V/26/700/8.

Public Works Letters from Madras, L/PWD/3/190.

Views and Proceedings of the Madras Government on the First Report of the Commission of Public Works (Madras, 1853), V/26/700/6.

Newpapers

Athenaeum.

Jaridai-i-Rozigar.

Madras Times.

The Sunday Times.

The Times of India.

Contemporary Work

A Gazetteer of Southern India with the Tenasserim Provinces and Singapore (Madras, 1855).

A Guide to the City of Madras and its Suburbs, 2nd edn. (Madras, 1881).

A Visit to Madras Being a Sketch of the Local Characteristics and Peculiarities of that Presidency in the Year 1811 (London, 1821).

An Accurate and Authentic Narrative of the Origins and Progress of the Dissensions at the Presidency of Madras Founded on the Original Papers and Correspondence (London, 1810).

Asylum Press Almanac (Madras, 1874).

The East India Register and Army List (Madras, 1846).

Acland, Charles, *A Popular Account of the Manners and Customs of India* (London, 1847).

Arbuthnot, Alexander, *Major General Sir Thomas Munro Governor of Madras,* new edn. (3 vols., Madras, 1886).

Bell, Andrew, *The Madras School or Elements of Tuition*, reprint (London, 2000).

Bell, Evans, *The Empire in India: Letters from Madras and Other Places* (London, M.DCCC.LXIV).

Blagdon, Francis, *A Brief History of Ancient and Modern India* (3 vols., London, 1804).

Buchanan, F., *A Journey from Madras through the Countries of Mysore, Canara and Malabar* (3 vols., London, 1807).

Buckley, Robert, *The Irrigation Works of India* (London, 1880).

Burhan-ibn-Hasan, *Tuzak-i-Walajahi*, transl. H.M. Nainar (Part 1, Madras, 1934).

Chariar, Krishnama, *Select Papers, Speeches and Poems Connected with Pachaiyappa Mudaliar* (Madras, 1892).

Charier, S.C. Srinivasa, *Opinions on Social Matters of Raja Sir T. Madava Rao KCSI Fellow of the Madras and Bombay Universities Compiled from His Public Addresses and Newspaper Contributions* (Madras, 1890).

Chisholm, Robert, 'Tiroomal Naik's Palace, Madura', *TRIBA* (1875–76), pp. 159–77.

————, 'New College for the Gaekwar of Baroda with Notes on Style and Domical Construction', *TRIBA* (1882–83), pp. 41–146.

————, 'The Old Palace of Chandragiri' *Indian Antiquary* (November, 1883), pp. 295–96, with illustrations 1–4.

————, 'Baroda Palace: The Town Residence of H.H. Sir Syaji Rao-I' *JRIBA*, vol. 3, Third Series (1896), pp. 421–33, 445–50.

Cotton, Sir A.T., *Public Works in India: Their Importance with Suggestions for Their Extension and Improvement*, 3rd edn. (London, 1885).

Daniell, Thomas and William, *A Picturesque Voyage to India by Way of China* (London, 1810).

de Havilland, T.F., *An Account of St. Andrews* (Madras, 1821).

————, *The Public Edifices of Madras* (Kingsbury, 1826).

Denison, W., *Varieties of Vice Regal Life* (2 vols., London, 1870).

Emerson, W., 'On the Taj Mahal at Agra', *TRIBA, 1st Series*, vol. 20, (1869–70), pp. 195–203.

————, 'A Description of Some Buildings Recently Erected in India with Some Remarks on Domes and the Mingling of Styles of Architecture' *TRIBA, 1st Series* (1883–84), pp. 149–63.

Fay, Eliza, *The Original Letters from India 1779–1815*, 2nd edn. (Calcutta, 1908).

Fergusson, James, *History of Architecture in All Countries from Earliest Times to the Present Day,* 2nd edn. (London, 1874).

————, *On the Rock-Cut Temples of India* (London, 1845).

————, *Illustrated Handbook of Architecture: Being a Concise and Popular Account of the Different Styles of Architecture Prevailing in All Ages and Countries* (2 vols., London, 1855).

————, (ed.), *Architectural Illustrations of the Principal Mahometan Buildings of Beejapore* (London, 1859).

————, *History of the Modern Styles of Architecture* (London, 1862).

————, *History of Architecture in All Countries from the Earliest Times to the Present Day* (3 vols., London, 1865–67).

Gibbs, James, *A Book of Architecture* (London, 1728).

————, *A Short Description of the Radcliffe Library at Oxford* (London, 1750).

G.P., *Representative Men of Southern India* (Madras, 1896).

Graham, Maria, *Journal of Residence in India* (Edinburgh, 1812).

Hamilton, Walter, *The East India Gazetteer* (London, 1815).

Heber, Reginald, *Narrative of a Journey through the Upper Provinces of India from Calcutta to Bombay 1824–1825* (2 vols., London, 1928).

Hendley, T.H., 'Decorative Arts in Rajputana' *Journal of Indian Art and Industry*, vol. 3 (1898).

Karim, Muhammad, *Swanihat-I-Mumtaz* (2 vols., Madras, 1940–44).

Kipling, J.L., 'Indian Architecture of Today', *The Journal of Indian Art*, 3, July (1881), pp. 1–5.

Kipling, Rudyard, *The Bridge Builders*, (London, 1898).

Maitland, Julia Charlotte, *Letters from Madras during the Years 1836–39* (London, 1843).

MacGeorge, G.W., *Ways and Works in India Being an Account of the Public Works in that Country from the Earliest Times up to the Present Day* (Westminster, 1894).

McLean, C.D., *Manual of Administration of the Madras Presidency* (3 vols., Madras, 1885).

Taylor, Philip Meadows, *Architecture at Beejapoor; Architectural Notes by James Fergusson* (London, 1866).

Mill, James., The History of British India (3 vols., London, 1817).

Munro, W.T., *Madrasiana* (Madras, 1889).

Murray, John, *A Handbook for India, Part I, Madras* (London, 1859).

Norton, George, *Speech at the Fourteenth Anniversary Meeting of the Patcheapah Moodelliar's Institution in Madras on Thursday April 23, 1857* (London, 1857).

Norton, John Bruce, *A Letter to Sir Robert Lowe Esq. from John Bruce Norton Esq. On the Condition and Requirements of the Presidency of Madras* (Madras, 1854).

————, *The Rebellion in India: How to Prevent Another* (London, 1857).

Pasley, C.W., *Outline Course of Architecture Compiled for the Use of Junior Officers of the Royal Engineers* (Chatham, 1826).

Phene Spiers, R., 'The Late Major Mant, Fellow', *TRIBA*, *1st Series* (1881–82), pp. 100–111.

Pillai, A. Muttasami, 'A Brief Sketch of the Life and Writings of Father C.J. Beschi, or Viramuni', *Madras Journal of Literature and Science*, XI, January–June (1840), pp. 250–301.

Raghavaiyangar, Srinivasa, *Memorandum of the Progress of the Madras Presidency During the Last Forty Years* (Madras, 1892).

Raz, Ram, *Essays on the Architecture of the Hindus* (London, 1834).

Row, Venkasami T., *Manual of the District of Tanjore in the Madras Presidency* (Madras, 1883).

Stuart, James and Nicholas Revett, *The Antiquities of Athens and Other Monuments of Greece* (London, 1837).

Satthianadhan, S., *History of Education in the Madras Presidency* (Madras, 1894).

Sayer, Robert, *Ruins of Athens,* reprint (London, 1969).

Srinivasachariar, S.C., *Opinions on Social Matters of Raja Sir T. Madava Raw KCSI Fellow of the Madras and Bombay Universities* (Madras, 1890).

Sullivan, John, *Tracts Upon India; Written in the Years 1779, 1780 and 1788 with Subsequent Observations* (London, 1795).

Underwood, George, 'Memorandum Regarding Syrian or Cylinder Roofs', *Professional Papers of the Madras Engineers* (London, 1836), pp. 92–95.

Valentia, Viscount George, *Voyages and Travels to India, Ceylon, the Red Sea, Abyssinia and Egypt in 1802–1807* (3 vols., London, 1809).

Vibart, Henry Meredith, *Addiscombe: Its Heroes and Men of Note* (Westminster, 1894).

————, 'The East India Company's Military Seminary at Addiscombe', *United Services Journal*, 2 (1829), pp. 225–29.

————, *The Military History of the Madras Engineers and Pioneers from 1734 up to the Present Time* (2 vols., London, 1881–83).

Wathen, James, *Journal of a Voyage in 1811 and 1812 to Madras and China* (London, 1814).

Wheeler, J. Talboys, *Madras in the Olden Time* (3 vols., Madras, 1862).

Tamil Nadu State Archives

Madras Courier.

Minutes Recorded by the Rt. Honble. Francis Baron Napier and Ettrick, K.T. During the Administration of the Government of the Madras Presidency (Madras, 1872).

Proceedings Madras Public Works Department.

Public Consultations.

Selections From the Records of the Madras Government No.XXV, Report on Important Public Works for 1854 (Madras, 1856).

Bodleian Library

Parliamentary Papers, East India-Lords Second Report (25) 1852–53.

Professional Papers on Indian Engineering.

The Builder.

Transactions of the Royal Institute of British Architects.

Royal Institute of British Architects, British Architectural Library

Chisholm, R.F., *The Napier Museum, Trevandrum*, RIBA Pamphlet (1873).

————, *Notes on Technical Education Addressed to His Highness Sir Syaji Rao, K.C.S.I., Gaekwar of Baroda* (Bombay, 1888).

————, biography file.

Manuscript

A Narrative by Captain (later Colonel) Thomas Fiott de Havilland (1755–1866) Madras Army 1793–1825, of his part in the mutiny of European Officers of the Madras Army at Seringapatam 1809 and subsequent events up to the court-martial ordered, MSS Eur E232.

Aberdeen Papers, Add MS 43240, 1842–53.

Blechynden Papers, Add MS 45,645; 45,646; 45,647.
British Library.
Clive, C.F., *Journal of a Voyage to the East Indies and During a Residence there A Tour Through Mysore and Tanjore Countries etc.*, WD4235.
Elphinstone Papers, MSS Eur F/87/33.
Fiebig Collection.
Iddelsleigh Papers, Add MS 50,027, ff 121–51.
John Lawrence Collection, MSS Eur F 90,43; F 90 44.
Layard Papers, Add MS 39112, 39115, 39116.
Mackenzie Collection General, MSS Eur/MackGen 3, pp. 483–89.
Nightingale Papers, Add MS 45779, ff 215.
Papers Relating to the Madras Military Fund of Lt. Col. F. de Havilland, MSS Eur F344.
Paterson Collection, MSS Eur E379/4.
Photographs Catalogue.
Prints and Drawings Catalogue.
Salisbury Collection, IOR Negative 11672.
Walter Elliot Collection, MSS Eur J 684–705.

Royal Institute of British Architects, British Architectural Library

Drawings—two rolls, 4 by 10 foot, of the Tiroomal Naik's Palace, 3–4 cupboard, lower mezzanine, roll 2.
Fellows Nomination papers, 4, 4.12.1865 and 9.6.1873.
Letters to Council, LC/2/1/6 1838; LC/1/1/24 1836.

SECONDARY WORKS

A Guide to Madras (Higginbothams) (Madras, 1903).
Concise Dictionary of National Biography (Oxford, 1948).
Dictionary of National Biography (Oxford, 1885–1901).
Educational Buildings in India, Department of Education Occasional Papers No. 6 (Calcutta, 1911).
History of Higher Education in South India (2 vols., Madras, 1957).
Acharya, P.K. (ed.), *Manasara on Architecture and Sculpture* (4 vols., Allahabad, 1927).
Alder, Ken, *Engineering the Revolution Arms and Enlightenment in France 1763–1815* (Princeton, 1997).
Ambirajan, S., 'Science and Technology Education in South India', in Roy MacLeod and Deepak Kumar (eds.), *Technology and the Raj* (New Delhi, 1995), pp. 112–33.

Anderson, B., *Imagined Communities*, revised edn. (London, 1991).

Appadurai, Arjun, *Worship and Conflict Under Colonial Rule* (Cambridge, 1981).

Arbuthnot, Alexander, *Memories of Rugby and India* (London, 1910).

Archer, Mildred, *Company Drawings in the India Office Library* (London, 1972).

————, *India and British Portraiture 1770–1825* (London, 1979).

————, 'Serfogee: An Enlightened Tanjore Ruler and his Patronage of the Arts', in *The India Magazine* (1985), pp. 9–19.

————, *Company Paintings: Indian Paintings of the British Period* (New Jersey, 1992).

Arnold, Dana (ed.), *Cultural Identities and the Aesthetics of Britishness* (Manchester, 2004).

Arnold, David, *The New Cambridge History of India III.5: Science, Technology and Medicine in Colonial India*, reprint (Cambridge, 2002).

Asher, Catherine, *The New Cambridge History of India I.4: Architecture of Mughal India* (Cambridge, 1992).

Baliga, B.S., 'British Relations With the Nawabs and Princes of Arcot' in B.S. Baliga (ed.), *Studies in Madras Administration* (Madras, 1960), pp. 310–29.

————, 'Sir Charles Trevelyan, Governor of Madras 1859–60' in B.S. Baliga (ed.), *Studies in Madras Administration* (Madras, 1960), pp. 338–86.

Barringer, Tim amd Tom Flynn (eds.), *Colonialism and the Object: Empire, Material Culture and the Museum* (London, 1997).

Barringer, Tim, *Men at Work: Art and Labour in Mid-Victorian Britain* (New Haven and London, 2005).

Baucom, Ian, *Out of Place: Englishness, Empire and the Location of Identity* (Princeton, 1999).

Bayly, Christopher, *The New Cambridge History of India II.1, Indian Society and the Making of the British Empire*, paperback edn. (Cambridge, 1990).

————, *Origins of Nationality in South Asia* (New Delhi, 1998).

Bayly, Susan, *Saints, Goddesses and Kings: Muslims and Christians in South Indian Society 1700–1900* (Cambridge, 1989).

Beard, Mary, *The Parthenon* (London, 2002).

Begde, Prabhakar, *Ancient and Medieval Town-Planning in India* (New Delhi, 1978).

Boner, Alice, 'Economic and Organizational Aspects of the Building Operations of the Sun Temple at Konarka', *Journal of Economic and Social History of the Orient*, 13 (1970), pp. 257–72.

Borden, Iain and David Dunster (eds.), *Architecture and the Sites of History* (Oxford, 1995).

Bradley, Margaret, 'Scientific Education versus Military Training: The Influence of Napoleon Bonaparte on the Ecole Polytechnique', *Annals of Science*, 32 (1975), pp. 415–49.

Brantlinger, Patrick, 'A Postindustrial Prelude to Postcolonialism: John Ruskin, William Morris and Gandhism' in *Critical Inquiry*, 22, 3 (Spring, 1996), pp. 466–85.

Bravo, Michael T., *The Accuracy of Ethnoscience: A Study of Inuit Cartography and Cross Cultural Commensurability* (Manchester, 1996).

Bremner, Alex G., 'Nation and Empire in the Government Architecture of Mid-Victorian London: The Foreign and India Office Reconsidered', in *The Historical Journal*, 48, 3 (2005), pp. 703–42.

Brittlebank, Kate, *Tipu Sultan's Search for Legitimacy: Islam and Kingship in a Hindu Domain* (Delhi, 1997).

Brown, Percy, *Indian Architecture (Islamic Period)* 4th edn. (Bombay, 1964).

————, *Indian Architecture (Buddhist and Hindu)*, 3rd revised edn. (Bombay, 1983).

Buchanan, Alexandrina, 'The Power and the Glory: the Meanings of Medieval Architecture', in Iain Borden and David Dunster (eds.), *Architecture and the Sites of History* (Oxford, 1995), pp. 78–92.

Buddle, Anne with Pauline Rohatgi, 'The Scots in India', in *The Tiger and the Thistle: Tipu Sultan and the Scots in India 1760–1800* (Edinburgh, 1999), pp. 55–58.

Cannadine, David, *Aspects of Aristocracy* (London, 1995).

————, *Ornamentalism: How the British Saw Their Empire* (London, 2001).

Chatterjee, Indrani, 'Colouring Subalternity: Slaves, Concubines and Social Orphans in Early Colonial India', *Subaltern Studies*, X (1999), pp. 49–97.

Codell, J.F. and D.S. MacLeod (ed.), *Orientalism Transposed: The Impact of Colonialism on British Culture* (Aldershot, 1998).

Colley, Linda, *Britons Forging the Nation 1707–1837* (London, 1992).

————, *Captives: Britain, Empire and the World 1600–1850* (London, 2002), p. 110.

Collyer, Kellson, *The Hoysala Artists: Their Identity and Styles* (Mysore, 1990).

Conner, Patrick, *George Chinnery 1774–1852: Artists of India and the China Coast* (Suffolk, 1993).

Coomaraswamy, Ananda, *Medieval Sinhalese Art,* 2nd edn. (New York, 1956).

Copland, Ian, *The British Raj and the Indian Princes: Paramountcy in Western India 1857–1930* (Bombay, 1982).

Corfield, P.J., *Power and the Professions in Britian 1700–1850*, 2nd edn. (London, 2000).

Crinson, Mark, and Jules Lubbock, *Architecture, Art or Profession? Three Hundred Years of Architectural Education in Britain* (Manchester, 1994).

Crinson, Mark, *Empire Building: Orientalism and Victorian Architecture* (London, 1996).

Cronin, Vincent, *A Pearl to India: The Life of Roberto de Nobili* (London, 1959).

Curl, James Stevens, *The Art and Architecture of Free Masonry* (London, 1991).

Dakers, Caroline, *The Holland Park Circle: Artists and Victorian Society* (London, 1999).

Dalrymple, William, *White Mughals: Love and Betrayal in Eighteenth Century India* (London, 2002).

Dagens, Bruno, *Mayamata: An Indian Treatise on Housing Architecture and Iconography* (New Delhi, 1985).

Darley, Gillian, *John Soane: An Accidental Romantic* (New Haven, 1999).

Das, Neeta, *Indian Architecture: Problems in the Interpretation of 18th and 19th Century Architecture, A Study of Dilkusha Palace Lucknow* (New Delhi, 1998).

Davies, Philip, *Splendours of the Raj* (London, 1985).

Desmond, Ray, *The India Museum, 1801–1879* (London, 1982).

Dewan, Janet, 'Linnaeus Tripe; Documenting South Indian Architecture' *History of Photography*, 13, 2, (April–June, 1989), pp. 147–54.

Dirks, Nicholas B., *The Hollow Crown: Ethnohistory of an Indian Kingdom* (Cambridge, 1987).

Dodwell, Henry, *The Nabobs of Madras* (London, 1926).

Eaton, Richard Maxwell (ed.), 'The Articulation of Islamic Space in the Medieval Deccan', *Essays on Islam and Indian History* (New Delhi, 2000), pp. 159–75.

Edney, Matthew E., *Mapping an Empire: The Geographical Construction of British India 1765–1834* (Chicago, 1997).

Escrig, Felix, *Towers and Domes* (Southampton, 1998).

Evenson, Norma, *The Indian Metropolis: A View toward the West* (New Haven, 1989).

Fass, Virginia, *The Forts of India* (London, 1986).

Flaubert, Gustave, *Dictionary of Received Ideas*, first publd. 1913 (London, 1934).

Forty, Adrian, 'Commonsense and the picturesque' in David Dunster and Iain Borden (eds.), *Architecture and the Sites of History* (Oxford, 1995), pp. 176–88.

Francis, W., *Madras District Gazatteer, Madura* (Madras, 1906).

Friedman, T., *James Gibbs* (New Haven, 1984).

Frykenberg, Robert, E., 'The Socio-politcal Morphology of Madras', in Kenneth Ballhatchet (ed.), *Changing South Asia* (London, 1984), pp. 20–41.

————, 'Modern Education in South India, 1754–1854: Its Roots and Its Role as a Vehicle of Integration Under Company Raj', *American Historical Review*, 96, 1 (1986), pp. 37–65.

————, 'The Construction of Hinduism as a "Public" Religion: Looking Again at the Religious Roots of Company Raj in South India', in Keith Yandell and John Paul (eds.), *Religion and Public Culture Encounters and Identities in Modern South India* (Surrey, 2000), pp. 3–26.

Gasparini, D.A., and Caterina Provost, 'Early Nineteenth Century Development in Truss Design in Britain, France and the United States', *Construction History*, 5 (1989), pp. 21–33.

Ghosh, Suresh Chandra, 'The Utilitarianism of Dalhousie and the Material Improvement of India', *Modern Asian Studies*, 12, 1 (1978), pp. 97–110.

Gilmartin, David, 'Models of the Hydraulic Environment: Colonial Irrigation, State Power and Community in the Indus Basin', in David Arnold (ed.), *Nature, Culture and Imperialism: Essays on the Environmental History of South Asia* (Delhi, 1996), pp. 210–36.

Goetz, Hermann, *The Crisis of Indian Civilisation in the Eighteenth and Early Nineteenth-Century and the Genesis of Indo-Muslim Civilisation* (Calcutta, 1938).

Goswamy, B.N., 'The Pahari Artists: A Study', *Roopa Lekha*, xxxii, 2 (1961), pp. 31–50.

Govindaswami, S.K. (ed.), 'Some Unpublished Letters of Charles Bourchier and George Stratton', *Madras Tercentenary Commemoration Volume* (New Delhi, 1939, 1999), pp. 27–33.

Guha-Thakurta, Tapati, 'Westernisation and Tradition in South Indian Painting in the Nineteenth Century: The Case of Raja Ravi Varma (1848–1906)', *Studies in History*, 2, 2 (1986), pp. 165–95.

———, *The Making of a New Indian Art: Artists, Aesthetics and Nationalism in Bengal 1850–1920* (Cambridge, 1992).

———, 'The Museumised Relic: Archaeology and the First Museum of Colonial India', *Indian Economic and Social History Review*, 34, 1 (1997), pp. 21–51.

Habib, Irfan, *Essays in Indian History: Towards a Marxist Perception* (New Delhi, 1995).

Hardy, Adam, 'Form, Transformation and Meaning in Indian Temple Architecture', in Giles Tillotson (ed.), *Paradigms of Indian Architecture* (London, 1998), pp. 107–35.

Harle, J., *Temple Gateways in South India* (London, 1963).

Harris, Steven J., 'Jesuit Activity in the Overseas Mission', *Isis*, 96, (2005), pp. 71–79.

Harrison, M.,'Colonial Science and the British Empire', *Isis*, 96 (2005), pp. 56–63.

Havell, E.B., *Indian Architecture* (London, 1913).

Hay, George, *The Architecture of the Scottish Post-Reformation Churches 1560–1843* (Oxford, 1957).

Herbert, Gilbert, *Pioneers of Prefabrication* (Baltimore, 1978).

'Historicus', *Sawmy Naick and his Family* (Madras, 1951).

Irschick, Eugene, *Dialogue and History: Constructing South India 1795–1895* (Berkeley, 1994).

Kalpana, K. and Frank Schiffer, *Madras: The Architectural Heritage* (Chennai, 2003).

Kerr, Ian, *Building the Railways of the Raj* (London, 1995).

King, Anthony, *Colonial Urban Development: Culture, Social Power and Environment* (London, 1976).

———, 'Writing Colonial Space: A Review Article', *Comparative Studies in Society and History*, 37, 3 (July, 1995), pp. 541–54.

———, (ed.), *Culture, Globalisation, and the World System* (Binghampton, 1991).

King, Ross, *Brunelleschi's Dome* (London, 2000).

Kopf, David, *The Brahmo Samaj* (Princeton, 1979).

———, *British Orientalism and the Bengal Renaissance: The Dynamics of Indian Modernization 1773–1835* (California, 1969).

Krishnaswami, P.R., *Tom Munro Saheb: Governor of Madras* (Madras, 1947).

Kumar, Arun, 'Colonial Requirements and Engineering Education: The Public Works Department, 1847–1947', in Roy MacLeod and Deepak Kumar (eds.), *Technology and the Raj* (New Delhi, 1995), pp. 216–32.

Lafont, Jean-Marie, *Chitra: Cities and Monuments of Eighteenth-century India from French Archives* (New Delhi, 2001).

———, *Indika—Essays in Indo-French Relations, 1630–1976* (New Delhi, 2000).

Lang, Jon, Madhavi Desai, and Miki Desai, *Architecture and Independence: The Search for Identity, India 1880–1980* (New Delhi, 1997).

Lewandowski, Susan, 'Changing Form and Function in the Ceremonial and the Colonial Port City in India: An Historical Analysis of Madurai and Madras', *Modern Asian Studies*, 11, 2 (1977), pp. 83–212.

Llewellyn-Jones, Rosie, *A Fatal Friendship: The Nawabs, the British and the City of Lucknow* (Oxford, 1985).

London, Christopher, *Architecture in Victorian and Edwardian India* (Bombay, 1994).

Losty, Jeremiah, *Calcutta: City of Palaces* (London, 1990).

————, 'The Mahabodhi Temple Before its Restorarion', in Gouriswas Bhattacharya (ed.), *Aksayanivi:Essays Presented to Dr. Debala Mitra in Admiration of her Scholarly Contribution* (New Delhi, 1991), pp. 233–58.

Love, H.D., *Vestiges of Old Madras* (3 vols., London, 1913).

————, *Descriptive List of Pictures in Government House and the Banqueting Hall, Madras* (Madras, 1903).

MacKenzie, John, *Orientalism: History, Theory and the Arts* (Manchester, 1995).

Marsh, Jan, *William Morris and Red House* (London, 2005).

Marshall, P.J., 'British Society in India Under the East India Company', *Modern Asian Studies*, 31, 1 (1997), pp. 89–108.

————, (ed.), *The Writing and Speeches of Edmund Burke* (5 vols., Oxford, 1981).

Merklinger, Elizabeth, *Indian Islamic Architecture: The Deccan 1437–1686* (Warminster, 1981).

Metcalf, Thomas, *Ideologies of the Raj* (Cambridge, 1997).

————, *An Imperial Vision: Indian Architecture and Britain's Raj* (London, 1989).

Michell, George (ed.), *Islamic Heritage of the Deccan* (Bombay, 1986).

————, *The New Cambridge History of India I.6: Architecture and Art of Southern India* (Cambridge, 1995).

Michell, George and Mark Zebrowski, *The New Cambridge History of India I.7: Architecture and Art of the Deccan Sultanates* (Cambridge, 1999).

Mitra, Debala, *Buddhist Monuments* (Calcutta, 1971).

Mitter, Partha, *Much Maligned Monsters: European Reactions to Indian Art* (Oxford, 1977).

————, 'The Formative Period c. 1856–1900: Sir J J School of Art and the Raj', in Christopher London (ed.), *Architecture in Victorian and Edwardian India* (Bombay, 1994), pp. 1–14.

————, *Art and Nationalism in Colonial India 1850–1922* (Cambridge, 1994).

Mizushima, Tsukasa, *Nattar and the Socio-economic Change in South India in the 18th–19th Centuries* (Tokyo, 1986).

Mukerji, Chandra, *Territorial Ambitions and the Gardens of Versailles* (Cambridge, 1997).

Muthiah, S., *Madras Discovered* (New Delhi, 1992).

————, *Madras: Its Past and Its Present* (New Delhi, 1995).

Nagam Aiya, V., *The Travancore State Manual* (3 vols., Trivandrum, 1906).

Necipoglu-Kafadar, Gulru, 'Plans and Models in 15th and 16th Century Ottoman Architectural Practice', *Journal of the Society of Architectural Historians*, XLV (September, 1986), pp. 224–43.

Neild, Susan, 'Colonial Urbanism: The Development of Madras City in the Eighteenth Century and Nineteenth Centuries', *Modern Asian Studies*, 13, 2 (1979), pp. 217–46.

Neild-Basu, Susan, 'The Dubashes of Madras', *Modern Asian Studies*, 18, 1 (1984), pp. 1–31.

Nilsson, Sten, *European Architecture in India 1750–1850* (London, 1968).

Oldenberg, Veena Talwar, 'The Making of Colonial Lucknow 1856–77', *The Lucknow Omnibus* (New Delhi, 2001).

Page, Jesse, *Schwartz of Tanjore* (London, 1921).

Pal, Pratapaditiya and V. Dehejiya, *From Merchants to Emperors British Artists in India 1757–1930* (Ithaca, 1986).

Pannikkar, K.N., *Culture, Ideology, and Hegemony: Intellectuals and Social Consciousness in Colonial India* (New Delhi, 1995).

Parry, Linda, *William Morris Textiles* (London, 1983).

Parsons, Constance, *Mysore City* (Oxford, 1930).

Parthasarathi, Prasanna, *The Transition to a Colonial Economy: Weavers Merchants and Kings in South India, 1720–1800* (Cambridge, 2000).

Peers, Douglas M., 'Colonial Knowledge and the Military in India 1780–1860,' *The Journal of Imperial and Commonwealth History*, 33, 2 (May 2005), pp. 157–80.

Penner, Peter, *The Patronage Bureaucracy in North India* (New Delhi, 1986).

Penny, Frank, *The Church in Madras* (2 vols., London, 1904).

Phillimore, R.H., *Historical Records of the Survey of India* (3 vols., Dehra Dun, 1950).

Physick, John, *The Victoria and Albert Museum: The History of its Building* (London, 1982).

Pichard, Pierre, *Brhadisvara: An Architectural Study* (Pondicherry, 1995).

Picon, Antoine, *French Architects and Engineers in the Age of Enlightenment* (Cambridge, 1992).

Pillai, Parameswaran, *Representative Indians*, 2nd edn. (London, 1902).

Pope, Arthur Upham, *Introducing Persian Architecture* (Teheran, 1976).

Port, M.H., *Imperial London: Civil Government Buildings in London 1851–1915* (New Haven, 1995).

Price, Pamela, *Kingship and Political Practice in Colonial India* (Cambridge, 1996).

Pyper, Robert, *The British Civil Service* (London, 1995).

Qaisar, Ahsan Jan, *Building Construction in Mughal India: The Evidence from Painting* (Delhi, 1988).

Raby, Peter, *Bright Paradise: Victorian Scientific Travellers* (London, 1996).

Raghavan, V. (ed.), 'The Sarva Deva Vilasa: a Critical Historical Study', *The Adayar Library Bulletin*, vols. 21.3–4 and 22.1–2 (Madras, 1958).

Rajayyan, K., *Administration and Society in the Carnatic 1701–1801* (Tirupati, 1969).

———, *South Indian Rebellion: The First War of Independence 1800–1801* (Mysore, 1971).

Ramaswami, N.S., *Pachaiyappa and His Institutions* (Madras, 1986).

Ramaswamy, Vijaya, 'Craft Work and Wages in Medieval Tamilnadu', in Narayani Gupta (ed.), *Craftsmen and Merchants: Essays in South Indian Urbanism* (Chandigarh, 1993), pp. 27–43.

Ramusack, Barbara, *The New Cambridge History of India lll.6: The Indian Princes and their States* (Cambridge, 2004).

Ransome, James, 'European Architecture in India', *Journal of the Royal Institute of British Architects*, Third Series, XII, 6 (January 1905), pp. 85–204.

Rao, Velcheru Narayana, David Shulman and Sanjay Subrahmanyam, *Symbols of Substance: Court and State in Nayaka Period Tamil Nadu* (Delhi, 1992).

Reid, *The Story of Fort St. George,* 2nd edn. (New Delhi, 1999).

Ridgway, Christopher and Robert Williams (eds.), *Sir John Vanbrugh and Landscape Architecture in Baroque England* (Stroud, 2000).

Ridley, Jane, 'Edwin Lutyens, New Delhi, and the Architecture of Imperialism' in Peter Burroughs and A.J. Stockwell (eds.), *Managing the Business of Empire: Essays in Honour of David Fieldhouse* (London, 1998).

Robb, Peter, *Clash of Cultures? An Englishman in Calcutta*, pamphlet, School of Oriental and African Studies (London, 1998).

————, 'Mysore, 1799–1810', *Journal of the Royal Asiatic Society,* Series 3, 8, 2 (1998), pp. 81–206.

Robinson, Francis, 'Problems in the History of the Farangi Mahall: Family of Learned and Holymen', *Oxford University Papers on India*, vol. 1, part 2 (New Delhi, 1987), pp. 1–25.

Rolt, L.T.C., *Thomas Telford* (London, 1958).

Rowland, Benjamin, *Art and Architecture of India: Hindu-Buddhist-Jain,* 3rd revised edn. (Middlesex, 1967).

Rudner, David, *Caste and Capitalism in Colonial India: The Nattukottai Chettiars* (Berkeley, 1994).

Said, Edward, *Culture and Imperialism* (London, 1994).

Sandes, E.W., *Military Engineer in India* (2 vols., Chatham, 1933).

Shukla, D.N. (ed.), 'Hindu Science of Architecture', *Vastu Sastra* (5 vols., Lucknow, 1960).

Sicca, Cinzia Maria, *Committed to Classicism: The Building of Downing College Cambridge* (Cambridge, 1987).

Singh, Brijraj, *The First Protestant Missionary in India* (Delhi, 1999).

Sivakumar, Chitra and S. Sivakumar, *Peasants and Nabobs: Agrarian Radicalism in late 18th Century Tamil Country* (Delhi, 1993).

Shallat, Todd, *Structures in the Stream: Water and the Rise of the US Army Corps of Engineers* (Austin, Texas, 1994).

Sivasundaram, Sujit, 'Trading Knowledge: The East India Company's Elephants in Britain', *The Historical Journal*, 48 (2005), pp. 27–63.

Skempton, A.W., *Civil Engineers and Engineering in Britian 1600–1830* (Aldershot, 1996).

Srinivasachari, C.S., *The Inwardness of British Annexations in India: Sir William Meyer Endowment Lectures 1948–49* (Madras, 1950).

Srinivasan, T.M., *Irrigation and Water Supply South India 200 BC–1600 AD* (Madras, 1991).
Stamp, Gavin, *Alexander Greek Thomson* (London, 1999).
Stein, Burton, *Sir Thomas Munro: The Colonial State and His Vision of Empire* (Delhi, 1989).
———, *The New Cambridge History of India I.2: Vijayanagara* (Cambridge, 1989).
Stierlin, Henri, *Islam from Baghdad to Cordoba: Early Architecture from the 7th to the 13th Century* (Koln, 2002).
Stone, Ian, *Canal Irrigation in British India* (Cambridge, 1984).
Subrahmanyam, Sanjay, *Explorations in Connected Histories: Mughals and Franks* (New Delhi, 2005).
Summerson, John, *Architecture in Britain 1530–1830, Pelican History of Art* (Somerset, 1977).
——— (ed.), 'The London Building World of the 1860s', *The Unromantic Castle and Other Essays* (London, 1990), pp. 175–92.
Sundararaja, M., *Prostitution in Madras: A Study in Historical Perspective* (New Delhi, 1993).
Sundaram, K., 'The Artisan Community of Medieval Andhra (A.D.1000–1600)', *Journal of Indian History*, 43 (1965), pp. 905–15.
Suntheralingam, R., *Politics and Nationalist Awakening in South India 1852–1891* (Arizona, 1974).
Swenarton, Mark, *Artisans and Architects: The Ruskinian Tradition in Architectural Thought* (London, 1989).
Szambien, Werner, 'Durand and the Continuity of Tradition', in Robin Middleton (ed.), *The Beaux-Arts and Nineteenth-century French Architecture* (London, 1984,) pp. 18–33.
Tandan, Banmali, *The Architecture of Lucknow and Its Dependencies 1722–1856* (New Delhi, 2001).
Thomas, P. Rev., 'The Catholic Mission in Madras' in *Madras Centenary Commemoration Volume*, 3rd revised edn. (New Delhi, 1999), pp. 375–82.
Thompson, E.P., *William Morris: Romantic to Revolutionary* (New York, 1976).
Thurston, Edgar, *Castes and Tribes of South India* (Madras, 1909).
Tillotson, Giles, *The Rajput Palaces: the Development of an Architectural Style 1450–1750* (New Haven, 1987).
———, *The Tradition of Indian Architecture: Continuity, Controversy and Change since 1850* (New Haven, 1989).
——— (ed.), *Paradigms of Indian Architecture: Space and Time in Representation and Design, Collected Papers on South Asia*, no. 13 (Surrey, 1998).
———, 'Orientalising the Raj' in Christopher London (ed.), *Architecture in Victorian and Edwardian India* (London, 1994), pp. 15–31.
Tomlinson, John, *Globalization and Culture* (Oxford, 1999).
Trautmann, T.R., 'Hullabaloo about Telugu', *South Asia Research*, 19, 1 (1999), pp. 53–70.
Trivedi, Madhu, 'Encounter and Transition—European Impact in Awadh (1765–1856)' in Ahsan Jan Qaisar and Som Prakash Varma (ed.), *Art and Culture: Endeavours in Interpretation* (New Delhi, 1996), pp. 17–48.
Trodd, Colin and Stephanie Brown (eds.), *Representations of G.F. Watts Art Making in Victorian Culture* (Aldershot, 2004).

Vadivelu, C., *The Aristocracy of Southern India* (2 vols., Delhi, 1984).

Viswanathan, Gauri, *Masks of Conquest* (London, 1990).

Volwahsen, Andrea, *Splendours of Imperial India: British Architecture in the 18th and 19th Centuries* (Munich, 2004).

Washbrook, David, *The Emergence of Provincial Politics* (Cambridge, 1976).

————, 'Land and Labour in Late Eighteenth-Century South India: The Golden Age of the Paraiah?' in Peter Robb (ed.), *Dalit Movements and the Meanings of Labour in India* (Delhi, 1993), pp. 68–86.

————, 'India, 1818–60: The Two Faces of Colonialism' in Andrew Porter (ed.), *Oxford History of the British Empire, vol. III, the 19th Century* (Oxford, 1999), pp. 395–421.

Watkin, David, *English Architecture: A Concise History* (London, 1979).

————, *Sir John Soane: Enlightenment Thought and the Royal Academy* (Cambridge, 1996).

Weiler, John, 'Colonial Connections: Royal Engineers and Building Technology Transfer in the Nineteenth Century', *Construction History*, 12 (1996), pp. 3–18.

White, G.S., (ed.), 'The Norton Family and Pachaiyappa's', *Pachaiyappa's Charities 125th Year Foundation Celebrations Commemoration Volume* (Madras, 1968), pp. 89–95.

Woodruff, Philip, *The Men Who Ruled India: The Founders* (London, 1953).

Woodward, Christopher, '"Wall, Ceiling, Enclosure and Light"; Soane's Designs for Domes', in M. Richardson and Mary-Anne Stevens (eds.), *John Soane Architect: Master of Space and Light* (London, 1999), pp. 62–67.

Wright, Gwendolyn, *Politics of Design in French Colonial Urbanism* (Chicago, 1991).

UNPUBLISHED THESES

Gurney, J.D., 'The Debts of the Nawab of Arcot' (University of Oxford, D.Phil., 1968).

Howes, Jennifer, 'Kings, Things and the Courtly Ideal in Pre-Colonial South India 1500–1800' (University of London, Ph.D., 1999).

Menon, Vikram, 'Popular Princes: Kingship and Social Change in Travancore and Cochin 1870–1930' (University of Oxford, D.Phil., 1998).

Montgomery, Carina, 'The Sepoy Army in Colonial Madras 1806–57' (University of Oxford, D.Phil., 2002).

Scriver, Peter, 'Rationalisation, Standardisation, and Control of Design: A Cognitive Historical Study of Architectural Design and Planning in the Public Works Department of British India 1855–1900' (University of Delft, Ph.D., 1994).

Sivasankaran, A., 'History of the Public Works Department of the Madras Presidency 1858–1947' (University of Madras, Ph.D., 1985).

Index